D1553199

Collectors' Guide
To American Recordings
1895 - 1925

by *Julian Morton Moses*

Foreword by Giuseppe De Luca

Dover Publications, Inc., New York

This Dover edition, first published in 1977, is an unabridged and slightly corrected republication of the work originally published by the American Record Collectors' Exchange, New York, in 1949.

International Standard Book Number: 0-486-23448-7
Library of Congress Catalog Card Number: 76-27456

Manufactured in the United States of America
Dover Publications, Inc.
180 Varick Street
New York, N.Y. 10014

CONCERNING THIS BOOK

Though the interest in collectors' recordings has increased immeasurably since this author's "Record Collector's Guide" appeared over thirteen years ago, no other book has been published in this country continuing the research into this fascinating field. Even the requests for a re-printing of that material have hitherto remained unsatisfied, much more the manifold enlargement this present work also attempts. Yet, as we move farther away from the early days of the phonograph record, information on the subject becomes more elusive just as the demand for it becomes more widespread. Especially is this true of the entire quarter of a century which comprised the era of acoustic recording and where the standards for musical performance were in the hands and throats of the artists themselves rather than in technical devices and electrical amplification. That these artists comprised a galaxy of superlative greatness may be surmised from the enduring fame their names enjoy; it can be proven by their performances upon the recordings listed herein. To bring to light these important facts is the purpose of this book.

Giuseppe De Luca, one of the immortal names in the history of grand opera, has entrenched himself in the hearts of all collectors through his superb recordings extending from the dawn of celebrity discs down to the present. Our indebtedness to him for a foreword full of wisdom on the value of historical records to the musician is gratefully acknowledged; our appreciation also to Christopher Bruno as well as to the author's ever helpful father for many excellent suggestions.

JULIAN MORTON MOSES

New York, December, 1949.

FOREWORD

by GIUSEPPE DE LUCA

While it is regrettable that the phonograph was not invented a century—or centuries—earlier, we are fortunate that it came in time to record the assortment of fabulous names that this book contains. Artists like Caruso, Destinn, Melba, Rachmaninoff, Schumann-Heink and Ysaye are worthy of study on the part of all those preparing for musical careers, even of those who have already established their fame, for the truly finished artist never considers himself as having finished studying. Much can be learned from the high standards and musicianship of the great celebrities who flourished in the first quarter of this century.

In addition to the breadth of their musical capabilities, the result of long, very intensive study, the singers of what we now call the "Golden Age of Opera" were recipients as well of direct, or almost direct, instruction at the hands of great composers themselves or their immediate disciples. This is equally true, of course, of instrumentalists such as those pianists who were pupils of Liszt. Tradition may live on, but the authority to re-enact it fades as it becomes more and more removed from the actual source. When we can hear, via the phonograph, the creators of Falstaff and Otello, we know that we are experiencing interpretations immortal in their concept because they were formed under the rigorous supervision of the exacting composer himself.

Music, being the most intangible of all the arts in spite of the written notes, stands in danger of having authentic qualities and nuances disappear forever with the performances unless something exists to perpetuate them. Acoustic recordings afford us a living re-creation of famous performances and thus constitute a direct link to the musical heritage we have received from the past, just as those of the present will link the future back to today. As such these prized discs are to be treasured.

Giuseppe De Luca

TABLE OF CONTENTS

[4]

NUMERICAL GUIDE

INDEX OF OPERAS

INSTRUMENTAL INDEX

INTRODUCTION

Acoustic Records of Permanent Value

In the realm of recorded sound, hearing is believing. Any record which cannot be heard might just as well be traded for a match-box cover and so it is that those records which require uncommon equipment to attain their translation into meaningful tones are of little interest to collectors in general except as subjects for subsequent re-recordings. In this category are all cylindrical records as well as those flat ones, notably Edison and Pathe, wherein the grooves vary in depth and the movement up and down of the special pick-up required causes them to be called hill-and-dale, and produces a lot of extraneous noise as well. While reference is occasionally made to these outmoded types, particularly the cylinders issued during the earliest decade of commercial recording, it is the lateral-cut disc with its sound-track cut into the sides rather than the bottom of the grooves thus guiding the tone-arm in smooth travel, which endured permanently and constitutes the form still in use today. Invented by Berliner almost ten years earlier, it was first sold to the public in 1895 but did not enjoy general acceptance until the turn of the century, when much needed improvements paved the way for great artists to condescend to lend it celebrity distinction. At this time, it became virtually the exclusive property of two companies, Columbia and the newly-formed Victor, both of which inaugurated a fabulous era, persisting, if not with uniform glamour, until 1925 when the advent of electrical recording brought dramatic changes— revolutionary and immediate technical improvement, insidious and gradual artistic decline, at least in realm of song.

Columbia Discs

The oldest name still extant in the record industry and the first on which appeared a sizeable number of domestically recorded celebrity discs is Columbia. Founded in 1889 as a local unit for Washington (hence its name) and nearby cities, it first made cylinders under license from the American Graphophone Company and others. Through its early acquisition of certain patent rights later pooled with those under which Victor had begun to issue discs, it turned to this more lasting medium and brought forth in 1903 a group of red label, ten-inch "Grand Opera Discs" by Edouard de Reszke, Schumann-Heink, Sembrich and others. A notable achievement, Columbia did not seek to expand or even match it for three years. Meanwhile, all other records and even these in time, were issued with conventional black and silver labels and are undistinguishable on this basis or through catalogue number as to whether the selections and performers were of permanent or transient importance.

It is this failure, which persisted for over twenty years, to identify by number its celebrity groups which makes the choice of Columbia records for inclusion in a collectors' guide a difficult one, the more so since the tricolor or Symphony Series or banner label, as it is variously called, in use for most of this time, covered many and frequently changing price categories. Only in 1925, after a year of a florid label with varying silver and gold background, did this company settle down to purple, blue and black labels with corresponding numerical differences akin to Victor's long-standing system. No criticism is intended of Columbia's past management, wholly different from that existing today, but all the above is necessary to explain the inclusion of certain artists and the relegation of others to mere mention, if any.

In brief, and this same system has been used in the case of later Vocalion and Brunswick discs as well, since they, too, afford a plethora of riches in putting practically everyone of slight importance into stellar classification, the artists who are chosen for complete listings are those who were consistently in the very top categories or those of slightly lesser stature whose recorded output was of a serious musical nature throughout. Those whose recordings were largely of semi-classical or standard pieces, particularly towards the less interesting period ushered in by the first World War, and those who had but temporary higher rank than they enjoyed in later re-numberings are omitted here in the expectancy that subsequent volumes will deal with this less important field.

In passing, examples of a few of the early artists contained in the domestic standard and foreign language Columbia series of the 1900-1908 period would include George Alexander (Baritone) 30017 Holy City (Adams); Alfredo Cibelli (Baritone) 1725 Maria, Mari (di Capua); Claude A. Cunningham (Baritone) 3162 When All the World is Young (Rogers); Eunice Clark Drake (Soprano) 1817 As the Dawn (Canton); Jeanne Ferenczy (Mezzo-Soprano) 1527 Stabat Mater: Fac ut portem; Sigmund Kundstadt (Tenor) 1480 Geisha: Kuss Duett (w. Mia Werber); Alexander Lyon (Leeuwin) (Bass) 1462 Zoovel liedjes (Brandts-Buys); J. W. Meyers (Baritone) 42 Robin Hood: Oh Promise Me; Joseph Saucier (Baritone) 1959 Les Rameaux (Faure); Mia Werber (Soprano) 1479 Boccaccio: Hab ich nur deine Liebe. Among those who came at a much later date may be mentioned such singers as Gates, Graveure, Macbeth, Barbara Maurel, Meader, Carmela Ponselle, Seagle and Van Gordon.

During the 1900-1908 period also, many Columbia records in lesser price categories were of European origin, a very few among them being: Romeo Berti (Tenor) 10531 Pearl Fishers: Mi par d'udir; Marja Bogucka (Soprano) 35250 Hrabina: Il Pionska Broni; Mary Boyer (Soprano) 50555 Manon: N'est-ce plus ma main; Lloyd Chandos (Tenor) 25114 I'll sing thee Songs of Araby (Clay); Horatio Connell (Baritone) 25976 Tannhauser: O Star of Eve; Paquita Correra (Soprano) 22594 Nueve de la Noche: Duo (w. Valls); Ingi Hedemark (Tenor) 41373 Norronakvod (Grieg); Margot Kaftal (Soprano) 35258 Mignon: Connais-tu le pays; Thorvald Lammers (Bass-Baritone) 41333 Veivseren Synger (Kjerulf); Gustalf Adolf Lund (Tenor) 41349 Du Gamla, du Friska; Carl Nebe (Bass) 40501 Im tiefen Keller (Fischer); Halfdan Rode (Bass) 41342 I djupar kallar (Fischer); M. Vallade (Tenor) 50240 Richard Coeur-de-Lion: Duo (w. Weber); Juan Valls (Tenor) 22579 Una Vieja (Gaztambide); Pietro Venerandi (Tenor) 10470 Otello: Morte d' Otello; Mizzi Zwerenz (Soprano) 12501 Donna Juanita: Kinder-Duett (w. Gutmann). While the preceding shows Columbia recording in several European capitals, it soon confined itself almost exclusively to London and Milan whence came most of the subsequent imports.

With the wholesale introduction of double-face discs in 1908, though a few had appeared four years earlier, letters were prefixed to catalogue numbers to denote points of sale. Of these, A stood for domestic issues, E for domestic foreign-language supplements, C, H, S for Latin-American release, etc. Since it was not unusual for one selection to be issued in five or more different couplings, only the numbers belonging to the A series are given in our listings except where the items were released exclusively in other groups. Following a later eight year period during which single-face records were again common, new double-face series ending in the letters D and M were inaugurated in 1924/5 and are still used today with minor modifications. Here, too, domestic numbers are the ones preferentially chosen for listing. For all Columbia recordings, single-face numbers are printed to the left of titles in BOLD type where the selection actually appeared in this form. In the case of noted singers with several selections not issued except as parts of double-face discs, numbers assigned to the designated sides are printed in light type.

Victor Red Seal

Outgrowth of a meeting between the inventor of the disc and the man who could produce a spring motor that played the pristine recordings with sufficient regularity to minimize their not inconsiderable defects, Victor was organized at the turn of the century but did not use the red label to denote celebrity classification until 1903. First assigned to selected items from domestic 2000 and imported 5000 series, the well-exploited color was soon transferred to exclusive groups with varying price differentials and all these, amounting to well over five thousand separate items, are listed in their entirety with artists' names in a Numerical Index of Victor Red Seal Records later in this book. Included are all single-face numbers assigned, whether they were actually released or not. Among the latter are items not published, which appear in the notes under various artists, as well as numbers set aside for selections which were later issued in double-face form only and are printed in the artists' section, to the left of the titles, in light type. The double-face series, running from 500 and 6000 etc., contain all acoustic Red Seals ever released in this form except the few additions made after 1925. Those not in the Index, are included in the artists' listings, where also will be found numbers belonging to other series, such as 61000, which utilized red labels in the specific instances only and these sometimes temporarily.

For lesser categories, Victor used black, blue and purple labels and fascinating as would be a complete listing of non-celebrity recordings, its inclusion in a prime guide for collectors would result in confusion and a lack of discrimination. While many domestic artists of importance graced these less expensive labels, their work upon them consisted largely of standard or semi-classical pieces. Yet among foreign recordings in these classifications, an especially large number of French, Italian and German items of note do appear. At best, however, these represent but a sampling of an artistic output often overwhelming in size and worthy of investigation but not through their very limited American representation. There are unexplored possibilities also in such 1900-1908 Victor black seal inclusions as Marino Aineto (Baritone) 52126 Aparacidos: Couplets de Crispulo; Lucrecia Arana (Soprano) 52108 Gigantes y Cabezudos: Jota final; Malka Bobkova 52804 Hubicka: Ukolebovka; Attilo Cancello (Tenor) 52535 Ave Maria (Mercadante); Maria Klanova (Contralto) 52822 V Studni: Quartet (w. Kubatova-Pollert-Stork) as well as later listings of Polish selections by de Bohus-Hellerowa on No. 65321 and by Korolewicz-Waydowa on No. 65203.

Earliest of the Victor records does not contain that name. It bears rather the title "Improved Record" with the name of its maker, Elridge R. Johnson. Soon the name Victor appears on the seven-inch records, the ten-inch being called Monarch and later, the twelve-inch, De Luxe, by which time also, the famous dog had made his appearance. These were superseded in 1905 by the "Grand Prize" label, so called because of these words appearing in the center, and this gave way in 1908 to the "Patents" label, adopted when the introduction of double-face records required the patents rights to be listed at the bottom of the label itself rather than on a sticker on the back of the record. In the main, these patent numbers end in three ways, according to the issue: Victor Talking Machine Company, Aug. 25, 1908; Emile Berliner, Victor Talking Machine Co. (June 1, 1910); Victor Talking Machine Company, May 1, 1912. Two years later the "No Patents" label omitted the patents inscription at the bottom while continuing the price listing but to the side of center. Subsequent plain labels of the "Victor" or "Victrola" variety were introduced, withdrawn, re-instated with little apparent interest to the average collector. Meanwhile, on its imports, Victor used varying means of additional identification. Earliest was mention of the origin of the recording on the label, soon the "angel" imprint was stamped on the back and later, a crown was placed alongside the stamp of the record number in the wax. Finally, the inscription "Recorded in Europe" or something similar was used once again.

Berliner-Zonophone

With patents the all-important key to the production of records, it is not at all surprising that Berliner gave his name to the first issue of commercial discs in the last half of the 1890s. These are crude affairs, with title, artist and catalogue number written or stamped into the center portion. Numbering seems an unreliable guide for dating as substitutions were frequently made and numerical changes appear at times even on the records themselves. Mentioned here chiefly because of their antiquity, these Berliner records had no celebrity classification and in 1900 the name was abandoned in favor of Zonophone, which had first been used two years earlier. This, likewise was never an important name in this country, being the property of the Universal Talking Machine Company, which released items of almost exclusively popular and semi-classical variety for over a decade.

Earliest Zonophone records appear with black etched labels, later replaced by printed ones, mostly green in color. While the Tetrazzini recordings did sell for a higher price, at least for a time, there was no actual American celebrity grouping and several of the Zonophone items on sale here were really of foreign origin. In addition to those mentioned under various footnotes, early releases included Vittoria Colombati (Contralto) 12604 Faust: Quando a te lieta; Orazio Cosentino (Tenor) 12700 Prophete: Sopra Berta; Eva Magliulo (Soprano) 24016 Trovatore: Miserere (w. Mieli); Carmen Melis (Soprano) 24010 Tosca: Non la sospiri (w. Gasparini); Giovanni Milani (Baritone) 15013 Lucia: Cruda funesta smania; Adolf Muhlmann (Baritone) 3537 Beiden Grenadiere (Schumann); Albert Quesnel (Baritone) 11003 Bonjour Suz_n (Delibes); Mme. E. Sardia (Soprano) 9158 Bohemian Girl: Then you'll remember me; Antonio Vargas (Baritone) 5525 Himno Bayames; Elvino Ventura (Tenor) 24008 Boheme: Mimi e una civetta.

Vocalion-Brunswick-Pathe-Actuelle

Since the success of the phonograph record has been largely determined by the great names to be found on its labels and greatness is both scarce and expensive, few indeed are the companies which survived the decade of their founding. Of the very many others, only passing mention can be made here and there, as they briefly enter the careers of certain artists whose chief work lies elsewhere. Emerson, founded in 1915 and publishing a few items of superior musical interest, is one such, as is Okeh, which sh.fted from vertical to lateral cut in 1919, at which time it also secured the rights for publication here of the masters made by the Fonotipia-Odeon affiliates, discussed later.

More prominence, by far, is given to Vocalion which likewise turned to lateral discs in 1920 bringing out single-face records, with blue labels, which soon gave way to dark brown and then a rust color. In 1923, they were doubled and subsequently issued in that form only but not for long, as in the next year, the company was bought out by Brunswick. Starting in 1920, this latter ou.fit had issued single-face discs with green labels for little over a year when it doubled them on a gold seal record. These celebrity doubles were numbered 15000 and 50000, some of which were changed over to a cheaper 10100 and 30100 purple seal group in 1924. No connection exists with the same numbers used on Vocalions, while it was still a separate company. In addition to artists listed, others such as May Peterson and Richard Bonelli appeared on these labels, mostly in standard selections.

In addition, a great number of the leading musicians whose records are listed in this book recorded as well for Pathe, one of the oldest and most prominent companies, but like Edison, another pioneer and ou.standing organization, their recordings were either cylinders or discs of the "hill-and-dale" variety. A few, however, were re-recorded or "dubbed" onto lateral-cut records bearing the name Pathe-Actuelle and later Perfect. After 1920, Pathe issued some of its records simultaneously in the old and new forms, the zero in front of the catalogue number signifying the latter. Previously issued selections were also introduced in small number in the 025000 Actuelle series, most of which became 11500s when the name was changed to Perfect. A sampling of these will be found under Muzio and a few other artists. Her name, and many more beside, would be prominently featured if Edison records were of more general interest. As it is, current re-recordings by various organizations like the Collectors Record Shop have restored some life to this quiescent group.

Imported Recordings: Gramophone

The importance of European affiliates to American recording interests lies in the valuable material made available for pressing here. Particularly was this of great impetus to Victor for the Gramophone Company was especially active right from the start. In Germany, for instance, where its original plant was established in Hanover, the birthplace of Berliner, it was already using in its advertisements of 1900, the familiar dog, angel and slogan "His Master's Voice." By the end of 1901, its catalogue included over thirty selections by Alma, over twenty by Berger, over a dozen by Dirkens and half a dozen each by Fischer, Greef-Andriessen, Meyerhofer, etc. Typical of still other artists were: Ungeduld sung by Knupfer (42527), the Faust Flohlied by Hauser (42287), Franz' Widmung by Nowak (42519) and the Meistersinger Fliedermonolog by Prell (42292). Further indication of German interest in its record industry of 1901 may be seen from the lists of the newly formed Zonophone outfit which already included ten or more items by Hoffmann, Schot and the ever present Carl Nebe whose Lohengrin Konigsgebet (X32) was to be repeated on ever so many labels including Gramophone, which bought out the International Zonophone Co. two years later. Meanwhile from Russia came the red label to denote celebrity and thereby higher-priced issues. By the time a second continental plant was in operation at Riga, the Russian catalogue contained many fascinating names, some of whom were found alongside of operatic titles representing important native works. Among these were Damaev 022142 May Night; Figner 22549 Opritchnik; Kamionsky 3-22774 Don Juan; Karensky 022089 Demon; Kastorsky 3-22832 Judith; Klementiev 022131 Masked Ball; Koralenko 2-23515 Iolanta; Labinski 3-22557 Askold's Tomb; Lejin 2-23061 Faust; Orlow 2-22737 Pique Dame; Osipow 022104 Rognida; Panina 2-23106 Pique Dame; Schewelev 022136 Khowantchina; Sewersky 2-22780 Gasparone; Sibriakow 022197 Lakme; Van Brandt 053125 Traviata; Witting 022178 Nischigorods; Zbrujewa 2-23172 Carmen.

Regarding the numbering system used by the Gramophone Company, it should be noted that the digit fourth from the right indicates type of voice or instrument (2 = male, 3 = female, 4 = concerted, 5 = piano, 7 = violin, etc.) while the number before that refers to the language group (2 = Russian, 3 =: French, 4 = German, 5 = Italian, etc.) and a zero in sixth place from the right signifies a twelve-inch record. Thus, the first item above is a twelve-inch record (O) in Russian (first 2) by a male singer (second 2); the last three digits and those which occur before the dash do not apply to this scheme.

In other lands, Arnoldson, Bellincioni, Bruno, Cucini, Fabbri, Kaschmann, Pandolfini, Pinto, Rousseliere, Russitano, Saltzmann-Stevens, Santley, Saville, Strong, Valero and a host of others made Gramophone masters which Victor did not import. However, the Deutsche Grammophon company which was separated from the rest of the Gramophone affiliates after the first World War, made an abortive attempt to compete directly in the American market by means of the Opera Disc label, on which it included not only German recordings to which it had exclusive rights but a great many Victor items, particularly of Caruso, whose masters it had preserved throughout hostilities. An end was soon brought to this particular competition but the Opera Discs introduced here during 1920/1 kept on turning up for many years and s ill do. Rights to the selections recorded by Deutsche Grammophon itself were assigned to Vocalion in 1924, then Brunswick and more recently, Decca and London.

Fonotipia-Odeon

The one very important group of European recordings not directly associated with any American series is that of the Fonotipia-Odeon affiliated companies, outgrowth of the International Talking Machine Company formed in 1903. During the first six years of their existence, a particularly impressive output of celebrity issues, notably on Fonotipia label, remained outside any domestic catalogue, except for the sparsest selection introduced as a Columbia adjunct. Even these were abandoned a few years later and the C-F and C-B numbers they bore by means of a small rubber stamp above the hole in the label seem to erase themselves in favor of the original numbers printed in far bolder type.

Collectors will be familiar with the leading names mentioned throughout this book and others such as Adini, Bassi, Carelli, Caron, Dani, Darclee, Labia, Magini-Coletti, Pacini, Parsi-Pettinella, Russ, Storchio, Van Dyck and Vignas, on the Fonotipia series which ran as follows in the period mentioned: 10¾-inch records, with piano accompaniment, exhausted a 39000 group and went some three hundred numbers into a 62000 group by 1909, by which time, the records of this size, with orchestral accompaniment, had reached 92237 in a 92000 series. 74000 was a twelve-inch series, the numbers from 74100 on being with orchestra, and the earlier 69000 group was fourteen-inch, while the items above 69050 came later as a continuation of 10¾-inch recordings.

While the Odeon label, common to several countries, covered all sorts of 1903-1908 items such as Madame Bernal-Resky 36562 Boheme: Addio; Hilgermann 38114 Tristan: Liebestod; Horsten 64153 Merry Widow Duett (w. Foerster); Hyde 44810 My Queen (Blumenthal); Maud Santley 57605 O Dry Those Tears (Del Riego); Thornton 66070 Faust: Flower Song and Watkins-Mills 44670 Acis and Galatea: O ruddier than the cherry as well as the many recordings of utmost importance noted under artists like Lilli Lehmann, its early use in Italy was mostly for lesser lights. These included Albinolo 37138 Favorita: Vien Lenora; Baldassare 37141 Gioconda: Ah Pescator; Colli 37767 Masked Ball: Non sai tu (w. Battaglioli); Dado 37702 Boheme: Vecchia zimarra; Ferraris 37391 Don Pasquale: So anch' io; Figoriti 37720 Tosca: Vissi d'arte; Gabardi 37591 Carmen: Canzone del fior; Lansi 37629 Traviata: Ah fors e lui; Mauro 37634 Aida: Celeste Aida; Minolfi 37041 Gioconda: O Monumento; Persichini 37355 Amico Fritz: Tutto tace (w. Sala); Pezzuti 37450 Traviata: Questa donna; Pini-Corsi 37183 Elisir d'Amore: Udite; Preve 37601 Juive: Voi che del Dio; Rota 37261 Voce 'e notte (de Curtis); Tebro 37036 Trovatore: Miserere (w. Cecchi-Cho.); Tessari 37182 Aida: Suo padre; Vecla 37462 Thais: Perche tanto severo.

With far-flung studios later turning out these labels as well as Parlophon and others, the much underused rights to them here became the property of Okeh, then once more Columbia, and recently Decca.

Favorite Records

Finally, as the briefest suggestion of the many smaller companies which sprang up throughout Europe in the 1900-1908 period, a sample of a few of the artists who appear in the early French Favorite catalogues with operatic and kindred selections, would include: Ananian 1-9027 Crucifix (w. Gautier); Belhomme 1-5313 Haydee: Air; Bensa 1-5341 Sigurd: Esprit gardien; Boyer 1-5321 Marriage of Jeannette: Enfin me voila; Boyer de Lafory 1-6041 O Salutaris; Cerdan 1-5339 Lakme: Lakme ton doux regard; Comes 1-6074 Carmen: Habanera; Dubois 1-5328 Romeo: Ah leve-toi soleil; Gilbert 1-5229 Roi d' Ys: Vainement; Laute-Brun 1-6066 Chanson de Florian; Leclerc 1-6076 Pearl of Brazil: Charmant oiseau; Magali-Muratore 1-6073 Fascination; Muratore 1-5291 Tosca: Le ciel luisait; Sardet 1-5430 Souvenir de Carmen; Vernet 1-5293 Africana: Conduisez-moi; Weber 1-5050 Herodiade: Vision fugitive.

In the above, a numeral one before the dash signifies a ten-inch record while a numeral two would indicate twelve-inch. Of the other numbers the fourth from the right indicates type of voice (5 = male, 6 = female, 9 = concerted, etc.) and where no number appears before that, the selection is French (otherwise, 1 = German, 3 = Italian, etc.). Thus 1-15270 is Tannhauser: Als du in kuhnem Sange by baritone Luria, 1-35096 is Ebreo: Mesta d' un certo by tenor Scalabrini and 1-66012 a selection from Veronique sung in English by soprano Jay.

A GOLDEN TREASURY OF RECORDS
Celebrity Discs

Listed in this section are all acoustic American celebrity discs belonging to those groups whose importance as outlined in the introduction, merits their complete inclusion in a listing of collectors' recordings. Every Victor Red Seal record of this period is thus included here and an exhaustive numerical study of this label is made in later pages. Likewise, the Columbia and other domestic recordings included in this section, except for those mentioned under "Notes", are complete for the artist under whom they appear. All artists are arranged alphabetically.

The records are grouped according to the years they were released, which, in several cases considerably post-dates the time of actual recording. In many instances, too, a subsequent re-recording of the same selection, was substituted under the same catalogue number as the original. These substitutions are not noted except where differentiation can be made through later numbering changes or through the type of accompaniment used; nor is the piano or orchestral background usually mentioned unless two different recordings of the same piece can be thus identified. The majority of items issued from mid-1905 onward do boast an orchestra of some sort.

In giving the title of selection, some attempt at space saving has been made by occasional condensation but it hoped not so much as to leave any doubt as to what composition it is. Also, there are omitted from the text the names of the composers of the larger vocal works, operas, oratorios, etc. These names are listed, however, in an appendix wherein all the large works in question are arranged alphabetically. Foreign accents must be assumed by those who know where they belong; to the collector merely intent upon identifying a piece, their absence is immaterial.

[14]

While an overall uniformity exists, such variations as occur in a few instances are but unwitting testimony to the number of years consumed in this compilation. Also, as collectors well know, there are rampant throughout record catalogues, and on labels themselves, idiosyncracies of the most violent nature; such outright errors as were detected have been corrected. Abbreviations are occasionally used, all, we trust, of a self-evident nature, such as:

w. for "with"	or. for "orchestra"
Cho. for "Chorus"	S. O. for "Symphony Orchestra"
p. for "piano"	att. for "attributed to"
Qt. for "Quartet"	arr. for "arranged by"

The numbering of the records receives the following treatment: Original single-face numbers appear in BOLD type to the left of the title. Where a given item did not ordinarily appear in single-face form, either no number is listed on the left or the one there appears in light type, signifying that this number had been assigned to the given side but that the selection was issued only as one-half of a double-face record. To the right of the title of the selection are any later single-face numbers, plus both original and subsequent double-face numbers except where Columbia assigned export series listings (H, S, M etc.) to items already having domestic representation.

Unpublished recordings are not listed but mention is made of those to which Victor Red Seal numbers were assigned so that there might be filled in the gaps which would otherwise appear in these series. Also omitted are any records which do not belong to domestic, celebrity groups though some slight indication of these may be had from the introductory sections and the necessarily brief notes about celebrity artists and others whose recording careers for various companies, particularly in the earlier days, makes such comment especially fitting.

In conclusion, it can be said that all this constitutes many years of research. Scarce as are most of these records, information regarding them is infinitely harder to come by. Catalogues were free and practically no one failed to throw them away. Even these, and no slightly complete set exists anywhere, could not tell the whole story. To attempt to do this, hundreds of sources of information as well as years of handling of records had to be utilized. Most of all, very long numerical lists had to be outlined and then the gaps filled in, some, alas, with the most persistent reluctance. The result, in any event, will enable those who love music to ferret out otherwise forgotten performances by some of its greatest artists.

ABOTT, Bessie (Soprano)

Like so many other artists in this book, Abott made a number of other interesting discs which were never released publicly. Those that were, represent not too successfully the operatic phase of her career while leaving to Bettini cylinders of the 1890's any indication of the days in musical comedy and vaudeville she shared with her sister, Jessie.

VICTOR RED SEAL 1907-1908

87003	Martha: Qui sola vergin rosa.	
87007	Romeo: Valse.	
87500	Rigoletto: Si vendetta (w. Ancona).	
88050	Rigoletto: Caro nome.	
88051	Magic Flute: Gli angui d'inferno.	
88084	Lakme: Ou va la jeune Hindoue.	
88110	Parla (Arditi).	
88129	Mireille: Valse.	
88171	Mignon: Io son Titania.	
89009	Martha: Mesta ognor (w. Homer).	
89013	Rigoletto: Tutte le feste (w. Ancona).	
96000	Rigoletto: Quartet (w. Homer-Caruso-Scotti).	(10011)

Note: The Bettini cylinders mentioned above also offered upon special order "Micro-Phonograph Excelsior Records" of Arnoldson, Calve, Campanari, Gilibert, Lassalle, Maurel, Melba, Plancon, Saleza, Saville, Tamagno, Van Dyck and many others noted elsewhere in this book.

ACKTE, Aino (Soprano)

This Finnish soprano had greatest success in Paris whence came these early celebrity discs, being but a few of those she recorded for this and other companies, notably Fonotipia-Odeon.

IMPORTED VICTOR RED SEAL 1903

5068	Herodiade: Il est doux.	
5072	A ma fiancee (Schumann).	(91042)
5074	Faust: Le Roi de Thule.	(91044)

Note: Among Ackte's other European discs were those she made for the International Zonophone Company, which, in a brief three year period, had also recorded Calve, Castellano, Delmas, Plancon, Slezak and a number of other celebrities, some of whom also come into the province of this book on the basis of their discs issued in America.

ADAMS, Suzanne (Soprano)

While on a concert tour with her husband, Leo Stern, whose death shortly thereafter caused her early retirement from the operatic stage, this youthful singer helped inaugurate the first extensive series of celebrity discs made in her native America. In spite of recording, poor even for its time, a substantial technique is evident in her authentic interpretations.

COLUMBIA RECORDS 1903

1193	Home, Sweet Home (Bishop).
1194	Sunbeams (Ronald).
1195	Printemps Nouveau (Stern).
1196	Obstination (Fontenailles).
1197	Romeo: Valse.
1198	Coquette (Stern).
1243	Faust: Air des bijoux.

IMPORTED VICTOR RED SEAL 1903

5004	Faust: Air des bijoux.	
5005	Coquette (Stern).	(91004)
5006	Home, Sweet Home (Bishop).	(91005)
5007	Romeo: Valse	(91006)

Note: Like so many important singers who appear here as well as many like Jean Lassalle who do not, Adams also recorded for Pathe.

AFFRE, Augustarello (Tenor)

An inveterate visitor to the recording studios of almost all the French companies of his day, Affre did not always enjoy such celebrity status as Victor awarded him in the novelty of its early operatic imports.

IMPORTED VICTOR RED SEAL 1903

5073   Faust: A moi les plaisirs (w. Gresse).   (91043)
5076   Romeo: Nuit d'hymenee (w. Agussol).   (91047)

Note: Affre appeared on all labels in solos and concerted pieces, a duet with the baritone Note from Masaniello being Odeon No. 36727.

AGOSTINI, Giuseppe (Tenor)

Note: This tenor, who is credited with being the first Rodolfo in New York, May 16, 1898, appears nearly two decades later on popular-price Columbia blue seal records in such perennials as Maria Mari (43760) and O Sole Mio (43761) coupled on No. A2350. In the interim, he had recorded abroad, notably for Fonotipia-Odeon including duets such as "Fia vero lasciarti" from Favorita, with Locatelli on No. 37099.

AGUSSOL, Charlotte Marie (Soprano)

IMPORTED VICTOR RED SEAL 1903

5076   Romeo: Nuit d'hymenee (w. Affre).   (91047)

Note: Like her partner, Agussol made a great number of recordings for all companies including smaller ones like Favorite of which one example occurs as No. 1—6031, this being the Hugenots: Nobles seigneurs. It will not be our practice, hereafter, even to list under more than one name such imported duets and other concerted pieces as the single Red Seal above. These very brief encounters upon celebrity label of foreign artists whose greater output in their native countries was in lesser category will be found, with slight exceptions, only under the name of the singer who accounts for their higher standing.

ALBANI, Carlo (Tenor)

VICTOR RED SEAL 1908

64081   Trovatore: Deserto sulla terra.
64082   Masked Ball: Barcarola.
74095   Forza del Destino: O tu che in seno.
74096   Lolita (Buzzi-Peccia).
74097   Pagliacci: Vesti la giubba.
74098   Lucrezia Borgia: Di pescatore.
74099   Otello: Ora e per sempre addio.

Note: Albani, a native of Trieste, is much better represented in the Odeon series of the Societa Italiana di Fonotipia which gave superior justice as well to many others of the Italian singers whose American celebrity recordings are contained in these lists.

ALDA, Frances (Soprano)

Frances Alda has written most frankly and authoritatively about her life, career and prejudices. Of her records, it can be said that they reveal a lovely quality and an even line, unmarred by any such emotional outbursts as her book might suggest.

VICTOR RED SEAL 1910-1912

87066　O si les fleurs (Massenet).
87079　Manon Lescaut: L'ora o Tirsi.
87086　The Cuckoo (Lehmann).
87090　Cradle Song (Humperdinck).
87096　Romance (Debussy).
87106　Manon Lescaut: In quelle trine.
87111　Manon: Gavotte.
87115　Dawn (d'Hardelot).
87116　Birth of Morn (Leoni).
87117　Ich liebe dich (Beethoven).
87118　Murmuring Zephyrs (Jensen).
88213　Otello: Ave Maria.　　(15-1000)
88214　Otello: Salce, salce.　　(15-1000)
88247　Falstaff: Sul fil d'un soffio.
88248　Serenata (Tosti).
88325　Loreley: Ah dunque ei m'amera.
88399　Tales of Hoffmann: Elle a fui.

VICTOR RED SEAL 1913-1916

64308　Mighty Lak' a Rose (Nevin).　　(535)
64334　Mme. Butterfly: Ancora un passo.　　(528)
64338　But lately in the dance (Arensky).
64339　Morgen (Strauss).　　(538)
64450　Melody in F (Rubenstein).　　(533)
64451　Ouvre tes Yeux (Massenet).
74335　Mme. Butterfly: Un bel di.　　(8044)　(6037)
74353　Carmen: Je dis que rien.　　(6038)
74385　Madeleine: A Perfect Day.　　(6370)
74388　Secret of Suzanne: O gioia, la nube.
74399　Panis Angelicus (Franck).　　(6353)
74400　Tosca: Vissi d'arte.　　(6037)
74401　Sari: Love's Own Sweet Song　　(6370)
74448　Boheme: Mi chiamano Mimi.　　(6038)
74449　Chanson Provencale (dell' Acqua).
87216　Tes Yeux (Rabey) (w. Elman).　　(87556)　(3030)
88521　Chanson d'amour (Hollman) (w. Elman).　　(89128)
88522　Ave Maria (Gounod) (w. Elman).　　(89129)　(8001)
88523　Angel's Serenade (Braga) (w. Elman).　　(89130)　(8001)

VICTOR RED SEAL 1917-1920

64653　Poor Butterfly (Hubbell).　　(530)
64654　Somewhere a Voice is Calling (Tate).　　(535)
64658　The Star (Rogers).
64662　I Love You Truly (Bond).　　(531)
64674　Just a-Wearyin' for You (Bond).　　(531)
64675　Love-Token (Thome).　　(538)
64687　Deep River (Coleridge-Taylor) (w. Qt.).　　(527)
64689　For Your Country (Berlin).
64692　Rule Brittania (Arne).
64693　La Marseillaise (de Lisle) (w. Cho.)　　(534)
64715　Lakme: Dans le foret.　　(533)
64716　Sing Me Love's Lullaby (Morse).　　(536)
64717　God Save the King (Carey) (w. Qt.).　　(534)
64779　Laddie o' Mine (Krams).
64780　Sorter Miss You (Smith).
64781　Laddie in Khaki (Novello).
64782　Magic of Your Eyes (Penn).　　(529)
64802　Gianni Schicchi: O mio babbino caro.　　(528)
64844　The Bells of St. Mary's (Adams).　　(525)
64859　If You Could Care (Darewski).　　(530)
64893　The Heart of a Rose (Nicholls).　　(529)

64908	By the Waters of Minnetonka (Lieurance).		(527)
74651	Mefistofele: L'altra notte		(6353)
88597	Mme. Butterfly: Tutti i fior (w. Braslau).	(89131)	(8044)
88598	Boheme: O soave fanciulla (w. Martinelli).	(89132)	(8002)

VICTOR RED SEAL 1921-1924

64927	Thoughts of You (Novello).	(526)
64948	I Passed by Your Window (Brahe).	(532)
64960	An Open Secret (Woodman).	(524)
64981	Wally: Ebben, ne andro.	(537)
64988	Mother of My Heart (Grey).	(536)
66027	Bless You (Novello).	(524)
66036	Carissima (Penn).	(897)
66056	Every Bit of Loving (Novello).	(526)
66093	The Singer (Maxwell).	(532)
66134	William Tell: Selva opaca.	(537)
66140	If Winter Comes (Tennent).	(525)
66152	Daddy (Behrend).	(897)
66174	Memory's Garden (Denni).	(946)
66175	Coming Home (Willeby).	(946)
66244	Vale (Russell).	(1005)
66245	I Heard You Go By (Wood)	(1005)
	What'll I Do (Berlin).	(1032)
	Love Has a Way (Schertzinger).	(1032)
89163	Mme. Butterfly: O quanti occhi (w. Martinelli).	(8002)

For other records, see CARUSO.

Note: Other Alda recordings to which catalogue numbers were assigned, though they were not publicly released, include the "Addio" from Boheme (64417), a twelve-inch Deep River (74507) and the final trio from Faust with Martinelli-Mardones (95214).

ALESSANDRONI, Cesare (Baritone)

None too impressive upon them, Alessandroni was yet one of the few members of the early "Columbia Italian Grand Opera Company" to make solo recordings.

COLUMBIA RECORDS 1912

19722	Faust: S'hai tu poter di Demon (w. Cho.).	(A1158)
19923	Favorita: Splendon piu belle (w. Cho.).	(A1218)
36396	Tosca: Te Deum (w. Cho.).	(A5430)

For other records, see CARTICA.

ALTHOUSE, Paul (Tenor)

VICTOR RED SEAL 1915

76031 Boris Godounow: Garden scene (in Ital.) (w. Ober).

Note: Because he makes but one appearance on Red Seal label, Althouse's blue seal records are worthy of slightly greater detail than usual for this series. They include: Pagliacci: Vesti la giubba and Tosca: E lucevan le stelle on No. 45055; Gioconda: Cielo e mar and Walkure: Siegmunds Liebeslied on No. 45076; Aida: Celeste Aida (55045); Duets from Aida (Fugglam gli ardori) with Marsh and Mme. Butterfly (O quanti occhi) with Kline on No. 55058; Onaway, Awake Beloved and Ah Moon of My Delight on No. 55059; and In Native Worth from The Creation (55076).

AMATO, Pasquale (Baritone)

A fine musician, Amato was one of the few of his compatriots to essay Wagnerian music drama in its original tongue. Though he also brought distinction to parts such as Cyrano, his recorded repertoire is more conventional, even on the several minor European labels he exalted by his presence.

VICTOR RED SEAL 1912-1914

87093	Gioconda: Ah Pescator (w. Cho.).	(539)
87097	Cavalleria Rusticana: Il cavallo (w. Cho.).	
87105	Guarany: Senza tetto (w. Cho.).	(940)
87180	Torna a Surriento (de Curtis).	(615)
87193	Jewels of the Madonna: Serenata (w. Cho.).	(539)
88326	Pagliacci: Prologo.	(6039)
88327	Carmen: Canzone del Toreador.	(6040)
88328	Otello: Credo	(6042)
88329	Barber of Seville: Largo al factotum.	(6039)
88338	Otello: Brindisi (w. Setti-Bada-Cho.).	
88340	Rigoletto: Povero Rigoletto (w. Setti-Bada-Cho.).	(6041)
88341	Rigoletto: Cortigiani.	(6041)
88437	Germania: Ferito prigionier.	(15-1005)
88438	Due Foscari: O vecchio cor.	(15-1005)
88464	Masked Ball: Eri tu.	(6040)
88473	Dinorah: Sei vendicata.	
88474	Traviata: Di Provenza.	(6042)
88489	Tosca: Te Deum (w. Cho.).	
88490	Africana: Adamastor (w. Cho.).	
89055	Faust: Scene des Epees (w. Journet-Cho.).	(8003)
89056	Puritani: Suoni la tromba (w. Journet).	(8061)
89061	Carmen: Si tu m'aimes (w. Matzenauer-Cho.).	
89062	Favorita: Ah l'alto ardor (w. Matzenauer).	(8003)

For other Victor records, see **CARUSO, FARRAR, GADSKI, HEMPEL.**

COLUMBIA RECORDS 1917

48942	Pagliacci: Prologo.
48944	Barber of Seville: Largo al factotum.

Note: Columbia also sold his imported Fonotipias ten years earlier, one of these being No. 92008 Zaza: Buona Zaza (C-F73).

ANCONA, Mario (Baritone)

Ancona was a most dignified artist and his discs exemplify the nobility of style so wonderfully characteristic of a bygone day, though the zenith of his notable career was more nearly approximated by the cylinders he made more than ten years earlier.

VICTOR RED SEAL 1907-1909

87006	Traviata: Di Provenza.	
87010	Mattinata (Tosti).	
87011	Invano (Tosti).	
87014	Puritani: Ah per sempre.	
87015	Otello: Era la notte.	
87500	Rigoletto: Si vendetta (w. Abott).	
88055	Pagliacci: Prologo.	
88056	Faust: Dio possente.	(15-1002)
88062	Ernani: O de' verd' anni.	
88063	Favorita: A tanto amor.	
88081	Masked Ball: Eri tu.	(15-1002)
88109	Faust: Morte di Valentino.	
88167	Mia sposa sara la mia bandiera (Rotoli).	

88168   Serenade de Don Juan (Tschaikowsky).
88169   Dinorah: Sei vendicata.
88170   Andrea Chernier: Nemico della patria.
88500   Puritani: Suoni la tromba (w. Journet).
89007   Pearl Fishers: Del tempio (w. Caruso).   (8036)
89013   Rigoletto: Tutte le feste (w. Abott).

ANDERSON, Marion (Contralto)

Note: Like a few other noted Red Seal artists of current popularity, Anderson's long recording career goes back to the tail-end of the acoustic era when a group of her incomparable spirituals first appeared on Victor black seal records and included Deep River and My Way's Cloudy on No. 19227, Go Down, Moses and Heav'n on No. 19370 and Nobody Knows de Trouble and My Lord, What a Morning on No. 19560.

ANSELMI, Giuseppe (Tenor)

Note: A singer of great appeal in vocal texture, style, even appearance, Anselmi was enormously popular in Spain and Russia as well as his native Italy. His very large number of Fonotipia discs include original compositions, songs in Russian and out of the ordinary operatic excerpts such as Manru: Come al sol No. 62289 (C-F66) and Marcella: O mia Marcella No. 62169 (C-F60).

ANSSEAU, Fernand (Tenor)

IMPORTED VICTOR RED SEAL 1922-1923

74738   Romeo: Ah leve-toi soleil.   (6348)
74739   Werther: O Nature.   (6104)
74763   Herodiade: Ne pouvant reprimer.   (6104)
74823   Carmen: Air de la fleur.   (6348)

ARABIAN-SYRIAN Records

Note: The higher price commanded by records imported for the Arabic language trade accounts for such Red Seal numbers as 6467, 6476-7, 6488 and many later ten and twelve-inch ones being set aside for these interesting recordings, which continued to be acoustic for some time after all the rest of the catalogue had gone over to the electric process. Most of the early selections were by Cheikh Youssef el Manialawi, who, on the last numbered record above, sings "Hawa Taaebou" and "Ya Salma" or Lovers Suffer and I Love You Salma, apparently universal sentiments.

ARIMONDI, Vittorio (Bass)

A member of the original cast of "Falstaff" at La Scala, Arimondi later spent four years at Covent Garden and came with this established background to both the Metropolitan and Chicago Opera companies.

COLUMBIA RECORDS 1907-1908

30090   Simon Boccanegra: Il lacerato spirito.
30099   Faust: Serenata.   (A5010)
30100   Requiem (Verdi): Confutatis.   (A5001)
30110   Martha: Canzone del porter.   (A5006)
30111   Mia sposa sara la mia bandiera (Rotoli).   (A5002)

ARRAL, Blanche (Soprano)

A vibrant personality in life as on records, Arral, after a youthful debut as Mignon at the Opera Comique, made known her unique interpretations throughout the remotest parts of the world. As Clara Lardenois, she had even made Bettini cylinders before the nineteenth century was over.

VICTOR RED SEAL 1909

64098	Beggar Student: Czardas (in French).	
64099	Amour Mouille: Valse d' oiseau.	(901)
64107	El Bolero Grande (Vasseur).	
74132	Traviata: Quel est donc.	
74142	Marriage of Jeannette: Chanson du rossignol.	
74146	Lombardi: Polonaise.	(15-1016)
74147	Faust: Air des bijoux.	(15-1016)
74151	Romeo: Valse	

AUMONNIER, Paul (Bass)

Note: Among the first Columbia imports from France was a group of no less than 140 solos by this famous basso on Nos. 50013-50152. On a dozen seven-inch records, many more ten-inch records and a still larger number issued simultaneously in both sizes were many songs and operatic arias including selections from such indigenous works as Charles VI, Domino Noir, Galathee, Petit Duc, Songe d' une Nuit d' Ete, Val d' Andorre. Songs like Les Boeufs, Columbia No. 50025, he recorded again for Favorite as No. 1-5028 not to mention numerous other makes he likewise favored.

AUSTRAL, Florence (Soprano)

Her native land apparent in her name, Austral was one of the last of those sopranos who could sing the Liebestod and follow it with Caro Nome.

IMPORTED VICTOR RED SEAL 1925

89164	Aida: Presago il core (w. Fleta-Cho.).	(8063)
89165	Aida: O terra addio (w. Thornton-Fleta-Cho.).	(8063)

Note: A group of blue seal imports Nos. 55203 through 55215 were issued the year before featuring the Brunnhilde of Austral and the superb conducting of Albert Coates in a series of scenes from the Ring of the Nibelungs. To this group belong also the last items listed under Whitehill which bore red seals because of his prior status here.

BACHAUS, Wilhelm (Pianist)

Though by no means the first to record, Bachaus was earliest among internationally renowned pianists to appear on Victor Red Seal records and his career upon them is not yet over.

IMPORTED VICTOR RED SEAL 1909-1910

71042	Norwegian Wedding March (Grieg).	
71043	Perpetuum Mobile (Weber).	
71044	Liebestraum (Liszt).	
71045	Prelude Op. 28 No. 1; Etude Op. 10 No. 1 (Chopin).	
71046	Prelude in C Sharp Minor (Rachmaninoff).	
74159	Etudes Op. 25 Nos. 6; 1 (Chopin).	
88158	Fantasie Impromptu (Chopin).	(71040)
88160	Harmonious Blacksmith (Handel).	(71041)

BADINI, Ernesto (Baritone)

For Imported Victor Red Seal records, see DE CASAS, DE LUCIA, DE MURO, DE TURA, DOMAR, PAOLI, RUSZCOWSKA.

Note: Badini appeared in solo and concerted pieces on very many other early Victor imports, including Don Pasquale: Son nov' ore on No. 58349 (68273) on which the fine buffo, Antonio Pini-Corsi, who scored so notably here in Maestro di Capella, sings the name part which Badini himself later assumed in the complete recording of the opera. His appearances on Columbia green label imported E series are likewise numerous.

BAKLANOFF, George (Baritone)

While appearing with the Boston Opera Company, Baklanoff made the first group of recordings below. Unfortunately, only the first two are from the much neglected masterpieces of his native Russia, but he did make up for this lack on later acoustic and electrical discs.

COLUMBIA RECORDS 1911

30617	Demon: The world's queen.	(A5271)
30618	Demon: The vow.	(A5271)
30619	Carmen: Chanson du Toreador.	(A5272)
30620	Gioconda: Ah Pescator.	(A5272)
30621	Otello: Credo.	(A5270)
30622	Otello: Era la notte.	(A5270)
30623	Rigoletto: Figlia, Mio Padre (w. Lipkowska).	(A5296)

COLUMBIA RECORDS 1918

49452	Hamlet: Brindisi.	(7028M)
77911	Gioconda: Ah Pescator (w. Cho.).	(2013M)

BARRIENTOS, Maria (Soprano)

COLUMBIA RECORDS 1916-1920

48627	Lucia: Mad scene.	(68040D)	
48628	Lucia: Regnava nel silenzio.	(68040D)	(8930M)
48649	Rigoletto: Caro nome.	(68041D)	(8905M)
48650	Mireille: Vals.	(68068D)	(8905M)
48651	Marriage of Figaro: Deh vieni.	(68057D)	(8930M)
49112	Pearl of Brazil: Charmant oiseau.	(68057D)	(7037M)
49113	Martha: Qui sola vergin rosa.	(68079D)	(8906M)
49151	Lakme: Ou va la jeune Hindoue.	(68041D)	(7037M)
49171	Voci di primavera (Strauss).	(68068D)	(7036M)
49354	Traviata: Parigi, o cara (w. Lazaro).	(71001D)	(8928M)
49370	Puritani: Qui la voce.	(68052D)	(8907M)
49371	Puritani: Vien diletto.	(68052D)	(8907M)
49372	Traviata: Ah fors e lui.		(8908M)
49386	Coq d' Or: Hymne au soleil.	(68053D)	(7069M)
49596	Dinorah: Ombra leggiera.	(68042D)	(8906M)
49598	Mignon: Io son Titania.	(68042D)	(8908M)
49611	Rigoletto: Tutte le feste (w. Stracciari).	(71003D)	(8928M)
49612	Barber of Seville: Dunque io son (w. Stracciari).	(71003D)	(8929M)
49616	Rigoletto: E il sol (w. Hackett).	(71002D)	(8929M)
49622	Traviata: Un di felice (w. Hackett).	(71001D)	(9009M)
49763	Sonnambula: Ah non giunge.	(68053D)	(7069M)
49766	Lucia: Verranno a te (w. Hackett).	(71002D)	
49768	Lucia: Sextet (w. Hackett-Stracciari-Mardones-Meader-Noe).		
		(74000D)	(9014M)
49782	Rigoletto: Quartet (w. Gordon-Hackett-Stracciari).	(74000D)	(9014M)
49793	Barber of Seville: Una voce poco fa.	(68085D)	(7070M)
49794	Barber of Seville: Io son docile.	(68085D)	(7070M)

| 49803 | Theme and Variations (Proch). | (68079D) (7036M) |
| 78363 | Rigoletto: Si vendetta (w. Stracciari). | (4010M) |

Note: No. 9014M above was later changed to 7180M. Her youthful Milan recordings, made for Fonotipia when she was but twenty years old, included Spanish zarzuelas in addition to repertoire such as above.

BATTISTINI, Mattia (Baritone)

Few fears of the sea have been as widely publicized as that which supposedly kept Battistini, the "Gloria d' Italia", from thrilling American audiences with his superb vocal style and technique except by means of those of his European discs which were issued here from time to time. Certainly, the magnificence of this voice, even in his mid-sixties, when the last group of records listed below were made, must prove incredible and exasperating to the many singers whose bad schooling wears them out before they have sung half so long as he.

IMPORTED VICTOR RED SEAL 1903

5113	Demon: Deh non plorar.	(91053)
5114	Faust: Dio possente.	(91054)
5115	Barber of Seville: Largo al factotum.	(91055)
5116	Eugen Onegin: Se dell' imen.	(91056)
5117	La Mantilla (Alvarez).	(91057)
5118	Don Giovanni: Fin ch' han dal vino.	(91058)
5119	Tannhauser: O tu bell' astro.	(91059)
5127	Don Giovanni: Serenata.	(91062)

IMPORTED VICTOR RED SEAL 1907-1909

92004	Zampa: Perche tremar.	
92005	Martha: Il mio Lionel.	(15-1010)
92006	Don Sebastiano: O Lisbona.	
92007	Ernani: Lo vedremo (w. Sillich).	
92008	Ernani: Vieni meco (w. Corsi-Cho.).	
92023	Damnation of Faust: Su queste rose.	
92024	Don Giovanni: La ci darem (w. Corsi).	
92044	Masked Ball: Eri tu.	(6408)
92045	Favorita: A tanto amor.	(0415) (15-1010)
92046	Ernani: O sommo Carlo (w. Corsi-Colazza-Sillich-Cho.).	
		(89135) (18144)

IMPORTED VICTOR RED SEAL 1910-1912

88232	Masked Ball: Alla vita.	(6408)
88350	Maria di Rohan: Bella e di.	(6043)
88351	Per la Patria: Bella Italia.	
88352	Puritani: Bel sogno.	
88353	Thais: D'acqua aspergimi (w. Janni).	(89123) (8061)
88354	Werther: Ah non mi ridestar.	(6045)
88374	Ernani: Da quel di (w. Corsi).	

IMPORTED VICTOR RED SEAL 1922

87338	Vittoria mio core (Carissimi).	(540)
87339	La Mantilla (Alvarez).	(540)
88649	Roi de Lahore: O casto fior.	(6046)
88650	Ruy Blas: A miei rivali.	(6045)
88651	Don Carlos: Per me giunto.	(6044)
88652	Maria di Rohan: Voce fatal.	(6043)
88653	Favorita: Vien Leonora.	(6044)
88654	Maria di Rudenz: Ah non avea piu lagrime.	(6046)
89135	Ernani: O sommo Carlo (w. De Witt-Taccani-Cho.).	(8037)

Note: Early labels went to unusual trouble to assure the listener that Battistini's modulation of the tenor aria from Werther into a baritone's range was done through a transcription by Massenet himself. Other liberties were rampant throughout the catalogues of that and previous days without so much as notice to the public, much less deference to the unwitting composer.

BAUER, Harold (Pianist)

VICTOR RED SEAL 1924-1925

Barbarini's Minuet (Bauer).	(1058)
Motley and Flourish (Bauer).	(1058)
Kamenoi Ostrow (Rubenstein).	(6468)
Impromptu in A Flat Op. 90 No. 4 (Schubert).	(6468)

BEDDOE, Daniel (Tenor)

Beddoe enjoyed a Welsh background as did so many other great oratorio singers. The combination may not be infallible but in this case it was certainly operative for a long time during which he recorded acoustically many a sacred song for small companies such as Rainbow and others.

VICTOR RED SEAL 1911-1914

64195	Irish Love Song (Lang).
64196	Elijah: Then shall the righteous.
64361	Yesterday and Today (Spross).
64391	A Moonlight Song (Cadman).
74244	Freischutz: Thro' the forest.

BEGUE, Bernard (Baritone)

Note: An early recording artist on both domestic and imported Columbia discs was this minor member of the Metropolitan Opera Company of that period. Included among his first records were operatic pieces like the Faust serenade— No. 301, and several songs such as La Marseillaise—No. 8, Noel—No. 50, Les Rameaux—No. 306, and Le Temps de Cerises—No. 50003.

BELLATTI, Virgilio (Baritone)

COLUMBIA RECORDS 1908

30116	Zaza: Zaza piccola zingara.	(A5076)
30117	Roland von Berlin: Preghiera di Giovanni.	(A5076)

Note: Bellatti came to this country with Mascagni, who was desirous of revealing his conducting ability as well as such works as Zanetto and Guglielmo Ratcliff, though the venture failed before he got around to the latter. However, even the excerpts above are from the pen of his chief rival, whose setting of Boheme was featured among earlier Bellatti imports on Columbia Nos. 10487/91.

BERL-RESKY, Gustave (Baritone)

Note: Although a celebrity on Edison cylinders as Gustavo Bernal-Resky, the name under which his many European releases appeared, his domestic discs of various makes were of lesser category as were his Columbia imports including Don Carlos: Per me giunto on No. 10556. In Russia, however, his Gramophone Company records were red seal and included arias from Masked Ball on No. 2-52649 and Hamlet on No. 2-52650 among others. Among the many other labels on which his name appears is a large group of Beka discs which include such items as Furioso: Raggio d' amor on No. 598 and the Don Giovanni: Serenata on No. 623.

BERTANA, Luisa (Mezzo-Soprano)
IMPORTED VICTOR RED SEAL 1925
Nerone: Padre nostro che sei nei Ciel. (6483)
Nerone: Or tutto e confessato (w. Galeffi). (6485)
Nerone: Laggiu tra i giunchi (w. Galeffi). (6485)

BERTHALD, Barron (Tenor)
Through a hasty, unscheduled appearance as Lohengrin with Damrosch's opera troupe, Berthald came into a fame which he carried over to the premiere of the former's Scarlet Letter.
COLUMBIA RECORDS 1912
30815 Lohengrin: Mein lieber Schwan. (A5382)
30816 Walkure: Siegmunds Liebeslied. (A5382)

BESANZONI, Gabriella (Contralto)
VICTOR RED SEAL 1920-1921
64875 Trovatore: Stride la vampa. (541)
64876 Gioconda: Voce di donna. (940)
64877 Samson: S' apre per te. (541)
74613 Carmen: Avanera. (6047)
74617 Samson: Aprile foriero. (6409)
74680 Favorita: O mio Fernando. (6047)
Note: No. 74677 was assigned to Prophete: Ah mon fils.

BISPHAM, David (Baritone)
Few singers have done such justice to the simple ballad as this great Quaker Singer, whose stirring recorded performances likewise make understandable his success in the spoken drama.
COLUMBIA RECORDS 1906-1910
30016 Danny Deever (Damrosch). (A5021)
30018 Der Wanderer (Schubert). (A5014)
30019 Erlkonig (Schubert). (A5023)
30020 Who is Sylvia (Schubert). (A5018)
30021 Hark, Hark, the Lark (Schubert). (A5020)
30023 Annie Laurie (Scott). (A5022)
30026 Pirate Song (Gilbert). (A5019)
30027 Drink to me only with thine eyes.
30036 Kathleen Mavourneen (Crouch). (A5016)
30037 Faust: Dio possente. (A5010)
30148 Down among the dead men. (A5503)
30149 Faithfu' Johnie (Beethoven). (A5121)
30210 Believe me if all those endearing young charms. (A5095) (5033M)
30211 Acis and Galatea: O Ruddier. (A5095) (5033M)
30212 Elijah: It is enough. (A5100)
30218 Ivanhoe: Ho, Jolly Jenkin. (A5099)
30219 Semele: Where'er you walk. (A5099)
30220 The Pretty Creature (Storace). (A5121)
30221 By Celia's Arbour (Mendelssohn). (A5100)
30284 Drink to me only with thine eyes (or.). (A5132)
30285 Mary of Argyle (Nelson). (A5132)
30286 Trovatore: Il balen. (A5137)
30287 Ivanhoe: Woo thy snowflake. (A5137)
30331 The Palms (Faure). (A5161)
30332 Boat Song (Ware). (A5166)
30333 The Pauper's Drive (Homer). (A5166)
30334 Ring Out, Wild Bells (Gounod). (A5161)

COLUMBIA RECORDS 1911-1915

30543	Elijah: Lord God of Abraham.			(A5258)
30544	Samson (Handel): Honor and Arms.			(A5332)
30545	Messiah: Why do the Nations.			(A5332)
30546	St. Paul: O God Have Mercy.			(A5258)
30767	Banjo Song (Homer).			(A5320)
30768	Who Knows (Heinrich).			(A5362)
30770	All through the Night.			(A5320)
30773	Danny Deever (Damrosch) (or.).	(A5021)	(A5778)	(5010M)
30774	Pirate Song (Gilbert) (or.).		(A5019)	(A5778)
30791	Banks of Allan Water (Horne).			(A5377)
30792	Oft in the Stilly Night (Stevenson).			(A5377)
30793	Yeoman's Wedding Song (Poniatowski).			(A5362)
36352	Loch Lomond.			(A5420)
36355	Hedge Roses (Schubert).			(A5420)
36473	Arrow and the Song (Balfe).		(A5437)	(5032M)
36474	Vicar of Bray.			(A5492)
36475	Annie Laurie (Scott) (or.).	(A5022)	(A5437)	(5032M)
36476	Der Wanderer (Schubert) (or.).		(A5014)	(A5503)
36681	Thursday (Molloy).			(A5492)
36682	Tell Me, Mary (Hodson).			(A5473)
36683	Who is Sylvia (Schubert) (or.).		(A5018)	(A5473)
37086	It's a Long, Long Way (Williams).			(A5629)
37087	Two Grenadiers (Schumann).			(A5629)
37207	Old Guard (Rodney).			(A5664)
37208	Route Marching (Stock).			(A5664)

Note: Banks of Allan Water was coupled with Rock'd in the cradle of the deep on English Columbia No. 385, issued Sept. 1913. Of Bispham's Pathe discs, a few were re-recorded onto lateral-cut Actuelles during 1920, including Duncan's Mistress Magrath on No. 025099; Perfect No. 11532.

BLANCHART, Ramon (Baritone)

Blanchart repeated the advance of so many Spaniards which lost them to their native country only to benefit the operatic world at large. In the group of recordings designed for Latin-American devotees, he gives at least some indication of a usually unexplored musical realm he had earlier touched, in far lesser degree, on imported Victor blue seal and Fonotipia recordings.

COLUMBIA RECORDS 1910-1911

4437	Masked Ball: Alla vita.	(A837)
30409	Puritani: Suoni la tromba (w. Mardones).	(A5184)
30413	Gioconda: Ah Pescator (w. Cho.).	(A5176)
30424	Pagliacci: Prologo.	(A5206)
30431	Masked Ball: Eri tu.	(A5207)
30433	Otello: Credo.	(A5208)
30441	Traviata: Di Provenza.	(A5207)
30450	Rigoletto: Pari siamo.	(A5206)
30451	Las Golondrinas (Alvarez).	(H1047)
30456	A Granada (Alvarez).	(H1047)
30457	Trovatore: Il balen.	(A5208)
19282	Los Ojos Negros (Alvarez).	(S1)
19283	La Partida (Alvarez).	(S9)
19285	Cuba Hermosa (Fuentes).	(S8)
19286	La Mantilla (Alvarez).	(S7)
19287	A una morena (Alvarez).	(S6)
19288	Anyoransa (Alvarez).	(S6)
19289	La Serrana (Alvarez).	(S9)

19290	Canto del Presidiario (Alvarez).	(S5)
19291	Recuerdos de Aragon (Alvarez).	(S2)
19292	Pesares (Alvarez).	(S8)
19293	Mi Patria (Alvarez).	(S7)
19294	Hijas de Eva: Romanza.	(S3)
19295	Grumete: Barcarola.	(S10)
19298	Juramento: Duo de la Diana*.	(S1)
19299	Merry Widow: Duo vals (Span.)*.	(S4)
19300	Mascotte: Duo de los Pavos*.	(S3)
19305	Campanone: Salida.	(S4)
19306	Juramento: Duo del Piano*.	(S2)
19307	Pepe Gallardo: Duo*.	(S5)

* These are duets with MME. DE LA ROCHE (Soprano).

For other records, see BRONSKAJA, CONSTANTINO, LIPKOWSKA, NIELSEN.

BLASS, Robert (Bass)

Blass' return to his native New York and the Metropolitan Opera was via Bayreuth where his study of Gurnemanz prepared him for the first performance of the role outside that sanctuary.

VICTOR RED SEAL 1903

81015	Der schlesische Zecher (Reissiger).	(64032)
81016	Magic Flute: In diesen heil' gen Hallen.	(64033)
81017	Lohengrin: Konigs Gebet.	(64034)
85007	Freischutz: Schweig, schweig.	(74028)
85008	Im tiefen Keller (Fischer).	(74029)
85009	Parsifal: Charfreitags-Zauber.	(74030)
85010	Beiden Grenadiere (Schumann).	(74031)
85011	Im wunderschonen Monat Mai, Ich grolle nicht (Schumann).	(74032)

BLAUVELT, Lillian (Soprano)

A native of Brooklyn, which much abused borough also gave De Lussan and De Gogorza to the pages of this book, Blauvelt seems to have encountered difficulties in recording for Victor since many earlier and later versions of the selections listed as well as others remained unpublished.

VICTOR RED SEAL 1905

81067	Vespri Siciliani: Bolero.	(64029)
81068	My Bairnie (Vannah): Comin' thro' the Rye.	(64031)
81069	Home, Sweet Home (Bishop).	(64030)
85070	Romeo: Valse.	(74027)

COLUMBIA RECORDS 1907-1909

30091	Vespri Siciliani: Bolero.	
30112	Cherry Ripe (Horn).	(A5017)
30113	Filles de Cadiz (Delibes).	(A5003)
30124	Romeo: Valse.	
30125	Home, Sweet Home (Bishop).	(A5008)
30126	Martha: Last rose of summer.	(A5019)
30150	Barber of Seville: Una voce poco fa.	(A5078)
30252	Rodelinda: Le Printemps.	(A5120)
30253	Ouvrez (Dessauer).	(A5119)
30254	When Celia Sings (Moir).	(A5119)
30262	Norwegian Song (Loge).	(A5120)

BLOCH, Max (Tenor)

See FLEISCHER, GERHARDT, SEMBACH.

Note: As soloist, mostly in German arias and songs, Bloch appears on a great
many Columbia green label and Victor black seal records as well as other
makes, including Emerson, where a slightly more unusual, for him, Pagliacci:
Vesti la giubba was listed as No. 41377 (mat. 10340).

BOHNEN, Michael (Bass-Baritone)

BRUNSWICK RECORDS 1923-1925

Freischutz: Hier im ird' schen Jammerthal.	(15074)
Wenn Ich einmal Der Herrgott War (Binder).	(15074)
Dinorah: Sei vendicata assai.	(15097)
Robert: Nonnes qui reposez.	(15097)
Beiden Grenadiere (Schumann).	(50033)
Tannhauser: Blick' ich umher.	(50033)
Goldene Kreuz: Bom Bom Bom.	(50037)
Goldene Kreuz: Wie anders war.	(50037)
Tannhauser: O du mein holder Abendstern.	(50048)
Walkure: Der Augen Leuchtendes Paar.	(50048)
Magic Flute: O Isis und Osiris.	(50056)
Magic Flute: In diesen heil' gen Hallen.	(50056)

Note: Bohnen's European recordings were introduced here slightly before the
above. His Odeon No. 76461 Parsifal: O wunden-wundervaller was doubled by
Okeh on No. 5041 while on Opera Disc No. 76357, Gr. 044299, Meistersinger:
Gut'n Abend, Meister, he was joined by none other than LOTTE LEHMANN.

BONCI, Alessandro (Tenor)

Hailed as outstanding competition for the overwhelming popularity of Caruso's records, though he does not appear too formidable in that role, this essen-
tially lyric tenor sounds his best on the earliest of his many Fonotipia Italian
recordings. Through its arrangements with that company, Columbia sold these
in a distinct series and did not include the name of Bonci in its own roster until
the many interesting items below were released.

COLUMBIA RECORDS 1913

36458	Boheme: Che gelida manina.	(H1102)	(A5449)
36459	Martha: M' appari.	(H1104)	(A5479)
36460	Elisir d'Amore: Una furtiva lagrima.	(H1102)	(A5449)
36461	Manon: Ah dispar.	(H1103)	
36534	Gioconda: Cielo e mar.	(H1104)	(A5479)
36535	Faust: Salve dimora.	(H1103)	
36656	Favorita: Spirto gentil.	(H1105)	(A5468)
36657	Africana: O Paradiso.	(H1105)	(A5468)
38320	Rigoletto: Questa o quella.	(H54)	(A1286)
38321	Fedora: Amor ti vieta.	(H56)	(A1408)
38555	Girl of the Golden West: Ch' ella mi creda.	(H59)	
38556	Manon Lescaut: Donna non vidi mai.	(H55)	(A1418)
38557	Luisa Miller: Quando le sere al placido.	(H55)	(A1287)
38561	Favorita: Una vergine.	(H56)	(A1287)
38562	Manon: Il sogno.	(H59)	
38563	Rigoletto: La donna e mobile.	(H54)	(A1286)
38586	Elisir d'Amore: Quant' e bella.	(H57)	(A1408)
38587	Tosca: E lucevan le stelle.	(H60)	(A1316)
38596	Tosca: Recondita armonia.	(H60)	(A1316)
38607	Masked Ball: Barcarola.	(H58)	(A1377)
38661	Mignon: La tua bell' alma.	(H58)	(A1418)
38666	Pagliacci: Vesti la giubba.	(H57)	(A1377)

Note: The Africana aria above persisted quite late in U. S. ca'alogues, being coupled with Constantino's Pearl Fishers on 7031M, later 5093M. Of this and the other selections, it seemed advisable to include earliest Latin American coupling numbers since several were not included in the domestic catalogue. Examples of his Fonot:pias made before 1909 would include arias from Tess on Nos. 92218-9 (CF83) and Martha on No. 74110 (CF 1005, also OK 52201).

BONINSEGNA, Celestina (Soprano)

In the opinion of many otherwise undemonstrative critics, Boninsegna's is the most thrilling dramatic soprano voice on records. Her American record:ngs are considered superior to those made abroad, of which only a part found their way here and these largely via South American series as with the second group of Columbia discs below.

IMPORTED VICTOR RED SEAL 1907-1910

91071	Trovatore: Vivra contende (w. Cigada).	(87560)	(3032)
91074	Ernani: Ernani involami.		
91075	Forza del Destino: La vergine (w. Cho.).		
91076	Trovatore: Miserere (w. Valls).		
91077	Trovatore: Mira d'acerbe (w. Cigada).	(87559)	(3032)
92000	Masked Ball: Ma dall' arido stelo.	(6414)	(15-1006)
92001	Africana: Gia l'odio.		
92025	Norma: Casta diva.		(6404)
92026	Trovatore: Tacea la notte.		(6415)
92027	Forza del Destino: Pace, Pace.		(6404)
92031	Forza del Destino: Madre Pietosa (w. Cho.).		(6351)
92034	Ruy Blas: O dolce volutta (w. Colazza).		
88223	Aida: I sacri nomi.		(6395)
88239	Aida: O patria mia.	(6395)	(15-1006)
88256	Faust: Ei m'ama.		

COLUMBIA RECORDS 1910

30351	Trovatore: D'amor sull'ali.	(A5194)	(5013M)
30352	Cavalleria Rusticana: Voi lo sapete.	(A5198)	(5035M)
30353	Boheme: Mi chiamano Mimi.	(A5195)	
30354	Trovatore: Tacea la notte.	(A5194)	
30355	Tosca: Vissi d'arte.	(A5195)	
30356	Norma: Casta diva.	(A5197)	(5034M)
30357	Norma: Bello a me ritorna.	(A5197)	(5034M)
30358	Gioconda: Suicidio.	(A5198)	(5035M)
30359	Semiramide: Bel raggio.	(H1016)	(5013M)
30380	Ernani: Ernani involami.	(A5199)	
30381	Aida: Ritorna vincitor.	(A5196)	
30382	Aida: O patria mia.	(A5196)	
30383	Forza del Destino: Pace, Pace.	(A5199)	

IMPORTED COLUMBIA RECORDS 1911-1914

11028	Faust: C'era un Re.	(H42)
11029	Faust: Aria dei gioelli.	(H42)
11034	Masked Ball: Morro, ma prima.	(H39)
11036	Lohengrin: Sola nei miei.	(H43)
11045	Forza del Destino: La vergine (w. Cho.).	(H44)
11046	Forza del Destino: Madre Pietosa (w. Cho.).	(H44)
11047	Mefistofele: Spunta l'aurora.	(H39)
11048	Faust: Ei m'ama.	(H43)
42127	Tosca: Vissi d'arte.	(S62)
42128	Ernani: Ernani involami.	(S62)
74711	Masked Ball: Non sai tu (w. Del Ry).	(H1067)
74712	Masked Ball: O qual soave (w. Del Ry).	(H1067)

BORELLO, Camille (Soprano)

A light and sweet voice well suited to pristine phonograph horns, Borello's soprano appeared on a host of Latin American couplings as well as the domestic ones that follow.

COLUMBIA RECORDS 1909

4035	Lucia: Mad scene.	(A691)
4036	Faust: Air des bijoux.	(A691)
4037	Mignon: Io son Titania.	(A684)
4039	Lakme: Ou va la jeune Hindoue.	(A685)
4040	Romeo: Valse.	(A686)
4077	Mireille: Vals.	(A684)
4078	Dinorah: Ombra leggiera.	(A685)
4087	Martha: Qui sola vergin rosa.	(A687)
4088	Rigoletto: Caro nome.	(A686)
4089	Marriage of Figaro: Deh vieni.	(A687)

BORI, Lucrezia (Soprano)

If there were any deficiencies in Bori's voice, you certainly could not remember them after her poignant final moments as Mimi, Violetta or any other portrayal she made. Only on records, perhaps, is there a tinge of hardness to make one feel that all has not been caught of one of the greatest singing actresses of our time.

VICTOR RED SEAL 1914-1915

87178	Traviata: Addio del passato.		(543)
87181	Danza (Rossini).		(546)
87188	I Hear You Calling Me (Marshall).		
87189	Nina Pancha: Habanera.		(898)
87190	Malaguena (Pagans).		(544)
87217	Clavelitos (Valverde).		(544)
87219	Iris: In pure stille.		(545)
87225	Punao de Rosas: Romanza (w. De Segurola).	(87557)	
88398	Pagliacci: Ballatella.		(6048)
88475	Boheme: Mi chiamano Mimi.		(6048)
88480	La Paloma (Yradier).		(6354)
88524	Iris: Un di al tempio.		
88525	Tales of Hoffmann: Elle a fui.		(6049)
88526	Revoltosa: Porque de mis ojos (w. De Segurola).	(89127)	(6354)

VICTOR RED SEAL 1921-1924

87328	Villanella (Sibella).	(546)
87333	Don Giovanni: Vedrai carino.	(543)
87344	When Love is Kind (Moore).	(898)
87346	Cosi Fan Tutte: In uomini.	(545)
87351	Romeo: Valse.	(542)
87356	Snow Maiden: Je connais.	(542)
87371	Amico Fritz: Son pochi fiori.	(967)
87372	Amico Fritz: Non mi resta.	(967)
87379	Ciribiribin (Pestalozzi).	(986)
87380	Il Bacio (Arditi).	(986)
87391	Manon: Adieu, notre petite table.	(1009)
87392	Lakme: Pourquoi dans les grands bois.	(1009)
	Milonguita (Delfino).	(1033)
	El Majo Discreto (Granados).	(1033)
	Boheme: Vals di Musetta.	(1053)
	Amour Mouille: Valse d'oiseau.	(1053)

87581	Romeo: Ah ne fuis pas (w. Gigli).	(3027)
88633	Marriage of Figaro: Deh vieni.	(6049)
88647	Secret of Suzanne: O gioia, la nube.	
89161	Don Pasquale: Pronta io son (w. De Luca).	(8004)
89162	Don Pasquale: Vado corro (w. De Luca).	(8004)

For other records, see McCORMACK.

BORONAT, Olimpia (Soprano)

IMPORTED VICTOR RED SEAL 1910

88242 Rigoletto: Tutte le feste.   (15-1023)

Note: The solitary Red Seal issue of this highly expressive singer was reinstated as a Heritage Series issue coupled with Don Pasquale: So anch'io.

BOSTON SYMPHONY ORCHESTRA (cond: Muck)

VICTOR RED SEAL 1918

64744	Lohengrin: Prelude to Act 3.	(547)
64766	Nutcracker Suite—Marche Miniature (Tschaikowsky).	(547)
74553	Symphony No. 4—Finale (part I) (Tschaikowsky).	(6050)
74554	Symphony No. 4—Finale (part II) (Tschaikowsky).	(6050)

Note: Several unreleased recordings were assigned numbers including the Secret of Suzanne Overture (64745), Ballet des Sylphes from Damnation of Faust (64746), the finale movement from the A Major Symphony (64754), Rakoczy March also from Damnation of Faust (74555) and Valse des Fleurs from the Nutcracker Suite (74561).

BOURCHIER, Arthur (Actor)

Note: Among the last assigned single-face Red Seal Victor numbers in 1924 was 88689 which was allotted to Bourchier's 1909 English recording of the Dagger Speech from Shakespeare's Macbeth. This was probably designed for Canadian trade or possibly even for an Historical Section.

BRANZELL, Karin (Contralto)

BRUNSWICK RECORDS 1924

Saetergjentens Sondag (Bull).	(15079)	(10122)
Synnoves Sang (Kjerulf).	(15079)	(10122)

Note: A sterling artist who brought to Wagner the same style of beautiful singing that Verdi more unashamedly called for, Branzell is more dramatically presented on other acoustic discs like the imported Homocord recording of the Suicidio from Gioconda, an opera in which she was more accustomed to let Rosa Ponselle sing this aria while she portrayed a fitting rival.

BRASLAU, Sophie (Contralto)

From minor parts in Julien and Oracolo, Braslau went on to the creation of Shanewis and a widespread fame on the concert platform.

VICTOR RED SEAL 1914-1918

64468	Lucrezia Borgia: Brindisi.	(550)
64469	Carmen: Habanera.	(550)
64470	Thy Beaming Eyes (MacDowell).	(557)
64475	Sweedish Love Song (Halsey).	
64478	Chant Juif (Mussorgsky) (in Russian).	
64539	Birds in the Night (Sullivan).	
64540	Last Night (Kjerulf).	(553)

64541	Bid Me Good Bye (Tosti).	(549)
64633	I Love You Truly (Bond).	(556)
64708	Sweetest Story Ever Told (Stults).	(553)
64718	Villanella (Sibella).	(548)
64742	My Lady Chlo (Leighter).	(552)
64747	I'm a-Longin' fo' You (Hathaway).	(552)
64757	Pirate Dreams (Huerter).	(554)
64799	Croon, Croon (Clutsam) (w. Cho.).	(551)
74456	Oh, Dry Those Tears (Del Riego).	(6052)
74577	Eili, Eili (arr. Shalitt).	(6051)

VICTOR RED SEAL 1919-1923

64810	Baby Mine (Johnston).	
64845	My Jesus, as Thou Wilt (Weber).	
64883	Ever of Thee (Hall).	(549)
64887	Greatest Miracle of All (Guion).	
64937	Just a Little House of Love (Wood).	(875)
64967	Girometta (Sibella).	(548)
64983	My Laddie Boy (Akst).	(554)
64996	Swingin' Vine (Grosvenor).	(555)
66035	Cradle Song (Iljinsky).	(551)
66044	Jasmine Door (Scott).	(875)
66083	Ma Li'l' Batteau (Strickland).	(555)
66084	Somebody Loves Me (Starr).	(556)
66115	Some Day You Will Miss Me (Darewski).	(557)
74595	Yohrzeit (Silberta).	(6051)
74681	Same Old, Dear Old Place (Wilson).	(6052)
88597	Mme. Butterfly: Tutti i fior (w. Alda).	(89131) (8044)

BRAUN, Carl (Bass)

COLUMBIA RECORDS 1916-1917

43950	Roslein rot (w. Sembach-Bloch-Goritz).	(E3515)
44003	Merry Wives of Windsor: Falstaffs Trinklied.	(E3097)
44196	Noch sind die Tage (Baumgartner).	(E3097)
44601	Daheim (Kaun).	(E3269)
44602	Rheinlied (Peters).	(E3269)
59428	Waffenschmied: Ach ich war Jungling.	(A5865)
59429	Im Kuhlen Keller (Fischer).	(A5865)

Note: Though he assisted in the German version of Iphigenia in Tauris, Carl Braun was recorded in selections of far inferior calibre, a practice Columbia used as well with most others of his Metropolitan Opera compatriots. Other similar items were undoubtedly made for cheaper foreign-language series.

BRONSKAJA, Eugenie (Soprano)

Unusual ability to cooperate without overpowering or undersinging her male companions on discs, a feat not performed by all sopranos of her day, made Bronskaja especially valuable for recorded ensembles.

COLUMBIA RECORDS 1910

4436	Rigoletto: Si vendetta (w. Blanchart).	(A837)
30422	Rigoletto: Quartet (w. Freeman-Constantino-Blanchart).	(A5177)
30426	Barber of Seville: Io sono docile.	(A5209) (5036M)
30427	Barber of Seville: Una voce poco fa.	(A5209) (5036M)
30428	Romeo: Vals.	(A5211)
30429	Traviata: Parigi, o cara (w. Constantino).	(A5181)
30434	Mignon: Io son Titania.	(A5210)
30435	Rigoletto: E il sol (w. Constantino).	(A5183)
30436	Rigoletto: Tutte le feste (w. Blanchart).	(A5183)

30439	Lucia: Verranno a te (w. Constantino).	(A5182)
30440	Faust: All'erta (w. Constantino-Mardones).	(A5187)
30442	Rigoletto: Figlia, Mio Padre (w. Blanchart).	(A5180)
30443	Lucia: Sextet (w. Freeman-Constantino-Blanchart-Mardones-Cilla)	
		(A5177)
30444	Boheme: O soave fanciulla (w. Constantino).	(A5185)
30445	Faust: Dammi ancor (w. Constantino).	(A5182)
30446	Dinorah: Ombra leggiera.	(A5210)
30447	Lucia: Regnava nel silenzio.	(A5211)
30448	Traviata: Ah, fors e lui.	(A5212)
30452	Traviata: Dite alla giovine (w. Blanchart).	(A5186)
30453	Rigoletto: Veglia o donna (w. Blanchart).	(A5180)
30454	Rigoletto: Caro nome.	(A5193)
30455	Traviata: Sempre libera.	(A5212)
30460	Traviata: Un di felice (w. Constantino).	(A5181)
30471	Lakme: Sous le dome (w. Freeman).	(A5186)
30472	Ave Maria (Gounod).	(A5193)

BROZIA, Zina (Soprano)

Brozia came to Columbia via Paris and Boston, a customary journey.

COLUMBIA RECORDS 1912-1913

19761	Faust: Air des bijoux.	(A1242)
19762	Thais: L'amour est une vertu.	(A1242)
30964	Herodiade: Il est doux.	(A5417)
30966	Mme. Butterfly: Ancora un passo.	(A5417)

BURZIO, Eugenia (Soprano)

IMPORTED COLUMBIA RECORDS 1911-1913

11043	Aida: O patria mia.	(H38)
11044	Africana: Figlio del sol.	(H37)
11049	Mefistofele: Spunta l'aurora.	(H38)
11050	Zulma: Da tanto tempo.	(H52)
11051	Zulma: Oh si ricordiamo.	(H52)
11052	Ave Maria (Gounod).	(H37)
11354	Norma: Casta diva.	(H47)
11355	Adriana Lecouvreur: Io son l'umile.	(H36)
11361	Adriana Lecouvreur: Poveri fiori.	(H36)
11362	Forza del Destino: Me pellegrina.	(H45)
11368	Girl of the Golden West: Laggiu nel Soledad.	(H45)
11369	Sapho: L'ama ognor.	(H50)
11370	Norma: Bello a me.	(H47)
11392	Norma: Qual cor tradisti.	(H46)
11393	Norma: Deh! non volerli (part I).	(H48)
11394	Norma: Deh! non volerli (part II).	(H48)
74715	Otello: Ave Maria.	(H1087)
74716	Mefistofele: L'altra notte.	(H1087)
74722	Norma: Casta diva.	(H1084)
74723	Adriana Lecouvreur: Io son l'umile.	(H1074)
74724	Forza del Destino: Me pellegrina.	(H1074)

Note: Among Burzio's pre-1909 Fonotipia recordings was the celebrated Voi lo sapete from Cavalleria Rusticana on No. 92160, into which role she threw herself with the same vibrant passion she showered on all others.

BUTT, Clara (Contralto)

The low tones of this wonderful contralto make one wish she had recorded in duet with Farinelli.

IMPORTED VICTOR RED SEAL 1912-1913

88385 Abide with Me (Liddle).
88386 Three Fishers (Hullah).
88411 Messiah: He Shall Feed.
88415 Elijah: Oh Rest in the Lord.

Note: In 1924, No. 88676 was assigned to A Summer Night (Goring Thomas), a 1910 English recording.

IMPORTED COLUMBIA RECORDS 1921-1925

6544	The Lost Chord (Sullivan)	(68067D)	(9004M)
29901	The Fairy Pipers (Brewer).	(33044D)	(4011M)
29903	My Treasure (Trevalsa).	(33044D)	
29904	Sweetest Flower That Blows (Hawley)	(33011D)	(4012M)
35935	The Rosary (Nevin).		
65521	Kathleen Mavourneen (Crouch).	(33012D)	
69149	Ye Banks and Braes o' Bonnie Doon	(33012D)	(4011M)
69999	Till I Wake (Woodforde-Finden).	(33011D)	(4012M)
75929	Land of Hope and Glory (Elgar).		
75930	Abide with Me (Liddle).	(68067D)	
	Messiah: He Shall Feed		(9004M)

CALLEJA, Icilio (Tenor)

IMPORTED COLUMBIA RECORDS 1913-1914

41915	Germania: Studenti udite.	(S57)
41916	Otello: Ora e per sempre.	(S58)
41917	Andrea Chernier: Improvviso.	(S60)
41918	Germania: Non chiuder.	(S57)
41919	Andrea Chernier: Come un bel di.	(S60)
41922	Pagliacci: No Pagliaccio.	(S59)
41924	Carmen: Mia tu sei.	(S58)
41925	Isabeau: Canzone del Falco.	(S59)

Note: Several of Calleja's Italian recordings above were issued here on double-faced A and E series, while others appeared in England, as did his arias from Girl of the Golden West issued June 1914 as Col. D9710. He was also a Fonotipia artist; his Otello: Addio being No. 92674 on that label.

CALVE, Emma (Soprano)

So inseparable are Calve and Carmen in many minds that the collector who thinks of her in this fairly low-voiced role will get a surprise and thrill when he first hears her rendition of Ma Lisette. He will then remember that she belonged to a day when the audience required versatility in singing as well as acting.

IMPORTED VICTOR RED SEAL 1903

5000	Carmen: Habanera	(91000)
5001	Enchantement (Massenet).	(91001)
5002	Carmen: Seguidilla.	(91002)
5003	Cavalleria Rusticana: Voi lo sapete.	(91003)

VICTOR RED SEAL 1907-1909

88085	Carmen: Habanera (or.).	(18144)
88086	Cavalleria Rusticana: Voi lo sapete.	(6053)
88087	Pearl of Brazil: Charmant oiseau (or.).	
88087	Pearl of Brazil: Charmant oiseau (p.).	(6054)
88089	Old Folks at Home (Foster) (or.).	
88089	Old Folks at Home (Foster) (p.).	(6056)

88119	Serenade (Gounod).	(6054)
88123	Ma Lisette; Le Printemps (Gounod).	
88124	Carmen: Chanson Boheme.	(6407)
88130	Herodiade: Il est doux.	(6055)
88134	Plaisir d'amour (Martini).	
89019	Carmen: La-bas (w. Dalmores).	

VICTOR RED SEAL 1916

88085	Carmen: Habanera (p.).	(6053)
88570	La Marseillaise (w. Cho.).	(6055)
88572	Trois chansons pour les petits.	(6056)

Note: As with many other singers, the Calve records were frequently remade at later dates, particularly in 1916, but only those with numerical or accompaniment differences are so noted in these listings.

CAMPAGNOLA, Leon (Tenor)

IMPORTED VICTOR RED SEAL 1912

64251	Favorita: Une ange.
74297	Sigurd: Esprits gardiens.

Note: The first act aria from Donizetti's French grand opera above was coupled with the last act "Ange si pur" on blue seal Victor No. 45119, issued in 1917 along with ten other Campagnola recordings including duets from Manon and Romeo with his wife Berthe Cesar.

CAMPANARI, Giuseppe (Baritone)

Campanari made a youthful debut in Masked Ball at Teatro Dal Verme but lost his voice and turned to the cello, which instrument he played in the Boston Symphony Orchestra. Regaining his voice, he continued in opera as a major participant in the glittering Metropolitan casts which Maurice Grau assembled.

COLUMBIA RECORDS 1903

1224	Faust: Dio possente.	
1225	Serenata (Sepilli).	
1226	Barber of Seville: Largo al factotum.	(A619)
1227	Carmen: Canzone del Toreador.	(A619)
1445	Africana: All'erta. Marinar.	(A620)

VICTOR RED SEAL 1903-1905

81010	Traviata: Di Provenza.
81011	Carmen: Canzone del Toreador.
81012	Barber of Seville: Largo al factotum.
81044	Mia sposa sara la mia bandiera (Rotoli).
81071	Traviata: Di Provenza.
81074	Gioconda: Ah Pescator.
81075	Mia sposa sara la mia bandiera (Rotoli).
81080	Barber of Seville: Largo al factotum.
81081	Danza (Rossini).
81082	Trovatore: Il balen.
85001	Masked Ball: Eri tu.
85002	Gloria a Te (Buzzi-Peccia).
85003	Carmen: Canzone del Toreador.
85026	Rigoletto: Pari siamo.
85027	Africana: Adamastor.
85028	Pagliacci: Prologo.
85073	Carmen: Canzone del Toreador.
85074	Gloria a Te (Buzzi-Peccia).

85078   Africana: Adamastor.
85079   Rigoletto: Pari siamo.
85080   Masked Ball: Eri tu.
85081   Pagliacci: Prologo.
85086   Faust: Dio possente.
85087   Ernani: O de' verd' anni miei.
85088   Herodiade: Visione fuggitiva.

COLUMBIA RECORDS 1909

4091	Marriage of Figaro: Se vuol ballare.		(A740)
4092	Marriage of Figaro: Non piu andrai.		(A740)
30243	Pagliacci: Prologo.		(A5126)
30244	Carmen: Canzone del Toreador.	(A5125)	(A5777)
30257	Barber of Seville: Largo al factotum.	(A5128)	(A5777)
30258	Danza (Rossini).		(A5128)
30263	Masked Ball: Eri tu.		(A5125)
30264	Myosotis (Tirindelli).		(A5126)
30265	Musica Proibita (Gastaldon).		(A5127)
30266	Herodiade: Visione fuggitiva.		(A5127)

Note: The earliest Columbias as well as Victors through 81044 and 85028 have piano accompaniments; those released after 1904 are with orchestra.

CAPRILE, Giorgina (Soprano)

IMPORTED VICTOR RED SEAL 1914-1915

88493   Traviata: Alfredo, Alfredo (w. De Gregorio-Maggi-Cho.).
88509   Traviata: Brindisi (w. De Gregorio-Cho.).

Note: Other Italian Gramophone records exist of this singer, the above concerted pieces being originally issued by that company as Nos. 054419/8; also a number of Fonotipias including rarely sung duets with Krismer from Damnation of Faust on Nos. 92574/7.

CARTICA, Carlo (Tenor)

As former member of La Scala Opera and possessor of a good, virile voice and style, Cartica seemed worthy of more exalted rank than his popular-priced blue label concerted discs.

COLUMBIA RECORDS 1911-1912

30709	Lucia: Sextet (w. Wright-Heims-Alessandroni, etc.).	(A5305)
30710	Rigoletto: Quartet (w. Wright-Heims-Alessandroni, etc.).	(A5306)
30795	Faust: All'erta (w. Wright-Heims-Alessandroni).	(A5381)
30809	Forza del Destino: Solenne (w. Alessandroni).	(A5343)
30817	Martha: Solo profugo (w. Alessandroni).	(A5343)
36426	Lombardi: Qual volutta (w. Kaestner-Alessandroni).	(A5446)
36503	Wm. Tell: Troncar suoi di (w. Alessandroni-Bauer).	(A5465)

For other records, see VILLANI

CARUSO, Enrico (Tenor)

The greatest testimony to the importance of the phonograph record lies in the name of Enrico Caruso. His was not the largest voice, the most beautiful or the best produced but it was the greatest combination of all three just as it most poignantly combined musical and dramatic feeling. No inadequacy of recording or reproducing equipment could throttle this voice, and it was the superlative ability to relive his greatness on all his records that made him the most widely known singer of the twentieth century.

IMPORTED VICTOR RED SEAL 1903

5008	Aida: Celeste Aida.	(91007)
5009	Gioconda: Cielo e mar.	(91008)
5010	Tosca: E lucevan le stelle.	(91009)
5011	La Mia Canzone (Tosti).	(91010)
5012	Cavalleria Rusticana: Siciliana.	(91011)
5014	Non t'amo piu (Denza).	(91013)
5016	Pagliacci: Vesti la giubba.	(91014)

VICTOR RED SEAL 1904-1905 (piano acc.)

81025	Rigoletto: Questa o quella.	(522)
81026	Rigoletto: La donna e mobile.	(522)
81027	Elisir d'Amore: Una furtiva lagrima (part I).	(930)
81028	Tosca: E lucevan le stelle.	(523)
81029	Tosca: Recondita armonia.	
81030	Cavalleria Rusticana: Siciliana.	(521)
81031	Manon: Il sogno.	(523)
81032	Pagliacci: Vesti la giubba.	(930)
81062	Cavalleria Rusticana: Brindisi.	(521)
85021	Elisir d'Amore: Una furtiva lagrima (part II).	
85022	Aida: Celeste Aida.	
85048	Don Pasquale: Com'e gentil.	(6036)
85049	Carmen: Canzone del fior.	
85055	Gioconda: Cielo e mar.	(6036)
85056	Hugenots: Bianca al par.	

VICTOR RED SEAL 1906-1908

87001	Trovatore: Di quella pira.	(512) (3031)
87017	Rigoletto: La donna e mobile.	(500)
87018	Rigoletto: Questa o quella.	(500)
88001	Martha: M'appari.	(15-1036)
88002	Boheme: Che gelida manina.	(6003)
88003	Faust: Salut demeure.	(6004)
88004	Favorita: Spirto gentil.	(6005) (15-1036)
88048	Triste Ritorno (Barthelemy).	(6030)
88049	Ideale (Tosti).	(6019)
88054	Africana: O Paradiso.	(6007)
88060	Andrea Chernier: Improvviso.	(6008)
88061	Pagliacci: Vesti la giubba.	(6001)
88106	Don Sebastiano: In terra sola.	(6014) (15-1037)
88115	Adorables tourments (Barthelemy).	(6006)
88120	Lolita (Buzzi-Peccia).	(6003)
88121	Trovatore: Ah si ben mio.	(6002)
88127	Aida: Celeste Aida (no recitative).	
89001	Forza del Destino: Solenne (w. Scotti).	(8000)
89006	Boheme: Ah Mimi (w. Scotti).	(8000)
89007	Pearl Fishers: Del tempio (w. Ancona).	(8036)
89017	Mme. Butterfly: O quanti occhi (w. Farrar).	(8011)
89018	Trovatore: Ai nostri monti (w. Homer).	(8013)
95200	Boheme: O soave fanciulla (w. Melba).	
96000	Rigoletto: Quartet (w. Abott-Homer-Scotti).	(10011)
96001	Rigoletto: Quartet (w. Sembrich-Severina-Scotti).	(10001) (16-5001)
96002	Boheme: Addio dolce (w. Farrar-Viafora-Scotti)	(10007) (16-5001)
96200	Lucia: Sextet (w. Sembrich-Severina-Scotti-Journet-Daddi).	(10001)

VICTOR RED SEAL 1909-1911

87041	Queen of Sheba (Goldmark): Magiche note.	(520)
87042	Pour un baiser (Tosti).	(517)
87043	Tosca: Recondita armonia.	(511)
87044	Tosca: E lucevan le stelle.	(511)

87053	Germania: Studenti, udite.		(508)
87054	Germania: Non chiuder.		(508)
87070	For You Alone (Giehl).		(507)
87071	Otello: Ora e per sempre addio.		(505)
87072	Cavalleria Rusticana: Siciliana.		(516)
88206	Mamma Mia (Nutile).		(6009)
88207	Forza del Destino: O tu che in seno.		(6000)
88208	Carmen: Air de la fleur.		(6004)
88209	Carmen: Canzone del fior.		(6007)
88210	Hugenots: Bianca al par.	(6005)	(15-1037)
88246	Gioconda: Cielo e mar.		(6020)
88279	Pagliacci: No, Pagliaccio non son.		(6001)
88280	Addio (Tosti).	(6021)	(7156)
89028	Aida: La fatal pietra (w. Gadski).		(8015)
89029	Aida: O terra addio (w. Gadski).		(8015)
89030	Trovatore: Miserere (w. Alda-Cho.).		(8042)
89031	Faust: Eternelle (w. Farrar).		(8009)
89032	Faust: Laisse-moi (w. Farrar).		(8009)
89033	Faust: Mon coeur (w. Farrar).		(8010)
89034	Faust: Voici la rue (w. Farrar).		(8010)
89036	Martha: Solo, profugo (w. Journet).		(8016)
89039	Faust: O Merveille (w. Journet).		(8016)
89043	Mme. Butterfly: Amore o grillo (w. Scotti).		(8014)
89047	Mme. Butterfly: Ve lo dissi (w. Scotti).		(8014)
89049	Trovatore: Mal reggendo (w. Homer).		(8013)
89050	Aida: Gia i sacerdoti (w. Homer).	(8012)	(15-1025)
89051	Aida: Aida a me togliesti (w. Homer).	(8012)	(15-1025)
95203	Faust: Alerte (w. Farrar-Journet).	(10008)	(16-5003)
95204	Faust: Seigneur Dieu (w. Farrar-Mme. Gilibert-Journet).		(10004)
95205	Faust: Eh quoi (w. Farrar-Mme. Gilibert-Journet).		(10004)
95206	Faust: Que voulez-vous (w. Scotti-Journet).		(10011)

VICTOR RED SEAL 1912-1915

87091	Masked Ball: Barcarola.		(512)
87092	Canta pe' me (de Curtis).		(502)
87095	Love is Mine (Gartner).		(510)
87122	Because (d'Hardelot).		(506)
87128	Pimpinella (Tschaikowsky).		(513)
87135	Manon Lescaut: Donna non vidi mai.		(505)
87159	Your Eyes Have Told (O'Hara).		(514)
87161	Lasciati amar (Leoncavallo).		(509)
87162	Guardann'a luna (de Crescenzo).		(509)
87169	Serenade Espagnole (Ronald).		(520)
87175	Serenade de Don Juan (Tschaikowsky).		(513)
87176	Amor Mio (Ricciardi).		(504)
87186	Parted (Tosti).		(510)
87187	Trusting Eyes (Gartner).		(514)
87211	Hantise d'amour (Szulc).		(506)
87213	La Mia Canzone (Tosti).		(503)
87218	Cielo Turchino (Ciociano).		(504)
87511	Traviata: Brindisi (w. Gluck-Cho.).		(3031)
88127	Aida: Celeste Aida (with recitative).		(6000)
88331	Boheme (Leoncavallo): Testa adorata.		(6012)
88333	Eternamente (Mascheroni).		(6034)
88334	Core 'ngrato (Cardillo).		(6032)
88335	Boheme (Leoncavallo): Io non ho.	(6012)	(15-1038)
88339	Elisir d'Amore: Una furtiva lagrima.		(6016)
88345	Lo Schiavo: Quando nascesti tu.		(6027)
88346	Masked Ball: Ma se m'e forza.		(6031)
88347	Tarantella Sincera (de Crescenzo).		(6031)
88348	Manon: Ah fuyez.	(6020)	(15-1004)
88355	Danza (Rossini).	(6031)	(15-1040)

88376	Dreams of Long Ago (Caruso).		(6015)
88378	Lost Chord (Sullivan).		(6023)
88403	Hosanna (Granier).		(6022)
88425	Agnus Dei (Bizet).		(6010)
88429	Rigoletto: Parmi veder le lagrime.		(6016)
88439	Fenesta che lucive.	(6019)	(15-1040)
88458	Cavalleria Rusticana: Addio alla madre.		(6008)
88459	Les Rameaux (Faure).		(6022)
88460	Stabat Mater: Cuius Animam.		(6028)
88465	Manella Mia (Valente).		(6025)
88472	Tiempo antico (Caruso) (1916).		(6033)
88514	Requiem (Verdi): Ingemisco.		(6028)
88516	Duca d'Alba: Angelo casto.		(6355)
88517	Pecche (Pennino).		(6025)
89052	Forza del Destino: Invano, Alvaro (w. Amato).		(8005)
89053	Forza del Destino: Le minaccie (w. Amato).		(8005)
89054	Crucifix (Faure) (w. Journet).		(6347)
89059	Manon: On l'appelle (w. Farrar).		(8011)
89060	Trovatore: Ai nostri monti (w. Schumann-Heink).		(8042)
89064	Don Carlos: Dio che nell'alma (w. Scotti).		(8036)
89065	Ave Maria (Kahn) (v. Elman).		(8007)
89066	Elegie (Massenet) (v. Elman).		(8007)
89075	Otello: Si per ciel (w. Ruffo).		(8045)
89076	Masked Ball: E scherzo (w. Hempel-Duchene-Rothier-De Segurola).		
		(10005)	(16-5000)
89077	Masked Ball: La rivedro (w. Hempel-Rothier-De Segurola).		(10005)
89078	Guarany: Sento un forza (w. Destinn).		(6355)
89084	Si vous l'avez compris (Denza) (v. Elman).		(8008)
89085	Deux Serenades (Leoncavallo) (v. Elman).		(8008)
95207	Martha: Siam giunti (w. Alda-Jacoby-Journet).		(10002)
95208	Martha: Che vuol dir (w. Alda-Jacoby-Journet).		(10002)
95209	Martha: Presto, Presto (w. Alda-Jacoby-Journet).		(10003)
95210	Martha: Quartetto Notturno (w. Alda-Jacoby-Journet).		
		(10003)	(16-5002)
95211	Lombardi: Qual volutta (w. Alda-Journet).	(10010)	(16-5002)
96201	Lucia: Sextet (w. Tetrazzini-Jacoby-Amato-Journet-Bada).		(16-5000)
	Rigoletto: Quartet (w. Tetrazzini-Jacoby-Amato).		(15-1019)

VICTOR RED SEAL 1916-1920 (and later releases)

87242	Luna d'estate (Tosti).	(519)
87243	O Sole Mio (di Capua).	(501)
87266	Andrea Chernier: Come un bel di.	(516)
87269	Pearl Fishers: De mon amie.	(513)
87271	Pourquoi (Tschaikowsky).	(517)
87272	L'Alba separa (Tosti).	(503)
87294	Over There (Cohan).	(515)
87297	Inno di Garibaldi (Olivieri).	(515)
87304	A Vucchella (Tosti).	(501)
87305	Vieni sul mar.	(518)
87312	Addio a Napoli (Cottrau).	(502)
87321	A Dream (Bartlett).	(507)
87335	Messe Solenelle (Rossini): Crucifixus.	
87358	Nina (att: Pergolesi).	(519)
87365	Tu, Ca Nun Chiange (de Curtis).	(958)
87366	Noche Feliz (Posadas).	(958)
87395	Scordame (Fucito).	(1007)
87396	Senza Nisciuno (de Curtis).	(1007)
	Vaghissima Sembianza (Donaudy).	(1117)
	Sultanto a te (Fucito).	(1117)
	Amadis: Bois epais.	(1437)
	Premiere caresse (de Crescenzo).	(1437)

88001	Martha: M'appari (1917 rec.).		(6002)
88552	Queen of Sheba: Inspirez-moi.		(6035)
88554	Cid: O Souverain.		(6013)
88555	Mia sposa sara la mia bandiera (Rotoli).		(6018)
88556	La Procession (Franck).		(6035)
88558	Macbeth: Ah la paterna mano.	(6014)	(15-1038)
88559	Sancta Maria (Faure).		(6029)
88560	Santa Lucia.		(6032)
88561	Noel (Adam).		(6029)
88579	Chanson de Juin (Godard).		(6006)
88580	Pearl Fishers: Je crois entendre.		(6026)
88581	Samson: Vois, ma misere (w. Cho.).	(6026)	(15-1039)
88582	Eugen Onegin: Echo lointain.		(6017)
88586	Musica Proibita (Gastaldon).		(6021)
88587	Uocchie Celeste (de Crescenzo).		(6030)
88589	Nero: Ah mon sort.	(6017)	(15-1039)
88599	Pieta Signore (att: Stradella).		(6024)
88600	Regiment de Sambre et Meuse (Planquette).		(6018)
88612	Campana de San Giusto (Arona).		(6011)
88615	Campane a Sera (Malfetti).		(6024)
88616	Love Me or Not (Secchi).		(6015)
88617	Serse: Largo.		(6023)
88623	A Granada (Alvarez).	(6011)	(8038)
88625	La Juive: Rachel quand du Seigneur.	(6013)	(15-1004)
88628	Serenata (Bracco).		(6033)
88629	Messe Solenelle (Rossini): Domine Deus.		(6010)
88635	I'm' Arricordo e Napule (Gioe).		(6009)
88638	Salvator Rosa: Mia piccirella.		(6034)
88670	La Partida (Alvarez).		(6458)
88671	El Milargo de una Virgen (Chapi).		(6458)
	Africana: Deh ch'io ritorna		(7156)
89083	A la luz de la Luna (Michelena) (w. De Gogorza).		(8038)
89087	Forza del Destino: Il segreto fu dunque (w. De Luca).		(8006)
89088	Samson: Je viens celebrer (w. Homer-Journet).	(10010)	(16-5003)
89089	Elisir d'Amore: Venti scudi (w. De Luca).		(8006)
95100	Rigoletto: Quartet (w. Galli-Curci, Perini, De Luca).		(10000)
95212	Lucia: Sextet (w. Galli-Curci, Egener, De Luca, Journet Bada).		(10000)

Note: Unreleased Caruso recordings to which numbers were assigned include Souviens-toi (87293), Celeste Aida (88025) and the barcarola from Masked Ball (88332). According to some lists, Victor No. 91012 was also assigned to the siciliana from Cavalleria Rusticana but may have concealed a different 1902/3 Milan issue. The slightly later twelve-inch recording of "Mi par d'udir ancor" from Pearl Fishers (G. & T. No. 052066) was assigned Victor No. 92036 at a much later date. Whether or not it so appeared, this interesting recording with its more youthful lyricism and hooted falsetto is quite common as Opera Disc No. 76062. In addition to several European Zonophone discs, Caruso appears on Pathe hill-and-dale. Of the latter, two otherwise unrecorded selections, the Qui sotto in ciel from Hugenots and Tu non mi vuoi piu bene by Pini-Corsi, have been re-recorded by Collectors Record Shop, while a Tosca: E lucevan le stelle was dubbed on Emerson. There are, of course, numerous Victor dubbings.

CASALS, Pablo (Cellist)

No musician of our time has excelled this Spaniard in the warm humanity of his interpretations and the perfection of his impeccable technique, as free of pedantry or carelessness in Kathleen Mavourneen as in the Bach C Major Suite.

COLUMBIA RECORDS 1915-1919

Largo (Handel).	(A5649)
Melody in F (Rubenstein).	(A5649)

Le Cygne (Saint-Saens).			(A5650)
Serenade—Spanish Dance No. 2 (Popper).			(A5650)
Concerto in D Minor—Adagio (Tartini).			(A5654)
Romanza (Campagnoli).			(A5654)
Traumerei (Schumann).			(A5679)
Salut d'amour (Elgar).			(A5679)
Suite in C—Bourree (Bach).			(A5697)
Mazurka (Popper).			(A5697)
Kol Nidre (part I) (Bruch).			(A5722)
Kol Nidre (part II) (Bruch).			(A5722)
Liebestraum (Liszt).			(A5756)
Air for G String (Bach).			(A5756)
Suite in C—Prelude (Bach).			(A5782)
Suite in C—Sarabande (Bach).			(A5782)
Allegro Appassionato (Saint-Saens).			(A5821)
Minuet in C (Haydn).			(A5821)
Spanish Dance (Granados-Casals).			(A5847)
Concerto in A Minor—Cantilena (Goltermann).			(A5847)
Concerto in D—Adagio (Haydn).			(A5875)
Suite in C—Gigue (Bach).			(A5875)
Abendlied (Schumann).			(A5907)
Chanson Louis XIII (Couperin-Kreisler).			(A5907)
Tannhauser: Evening Star.			(A5953)
Quintet in D—Larghetto (Mozart).			(A5953)
Spring Song (Mendelssohn).			(A6020)
Apres un Reve (Faure).			(A6020)

COLUMBIA RECORDS 1920-1925

48710	Sonata in A—Allegro (Boccherini).	(68025D)		
49795	Traumerei (Schumann).	(68023D)	(7020M)	(5091M)
49796	Le Cygne (Saint-Saens).	(68027D)	(7021M)	(5092M)
49801	Abendlied (Schumann).	(68024D)	(7020M)	(5091M)
49802	Serse: Largo.	(68061D)	(7053M)	
49804	Melody in F (Rubenstein).	(68026D)		
49812	Liebestraum (Liszt).	(68023D)		
49813	Tannhauser: Evening Star.	(68027D)	(7021M)	(5092M)
49814	Air for G String (Bach).	(68026D)		
49820	Nocturne in E Flat Op. 9 No. 2 (Chopin).	(68024D)	(8901M)	
98012	Gavotte in D (Popper).	(68025D)		
79147	Thine Eyes So Blue (Lassen).	(33032D)	(2009M)	
79154	Kathleen Mavourneen (Crouch).	(33008D)		
79155	Believe Me if All Those Endearing Young Charms.	(33008D)	(2021M)	
80158	Salut d'amour (Elgar).	(33031D)		
80159	Would God I Were the Tender Apple Blossom.	(33032D)	(2009M)	
80815	Romance (Rubenstein).	(33031D)	(2021M)	
80817	To a Wild Rose (MacDowell).	(33030D)	(2010M)	(184M)
80923	Arabian Melody (Glazounow).	(33030D)	(2010M)	(184M)
	Serenade-Romance Sans Paroles (Mendelssohn).	(33048D)	(2011M)	
	Melody in E Flat (Tschaikowsky).	(33048D)	(2011M)	
	Kol Nidre (part I) (Bruch).	(68019D)		
	Kol Nidre (part II) (Bruch).	(68019D)		
	Adagio Op. 101 (Haydn).	(68061D)	(7053M)	
	Sapphic Ode (Brahms).	(68089D)	(7075M)	
	Autumn Song Op. 37 No. 10 (Tschaikowsky).	(68089D)	(7075M)	
	Minuet (Handel).		(2036M)	
	Serenata Napoletana (Sgambati).		(2036M)	
	Berceuse (Cui).		(2037M)	
	Oh Dry Those Tears (Del Riego).		(2037M)	

VICTOR RED SEAL 1925

Toccata in C—Adagio (Bach).   (6501)
Goyescas: Intermezzo.   (6501)

CASAZZA, Elvira (Mezzo-Soprano)

For duets, see DE MURO, GIGLI.

Note: In Italy, Casazza appeared on other labels including La Fonografia
Nazionale-Milano on which she recorded a number of items from Nerone, issued
in 1924 when that posthumous work of Boito had its premiere under Toscanini
with Raisa and Pertile.

CASE, Anna (Soprano)

See GADSKI.

Note: This charming soprano was one of the leading lights on Edison cylinders
and discs.

CASTELLANO, Edoardo (Tenor)

COLUMBIA RECORDS 1907-1908

30064	Tosca: E lucevan le stelle.	
30065	Elisir d'Amore: Una furtiva lagrima.	
30085	Boheme: Mimi e una civetta.	
30093	Gioconda: Cielo e mar.	(A5006)
30094	Rigoletto: Questa o quella.	(A5005)
30118	Pagliacci: Vesti la giubba.	(A5002)
30120	Aprite la finestra (Cimmino).	(A5009)
30135	Tosca: Recondita armonia.	(A5070)

Note: Castellano was more noted in South America, where some of the selections listed were originally released, then later coupled on C series. Piano accompaniment versions of certain arias were also made, the one from Rigoletto
appearing as No. 010019 on the flexible Columbia-Marconi discs.

CAVALIERI, Elda (Soprano)

Though possessed of a thrilling voice, akin to that of Boninsegna, Elda
Cavalieri was reclassified into the blue seal category only a few years after her
fine records first appeared.

VICTOR RED SEAL 1906-1907

64056	Tu-Habanera (Fuentes) (p.).	
64057	Traviata: Addio del passato.	(45018)
64058	Boheme: Vals di Musetta.	(45020)
64059	Adriana Lecouvreur: Io son l'umile.	(45018)
64060	Fedora: O grandi occhi.	(45019)
64061	Manon Lescaut: In quelle trine.	(45020)
64062	Andrea Chernier: La mamma morta.	(45019)
64063	La Sevillana (Yradier).	(45022)
64064	Tu-Habanera (Fuentes) (or.).	(45022)
64065	Ultimo Bacio (Tosti).	(45021)
64066	A una Morena (Alvarez).	
64067	Non ti ricordi piu (Doda).	(45021)
74048	Gioconda: Suicidio.	(55015)
74049	Mefistofele: L'altra notte.	(55015)
74050	Forza del Destino: Pace, Pace.	(55013)
74054	Tosca: Vissi d'arte.	(55011)
74055	Aida: O Patria Mia.	(55013)

74056	Boheme: Mi chiamano Mimi.	(55011)
74057	Los Ojos Negros (Alvarez).	(55012)
74058	Trovatore: Tacea la notte.	(55014)
74059	Cavalleria Rusticana: Voi lo sapete.	(55014)
74060	La Paloma (Yradier).	(55012)
74061	Ave Maria (Tosti).	

CAVALIERI, Lina (Soprano)

While she figured most notably in the press of her day as "the most beautiful woman on the stage", Lina Cavalieri sang and acted with artistry in spite of it.

COLUMBIA RECORDS 1910-1913

30347	Boheme: Mi chiamano Mimi.		(A5172)
30372	Carmen: Habanera.		(A5179)
30376	Tosca: Vissi d'arte.		(A5178)
30378	Manon Lescaut: In quelle trine.		(A5178)
30396	Mefistofele: L'altra notte.		(A5172)
30397	Faust: Aria dei gioelli.	(H1053)	(7030M)
30400	Maria, Mari (di Capua).		(A5179)
38715	O Sole Mio (di Capua).		(A1434)
38717	Mattinata (Tosti).		(A1434)

CHALIA, Rosalia (Soprano)

Note: Chalia was a seasoned recorder for practically all outfits from Bettini cylinders on. Of the hundreds of selections she made, one especially interesting is Cavalleria Rusticana: Voi lo sapete, No. 68400, since she made her Metropol.tan Opera debut in this role in 1898, long before this black seal Victor was first released.

CHALIAPIN, Feodor (Bass)

Who can write dispassionately of Chaliapin? Only one who never saw him as Mephistopheles picking up a Siebel and carrying him (her) off the stage under his arm or as Boris surmounting all language barriers between himself and the chorus, not to mention the audience, could perhaps apply analytical criteria to his enthralling records. For the most of us, listening to practically any one he ever made, and there were hundreds, a captivating art, which defied many conventions and all recording difficulties, leaves only a grateful wonderment.

IMPORTED VICTOR RED SEAL 1914

| 88461 | Mefistofele: Ave Signor. | |
| 88462 | Norma: Ite sul colle (w. Cho.). | (15-1042) |

VICTOR RED SEAL 1923-1925

87349	Boris Godounow: In the town of Kazan.	(558)
87355	Sonnambula: Vi ravviso.	(981)
87361	Prince Igor: Air of Prince Galitsky.	(558)
87367	Faust: Le veau d'or (w. Cho.).	(960)
87368	Faust: Serenade.	(960)
87378	Mefistofele: Ave Signor.	(981)
87389	Pilgrim's Song (Tschaikowsky).	(1004)
87390	Siberian Prisoner's Song.	(1004)
	Down the Petersky.	(1050)
	Dubinushka (w. Cho.).	(1050)
	Don Giovanni: Madamina.	(1105)
	Don Giovanni: Nella bionda.	(1105)

88644	Song of the Flea (Moussorgsky).	(6416)
88645	Two Grenadiers (Schumann).	(6057)
88646	When the King Went Forth (Koenemann).	(6061)
88648	Barber of Seville: La calunnia.	(6059)
88655	The Prophet (Rimsky-Korsakoff).	(6058)
88656	Midnight Review (Glinka).	(6057)
88657	In questa tomba (Beethoven).	(6059)
88659	Trepak (Moussorgsky).	(6061)
88661	Boris Godounow: Farewell of Boris.	(6455)
88663	Song of the Volga Boatman.	(6058)
88665	Don Carlos: Ella giammai m'amo.	
88666	Sadko: Song of the Viking Guest.	(6416)
88669	Boris Godounow: Death of Boris (w. Cho.).	(6455)
	Boris Godounow: Pimen's Monologue.	(6489)
	Boris Godounow: I Have Attained the Highest Power.	(6489)
	Doubt (Glinka).	(6512)
	Le Cor (Flegier).	(6512)
	The Nightingale (Tschaikowsky).	(6532)
	The Last Voyage (Alnaes).	(6532)
	Oh Could I But Express (Malashkin).	(6533)
	Prince Igor: How Goes it, Prince.	(6533)
	Life for the Czar: Now I am far.	(6534)
	Life for the Czar: The truth is suspected.	(6534)
	Robert: Suore che riposate.	(15-1045)

Note: Most of the above were pressed from imported masters which, in a few
cases, soon gave way to domestic replacements under the same numbers. A group
of his 1909-1912 European recordings in Russian were also given catalogue
numbers in 1924 though they did not appear under them in this country. Included were Down the Volga: From under the oak (w. Cho.) as 88677, Power
of Evil: Merry Butterweek as 88678, Lakme: Lakme, a shadow as 88679
(15-1041), The Birches (w. Cho.) as 88680, Faust: It was high time as 88681
(15-1041), Faust: When the Book (w. Michailowa) as 88682, Dubinushka (w.
Cho.) as 88683, Night as 88684, The Tempest Rages (Sokoloff) as 88685 and
Not a Little Autumn Rain (w. Cho.) as 88686. As noted, two selections did
finally appear on Heritage Series, on which another early recording of the bass
aria from Don Carlos was issued as No. 15-1045. Since his later domestic rendition of this was equally good or even superior, it is unfortunate Victor did not
rather choose one of his 1908 Russian and Ludmilla pieces, either Gr. 022109 or
022113.

CHAMLEE, Mario (Tenor)

    As Archer Chamlee, preceding his very successful Metropolitan debut, he
was Brunswick's earliest celebrity; the more tenorish first name was soon
substituted.

BRUNSWICK RECORDS 1920-1925

10000	For You Alone (Giehl).	(15012)	(10105)
10001	Absent (Metcalf).	(15011)	(10104)
10002	A Perfect Day (Bond).	(15011)	(10104)
10003	Elegie (Massenet).		
10005	Pagliacci: Vesti la giubba.	(15007)	
10006	Who Knows (Ball).		
10008	Cavalleria Rusticana: Siciliana.	(15008)	
10014	Rigoletto: Questa o quella.		
10016	Martha: M'appari.		
10018	Your Eyes Have Told Me (O'Hara).		
10020	Tosca: Recondita armonia.	(15008)	
10024	Tosca: E lucevan le stelle.	(15007)	
10026	Thank God for a Garden (Del Riego).		

10030	Santa Lucia.	(15010)	(10103)
10033	Love is Mine (Gartner).		
10040	Dreams of Long Ago (Caruso).	(15012)	(10105)
10042	O Sole Mio (di Capua).	(15010)	(10103)
10045	Holy Night (Adam) (w. Cho.).		
10049	Rigoletto: La donna e mobile.		
	My Dreams (Tosti).	(15023)	(10107)
	Parted (Tosti).	(15023)	(10107)
	Lolita (Buzzi-Peccia).	(15037)	(10109)
	Mattinata (Leoncavallo).	(15037)	(10109)
	Africana: O Paradiso.	(15040)	
	Manon: Le reve.	(15040)	
	Call Me No More (Cadman).	(15051)	(10111)
	Your Voice (Quirke).	(15051)	(10111)
	Cavalleria Rusticana: Brindisi.	(15056)	
	Gioconda: Cielo e mar.	(15056)	
	Dreams Dimly Lying (Roxas).	(15065)	(10115)
	Last Hour (Kramer).	(15065)	(10115)
	Moon Dream Shore (Lockhart).	(15071)	(10117)
	Out of the Dusk to You (Lee).	(15071)	(10117)
	The Old Refrain (Kreisler).	(15077)	(10121)
	Serenade (Drigo).	(15077)	(10121)
	At Night (Rachmaninoff).	(15080)	(10123)
	Tell Me Why (Tschaikowsky).	(15080)	(10123)
	Paquita (Buzzi-Peccia).	(15084)	(10126)
	Jocelyn: Berceuse (viol. Fradkin).	(15084)	(10126)
	Marcheta (Schertzinger).		(10101)
	Memory Lane (Spier).		(10101)
	Dream On (Herbert).		(10158)
	Me Neenyah (Spencer).		(10158)
	My Desire (Cadman).		(10188)
	Mother, O My Mother (Ball).		(10188)
	I Look into Your Garden (Wood).		(10201)
	Give Me One Rose (Grey).		(10201)
	Goin' Home (Dvorak-Fisher).		(10212)
	Liebestraum (Liszt-Schipa).		(10212)
30018	Carmen: Air de la fleur.		
	L'alba separa dalla luce (Tosti).	(50020)	
	Triste Ritorno (Barthelemy).	(50020)	
	Agnus Dei (Bizet) (viol. Fradkin).	(50021)	
	Ave Maria (Kahn) (viol. Fradkin).	(50021)	
	Elisir d'Amore: Una furtiva lagrima.	(50030)	
	Faust: Salut demeure.	(50030)	
	Ah Moon of My Delight (Lehmann).	(50040)	(30103)
	When My Ships Come Sailing (Dorel).	(50040)	(30103)
	On the Road to Mandalay (Speaks).	(50046)	(30104)
	Oh Dry Those Tears (Del Riego).	(50046)	(30104)
	Boheme: Che gelida manina.	(50003)	
	Manon: Ah fuyez.	(50003)	
	Open the Gates of the Temple (Knapp).		(30110)
	Hosanna (Granier).		(30110)

For other records, see ONEGIN.

CHEMET, Renee (Violinist)
            IMPORTED VICTOR RED SEAL 1922-1925
66043	Waltz (Weber).	(613)
66063	Bourree (arr. Moffat).	
66076	Sonata in G Minor—Presto non troppo (Tartini).	(613)
66259	By the Waters of Minnetonka (Lieurance).	(1015)
66260	Under the leaves (Thome).	(1015)

74751	Sonata in G Minor—Andante con moto (Tartini).	(6349)
74752	Sonata in G Minor—Largo; allegro (Tartini).	(6349)
	Adoration (Borowski).	(6473)
	Romance (d'Ambrosio).	(6473)
	Rondo (Mozart-Kreisler).	(6497)
	Sonata in E—Adagio; Allegro (Handel).	(6497)

CIAPARELLI-VIAFORA, Gina

Since Victor gave this singer Red Seal billing under her marriage name of Viafora, it is only fair that the equally good Columbia domestic recordings of Ciaparelli be listed though they belonged to a lower-priced category.

COLUMBIA RECORDS 1905-1907

3144	Carmen: Avanera.		
3145	Faust: Aria dei gioelli.		(A534)
3158	Trovatore: Mira d'acerbe (w. Parvis) (p.).		(A536)
3160	Semiramide: Bel raggio.		(A535)
3161	Trovatore: Di tal amor.		(A541)
3163	Traviata: Dite alla giovine (w. Parvis).		(A539)
3164	Barber of Seville: Io son docile (p.).		(C138)
3169	Traviata: Brindisi.		(A539)
3177	Mare Azzuro (Collena).		(A525)
3178	Boheme: Vals di Musetta.		(A580)
3179	Cavalleria Rusticana: Voi lo sapete.		(A544)
3197	Boheme: Mi chiamano Mimi.		
3232	Mattinata (Leoncavallo).		(C144)
3255	Barber of Seville: Io son docile (or.).		(A537)
3274	Addio (Tosti).		(C136)
3307	Ernani: Ernani involami.	(A540)	(A858)
3308	Traviata: Ah fors e lui.	(A532)	(A858)
3309	Tosca: Vissi d'arte.		(A538)
3495	Morremo (att: Mozart) (w. Parvis).		(A528)
3496	Carmen: Se tu m'ami (w. Parvis).		(A527)
3524	Trovatore: Mira d'acerbe (w. Parvis) (or.).		(A530)
3525	Trovatore: Vivra contende (w. Parvis) (or.).		(A536)
30030	Don Giovanni: La ci darem (w. Parvis).		(A5026)
30032	Ernani: Da quel di (w. Parvis).		(A5025)
30033	Aida: Rivedrai le foreste (w. Parvis).		(A5012)
30035	Pagliacci: Sei la (w. Parvis).		(A5011)
30049	Mme. Butterfly: Che tua madre.		(A5024)
30050	Serenata (Schubert) (w. Parvis).		(A5023)

VICTOR RED SEAL 1908

64085	Boheme: Vals di Musetta.		
64094	Manon Lescaut: In quelle trine.		
74116	Trovatore: Tacea la notte.		
96002	Boheme: Addio, dolce (w. Farrar-Caruso-Scotti).	(10007)	(16-5001)

Note: The Ciaparelli Columbia records were doubled in many ways, only a few of which are noted; also presented were a number of her Milan recordings including concerted pieces such as the Rigoletto quartet with Correa, Mieli and Baldassare on No. 10633.

CLAUSSEN, Julia (Contralto)

COLUMBIA RECORDS 1915

37361	Shadows (Bond).	(A5732)
37364	Ach wie ist's Moglich.	(A5719)
37365	Rinaldo: Ah let me weep.	(A5732)
37366	Good Bye Sweet Day (Vannah).	(A5719)

Note: Affording a far better appraisal of this valuable member of both leading American opera companies was an earlier group of discs made in her native Sweden and including big contralto arias like Prophete: Ach mein Sohn on Gr. 083023.

CLEMENT, Edmond (Tenor)

How the French language, nowadays an excuse for poor singing in the name of proper pronunciation, can be sung with perfect diction, beautiful tone and impeccable style, can be ascertained from the recordings of this wonderful tenor. His American discs are, by and large, much superior to the Odeon and other European issues.

VICTOR RED SEAL 1912-1913

64223	Bergere legere; L'adieu (Pessard).	(559)
64226	Ca fait peur aux oiseaux (Bemberg).	
64232	Chanson Lorraine (Arcadet).	
64233	Jocelyn: Berceuse.	(559)
64234	Werther: Pourquoi me reveiller.	(902)
64294	Sonnet (Massenet): La niege (Bemberg).	
74258	Manon: Le reve.	(6062)
74264	Roi d'Ys: Vainement.	(6062)
74319	Les Rameaux (Faure).	
76020	Robert: Du rendezvous (w. Journet).	
76021	Robert: Le Bonheur (w. Journet).	
76022	Pearl Fishers: Au fond (w. Journet).	(8017)

For other records, see **FARRAR.**

Note: In Canada, with its large French speaking population, a small number of Red Seal records, mostly in this language, were coupled differently than in the United States. On one such, No. 20500, Clement's Werther aria above was backed by his exquisitely performed "Ca fait peur aux oiseaux".

CONSTANTINO, Florencio (Tenor)

A misreading of stifle for style in the discussion of Constantino in a previous publication was no doubt a Freudian slip but, whichever is really more apt, both leading American companies as well as several European ones made considerable use of this serviceable tenor.

VICTOR RED SEAL 1907-1910

64069	Rigoletto: Questa o quella.
64070	Gioconda: Cielo e mar.
64072	Rigoletto: La donna e mobile.
64090	Favorita: Una vergine.
74065	Elisir d'Amore: Una furtiva lagrima.
74066	Lucia: Tu che a Dio.
74067	Pearl Fishers: Mi par d'udir.
74073	Barber of Seville: Ecco ridente.
74083	Traviata: De'miei bollenti.
74084	Mefistofele: Giunto sul passo.
74085	Africana: O Paradiso.
74106	Boheme: Che gelida manina.
74174	Manon: Ah dispar.

For other Victor Red Seal, see **NIELSEN.**

COLUMBIA RECORDS 1909-1910

4043	La Milonga (Cancion Argentina).		(A693)
4044	Rigoletto: La donna e mobile.	(A680)	(1902M)
4045	Rigoletto: Questa o quella.	(A680)	(1902M)

4046	Tosca: Recondita armonia.	(A682)	(1903M)
4047	Tosca: E lucevan le stelle.	(A682)	(1903M)
4048	Triste (Republicas de Plata).		(A693)
4049	Iris: Apri la tua finestra.		(A689)
4052	Nina Pancha: Habanera.		(A688)
4053	Favorita: Una vergine.		(A683)
4054	Barber of Seville: Ecco ridente.		(A706)
4056	Vidalita (Cancion).		(A688)
4057	Cavalleria Rusticana: Siciliana.	(A681)	(1904M)
4058	Lucia: Tu che a Dio.		(A692)
4059	Manon: Il sogno.		(A689)
4061	Martha: M'appari.		(A683)
4062	Aida: Celeste Aida.		(A679)
4063	Carmen: Air de la fleur.		(A692)
4064	Cavalleria Rusticana: Brindisi.	(A681)	(1904M)
4065	Pagliacci: Vesti la giubba.		(A679)
4069	Lolita (Buzzi-Peccia).		(A706)
4071	Trovatore: Di quella pira.		(A690)
4072	Trovatore: Deserto sulla terra.		(A690)
4440	Prophete: Re del ciel.		(A848)
4441	Werther: Ah non mi ridestar.		(A848)
4442	El Roble y el Ombu (Garcia).		(H34)
30225	Favorita: Spirto gentil.		(A5107)
30226	Vorrei (Tosti).		(A5108)
30227	Elisir d'Amore: Una furtiva lagrima.		(A5109)
30231	La Paloma (Yradier).	(A5111)	(6903M)
30232	Boheme: Che gelida manina.		(A5110)
30233	Gioconda: Cielo e mar.		(A5107)
30234	Romeo: Ah, leve-toi soleil.		(A5110)
30236	Adorables Tourments (Barthelemy).		(A5108)
30237	Marina: Cosa la de levante.	(A5111)	(6903M)
30238	Otello: Morte d'Otello.		(A5113)
30245	Africana: O Paradiso.		(A5109)
30246	Duca d'Alba: Angelo casto.		(A5112)
30247	Lucia: Tu che a Dio.		(A5112)
30248	Sempre Amarti (Vallini).		(A5113)
30410	Faust: Io voglio il piacer (w. Mardones).		(H1053)
30411	Faust: Che fati qui (w. Blanchart-Mardones).		(A5187)
30419	Forza del Destino: Solenne (w. Blanchart).		(A5184)
30420	Boheme: Ah Mimi (w. Blanchart).		(A5185)
30421	Mefistofele: Giunto sul passo.		(A5203)
30430	Mefistofele: Dai campi.		(A5203)
30437	Cavalleria Rusticana: Addio alla madre.		(A5205)
30438	Hugenots: Bianca al par.		(A5204)
30461	Aurora: La Bandiera.		(H1066)
30462	Lucia: Fra poco a me.		(A5217)
30463	Rigoletto: Parmi veder le lagrime.		(A5217)
30464	Faust: Salve dimora.		(A5204)
30465	Mignon: Ah non credevi tu.		(A5205)
30466	Pearl Fishers: Mi par d'udir.	(H1033) (7031M)	(5093M)
30467	Mi Nina (Guetary).		(H1052)

For other Columbia Records, see BRONSKAJA.

Note: Among his European issues is a group of ten solos on Favorite, Nos. 1-35050 through 35059, the first of which is the opening aria from Barber of Seville.

CORRADETTI, Ferruccio (Baritone)

Note: Long a teacher in this country, Corradetti was a prolific recording artist in his native Italy, where early items appeared among others in both Fonotipia and cheaper Odeon series. Among the latter were solos such as Don Giovanni:

Serenata on No. 37071; duets with Adami-Educande di Sorrento: Un bacio on No. 37179, with Pintucci—Barber of Seville: Voi dovreste on No. 37175, with Tromben—Barber of Seville: Dunque io son on No. 37121; trios with Ventura and Luppi-Fra Diavolo: Del Capitano on No. 37017; even a number of selections like Due Foscari: O vecchio cor, issued as No. 37226 under the pseudonym of Corrado Ferretti.

CORTOT, Alfred (Pianist)

VICTOR RED SEAL 1919-1923

64819	Seguidilla (Albeniz).	(560)
64846	Malaguena (Albeniz).	(560)
64910	Tarantelle Op. 43 (Chopin).	(561)
64956	Fille aux cheveux de lin; Menestrels (Debussy).	(562)
64973	Melody Polonaise Op. 74 No. 5 (Chopin-Liszt).	(562)
64989	Etudes in G Flat Op. 10; Butterfly Op. 25 (Chopin).	(561)
66213	Au bord d'une source (Liszt).	(982)
66214	Pathetic Study Op. 8 No. 12 (Scriabin).	(982)
66261	Scherzo Op. 16 No. 12 (Mendelssohn).	(1016)
66262	Bourree (Saint-Saens).	(1016)
74588	Waltz Etude (Saint-Saens).	(6063)
74589	La Leggierezza (Liszt).	(6065)
74623	Berceuse Op. 57 (Chopin).	(6063)
74636	Rigoletto Paraphrase (Verdi-Liszt).	(6064)
74659	Jeux d'eau (Ravel).	(6065)
74670	Hungarian Rhapsody No. 2 (part I) (Liszt).	(6335)
74798	Invitation to the Waltz (Weber).	(6064)
74810	Rondo Capriccioso (Mendelssohn).	(6358)
74822	Hungarian Rhapsody No. 2 (part II) (Liszt).	(6335)
74824	Polonaise Op. 22 (Chopin).	(6358)
74829	Etude in A Minor Op. 25 No. 11 (Chopin).	(6417)
74830	Impromptu in A Flat Op. 29 (Chopin).	(6417)

IMPORTED VICTOR RED SEAL 1925

Concerto in A Minor (Schumann) (w. Royal Orch.).	(6516/7/8/9)
Sonata in A (Franck) (w. Thibaud).	(6524/5/6/7)

Note: Numbers were also assigned to a Sonata finale (74584) and the Liszt Hungarian Rhapsody No. 11 (74587).

CRABBE, Armand (Baritone)

Note: Some twenty years before his appearance on Victor Red Seal among its earliest electrical recordings, Crabbe was a youthful member of Hammerstein's remarkable French contingent and as such, made a group of songs which were issued first on single-face black seal, as was d'Hardelot's Because, No. 3640, and later double-face, the former selection on No. 63407, and, among the twelve-inch, Massenet's Pensee d'Automne on No. 68303.

CRIMI, Giulio (Tenor)

Why Crimi was a leading tenor in first the Chicago Opera and then the Metropolitan, is hard to determine from his recordings below but the fault might be somewhat due to Vocalion's harsh process which even played havoc with the superlative talents of Rosa Raisa.

VOCALION RECORDS 1920-1924

30105	Pecche (Pennino).	(60017)
30119	Manon Lescaut: Donna non vidi mai.	(60030)
30123	Santa Lucia Luntana (Mario).	(60028)

30128	Ninna-Nanna (Tirindelli).		(60028)
30137	Tosca: Recondita armonia.		(60030)
30142	Ay, Ay, Ay (Perez).		
30151	Pagliacci: Vesti la giubba.		(60039)
30153	O Sole Mio (di Capua).		(60040)
30154	Tosca: E lucevan le stelle.		(60039)
30158	Zaza: Canzone di Milio.		(60017)
30170	Rigoletto: La donna e mobile.		(60035)
30174	Martha: M'appari.		(60044)
30175	Torna a Surriento (de Curtis).		(60040)
30176	Manon: Il sogno.		(60035)
52004	Favorita: Spirto gentil.		
52011	Trovatore: Ai nostri monti (w. D'Alvarez).		(70027)
52014	Mme. Butterfly: O quanti occhi (w. Sundelius).		(70027)
52032	Aida: Celeste Aida.		(70023)
52042	Cavalleria Rusticana: Addio alla madre.		(70023)
52045	Boheme: Che gelida manina.		(70026)
55003	L'Ultima Canzone (Tosti).		
55005	Africana: O Paradiso.	(52044)	(70026)
55006	Zaza: O mio piccolo tavolo.		
	Trovatore: Di quella pira.		(60049)
	Trovatore: Ah si ben mio.		(60049)

For other records, see RAISA.

CROOKS, Richard (Tenor)

Note: Advanced to Red Seal in 1926 on the newly introduced electrical 4000/9000 series, Crooks' records of the previous three years were Victor blue seal, among which, the acoustics included: Colleen Aroon by Strickland and Lang's Irish Love Song on No. 45373, Love is Mine by Gartner and For You Alone by Giehl on No. 45422 and Shaver's Red, Red Rose and Sun Girl by Tours on No. 45481.

CROSSLEY, Ada (Contralto)

Another Australian pupil of Marchesi, Ada Crossley concertized for the first time at Queens Hall, London, in 1895 and so won the admiration of the music-loving Victora, she was called to five command performances during the next two years.

VICTOR RED SEAL 1903

2186	Caro Mio Ben (Giordano).	(81001)	(64007)
2189	Four Leaf Clover (Willeby).	(81004)	(64008)
2190	Paysage (Hahn).	(81005)	(64010)
2191	New Year's Song (Mallinson).	(81006)	(64009)

CULP, Julia (Contralto)

In Culp's art, a song was sung with full, even, wonderfully modulated tones. To more modern listeners, used to lieder that is crooned, aspirated, declaimed, the above must sound like sacrilege.

VICTOR RED SEAL 1914-1918

64396	Haidenroslein (Schubert).	(567)
64397	Stille Nacht (Gruber).	(566)
64401	Drink to me only with thine eyes.	
64402	Wiegenlied (Brahms).	(566)
64403	Mignonette (Weckerlin).	(568)
64404	I've been roaming (Horn).	
64414	All Through the Night.	(563)
64418	Auld Lang Syne.	(565)
64419	Long, Long Ago (Bayley).	(563)

64441	At Parting (Rogers).	
64489	Ave Maria (Schubert).	(569)
64490	Samson: Mon coeur.	(568)
64491	Lullaby (Lieurance).	(564)
64492	Im Abendrot (Schubert).	(567)
64493	Cottage Maid (Beethoven).	(570)
64550	Passing By (Purcell).	
64551	Geluckig Vaderland ("Gedenck-Clanck").	(570)
64552	Dutch Serenade (de Lange).	
64553	Immer leiser (Brahms).	
64554	Mondnacht (Schumann).	(569)
64667	Old Refrain (Kreisler).	
64676	Nuit d'etoiles (Debussy).	
64683	Virgin's Slumber Song (Reger).	
64720	Bendemeer's Stream (arr. Gatty).	(565)
64721	By the Waters of Minnetonka (Lieurance).	(564)
74427	Elijah: Oh Rest in the Lord.	
74429	Faithfu' Johnie (Beethoven).	
74430	Samson: Printemps qui commence.	
74431	Standchen (Schubert).	(6066)
74460	Cradle Song 1915 (Kreisler).	(6359)
74461	Du bist die Ruh (Schubert).	(6066)
74462	Dank sei dir (Handel).	
74523	Blue Paradise: Auf Wiedersehn.	(6359)
74527	Silver Threads Among the Gold (Danks).	(6067)
74540	Love's Old Sweet Song (Molloy).	(6067)

VICTOR RED SEAL 1924

Auf Flugeln des Gesanges (Mendelssohn).	(1041)
Es muss ein Wunderbares sein (Liszt).	(1041)

Note: Culp's accompanist on several of the above including 64676 was Conrad V. Bos, not Debussy. Unpublished items include Silent Night (64672) and Traume (74358), which last selection she had at least recorded in Europe on Gr. No. 2-043009, Opera Disc No. 72557.

DADDI, Francesco (Tenor)

See CARUSO.

Note: Aside from his intelligent performances in a gigantic number of small operatic roles, Daddi was noted as an interpreter of Neopolitan songs, which art he practiced on all domestic labels. Among the pre-1909 recordings of world-popular pieces were Carmela Mia on Columbia 3807, Torna a Surriento on Victor 3813, Birbantella on Zonophone 3606, a coincidence of similar catalogue numbers that was soon dispelled on double-face couplings.

DAL MONTE, Toti (Soprano)

VICTOR RED SEAL 1924-1925

A Rosina (Fabris).	(1106)
Magari (Filippi).	(1106)
Lucia: Mad scene (w. Cho.).	(6466)
Lucia: Spargi d'amaro pianto (w. Cho.).	(6466)
Carnival of Venice (part I) (Benedict).	(6487)
Carnival of Venice (part II) (Benedict).	(6487)
Barber of Seville: Una voce poco fa.	(6495)
Rigoletto: Caro nome.	(6495)

Note: The Lucia mad scene and rondo were imported recordings, issued here in connection with her Metropolitan Opera debut.

DALMORES, Charles (Tenor)

While Dalmores created many roles in America, his interpretations even of the more traditional pieces are of memorable distinction.

VICTOR RED SEAL 1907-1908

81088	Tales of Hoffmann: C'est elle.	
85114	Carmen: Je suis Escamillo (w. Journet).	
85115	Faust: O Merveille (w. Journet).	
85121	Romeo: Ah, leve-toi soleil.	
85122	Carmen: Air de la fleur.	(18141)
85123	Trovatore: Ah si ben mio.	
89019	Carmen: La-bas (w. Calve).	
95300	Faust: Alerte (w. Eames-Plancon).	

VICTOR RED SEAL 1912-1913

85121	Romeo: Ah, leve-toi soleil.	(15-1013)
85122	Carmen: Air de la fleur.	(15-1013)
87087	Samson: Arretez, O mes freres.	
87088	Lohengrin: Atmest du nicht.	(571)
87089	Tales of Hoffmann: C'est elle.	(571)
87119	Bonjour Suzon (Delibes).	
87120	Je t'aime (Massenet).	
88330	Ninon (Tosti).	
88397	Griseledis: Ouvrez-vous.	

D'ALVAREZ, Marguerite (Contralto)

VOCALION RECORDS 1920-1922

30121	Homing (Del Riego).	(60029)
30124	Carmen: Seguidilla.	(60031)
30129	El Relicario (Padilla).	(60029)
30143	Mira la bien (Pedrell).	(60031)
45000	Prophete: Ah mon fils.	(70010)
52000	Samson: Mon coeur.	(70010)
52011	Trovatore: Ai nostri monti (w. Crimi).	(70027)
52018	Elijah: Oh Rest in the Lord.	(70020)
52020	Silent Night (Gruber).	(70020)
55008	Carmen: Habanera.	

DANISE, Giuseppe (Baritone)

BRUNSWICK RECORDS 1921-1925

10035	Marechiare (Tosti).		
30007	Andrea Chernier: Nemico della Patria.	(50004)	
30008	Faust: Avant de quitter.	(50007)	
30010	Traviata: Di Provenza.	(50007)	
30012	Masked Ball: Eri tu.	(50006)	
30020	Pagliacci: Prologo.	(50006)	
	Zaza: Zaza piccola zingara.	(15025)	
	Zaza: Buona Zaza.	(15025)	
	Voi ed Io (de Curtis).	(15028)	(10108)
	Luntananza (de Curtis).	(15028)	(10108)
	Forza del Destino: Urna fatal.	(15045)	
	Herodiade: Vision fugitive.	(15045)	
	L'Ultima Canzone (Tosti).	(15064)	(10128)
	Campana di San Giusto (Arona).	(15064)	(10128)
	Noche Serena.	(15078)	(10129)
	Linda Mia.	(15078)	(10129)

Otello: Credo.	(50004)	
Barber of Seville: Largo al factotum.	(50013)	
Ernani: O de' verd' anni miei.	(50013)	
La Paloma (Yradier).	(50014)	(30100)
Torna a Surriento (de Curtis).	(50014)	(30100)
La Partida (Alvarez).	(50011)	
La Danza (Rossini).	(50011)	
Canta pe' me (de Curtis).	(50034)	(30102)
Core 'ngrato (Cardillo).	(50034)	(30102)
Song of Volga Boatman (in Russ.).		(10150)
When the King Went Forth (Koenemann) (Fre.).		(10150)
Requiem du Coeur (Pessard).		(10181)
Fortunio: La Maison Grise.		(10181)

DE BASSINI, Alberto (Baritone)

Note: Announced as a star of the Royal Opera of Lisbon for his early Bettini cylinders, De Bassini, though not a very important singer, made over forty early Columbia discs, including many arias such as Masked Ball: Eri tu on No. 1500 as well as duets with Giannini such as Boheme: Ah Mimi on No. 1770, and with Ferenczy, whom he also joined on Zonophone and other makes. Among their several Columbia duets are Don Giovanni: La ci darem on No. 1244 and Carmen: Se tu m'ami on No. 1247. Other De Bassini recordings include at least some of the numbers listed in the 1898 Berliner catalogue and elsewhere under the name of Signor A. del Campo, also of the Royal Opera Lisbon. These early Berliners, for instance, numbering over half a dozen included arias like the Don Giovanni: Serenata on No. 1111 which might be his and still others like the Carmen Toreador Song on No. 909, the same number as was used for the Dec. 1, 1895 Meyers recording of this selection. Likewise, this very aria on Columbia No. 309 is listed in some places under Del Campo, in others under De Bassini.

DE CASAS, Bianca Lavin (Contralto)

IMPORTED VICTOR RED SEAL 1910-1911

87068	Mefistofele: La luna (w. Ardoni-Pini-Corsi).	(87561)
88264	Aida: Quest'assisa (w. Fabris Cunego-Badini-Sant' Elia-Cho.).	
		(89144) (8052)
88270	Aida: Ohime, Morir (w. Sant' Elia-Cho.).	(6351)
88323	Aida: Sacerdoti (W. Sant' Elia-Cho.)	(89122)

For other records, see RUSZCOWSKA

Note: Though she sang at La Scala in 1902, the earliest imports of Lavin de Casas were put into the black seal section, including arias such as the card scene from Carmen on No. 52404, doubled on 62617, and songs Lke Trimarchi's Pallide Mammole on No. 52405, doubled on 63424.

DE CISNEROS, Eleonora (Contralto)

Anyone privileged to glimpse at the scrap-books of this famous American singer would see revealed a meteoric career which took her throughout the great opera-houses of every country while still of an age at which most contraltos find themselves in local choirs. Further perusal of her diaries and extended disertations would lend deep insight into the sincerity and application such great successes require. Only her recordings, made for many companies and all styles of equipment here and abroad, fail to mirror the acclaim she received.

COLUMBIA RECORDS 1915

37075	Gioconda: Voce di donna.	(A5640)
37076	Favorita: O mio Fernando.	(A5653)

37077	Don Carlos: O don fatale.		(A5626)
37078	Hugenots: Nobil signori.		(A5626)
37098	Orfeo: Che faro senza Euridice.		(A5640)
37117	Carmen: Canzone Boema.		(A5653)

Note: Her excursions into Wagnerian characterization and a higher tessitura are suggested by the re-recording of Walkure: Ho yo to ho on Pathe-Actuelle 025073 (11513). Among early Nicoles, 15633 is Trovatore: Stride.

DE GOGORZA, Emilio (Baritone)

No name contained in this book is more intimately connected with the events it describes than is that of De Gogorza who died in the year it was published. As singer under his own name and several others, especially Senor Francisco, he recorded hundreds of times for practically every company, large and small of the 1895-1902 period, so much so that many items of Meyers, etc. are erroneously ascribed to him. From 1903 on, he was most closely aligned with Victor, which used his many talents for raproachment with its growing roster of celebrity artists as well as including him among them. Red Seal De Gogorza records or those which made their way into that category are listed in full below. They represent a far greater expression, artistically and technically, of his vocal art, than all the interesting incunabula that went before.

VICTOR RED SEAL 1904-1909

4084	For All Eternity (Mascheroni).		(64038)	(584)
4102	Clang of the Forge (Rodney).		(64037)	(575)
4162	La Sevillana (Yradier).		(64041)	(580)
4163	Holy City (Adams).		(64039)	
4292	Teresita Mia (Nicto).		(64043)	
4307	Linda Mia.		(64042)	(582)
4327	Barber of Seville: Largo al factotum.		(64040)	
4403	Tempestad: Monologo.		(64045)	(589)
4405	Canto del Presidiario (Alvarez).		(64044)	
31327	Holy City (Adams).		(74041)	(6071)
31436	Canto del Presidiario (Alvarez).		(74042)	(6074)
31446	Pagliacci: Prologo.	(74040)	(88176)	(6070)
64051	Martha: Canzone del porter (w. Cho.).			
74043	Roi de Lahore: Promesse de mon avenir.		(88172)	
74046	Carmen: Chanson du Toreador (w. Cho.).		(88178)	
74047	Dormi pure (Scuderi).			(6362)
74068	Caro Mio Ben (Giordano).		(88173)	(6362)
74069	God, My Father (Dubois).		(88177)	(6071)
74077	Drink To Me Only With Thine Eyes.			(6072)
74086	Semele: Where'er You Walk.			
74102	Faust: Dio Possente.		(88174)	(6069)
74105	O Sole Mio (di Capua).			(6075)
74110	Rigoletto: Pari siamo.		(88179)	
74114	Hamlet: Brindisi.		(88180)	
74118	Mother o'Mine (Tours); The Lark (Parker).			(6072)
74124	Trovatore: Il balen.		(88175)	(6069)
81092	Lina (Symiane).		(64101)	(574)
87501	Samson: Vengeance at last (w. Homer).			
88153	Herodiade: Vision fugitive.			(6352)
88154	Tannhauser: O du mein holder Abendstern.			(6352)
88181	Barber of Seville: Largo al factotum.			(6068)
89010	Hamlet: Doute de la lumiere (w. Sembrich).			

VICTOR RED SEAL 1910-1915

| 64110 | Tavira o' la Romeria (Encilla). | |
| 64136 | O Sole Mio (di Capua). | (583) |

64160	Mandolinata (Paladilhe).	(576)
64242	Malgre Moi (Pfeiffer).	
64372	Beauty's Eyes (Tosti).	(573)
64479	Comme se canta (Mario).	(576)
64480	Noche Serena.	(579)
64482	El Celoso (Alvarez).	(582)
64501	Sally in Our Alley (Carey).	(590)
74149	Mi Nina (Guetary).	(6074)
74209	A Granada (Alvarez).	
74229	Patrie: Air du sonneur.	
74234	Alleluja d'amour (Faure).	
74262	Cantares (Alvarez).	
74359	Lost Chord (Sullivan).	(6076)
74360	La Partida (Alvarez).	(6073)
74379	La Paloma (Yradier).	(6073)
74421	Non e ver (Mattei).	(6075)
74422	'Mong the Green Irish Hills (Freese).	
74438	Pipes of Pan (Elgar).	
88324	Masked Ball: Eri tu.	(6068)
88447	Don Giovanni: Serenata; Damnation of Faust: Serenade.	(6070)

VICTOR RED SEAL 1916-1920

64584	Pagliacci: Prologo.	(899)
64596	Musica Proibita (Gastaldon).	
64597	Preguntale a las Estrellas.	(579)
64598	Je sais que vous etes jolie (Christine).	(591)
64624	Since Molly Went Away (Burleigh).	(588)
64628	Absent (Tirindelli).	(572)
64629	When Dull Care (Wilson).	(587)
64632	Chanson de Fortunio: Serenade.	(574)
64663	Santa Lucia.	(583)
64688	All the World (Ball).	
64690	That's Why My Heart (Motzan).	
64698	Garden of Sleep (de Lara).	(578)
64722	Thou Art Near Me (Meyer-Helmund).	(586)
64786	Viking Song (Coleridge-Taylor).	(575)
64794	Could I (Tosti).	(573)
64797	Himnos Bayames (Figueredo).	(924)
64798	Clavelitos (Valverde).	(924)
64812	Juanita (Norton).	(581)
64816	For You a Rose (Edwards).	(585)
64836	Dear Heart (Mattei).	(577)
64847	A La Luna (Zapata).	
64862	Panurge: Chanson de la Touraine.	
64888	Each Shining Hour (Forster).	(577)
64898	En Calesa (Alvarez).	
64911	Garden of Memory (Phillips).	(584)
74478	Magic Song (Meyer-Helmund).	
74502	Oh Song Divine (Temple).	(6076)
89083	A la Luz de la Luna (w. Caruso).	(8038)

VICTOR RED SEAL 1921-1925

64928	John Peel.	(587)
64949	Dream Faces (Hutchinson).	(578)
64953	In Old Madrid (Trotere).	(581)
64984	Florodora: In the Shade of the Palm.	(588)
64997	Song of the Volga Boatmen.	(899)
66019	For Ever and For Ever (Tosti).	(585)
66033	Teresita Mia (Nicto).	(580)
66046	Lasciali dir, tu m'ami (Quaranta).	(591)
66072	I Know a Lovely Garden (d' Hardelot).	(586)

66094	Waiting for Your Return (Caesar).	(572)
66103	Madoline (Nelson).	(903)
66126	Blue Bells of Scotland.	(590)
66135	Boca de Pepita; Bolero (arr. Blake).	(589)
66164	My Black Haired Mary (North).	(903)
64477	Invictus (Huhn).	(992)
66228	Requiem (Homer).	(992)
	Drink To Me Only With Thine Eyes.	(1061)
	In The Gloaming (Harrison).	(1061)
	Mother o'Mine (Tours).	(1107)
	Unknown Soldier (O'Hara).	(1107)
	Bergere legere (Weckerlin).	(1108)
	Menuet (Favart-Exaudet).	(1108)
	De Captaine of de Marguerite (O'Hara).	(6535)
	Leetle Bateese (O'Hara).	(6535)

For other records, see EAMES, VAN HOOSE

Note: Other numbers assigned include En Calesa (64159), A Perfect Day (64481), Cantares (74120).

DE HIDALGO, Elvira (Soprano)

Note: Both early and late acoustic recordings of De Hidalgo appear on imported Columbia, the second group of which contained her celebrated Dinorah; Ombra leggiera spread over both sides of a twelve-inch record No. 65033D, changed in the same year to No. 7076M (matrices AX 378/386). Meanwhile she had made a large group of early Fonotipias including Don Pasquale: Quel guardo on No. 92302 (C-F 133).

DELLA TORRE, Nestore (Baritone)

IMPORTED VICTOR RED SEAL 1912

76013 Wm. Tell: Domo, o Ciel (w. Cho.).

Note: The above is but a single example of the work he did for the Gramophone Company in Italy, where he was listed on the roster of La Scala in 1902.

DELMAS, Jean Francois (Bass-Baritone)

A famous French singer and creator of many roles, Delmas appeared on most leading Paris labels of the early decade.

IMPORTED VICTOR RED SEAL 1903

5077	Patrie: Pauvre martyr obscur.	(91046)
5078	Don Giovanni: Serenade.	
5080	Walkure: Les Adieux de Wotan.	(91048)
5081	Jolie Fille de Perth: Quand la flamme.	(91049)
5083	Toussaint: Conte bleu.	(91050)

DE LUCA, Giuseppe (Baritone)

Anyone possessing one of the earliest items below and the remarkable Collectors Record Shop recordings of De Luca, made at Town Hall, New York, on November 7, 1947, will encompass, in one career, practically the entire history of celebrity recording. What is more, the "Quand' ero paggio" from Falstaff on C. R. S. No. 55, as sung when he was a mere 71, is as vibrant and youthful as anything during the preceding forty-five years. As does the audience at the end of this record, we can only applaud and applaud.

IMPORTED VICTOR RED SEAL 1903

5039	Hamlet: Come il romito.	(91031)
5040	Roi de Lahore: O casto fior.	(91032)
5041	Don Giovanni: Serenata.	(91033)

VICTOR RED SEAL 1917-1925

64668	Trovatore: Il balen.	(593)
64673	Marriage of Figaro: Se vuol ballare.	(596)
64685	Nuttata 'e Sentimento (Capolongo).	(594)
64686	Pastorale (de Leva).	
64775	God Bless You (Edwards).	
64776	Ultima Rosa (Sibella).	(595)
64912	Oi Luna (Cardillo).	(594)
64934	Beau Soir (Debussy).	(902)
64957	Don Carlos: O Carlo, ascolta.	(593)
64990	Mattinata (Fatuo).	(595)
66068	Marietta (Romilli).	(592)
66133	Wm. Tell: Resta immobile.	(596)
66158	Rosa (Romilli).	(592)
66050	Berceuse (Gretchaninoff).	(955)
66184	Voi dormite, Signora (Tosti).	(955)
	Canta il Mare (de Leva).	(1036)
	Occhi di Fata (Denza).	(1036)
	Siviglia (Fatuo).	(1109)
	Stornello (Cimara).	(1109)
74506	Ernani: O de' verd' anni miei.	(6077)
74514	Barber of Seville: Largo al factotum.	(6077)
74526	Masked Ball: Eri tu.	(6078)
74528	Traviata: Di Provenza.	(6079)
74572	Rinaldo: Lascia ch io pianga.	(6081)
74591	Favorita: A tanto amor.	(6080)
74633	Faust: Dio possente.	(6079)
74697	Don Carlos: Per me giunto.	(6078)
74744	Herodiade: Vision fugitive.	(6081)
74787	Puritani: Ah per sempre.	(6080)
74872	Dinorah: Sei vendicata assai.	(6443)
74873	Benvenuto Cellini: De l'art.	(6443)
87568	Zaza: Il bacio (w. Farrar).	(625)
89160	Don Carlos: Dio, che nell' alma (w. Martinelli).	(8047)
89161	Don Pasquale: Pronta io son (w. Bori).	(8004)
89162	Don Pasquale: Vado corro (w. Bori).	(8004)
95213	Wm. Tell: Troncar suoi di (w. Martinelli-Mardones).	(10009)

For other records, see CARUSO, GALLI-CURCI

Note: No. 64684 was assigned to Serenata Gelata. In between his rightful appearances as a Red Seal artist, De Luca could be found on black face Victor records. His early Don Giovanni: Serenata, for instance was re-numbered 52440 and even doubled under No. 62623, while a 1903 Eri tu from Masked Ball appeared in 1906 as No. 52439, then later in 1908 as a double-faced record No. 62086. Meanwhile, Fonotipia in Italy had recorded a large number of solos and duets including one with Burzio in the final scene from Gioconda on No. 74043; many of these also appeared as Odeons.

DE LUCIA, Fernando (Tenor)

Rabid partisanship is most apt to be aroused in collectors by the mention of the name of De Lucia. Creator of several roles of great importance, this famous singer was among the most versatile of Italian tenors. His command of the fioriture needed for Rossini and sensitive rubato so helpful to Bellini and Donizetti are unmatched on records, as is the dramatic impact he achieves in a Bizet largato. Only his voice is assailable and that because of a vibrato, excessive to some, suggestive of a great power to others.

IMPORTED VICTOR RED SEAL 1903

5025	Manon: Il sogno.		(91020)
5026	Rigoletto: La donna e mobile.		(91021)
5027	L'Ideale (Tosti).		(91022)
5028	Tosca: Recondita armonia.		(91023)
5049	Barber of Seville: Se il mio nome.		(91038)

IMPORTED VICTOR RED SEAL 1907-1912

91079	Elisir d'Amore: Obbligato (w. Badini).			(87562)
92028	Carmen: Canzone del fior.			(76001)
92029	Barber of Seville: Ecco ridente.	(76000)	(88602)	(6399)
92033	Lohengrin: Cigno gentil (w. Chorus).	(76002)	(88603)	(6399)
92052	Carmen: Mia Madre (w. Huguet).			(89140)
92053	Faust: Dammi ancor (w. Huguet).			
92054	Pearl Fishers: Non hai compreso (w. Huguet).		(89147)	(8058)
92055	Lohengrin: Cessaro i canti (w. Huguet).		(89141)	(8056)
92056	Rigoletto: E il sol (w. Huguet).			(89142)
88361	Traviata: Parigi, o cara (w. Huguet).			
89045	Sonnambula: Prendi l'anel (w. Galvany).			(8057)
87047	O Sole Mio (Di Capua).			(66004)
87048	Sulla bocca (Barthelemy).			(66002)
87049	Manon: Il sogno.			(66001)
66000	Barber of Seville: Se il mio nome.			
66003	Era di Maggio (Costa).			
66006	Carmela Mia (Cannio).			

Note: A Heritage Series doubling of Traviata: De miei bollenti spiriti and Mignon: Addio, Mignon on No. 15-1024 also reveals De Lucia as he sang in 1906. Four years later, some sixty Neapolitan canzonette, in which he also excelled, were released by Fonotipia. His most interesting group came later in the form of several hundred recordings for Phonotype, a Naples outfit, which also presented him in complete operas including Rigoletto and Barber of Seville with all its recitatives.

DE LUSSAN, Zelie (Mezzo-Soprano)

De Lussan attained the highest popularity both here and in London, where another small group of records were released in 1905 by the Beka company.

VICTOR RED SEAL 1903

2187	Lili (Guetary).	(81002)	(64002)
2188	Mignon: Connais-tu le pays.	(81003)	(64005)
2198	Carmen: Habanera.	(81007)	(64004)
2199	Rosy Morn (Ronald).	(81008)	(64006)
2301	La Paloma (Yradier).	(81009)	(64003)

DE MURO, Bernardo (Tenor)

When De Muro and Amato appeared at the New York Hippodrome some quarter of a century after their heyday elsewhere, it was evident that something was being enacted that harkened back to far more glorious times. The tenor, in particular, retained much of his vocal brilliance.

IMPORTED VICTOR RED SEAL 1914

74371	Isabeau: Tu ch' odi lo mio grido.		(6379)
74372	Isabeau: E passera la viva creatura.		(6379)
74373	Isabeau: Dormivi (w. Bartolomasi).		
74374	Isabeau: Fu vile l'editto.	(74762)	(6387)
74375	Isabeau: I tuoi occhi (w. Bartolomasi).		

74376	Andrea Chernier: Improvviso.	(6380)
74377	Carmen: Canzone del fior.	(6380)

IMPORTED VICTOR RED SEAL 1922-1925

66078	Girl of Golden West: Ch'ella mi creda.	(949)
66179	Aida: Pur ti riveggo (w. Vigano).	(949)
	Andrea Chernier: Vicino a te (w. Oltrabella).	(1129)
	Andrea Chernier: Ora soave (w. Oltrabella).	(1129)
74640	Trovatore: Miserere (w. Roggero-Cho.).	(6412)
74641	Andrea Chernier: Si fui soldato.	(6387)
74642	Carmen: Canzone del fior.	(6385)
74648	Otello: Dio mi potevi.	(6386)
74649	Carmen: Ho nome Escamillo (w. Janni).	(6385)
74650	Trovatore: E deggio (w. Baldini-Janni-Bettoni-Cho.).	(6410)
74664	Otello: Morte d' Otello.	(6386)
74665	Trovatore: Deserto sulla terra (w. Badini).	(6410)
74666	Trovatore: Mal reggendo (w. Casazza).	(6411)
74709	Trovatore: Prima che d'altri (w. Roggero-Badini).	(6412)
74714	Trovatore: Perigliarti ancor (w. Casazza).	(6411)
74715	Girl of Golden West: Sono Ramerrez.	(6422)
74834	Aida: Fuggiam gli adori (w. Vigano).	(6421)
74835	Aida: Si, fuggiam (w. Vigano-Gramegna-Baracchi).	(6421)
74836	Aida: De lei non piu (w. Gramegna).	(6422)
	Otello: Esultate (w. Cho.).	(6528)
	Otello: Ora e per sempre.	(6528)
	Trovatore: Ai nostri monti (w. Casazza).	(6529)
	Trovatore: Di quella pira (w. Cho.).	(6529)
	Andrea Chernier: Io no ho amato ancor.	(6551)
	Andrea Chernier: Vedi la luce (w. Oltrabella).	(6551)
	Gioconda: Gia ti veggo (w. Toninello-Badini-Quinzi-Tarpergi-Cho.).	(6552)
	Don Carlos: Io l'ho perduto.	(6552)
	Piccolo Marat: Va nella tua stanzetta (w. Vigano).	(6553)
	Iris: Or dammi il braccio tuo.	(6553)

DE PACHMANN, Vladimir (Piano)

VICTOR RED SEAL 1911-1913

64224	Mazurka in A Flat Op. 50 No. 2 (Chopin).	(907)
64263	Mazurka in F Sharp Minor Op. 59 No. 3 (Chopin).	(907)
64291	Etude in E Minor Op. 25 No. 5 (Chopin).	
74260	Prelude Op. 28, No. 24; Etude Op. 10 No. 5 (Chopin).	(6363)
74261	Rigoletto Paraphrase (Verdi-Liszt).	(6083)
74284	Impromptu in A Flat Op. 29; Prelude in F Op. 28 (Chopin).	(6363)
74285	Spring Song Op. 62 (Mendelssohn); Prophet Bird (Schumann).	(6082)
74293	Nocturne in F Major Op. 15 No. 1 (Chopin).	(6377)
74301	La Fileuse (Raff-Henselt).	
74302	Etude Op. 10 No. 12 (Chopin-Godowsky).	
74304	Funeral March Op. 35 No. 2 (Chopin).	(6083)
74309	Ballade in A Flat Op. 47 (Chopin).	
74313	Nocturne in G Op. 37 No. 2 (Chopin).	(6082)
74315	Venetian Gondola Op. 30 No. 6; Spinning Song Op. 67 No. 4 (Mendelssohn).	(6377)
74318	Etude in E Minor Op. 25 No. 5 (Chopin).	

VICTOR RED SEAL 1924-1925

	Prophet Bird (Schumann).	(1110)
	Spring Song Op. 62, No. 6 (Mendelssohn).	(1110)
74864	Impromptu in F Sharp Op. 36 (Chopin).	(6441)
74868	Nocturne in B Op. 32 No. 1 (Chopin).	(6441)

74865   Novelette Op. 21 No. 1 (Schumann).   (6480)
        Prelude in D Flat Op. 28 No. 15 (Chopin).   (6480)

Note: Other Chopin pieces to which catalogue numbers were assigned include Preludes No. 6, 7, 10 from Op. 28 (74311), Polonaise Op. 26 No. 1 (74312), Nocturne Op. 55 No. 2 (74314), Ballade Op. 47 (74316), Preludes Op. 28 Nos. 20, 16 (74317).

IMPORTED COLUMBIA RECORDS 1916

Etude Op. 25 No. 3; Prelude Op. 28 No. 16 (Chopin)   (A5831)
Polonaise-Cadenza (Liszt).   (A5831)

Note: Many other characteristic renditions remained a long time in English Columbia catalogues, to which collectors turned to see if the titles would suggest any running conversation with the music. Some did.

DE PASQUALI, Bernice   (Soprano)

This American coloratura had marked success at the Metropolitan Opera, no doubt owing to an ingratiating tonal color and a fine sense of phrasing.

COLUMBIA RECORDS 1912-1914

19709	Low Back'd Car (Lover).	(A1179)
19714	Will o' the Wisp (Spross).	(A1179)
19860	Tales of Hoffmann: Barcarola (w. De Segurola).	(A1214)
19876	Mignon: Leggiadre Rondinelle (w. De Segurola).	(A1215)
30873	Vals (part I) (Venzano).	(A5429)
30874	Vals (part II) (Venzano).	(A5429)
30875	Pearl of Brazil: Thou brilliant bird.	(A5350)
30876	Hamlet: Mad scene (part I) (Ital.).	(A5349)
30877	Hamlet: Mad scene (part II) (Ital.).	(A5349)
30880	Linda di Chamounix: O luce.	(A5350)
30881	Mignon: I am Titania.	(A5448)
30934	Se Saran Rose (Arditi).	(A5376)
30935	Il Bacio (Arditi).	(A5376)
30936	Villanelle (dell'Acqua) (Eng.).	(A5456)
30951	Lakme: Dov' e l'Indiana bruna.	(A5523)
30952	Mignon: Io son Titania.	(H1083)
36389	Faust: Jewel Song.	(A5448)
36390	Pagliacci: Ballatella.	(A5456)
36810	Guarany: C'era un volta.	(A5523)
36811	O Dolce Concento (Drouet).	(A5580)
36826	Lo, Here the Gentle Lark (Bishop).	(A5554)
36911	Carmen: I say to the dread.	(A5554)
36973	Rigoletto: Caro nome.	(A5580)
36983	Mary (Richardson).	(A5612)
36984	Swiss Echo Song (Eckert).	(A5612)
39071	The Last Dance (Ware).	(A1446)
39079	Call Me No More (Cadman).	(A1446)

Note: An Angel's Serenade in English, No. 25939, was among the imports which placed De Pasquali's name in the Columbia catalogue six years before her domestic recordings were released.

DE RESZKE, Edouard (Bass)

Throughout 1905, the Fontipia companies advertised extensively their exclusive contract with Jean de Reszke. Yet, the records themselves, seem to have had negligible distribution and almost no public sale. That the great tenor was dissatisfied with them, as with other records he made, seems evident. So to his beloved brother, and the three selections below, in original or re-recorded form, collectors must turn for any readily obtainable full-length representation of this family on discs.

COLUMBIA RECORDS 1903

1221   Ernani: Infelice.   (A617)
1222   Martha: Canzone del porter.
1223   Serenade de Don Juan (Tschaikowsky).   (A617)

DEREYNE, Fely (Soprano)

Dereyne was a light-voiced part of Henry Russell's contingent at the Boston Opera and came with him to Columbia's ranks.

COLUMBIA RECORDS 1912

19852   Manon: Je marche sur tous les chemins.   (A1234)
19853   Boheme: Valse de Musette.   (A1234)

DE SEGUROLA, Andrea Perello (Bass)

COLUMBIA RECORDS 1912-1913

19857   Faust: Serenata.   (A1215)
19858   Boheme: Vecchia zimarra.   (A1214)
19860   Tales of Hoffmann: Barcarola (w. De Pasquali).   (A1214)
19876   Mignon: Leggiadre Rondinelle (w. De Pasquali).   (A1215)
21588   Un Adios a Mariquina (Chane).   (S16)
21589   Clavelitos (Valverde).   (S16)
36375   Ernani: Infelice.   (H1070)

For Victor Red Seal, see BORI, CARUSO, PAOLI, RUFFO

Note: From August 1903 on, De Segurola appeared on many Victor black and blue seal records in Spanish songs such as Tus Ojos on No. 5188 and operatic solos like the bass aria from Favorita with chorus on No. 52450, coupled on 16551, and duets like Nella notte from Hugenots with Grisi on No. 52518, coupled on 63404.

DESMOND, Mary (Contralto)

Mary Desmond was possessor of a lovely contralto voice well suited to both opera and song.

COLUMBIA RECORDS 1911

30490   Samson :Mon coeur.   (A5259)
30493   Beloved It is Morn (Aylward).   (A5256)
30564   Mignon: Gavotte.   (A5259)
30565   Nadeshda: My heart is weary.   (A5256)

DESTINN, Emmy (Soprano)

Destinn appears as heroine of novels as well as studies of vocal technique. Fortunate it is that her records number in the hundreds and, of those made abroad, the first group listed below were incorporated into the domestic catalogue while earlier Berlin issues on Columbia label were available as imports, as were her later Odeon recordings. Her staunch Czech patriotism, which caused her such difficulties with those who pre-echoed the Nazi regime, is evidenced in the domestic Victor groups.

IMPORTED VICTOR RED SEAL 1908-1909

91083   Mignon: Kennst du das Land.
91084   Mme. Butterfly: Sai cos' ebbe.   (939)
91086   Mme. Butterfly: L'ultima scena.   (939)
92057   Mme. Butterfly: Un bel di.   (15-1014)
92058   Aida: O Vaterland.

DESTINN [63] DE TURA

COLUMBIA RECORDS 1912-1913

30970	Cavalleria Rusticana: Voi lo sapete.		(A5398)
30971	Aida: Ritorna vincitor.		(A5387)
30972	Aida: I sacri nomi.		(A5387)
30973	Aida: O patria mia.	(A5587)	(7030M)
30974	Freischutz: Wie nahte mir.		(A5605)
30975	Freischutz: Alles Pflegt.		(A5605)
30976	Boheme: Vals di Musetta.		(A5397)
30977	Pagliacci: Ballatella.		(A5397)
30998	Tosca: Vissi d'arte.		(A5587)
36360	Aida: O terra addio (w. Zenatello-Cho.).		(A5399)
36361	Trovatore: Miserere (w. Zenatello-Cho.).		(A5399)
36365	Forza del Destino: La Vergine (w. Cho.).		(A5398)

VICTOR RED SEAL 1914-1917

87197	Uz Mou Milou (The Wedding) (w. Gilly).	(87554)	(3002)
87207	Kde domov Muj (My Homeland) (w. Gilly).	(87555)	(3002)
87214	Wiegenlied (Schubert).		
87215	Nazarene: Slovacka Pisen (Slovak Song).		
87246	Wiegenlied (Mozart).		
88467	Mignon: Kennst du das Land.		(6085)
88468	Mme. Butterfly: Un bel di.		(6413)
88469	Aida: O patria mia.		(6084)
88478	Gioconda: Suicidio.	(6086)	(15-1014)
88487	Tosca: Vissi d'arte.		(6086)
88488	Tannhauser: Elisabeths Gebet.		(6085)
88498	Dobrou noc (Good Night) (w. Gilly).	(89116)	(8046)
88510	Magic Flute: Ach, ich fuhl's.		
88518	Pique Dame: Es geht auf mitternacht.		
88519	Rusalka: Lieblicher Mond.		
88520	Pique Dame: Es dammert (w. Duchene).	(89117)	
88529	Pique Dame: O viens (w. Duchene).	(89118)	(8017)
88530	Trovatore: Miserere (w. Martinelli-Cho.).	(89119)	(6190)
88557	Trovatore: D'amor sull'ali.		
88562	Ave Maria (Gounod).		
88563	L'Ultima Canzone (Tosti).		
88565	Die Bekherte (Stange).		
88568	O quand je dors (Liszt).		
89078	Guarany: Sento un forza (w. Caruso).		(6355)

VICTOR RED SEAL 1920-1923

87306	Posledni Slzy (Last Tears) (Destinn).		
87310	Domu (Home) (Hess).		
87314	Sila Kosilicku (My Sweetheart) (Jindrich).		(908)
87315	Kdyz jsem (On My Way) (Stepan).		
87316	Ej, hory (O Mountains).		
87317	Namluvy; Divici Popevek (Wooing; A Maiden's Song).		
87318	Ten ostrozsky zamek (The Ostroh Castle) (Jindrich).		
87324	Zalo dievca (The Mower) (Dvorak).		(908)
88624	Romance (Destinn).		(6087)
88634	Hubicka: Ukolebavka (Cradle Song).		(6087)
88636	Masked Ball: Morro ma prima.		(6084)
Note:	No. 87249 was assigned to Serenade (Gounod).		

DE TURA, Gennaro (Tenor).

IMPORTED VICTOR RED SEAL 1910-1912

87056	Mefistofele: Lontano (w. Huguet).		
87067	Mefistofele: Folletto (w. Mansueto-Cho.).		(87565)
88227	Boheme: Mimi e una civetta (w. Mellerio-Badini).	(89157)	(8062)

88233	Boheme: Questo mar rosso (w. Badini).	(89156) (8062)
88241	Cavalleria Rusticana: Addio alla madre.	(76015) (88609)
76012	Favorita: Spirto gentil.	(88611)
76019	Faust: La vaga pupilla (w. Cho.).	(88610)

Note: The above is but a part of a much larger group of Italian recordings which included still another Boheme duet with Badini, this being the more familiar Ah Mimi tu piu on No. 54398.

DIDUR, Adamo (Bass)

Note: This celebrated Polish singer, long a favorite at the Metropolitan Opera, was a great success earlier in Italy, where a large number of Fonotipias made before 1909 included Hugenots: Signor difesa on No. 92003 (C-F25). His recorded work in this country was largely for Pathe, some of which were "dubbed" on Actuelle, among them Marriage of Figaro: Non piu andrai on No. 025084 (Perfect 11530).

DOMAR, Dora (Soprano)

IMPORTED VICTOR RED SEAL 1910-1911

88228	Boheme: Mimi, io son (w. Badini).	(89143)
89048	Boheme: Addio, dolce (w. Santoro-Giovanelli-Badini).	

Note: A number of other recordings featuring Domar as Mimi were issued in Italy where the above two selections were numbered 054244 and 054253.

DONALDA, Pauline (Soprano)

IMPORTED VICTOR RED SEAL 1912

87108	Pagliacci: Ballatella.

Note: In Canada, where her famliy had changed its name from Lichtenstein to its English equ:valent and she once more to the above name, this selection was listed as X3204 and the half dozen others she had recorded in London were issued with like numbers, the twelve-inch Boheme aria being X03200. She also appeared here on Emerson label when her Carmen: Scena della carte, No. 7218, was put on sale September 1917 at a price of twenty-five cents, quite a bargain for an artist of her distinction.

DUCHENE, Maria (Contralto)

See CARUSO, DESTINN, GILIBERT.

Note: Duchene was the fifth servingwoman when Electra received its first American performance, this one in French. On records, at least, her roles are more imposing ones.

DUFRANNE, Hector (Baritone)

The history of modern French opera could almost be written around the roles sung by this fine baritone, who created many of them in Parisian or American premieres. It is unfortunate that details of such casts are so infrequently given in works of reference.

COLUMBIA RECORDS 1913-1914

36494	Lakme: Lakme, ton doux regard.	(A5444)
36495	Jolie Fille de Perth: Quand la flamme.	(A5455)
36496	Tales of Hoffmann: Scintille diamant.	(A5444)
36497	Jongleur de Notre Dame: Legende.	(A5455)

36880   Puritani: Suoni la tromba (w. Scott).   (A5558) (7032M)
36885   Thais: Voila donc la terrible cite.   (A5558)

Note: On Victor, Dufranne appeared in black and blue seal imports, among
the former being the tenor-baritone duet from Carmen with Beyle on No. 62750.

DUX, Claire (Soprano)

BRUNSWICK RECORDS 1921-1925

30022	Boheme: Mi chiamano Mimi.	
	Mondnacht (Schumann).	(15027) (10130)
	Morgen (Strauss) (viol. Fradkin).	(15027) (10130)
	Haidenrøslein (Schubert).	(15061) (10114)
	In einem Kuhlen Grunde (Gluck).	(15061) (10114)
	Standchen (Strauss).	(10156)
	Marias Wiegenlied (Reger).	(10156)
	Abendlied (Schumann).	(10205)
	Komm Liebe Zither (Mozart).	(10205)
	Marriage of Figaro: Deh vieni.	(50057)
	Marriage of Figaro: Voi che sapete.	(50057)

Note: Just prior to the release of Dux domestic recordings, the German Odeon
of her Mignon: Kennst du das Land was imported by Okeh as Am 44016, OK
50501. Of her many Deutsche Grammophon items, several appeared here on
whatever label had or exercised the rights to them at the time they were imported. Thus, the Boheme final duet with Jorn, Gr. 044187, became Victor No.
55071 and Trovatore: befreit with the excellent baritone Joseph Schwarz, Gr.
3-44157, was issued as Opera Disc No. 74593, then again as Vocalion No. 24062.

EAMES, Emma (Soprano)

Eames was so much the grand lady, in the best sense of the term, that her
interpretations are sometimes considered lacking in warmth, a claim easily
belied by both arias like the Faust jewel song and songs like the beautiful
Chanson d'amour below.

VICTOR RED SEAL 1905

85052	Still wie die Nacht (Bohm).	(88005)
85053	Faust: Air des bijoux.	(88006)
85054	Ave Maria (Gounod).	(88007)
85057	L'Incredule (Hahn); Year's at the Spring (Beach).	(88008)
85058	Good Bye (Tosti).	(88009)
85059	Tosca: Vissi d'arte.	(88010)
85060	Romeo: Valse.	(88011)
85061	Star Spangled Banner (Smith); Dixie (Emmett).	(88012)
85062	Who is Sylvia (Schubert).	(88013)
85063	Elegie (Massenet).	

VICTOR RED SEAL 1906-1909

85097	Chanson d'amour (Hollman) (w. Hollman).	(88015)
85098	Ave Maria (Gounod) (w. Hollman).	(88016) (6088)
88005	Still wie die Nacht (Bohm).	
88006	Faust: Air des bijoux.	
88008	Spring (Henschel): Year's at the Spring (Beach).	
88010	Tosca: Vissi d'arte.	
88011	Romeo: Valse.	
88014	Elegie (Massenet) (w. Hollman).	(6088)
88035	Otello: Ave Maria.	
88036	Carmen: Je dis que rien.	
88037	Cavalleria Rusticana: Voi lo sapete.	

88045 Faust: Le Roi de Thule.
88131 Love in May (Parker); I once had a doll (Nevin).
88133 Chanson des Baisers (Bemberg).
88135 Si tu le veux (Koechlin); Aubade cherubin (Massenet).
89003 Magic Flute: La dove prende (w. De Gogorza).   (8043)
89004 Crucifix (Faure) (w. De Gogorza).
89005 Don Giovanni: La ci darem (w. De Gogorza).
89020 Lakme: Dome epais (w. Homer).
89021 Lohengrin: Du Aermste (w. Homer).
89022 Trovatore: Mira d'acerbe (w. De Gogorza).
89023 Marriage of Figaro: Crudel perche (w. De Gogorza).
95202 Marriage of Figaro: Che soave (w. Sembrich).   (8043)
95300 Faust: Alerte (w. Dalmores-Plancon).

<h3 style="text-align:center">VICTOR RED SEAL 1912-1913</h3>

88344 Dopo (Tosti).
88367 Gretchen am Spinnrade (Schubert).
89063 Veronique: Swing Song (w. De Gogorza).

Note: A 1911 recording of Rameau's Vents furieux appeared in 1912 catalogue as No. 87106 but was probably unpublished as this number was assigned to another record (see Alda). The April 1909 recording of the Crucifix duet was tentatively assigned No. 88183 (see Gadski) but finally appeared as No. 89004 replacing the 1906 recording. Likewise, the duet from Don Giovanni was listed in April 1906 under 85099 (see Plancon), under 89005 three months later.

EASTON, Florence (Soprano)

Those who know Easton only from her splendid Siegfried set might be surprised at the repertoire below but the many who enjoyed the tremendous variety of her Metropolitan Opera performances will only wish a greater assortment existed on discs.

<h3 style="text-align:center">VOCALION RECORDS 1920</h3>

30100 Values (Vanderpool).
30103 Tosca: Vissi d'arte.
30106 My Curly-Headed Babby (Clutsam).

<h3 style="text-align:center">BRUNSWICK RECORDS 1921-1925</h3>

10036 My Laddie (Thayer).
10037 Faust: Air des bijoux.
10044 Tosca: Vissi d'arte.
10046 Silent Night (Gruber) (w. Trio).   (15058) (10113)
30011 Ave Maria (Gounod) (viol. Rosen).
30013 Mme. Butterfly: Un bel di.
     Carmen: Je dis que rien.   (50012)
     Pagliacci: Ballatella.   (50012)
     Ave Maria (Gounod) (viol. Fradkin).   (50025)
     O Divine Redeemer (Gounod).   (50025)
     Boheme: Addio.   (15000)
     Carmen: Habanera.   (15000)
     Sadko: Song of India.   (15020) (10106)
     Snow Maiden: Song of Shepherd Lehl.   (15020) (10106)
     Faust: Le Roi de Thule.   (15030)
     Mignon: Connais-tu le pays.   (15030)
     El Cefiro.   (15038) (10110)
     Preguntale a las Estrellas.   (15038) (10110)
     Treue Liebe (Kucken).   (15054) (10112)
     Still wie die Nacht (Bohm).   (15054) (10112)
     Holy Night (Adam) (w. Cho.).   (15058) (10113)
     Sing Me to Sleep (Greene).   (10100)

Mighty Lak' a Rose (Nevin).		(10100)
Cradle Song (Iljinsky).	(15066)	(10116)
Songs My Mother Taught Me (Dvorak).	(15066)	(10116)
Over the Hills (Logan).	(15076)	(10120)
Heart o' Mine (Herbert).	(15076)	(10120)
Old Folks at Home (Foster) (viol. Fradkin).		(10152)
Hard Times (Foster) (w. Trio).		(10152)

ELMAN, Mischa (Violinist)

VICTOR RED SEAL 1908-1913

61180	Moment Musical (Schubert); Perpetuo Mobile (Bohm).	
61182	Faust: Fantasie (arr. Wieniawski).	
61183	Swing Song (Barnes).	
61184	Gavotte (Bohm).	
61185	Serenade (Drigo).	
64121	Minuet in G No. 2 (Beethoven).	(607)
64122	Faust: Fantasie (arr. Wieniawski).	(601)
64123	Serenade (Drigo).	(600)
64128	Les Farfadets (Pente).	
64135	Minuet in F (Haydn).	
64140	Idomeneo: Gavotte in G (arr. Auer).	
64197	Traumerei (Schumann).	(600)
64198	Gavotte (Gretry); Tambourin (Gossec).	
64201	Rigaudon (Monsigny-Franko).	(606)
64204	Capricietto (Mendelssohn-Burmester).	(605)
64336	Waltz in E Flat (Hummel-Burmester).	(604)
71038	Rondo Capriccioso (Saint-Saens).	
71039	Gavotte (Gossec); German Dance (Dittersdorf).	
74051	Souvenir de Moscow (Wieniawski).	(6093)
74052	Nocturne in E Flat Op. 9 No. 2 (Chopin-Sarasate).	(6099)
74053	Melodie Op. 42 No. 3 (Tschaikowsky).	(6091)
74163	Humoresque Op. 101 No. 7 (Dvorak).	(6095)
74164	Gavotte (Gossec); German Dance (Dittersdorf).	(6424)
74165	Rondo Capriccioso (Saint-Saens).	(6089)
74167	Serenade (Schubert).	(6095)
74176	Caprice Basque (Sarasate).	(6094)
74178	Nur wer die Sehnsucht kennst (Tschaikowsky).	(6091)
74186	Meistersinger: Prize Song.	(6090)
74292	Suite in D—Air for G String (Bach-Wilhelmj).	(6101)
74308	Sicilienne and Rigaudon (Francoeur-Kreisler).	
74336	Cavatina Op. 85 No. 3 (Raff).	(6093)
74339	Ave Maria (Schubert-Wilhelmj).	(6101)
74340	Chanson Louis XIII (Couperin-Kreisler).	
74341	Thais: Meditation.	(6100)

VICTOR RED SEAL 1914-1919

64438	Vogel als Prophet Op. 82 No. 7 (Schumann).	
64439	Hungarian Dance No. 7 (Brahms-Joachim).	(597)
64530	In a Gondola—Impromptu (Elman).	(603)
64537	Country Dance (Weber-Elman).	(598)
64538	Minuet in D (Haydn-Burmester).	(607)
64547	Rondino on a theme by Beethoven (Kreisler).	(611)
64636	Pastorale (D. Scarlatti).	(609)
64639	Orientale (Cui).	(599)
64642	Capriccio (Scarlatti).	(602)
64643	Valse Caprice Op. 16 (Rissland).	(604)
64644	Souvenir (Drdla).	(599)
64821	Tango (Albeniz-Elman).	(610)
74392	Canto Amoroso (Sammartini-Elman).	(6092)
74395	Dans les Bois (Paganini-Vogrich).	(6096)

74455	Spanish Dance Op. 22 No. 3 (Sarasate).		(6094)
74459	Orfeo: Melodie (arr. Wilhelmj).		(6090)
74515	Simple Aveu (Thome).		(6097)
74590	Nocturne in D Flat Op. 27 No. 2 (Chopin-Wilhelmj).		(6099)

VICTOR RED SEAL 1920-1925

64829	Waltz in A (Hummel).		(610)
64884	Scotch Pastorale Op. 130 No. 2 (Saenger).		(609)
64894	Dew is Sparkling (Rubenstein-Elman).	(605)	(3030)
64903	Roi s'amuse: Passepied (arr. Elman).		(606)
64915	Ruins of Athens—Turkish March (Beethoven).		(598)
64958	Martha: Last Rose of Summer (arr. Auer).		(608)
64968	Country Dance (Beethoven-Elman).		(597)
64977	Hungarian Dance No. 17 in F Sharp Minor (Brahms-Joachim).		(611)
66008	Canzonetta Op. 6 (d'Ambrosio).		(602)
66048	Serenade (Drdla).		(601)
66073	La Cinquantaine (Gabriel-Marie).		(603)
66099	Fond Recollections (Popper).		(608)
66144	Blue Lagoon (Millocker-Winternitz).		(900)
66151	Landler (Mozart).		(900)
66205	Romance Op. 44 No. 1 (Rubenstein-Bonime).		(974)
66206	Souvenir Poetique (Fibich-Schindler).		(974)
	Valse Sentimentale (Schubert-Franko).		(1034)
	Valse Staccato (Ravina-Piastro).		(1034)
	Etude (Rode-Elman).		(1060)
	Minuet (Haydn-Burmester).		(1060)
	A la Valse (Herbert).		(1079)
	To Slumber-Land (Kopylow-Hartmann).		(1079)
74597	Coq d'Or: Hymn to the Sun.		(6100)
74601	Kol Nidre Op. 47 (Bruch).		(6098)
74607	Song Without Words Op. 67 No. 6 (Mendelssohn).		(6096)
74643	Nocturne Op. 54 No. 4 (Grieg-Elman).		(6092)
74724	Alice Where Art Thou (Ascher).		(6097)
74732	Eili, Eili (arr. Elman).		(6098)
74771	Symphonie Espagnole-Andante (Lalo).		(6089)
74837	Adagio (Mozart-Friedberg).		(6424)
74892	Albumblatt (Wagner-Wilhelmj).		(6457)
74893	Gondoliera (Ries).		(6457)

For other records, see **ALDA, CARUSO.**

Note: The earliest Elman records are imports most of which were soon re-made in this country and inserted into the catalogue under the previous numbers or, in a majority of cases, new ones. Also assigned numbers were selections from Nuit de Mai (64536), Song Without Words (74393) and Martini's Minuette (74394).

ELMAN QUARTET

(Elman-Bak-Rissland-Nagel)

VICTOR RED SEAL 1917-1918

64661	Quartet in D Minor—Minuet (Mozart).	(612)
64671	Quartet in E Flat—Finale (Dittersdorf).	(612)
74516	Emperor Quartet—Theme and Var. (Haydn).	(6103)
74525	Quartet in G—Andante (Dittersdorf).	(6102)
74574	Quartet in A Minor Op. 29—Minuet (Schubert).	
74575	Quartet Op. 11—Andante cantabile (Tschaikowsky).	(6103)
74576	Quartet in E Flat—Minuet (Mozart).	(6102)

ENESCO, Georges (Violinist)

COLUMBIA RECORDS 1924-1925

Serenade Op. 4 (d'Ambrosio).	(20023D) (2008M)
Aubade Provencale (Couperin-Kreisler).	(20023D) (2008M)
Albumblatt (Wagner).	(20029D) (2026M)
Ruins of Athens—Chorus (Beethoven).	(20029D) (2026M)

FARRAR, Geraldine (Soprano)

A winning personality which came through the silent screen as it did across the footlights, coupled with an appearance of great beauty, and a voice of considerable warmth, if not impeccable technique or style, marked Farrar as an idol of countless operagoers and movie fans. Enough likewise comes through the acoustics of these and earlier European recordings to capture her great appeal and make one wonder if electrical recording is such a boon to those well enough endowed to stand on their own merits.

VICTOR RED SEAL 1907-1911

87004	Mme. Butterfly: Ancora un passo.	(616)
87005	Comin' thro' the Rye.	(619)
87023	Manon: Gavotte.	
87024	Robin Adair (Keppel).	
87025	Believe me if all those endearing young charms.	(622)
87030	Mme. Butterfly: L'ultima scena.	(617)
87031	Mme. Butterfly: Ieri son salita.	(616)
87055	Mme. Butterfly: Sai cos' ebbe.	(617)
87062	Ye Banks and Braes o' Bonnie Doon.	(619)
87073	Hear My Prayer: Oh, for the wings.	(623)
87076	Abide With Me (Monk).	(618)
87502	Tales of Hoffmann: Barcarolle (w. Scotti).	(3025)
88052	Annie Laurie (Scott).	(6112)
88053	Tannhauser: Elisabeths Gebet.	
88113	Mme. Butterfly: Un bel di.	(18141)
88114	Mefistofele: L'altra notte.	(6394)
88125	Nymphes et Sylvains (Bemberg).	
88126	Don Giovanni: Batti, Batti.	
88144	Carmen: Je dis que rien.	(6113)
88145	Marriage of Figaro: Voi che sapete.	
88146	Manon: Adieu, notre petite table.	(6111)
88147	Faust: Air des bijoux.	(6107)
88152	Mignon: Styrienne—Je connais.	(6394)
88192	Tosca: Vissi d'arte.	(6110)
88193	Bonnie Sweet Bessie (Gilbert).	(6112)
88211	Mignon: Connais-tu le pays.	(6113)
88229	Faust: Le Roi de Thule.	(6107)
88238	My Old Kentucky Home (Foster).	
88283	Ben Bolt (Kneass).	
88287	Tosca: Ora stammi a sentir.	
88289	My Mother Bids Me (Haydn).	
89008	Mme. Butterfly: Tutti i fior (w. Homer).	
89014	Mme. Butterfly: Ora a noi (w. Scotti).	(8039)
89015	Don Giovanni: La ci darem (w. Scotti).	(8023)
89016	Boheme: Mimi, io son (w. Scotti).	(8023) (10007)
89026	Mme. Butterfly: Tutti i fior (w. Jacoby).	
89027	Marriage of Figaro: Crudel perche (w. Scotti).	(8039)
89035	Faust: Scene de l' Eglise (part I) (w. Journet-Cho.).	(8021)
89037	Faust: Scene de l' Eglise (part II) (w. Journet-Cho.).	(8021)
89038	Mignon: Les hirondelles (w. Journet).	(8022)
89040	Faust: Elle ouvre sa fenetre (w. Journet).	(8022) (10008)

VICTOR RED SEAL 1912-1917

87126	Exultate Jubilate: Alleluja.		
87127	Recontre Imprevue: Wonervoller Mai (arr. Sieber).		
87134	Liebe Augustin: Der Himmel.		
87136	Secret of Suzanne: Via cosi.		
87160	I've Been Roaming (Horn).	(909)	
87163	Long, Long Ago (Bayly).	(624)	
87164	Love Has Eyes (Bishop).		
87165	Modest Heart (Wolf).		
87210	Carmen: Habanera.	(621)	
87247	Star Spangled Banner (Smith).		
87248	Lead, Kindly Light (Dykes).	(618)	
87251	Murmuring Zephyr (Jensen).		
87253	Thy Dear Eyes (Bartlett).		
87254	All Through the Night.		
87256	Tu me dirais (Chaminade).		
87257	Serenade (Gounod).		
87504	Wanderers Nachtlied (Rubenstein) (w. Schumann-Heink).		
87505	How Can I Leave Thee (w. Homer).	(3026)	
87506	Sandmannchen (Becker) (w. Homer).	(3026)	
87507	Sous la fenetre (Schumann) (w. Clement).		
87508	Dante: Nous allons partir (w. Clement).		
87509	Au clair de la lune (Lully) (w. Clement).	(3025)	
88113	Mme. Butterfly: Un bel di.	(6110)	
88356	Donne Curiose: Tutta per te.		
88359	Donne Curiose: Il cor nel contento (w. Jadlowker).	(89115)	
88405	Konigskinder: Lieber Spielmann.		
88406	Boheme: Addio.	(6106)	
88409	Love's Like a Summer Rose (Chadwick).		
88412	Konigskinder: Weiss nicht.		
88413	Boheme: Mi chiamano Mimi.	(6106)	
88421	Romeo: Ange adorable (w. Clement).	(89113)	(8020)
88422	Mefistofele: Lontano (w. Clement).	(89114)	(8020)
88424	Secret of Suzanne: O gioia la nube.		
88511	Carmen: Seguidilla.	(6108)	
88512	Carmen: Chanson Boheme.	(6109)	
88513	Carmen: La-bas dans la montagne.	(6108)	
88531	Carmen: Je t'aime encore (w. Martinelli).	(89110)	(8018)
88532	Carmen: Au quartier (w. Martinelli).		
88533	Carmen: C'est toi (w. Martinelli).	(89111)	(8019)
88534	Carmen: Air des cartes.	(6109)	
88536	Carmen: Halte-la (w. Martinelli).	(89112)	(8019)
88537	Mighty Lak' a Rose (Nevin) (w. Kreisler).	(89108)	(8024)
88538	Mignon: Connais-tu le pays (w. Kreisler).	(89109)	(8024)
88569	Holy City (Adams).		
89057	Secret of Suzanne: Il dolce idillio (w. Amato).		
89071	Der Engel (Rubenstein) (w. Homer).		
89072	Alla Campanna andiamo (Campana) (w. Homer).		
89086	Carmen: Si tu m'aimes (w. Amato-Cho.).	(8018)	

VICTOR RED SEAL 1918-1923

87289	Boat Song (Romilli).	(909)
87290	War Baby's Lullaby (Farrington).	
87292	Sans Toi (d'Hardelot).	
87308	Apple Blossoms: Star of Love.	
87311	Zaza: Mamma usciva di casa.	(625)
87313	Au Printemps (Gounod).	(621)
87319	At Parting (Rogers).	(624)
87322	Si j'etais Jardinier (Chaminade).	(620)
87348	Si mes vers (Hahn).	(620)

87350	Songs My Mother Taught Me (Dvorak).	(622)
87357	Ye Who Have Yearned Alone (Tschaikowsky).	(623)
87362	Serenata (Tosti).	(953)
87364	Madrigal (Chaminade).	(953)
87568	Zaza: Il bacio (w. De Luca).	(625)
88594	Thais: Meditation.	(6111)

For other records, see CARUSO.

Note: Except to distinguish the two recordings of "Un bel di" from Mme. Butterfly, a justifiably celebrated rendition, both of which were pressed onto double discs at different times, no indication has been given above that Farrar, like so many others, re-made a number of her early recordings at various times. Other Farrar items to which numbers had been assigned include a ten-inch My Old Kentucky Home (87029), The Star (87291), Chant Venetian (87347) and Serenata (with Kreisler) (88535).

FERRARI-FONTANA Edoardo (Tenor)

Ferrari-Fontana was a most intelligent singer who created important roles in Zanella's Aura in 1907, and more enduring works later.

COLUMBIA RECORDS 1915

36877	Jewels of the Madonna: Madonna con sospiri.	(A5663)
36878	Jewels of the Madonna: Madonna dei dolori.	(A5663)
37235	Otello: Morte d'Otello.	(A5721)
37236	Carmen: Air de la fleur.	(A5721)
39259	Tristan: Noto Regina e a me.	(A1731)
39260	Pagliacci: Un tal gioco.	(A1731)

FINZI-MAGRINI Giuseppina (Soprano)

IMPORTED VICTOR RED SEAL 1912

| 89058 | Rigoletto: Deh non parlare (w. Ruffo). | (8059) |

Note: Among a host of other selections, this fine soprano sang the usual coloratura aria from the above opera both for Fonotipia before 1909 on No. 92276 and for Columbia after that date on No. 11162, the latter imported here and coupled on A1392 and other popular priced discs.

FLEISCHER, Editha (Soprano)

Note: Anyone who recalls the Metropolitan Opera performances of Don Giovanni conducted by Serafin in which Editha Fleischer, as Zerlina, would practically steal the show from a cast which included Ponselle, Rethberg, Gigli and Pinza, this, of course, was over twenty years ago, will regret her great neglect by record companies. To match her few European recordings, mostly on inferior labels but including, at least, arias like the florid cavatina of Rosina from the Barber of Sev.lle, are several 1925 Victor black seal couplings, both of solos as the Vilja-Lied from Merry Widow and Sommers letzte Rose from Martha on No. 77856 and duets with Bloch from Schwarzwaldmadel on No. 77902, also from Gypsy Baron backed by an arrangement of the Blue Danube Waltz on No. 68660.

FLETA, Miguel (Tenor)

Earliest and latest of the items below were imports while others were made during his stay at the Metropolitan Opera, which Fleta terminated with characteristic abruptness; on records, he lingers much longer, particularly on a note he likes.

VICTOR RED SEAL 1922-1925

66090	Trust de los Tenorios: Te quiero.	(950)
66091	Tosca: E lucevan le stelle.	(950)
66177	Rigoletto: La donna e mobile.	(948)
66178	Puritani: A te o cara.	(948)
66229	Mi Tierra (Mediavilla).	(993)
66230	Adios Triguena (Robles).	(993)
	La Calle Mayor de Jaca-Jota.	(1065)
	Si fuera un aeroplano; Manica-Jotas.	(1065)
	Dolores: Jota.	(1066)
	La Fematera; La Virgen-Jotas.	(1066)
	Amapola (Lacalle).	(1073)
	Bimba non t'avvicinar (Bettinelli).	(1073)
74774	Ay Ay Ay (Perez).	(6392)
74775	Giulietta e Romeo: Giuletta, son io.	(6391)
74778	Carmen: Canzone del fior.	(6391)
74828	Dolores: Henchido de amor santo.	(6392)
	Dona Francisquita: Mujer fatal.	(6549)
	Gavilanes: Flor roja.	(6549)
89164	Aida: Presago il core (w. Austral-Cho.).	(8063)
89165	Aida: O terra addio (w. Austral-Thornton-Cho.).	(8063)

FLONZALEY QUARTET

(Betti-Pochon-Bailly-d'Archambeau)

VICTOR RED SEAL 1918-1925

64784	Quartet in E Flat Op. 12—Canzonetta (Mendelssohn).	(626)
64874	Drink to Me Only (arr. Pochon).	(626)
64889	Quartet in E Flat Minor Op. 30—Scherzo (Tschaikowsky)	(1012)
66254	Spharenmusik (Rubenstein).	(1012)
74578	Quartet in A Minor Op. 41 No. 1—Scherzo (Schumann).	(6115)
74579	Quartet in D—Andante (Mozart).	(6115)
74580	Molly on the Shore (Grainger).	(6121)
74592	Quartet in C Op. 59 No. 3—Fugue (Beethoven).	(6114)
74596	Quartet in D—Minuet (Mozart).	(6121)
74611	Quartet in F Op. 96—Lento (Dvorak).	(6449)
74634	Quartet in E Minor—Allegro Moderato (Smetana).	(6449)
74652	Quartet in D Minor—Allegretto (Mozart).	(6117)
74667	Interludium in Modo Antico (Glazounow).	(6117)
74685	Quartet in C Minor Op. 51 No. 1—Allegretto (Brahms).	(6120)
74693	Quartet in G—Finale (Mozart).	(6118)
74710	Quartet in A Op. 41 No. 3—Assai agitato (Schumann).	(6118)
74726	Quartet in D Op. 64 No. 5—Allegro Moderato (Haydn).	(6116)
74733	Quartet in D—Nocturne (Borodin).	(6361)
74746	Quartet in D Op. 64 No. 5—Adagio cantabile (Haydn).	(6116)
74754	Quartet in A Op. 18 No. 5—Theme and Var. (Beethoven).	(6114)
74755	Quartet in E Minor Op. 44 No. 2—Scherzo (Mendelssohn).	(6119)
74792	Quartet in D—Presto (Beethoven).	(6119)
74801	Quartet in C Minor Op. 18 No 4—Scherzo (Beethoven).	(6120)
74825	Quartet in D Op. 64 No. 5—Minuetto; Finale (Haydn).	(6361)
74840	Quartet in D—Adagio (Mozart).	(6425)
74841	Quartet in A Minor—Adagio (Schumann).	(6425)
	Quartet in G Op. 77 No. 1—Allegro (Haydn).	(6486)
	Quartet in G Op. 77 No. 1—Minuetto (Haydn).	(6486)

For other records, see GABRILOWITSCH.

No. 66009 was assigned to Lonely Shepherd—Shakespeare Fairy Character.

FORMICHI, Cesare (Baritone)

Note: A splendid, resounding baritone who had many notable successes at the Chicago Opera, Formichi was, by far, Columbia's most prolific recorder for the imported Italian E and related series, which included a complete Aida in which he figures as well as a complete Rigoletto which he dominates. At the very end of the acoustic period, several of his later European recordings were given higher recognition, among them Samson: Maudite a jamais on No. 2030M (mat. A896).

FORNIA, Rita (Contralto)

VICTOR RED SEAL 1911-1912

64162	Faust: Faites-lui mes aveux.
64244	Chanson de Florian (Meyer-Helmund).
64283	Zauberlied (Meyer-Helmund).
64284	Aime-moi (Chopin-Viardot).
64288	Madrigal (Chaminade).
64289	Allerseelen (Lassen).
64290	Dein gedenk'ich (Meyer-Helmund).
64299	Fruhlingzeit (Becker).
74211	Romeo: Chanson de Stephano.
74227	Der Spielmann (Hildach).
87503	Mme. Butterfly: Lo so che (w. Martin-Scotti).

Note: No. 64285 was assigned to a Lullaby with 'cello accompaniment by Rosario Bourdon; regarding No. 64287, see note under Martinelli. A 1920 Vocal.on record of Quis est homo from Rossini's Stabat Mater joins Fornia in duet with May Peterson on No. 52003. Her untimely death at the age of 43 two years later robbed us of further representations of her versatile art.

FREEMAN, Bettina (Mezzo-Soprano)

While a member of the Boston Opera Company, Freeman recorded for domestic Columbia. Later, she made several discs for its affiliate in London, where she starred in English versions of Wagnerian opera under Sir Thomas Beecham.

COLUMBIA RECORDS 1910

4451	The Little Irish Girl (Lohr).	(A856)
4452	A Little Thief (Stern).	(A856)
30387	Addio (Tosti).	(A5225)
30388	Marriage of Figaro: Voi che sapete.	(A5214)
30393	Hugenots: Nobil Signori.	(A5215)
30394	L'Ardita Waltz (Arditi).	(A5213)
30395	Carmena Waltz (Wilson).	(A5213)
30398	Faust: Le parlate d'amor.	(A5214)
30399	Trovatore: Stride la vampa.	(A5215)
30475	Mignon: Connais-tu le pays.	(H1056)
30476	Bohemian Girl: I dreamt I dwelt.	(A5225)

For other records, see BRONSKAJA.

FREMSTAD, Olive (Soprano)

A name most memorable in operatic history is that of Fremstad. Of mixed Scandanavian ancestry, she had first come here as a child, later as a mature singer of tremendous insight and capability.

COLUMBIA RECORDS 1911-1914

30635	Tannhauser: Dich teure Halle.	(A5281)
30636	Long, Long Ago (Bayly).	(A5273)

30637	Annie Laurie (Scott).	(A5273)
30644	Tosca: Vissi d'arte.	(A5282)
30645	Lohengrin: Elsas Traum.	(A5281)
30646	Carmen: Seguidilla.	(A5282)
30707	Tristan: Liebestod.	(A5521)
30708	Stille Nacht (Gruber).	
36807	Don Carlos: O don fatale.	(A5521)
39060	Mignon: Connais-tu le pays.	(A1505)
39061	Tosca: Ora stammi a sentir.	(A1505)
39062	Wiegenlied (Brahms).	(A1488)
39073	Walkure: Ho yo to ho.	(A1451)
39074	Ach, wie ist moglich.	(A1488)
39081	Walkure: Du bist der Lenz.	(A1451)

FRIEDHEIM, Arthur (Pianist)

COLUMBIA RECORDS 1912-1913

Sonata Op. 35—Funeral March (Chopin).	(A5416)
Moto Perpetuo (Weber).	(A5416)
Scherzo in B Flat Minor (part I) (Chopin).	(A5458)
Scherzo in B Flat Minor (part II) (Chopin).	(A5458)
Hungarian Rhapsody No. 6 (part I) (Liszt).	(A5491)
Hungarian Rhapsody No. 6 (part II) (Liszt).	(A5491)

Note: **Beethoven's Moonlight Sonata was issued in England November 1913 on English Columbia 410. Friedheim was also included in the Emerson catalogue where his rendition of the Liszt Second Hungarian Rhapsody bore No. 7235 (Matrices 2616/7).**

FRIEDMAN, Ignaz (Pianist)

COLUMBIA RECORDS 1924-1925

Hark Hark the Lark (Schubert-Liszt).	(33007D)	(30005D)	(2007M)
Mazurka Op. 63 No. 3; Waltz Op. 64 No. 1 (Chopin).	(33007D)	(30005D)	(2007M)
Mazurka Op. 35 No. 2 (Chopin).	(30011D)		
Prelude Op. 28 No. 19; Etude Op. 25 No. 6 (Chopin).	(30011D)		

GABRILOWITSCH, Ossip (Pianist)

VICTOR RED SEAL 1924

	En Automne Op. 36 No. 4 (Moszkowski).	(1042)
	Novelette Op. 99 No. 9 (Schumann).	(1042)
74900	Quintet Op. 44 (Schumann) (part I) (w. Flonzaley Qt.).	(6462)
74901	Quintet Op. 44 (Schumann) (part II) (w. Flonzaley Qt.).	(6462)
74902	Quintet Op. 44 (Schumann) (part III) (w. Flonzaley Qt.).	(6463)
74903	Quintet Op. 44 (Schumann) (part IV) (w. Flonzaley Qt.).	(6463)

GADSKI, Johanna (Soprano)

It is said that Gadski synchronized her body movements with exact notes in the score, a mechanical bent, which, for all their vocal excellence, leaves a great many of her records somewhat lacking in that spark which was Destinn's, for instance. This, however, did not hold true for an equal number of superb renditions among so numerous and varied an output.

VICTOR RED SEAL 1903-1904

81018	Walkure: Ho yo to ho.
81019	Widmung (Schumann).
81024	Der Nussbaum (Schumann).

81045	Ave Maria (Gounod).	
85012	Aida: O Patria Mia.	
85013	Tannhauser: Dich teure Halle.	
85025	Du bist die Ruh (Schubert).	
85029	Lohengrin: Elsas Traum.	
85032	Aus meinen grossen Schmerzen; Liebchen ist da (Franz).	

VICTOR RED SEAL 1907-1910

81089	Salome: Jochanaan, ich bin verliebt.	(87028)
87002	Walkure: Ho yo to ho.	(904)
87016	Standchen (Strauss).	
87019	Widmung (Schumann).	
87026	How much I love you (La Forge); Year's at Spring (Beach).	
87052	Gotterdammerung: Helle Wehr.	
88038	Lohengrin: Elsas Traum.	
88039	Ave Maria (Gounod).	
88040	Erlkonig (Schubert).	(6122)
88041	Verborgene Wunden; Like the Rose Bud (La Forge).	
88042	Aida: O Patria Mia.	(6413)
88057	Tannhauser: Dich teure Halle.	(18142)
88058	Tristan: Liebestod.	
88059	Stabat Mater: Inflammatus.	
88111	Gretchen am Spinnrade (Schubert).	
88112	Standchen (Schubert).	
88116	Flying Dutchman: Traft ihr das Schiff.	
88117	Irish Folk Song (Foote).	
88136	Cavalleria Rusticana: Voi lo sapete.	
88137	Aida: Ritorna vincitor.	(6122)
88163	Aida: Fu la sorte (w. Homer).	(89024)
88164	Aida: Alla pompa (w. Homer).	(89025)
88165	Tristan: Dein Werk.	
88183	Walkure: Brunnhildes Bitte.	
88185	Gotterdammerung: Fliegt heim.	
88186	Siegfried: Ewig war ich.	
88253	Don Giovanni: In quali eccessi.	
88254	Magic Flute: Ah lo so.	
88275	Marriage of Figaro: Porgi amor.	
89028	Aida: La fatal pietra (w. Caruso).	(8015)
89029	Aida: O terra addio (w. Caruso).	(8015)
89041	Orfeo: Su e con me (w. Homer).	
95201	Meistersinger: Quintet (w. Mattfield-Van Hoose-Journet-Reiss).	

VICTOR RED SEAL 1912-1917

87098	Gotterdammerung: Zu neuen Taten.	
87099	Auf dem Kirchhofe (Brahms).	
87100	Auf Flugeln des Gesanges (Mendelssohn).	
87167	Walkure: Du bist der Lenz.	
87173	Annie Laurie (Scott).	
87252	Slumber Song (Gilmour).	
87273	Der Engel (Wagner).	
87274	Schmerzen (Wagner).	
87275	Stehe Still (Wagner).	
87281	Walkure: Fort denn eile.	
87510	Magic Flute: Papagena, Papageno (w. Goritz).	
88362	Lobetanz: Am allen Zweigen.	
88369	Magic Flute: Bei mannern (w. Goritz).	(89124)
88370	Flying Dutchman: Versank ich jetzt (w. Goritz).	
88371	Flying Dutchman: Wohl komm' ich (w. Goritz).	
88377	Lohengrin: Euch luften.	
88379	Trovatore: D'amor sull'ali.	
88440	Still wie die Nacht (Goetze) (w. Goritz).	(89125)

88441	Magic Flute: Du also bist (w. Sparkes-Case-Mattfield).	
88442	Tannhauser: Verzeiht wenn ich.	
88443	Tannhauser: Zuruck von ihn.	
88495	Oberon: Ozean (part I).	
88496	Masked Ball: Ma dall'arido.	
88497	Masked Ball: Morro, ma prima.	
88515	Wacht am Rhein (Wilhelm).	
88542	Im Herbst (Franz).	
88545	Oberon: Ozean (part II).	
88546	Kathleen Mavourneen (Crouch).	
88564	Lorelei (Silcher).	
88566	Haidenroslein (Werner).	
88571	Messiah: He Shall Feed.	
88578	Lotosblume (Schumann).	
88590	Im Treibhaus (Wagner).	
88591	Traume (Wagner).	
89067	Aida: Ciel mio Padre (w. Amato).	(8048)
89068	Aida: Su dunque (w. Amato).	(8048)
89069	Trovatore: Mira d'acerbe (w. Amato).	(8060)
89070	Trovatore: Vivra contende (w. Amato).	(8060)

Note: Other Gadski recordings to which numbers were assigned include Tannhauser: Dich teure Halle (88043), Tannhauser: Elisabeths Gebet (88044), Flying Dutchmann duet with Goritz (88372) and Mondnacht (88499).

GALEFFI, Carlo (Baritone)

IMPORTED VICTOR RED SEAL 1925

	Nerone: Non resistete al malvagio.	(6484)
	Nerone: V'amai dal di che il cor (w. Cho.).	(6484)
	Nerone: Laggiu tra i giunchi (w. Bertana).	(6485)
	Nerone: Or tutto e confessato (w. Bertana).	(6485)

Note: More conventional baritone fare appeared earlier on Columbia buff seal records among which the imported recordings of Galeffi singing the Pagliacci Prologo (74804) and "O Monumento" from Gioconda (74805) were coupled on S5133, later 8926M.

GALLI-CURCI, Amelita (Soprano)

A most appealing quality and smooth legato mark the singing of Galli-Curci, who was likewise capable of considerable brilliance, though not of the spontaneous variety of her more illustrious predecessors.

VICTOR RED SEAL 1917-1920

64669	Manon Lescaut (Auber): L'Eclat de rire.	(635)
64723	Caro mio ben (Giordani).	(629)
64724	Little Birdies (Buzzi-Peccia).	(630)
64748	Marriage of Figaro: Non so piu.	(634)
64749	Little Dorry (Seppilli).	
64792	La Capinera (Benedict).	(629)
64807	Crepuscule (Massenet).	(632)
64820	Traviata: Sempre libera.	(627)
64885	Filles de Cadiz (Delibes).	(632)
64904	Clavelitos (Valverde).	(635)
64918	Sonnambula: Sovra il sen.	(633)
74499	Rigoletto: Caro nome.	(6126)
74500	La Partida (Alvarez).	(6134)
74509	Lucia: Mad Scene.	(6129)
74510	Lakme: Dov' e l'Indiana bruna.	(6132)
74511	Home, Sweet Home (Bishop).	(6123)
74512	Romeo: Valse.	(6133)

74522	Solvejg's Song (Grieg) (in French).		(6132)
74532	Dinorah: Ombra leggiera.		(6129)
74536	Martha: Last Rose of Summer.		(6123)
74538	Sonnambula: Ah non credea.		(6125)
74541	Barber of Seville: Una voce poco fa.		(6130)
74552	Pearl of Brazil: Charmant oiseau.		(6124)
74557	Air and Variations (Proch).		(6134)
74558	Puritani: Qui la voce.		(6128)
74594	Traviata: Ah fors e lui.		(6126)
74599	Don Pasquale: Quel guardo.		(6128)
74608	Lo, Here the Gentle Lark (Bishop).		(6127)
74639	Villanelle (Dell'Acqua).		(6131)
74644	Sonnambula: Come per me sereno.		(6125)
74653	Mignon: Io son Titania.		(6133)
87567	Rigoletto: Piangi fanciulla (w. De Luca).		(3027)
88596	Traviata: Imponete (w. De Luca).	(89133)	(8025)
88601	Traviata: Dite alla giovine (w. De Luca).	(89134)	(8025)

VICTOR RED SEAL 1921-1925

64929	When Chloris Sleeps (Samuels).	(630)
64945	Traviata: Addio del passato.	(627)
64991	Messaggero Amoroso (Chopin-Buzzi-Peccia).	(633)
66014	Ol' Car' lina (Cooke).	(628)
66069	Coq d'Or: Hymne au Soleil.	(631)
66092	Old Folks at Home (Foster).	(628)
66125	Lucia: Spargi d'amaro pianto.	(634)
66136	Sadko: Chanson Indoue.	(631)
66187	Orange Blossoms: A Kiss in the Dark.	(959)
66188	Mlle. Modiste: Kiss Me Again.	(959)
66235	Silver Threads Among the Gold (Danks).	(998)
66236	Love's Old Sweet Song (Molloy).	(998)
66265	Manon: Gavotte.	(1018)
66266	Don Cesar: Sevillana.	(1018)
	Memory Lane (Conrad).	(1047)
	Mah Lindy Lou (Strickland).	(1047)
	Coppelia-Valse (Delibes).	(1068)
	Serenade (Pierne).	(1068)
	Estrellita (Ponce).	(1097)
	Non te vayas te lo pido (arr. Guervos).	(1097)
	Don Pasquale: Torami a dir (w. Schipa).	(3034)
	Rigoletto: E il sol (w. Schipa).	(3034)
	Traviata: Un di felice (w. Schipa).	(3038)
	Traviata: Parigi o cara (w. Schipa).	(3038)
74718	Pearl Fishers: Comme autrefois.	(6124)
74734	Variations on Mozart Air (Adam).	(6131)
74743	Echo Song (Bishop).	(6127)
74784	Star of the North: Prayer; Barcarolle.	(6357)
74786	Mme. Butterfly: Un bel di.	(6130)
74812	Linda di Chamounix: O luce.	(6357)
74850	Rigoletto: Tutte le feste.	(6432)
74851	Puritani: Son vergin vezzosa.	(6432)
	Dinorah: Si carina.	(6469)
	Pretty Mocking Bird (Bishop).	(6469)
	Lucia: Verranno a te (w. Schipa).	(8067)
	Sonnambula: Son geloso (w. Schipa).	(8067)

For other records, see CARUSO.

Note: A more distinguishable difference than usual between different recordings of the same selection bearing the same catalogue number can be found in the "Caro nome" from Rigoletto listed above, the first recording of which starts with the short recitative "Gualtier Malde" whereas the others start at the aria proper ten bars later.

GALVANY, Maria (Soprano)

With a style galvanic in more ways than one, this big-voiced coloratura gave off some startling staccati which, when not played so fast that they resemble a cackle, are quite thrilling indeed. But De Lucia, for one, could tone her down considerably.

IMPORTED VICTOR RED SEAL 1910-1914

87057	Hijas del Zebedeo: Carceleras.	
87058	Air and Variations (Proch).	
87059	Magic Flute: Gli angui d'inferno.	(931)
87060	Barber of Seville: Una voce poco fa.	(931)
87061	Fado Portuguez (Neupatk).	
88219	Lakme: Dov' e l'Indiana bruna.	
88220	Maggio Valzer (Dufau).	
88221	Lucia: Spargi d'amaro pianto.	
88222	Dinorah: Ombra leggiera.	
88234	Hugenots: O vago suol.	
88235	Hamlet: Mad Scene (Ital.).	
88236	L'Incantatrice (Arditi).	(6414)
88507	Traviata: Sempre libera (w. Andreini).	(89145) (8058)
89045	Sonnambula: Prendi l'anel (w. De Lucia).	(8057)
89046	Puritani: Vieni fra questa (w. Marconi).	

For other records, see RUFFO.

GARBIN, Edoardo (Tenor)

IMPORTED VICTOR RED SEAL 1903

5037	Manon Lescaut: Donna non vidi mai.	(91029)
5038	Favorita: Una vergine.	(91030)

Note: Many interesting imported Columbias were presented as part of the popular priced foreign series, among them Boheme: Che gelida manina on Nos. 41941/79 (E1808), also Lucrezia Borgia: Di pescatore on No. 41949 (E2280), which selection had been recorded by Fonotipia as No. 92033 (C-F68) among a large number of 1905/08 items.

GARDEN, Mary (Soprano)

Garden was a cause celebre for so long, we are apt to forget she was also a singer of no meager ability. When Debussy accompanied her to Parisian recording studios for a group of his songs and an excerpt from the part of Melisande she had recently created, he added but another feather to the cap of an immensely successful operatic personality.

COLUMBIA RECORDS 1911-1913

19886	John Anderson, My Jo.	(A1190)
19887	Comin' thro' the Rye.	(A1190) (2012M)
19888	Jack o' Hazeldean (Hewitt).	(A1191)
19891	Blue Bells of Scotland.	(A1191)
30695	Traviata: Quel est donc.	(A5284)
30696	Traviata: Pour jamais.	(A5284)
30699	Jongleur de Notre Dame: Liberte.	(A5289)
30701	Herodiade: Il est doux.	(A5289)
36385	Louise: Depuis le jour.	(A5440)
36386	Thais: L'amour est une vertu rare.	(A5440)

Note: In England, the first selection above was coupled with Irish Love Song (Lang) on English Columbia D9703, later D1363.

GARRISON, Mabel (Soprano)
VICTOR RED SEAL 1916-1920
64616	Happy Days (Strelezski).	
64637	Dixie (Emmett) (w. Qt.).	
64641	Bohemian Girl: I Dreamt I Dwelt.	(641)
64695	Lullaby (Emmett).	(642)
64697	Little Alabama Coon (Starr) (w. Qt.).	(640)
64714	Norwegian Echo Song (Thrane).	(639)
64783	Khaki Sammy (Carpenter).	
64790	Coq d' Or: Hymne au Soleil.	(638)
64795	Mlle. Modiste: Kiss Me Again.	(636)
64808	When I Was Seventeen (Lilljebjorn).	(639)
64811	Vous dansez, Marquise (Lemaire).	(638)
64815	Quilting Party (Fletcher) (w. Qt.).	(642)
64891	Heaven is My Home (Sullivan).	(637)
64899	Only Girl: When You're Away.	(636)
74481	Erminie: Lullaby (w. Cho.).	(6137)
74482	Tales of Hoffmann Les oiseaux.	(6135)
74488	Voci di primavera (Strauss).	(6137)
74489	Mignon: Je suis Titania.	(6136)
74491	Lakme: Ou va la jeune Hindoue.	(6135)
74542	Pearl of Brazil: Charmant oiseau.	(6136)
74612	Eclair: Call Me Thine Own.	
87569	Don Giovanni: La ci darem (w. Werrenrath).	

VICTOR RED SEAL 1921-1924
64920	Come Ye Disconsolate (Webbe).	(637)
64966	Serenade (Moszkowski).	(905)
64969	Swing Low, Sweet Chariot.	(640)
64978	Parysatis: Nightingale and the Rose.	(641)
66165	Serenade (Nevin).	(905)
66168	Since First I Met Thee (Rubenstein).	(941)
66169	Gay Butterfly (Hawley).	(941)
66246	Spring (Henschel).	(1006)
66247	Star Eyes (Speaks).	(1006)

Note: Interesting items to which numbers were assigned include Hymn to the Sun (64293), Magic Flute (64725) and Variations on a theme by Mozart (74625).

GAUTHIER, Eva (Soprano)
VICTOR RED SEAL 1921
74716 Louise: Depuis longtemps (w. Harrold).   (6151)

Note: This all too brief appearance on Red Seal was preceded by many such on Columbia green label and especially Victor black seal where over a score of interesting recordings included arias such as Souvenirs de jeune age from Le Pre-aux-clercs, often coupled with songs like La chere maison by Jacques-Dalcroze as on No. 69223.

GAY, Maria (Contralto)
IMPORTED VICTOR RED SEAL 1908
91085	Carmen: Seguidilla.	
92059	Carmen: Habanera.	(6407)

COLUMBIA RECORDS 1911-1913
19854	Trovatore: Stride la vampa.	(H51)
30664	Samson: Mon coeur.	(A5280)
30665	Carmen: Habanera.	(A5279)

30667 Carmen: Air des cartes. (A5279)
30669 Samson: Printemps qui commence. (A5280)
30892 Trovatore: Ai nostri monti (w. Zenatello). (A5370)
30895 Trovatore: Perigliarti ancor (w. Zenatello). (A5370)
30896 Aida: Misero appien (w. Zenatello). (A5406)
30920 Aida: Gia i sacerdoti (w. Zenatello). (A5406)
30921 Cavalleria Rusticana: Tu qui, Santuzza (w. Zenatello). (A5426)
36374 Orfeo: Che faro senza Euridice. (H1101)
       Trovatore: Condotta ell'era (w. Zenatello). (S5072)

Note: Unfortunately, none of her native Spanish songs appear among Maria Gay's records listed above as they had among earlier Favorites, including L'Hereu Riera, etc.

GERHARDT, Elena (Soprano)

That expressiveness in lieder need not signify a lack of purity of tone or rhythm of phrasing but is rather dependent upon these very attributes can be learned from the records of Gerhardt by those who are unacquainted with good singing as a means of musico-dramatic interpretation.

COLUMBIA RECORDS 1917-1918

44963 Gypsy Baron: Zigeunerlied. (E3515)
44964 Gypsy Baron: Wer uns getraut (w. Bloch). (E4854)
47350 Am Sylvesterabend (Schulz). (20015D)
58246 Stille Nacht (Gruber).
58256 Der Tannenbaum (w. Bloch). (20015D)
58257 Du, du liegst mir im Herzen (w. Bloch). (E4854)

Note: Later, Columbia issued on popular priced green label discs other songs such as Lang, lang ist's her and Heidenroslein, coupled on No. E4856. Far superior are her still later Vocalion imports which were recorded in their London studios though such an item as Sapphische Ode on Voc. 28017 was also available to them in a much earlier version on Gr. 2-43444 (70530).

GERVILLE-REACHE, Jeanne (Contralto)

VICTOR RED SEAL 1909-1912

81091 Werther: Va laisse couler mes larmes. (87027)
87035 Chanson Slave (Chaminade).
87039 Carmen: Air des cartes.
87065 Trovatore: Stride la vampa.
87080 Vivandiere: Viens avec nous.
87085 Ich grolle nicht (Schumann).
88166 Sapho: O ma lyre.
88184 Samson: Mon coeur.
88198 Orfeo: J'ai perdu mon Euridice.
88205 Queen of Sheba: Plus grand.
88244 Samson: Printemps qui commence.
88278 Carmen: Habanera. (15-1008)
88281 Enfant Prodigue: Air de Lia.
88317 Paul et Virginie: Chanson du tigre. (15-1008)
88368 D'une prison (Hahn).

COLUMBIA RECORDS 1914

36825 Samson: Amour, viens aider. (A5533)
36832 Samson: Mon coeur. (A5533)

Note: A ten-inch version of the Carmen habanera was assigned No. 87038. Gerville-Reache possessed both voice and artistry of the highest calibre. Her repertoire was most unusually eclectic and her untimely death here in 1915 left the entire musical world in grief, consoled only by her wonderful recordings. Such was the sad fate more recently of another versatile, though lighter contralto, the inimitable Conchita Supervia, who, in 1915, was just beginning to show American audiences what she, in turn, could do with Bizet's heroine.

GIANNINI, Dusolina (Soprano)

Note: Coming at the end of the acoustic era as her father had at its very beginning, this famous American prima donna, was first listed in non-celebrity category, that of blue seal, though she was promoted electrically to Red Seal. Among her 1924 recordings of Italian songs were Sadero's In mezo al mar and Fa' la nana bambin on No. 45413 and Tosti's Non me lo dite and Penso on No. 45427.

GIANNINI, Ferruccio (Tenor)

Note: By no means a widely celebrated musician, though he fathered two such, Ferruccio Giannini is probably the earliest recorder of the standard operatic repertoire on discs, albeit some of it is altered slightly from the original score in providing a cornet or trombone in duet in lieu of the more customary vocal partner. His Berliner discs of the 1895-1899 period number well over thirty and include tenor arias like Fra poco a me from Lucia on No. 923 and Quando le sere al placido from Luisa Miller on No. 1740 as well as songs such as The Palms on No. 971 and Pieta Signore on No. 979. He also appears on Zonophone as in the Pagliacci arioso, for example, on No. 12518, on Columbia as in the Mefistofele: Giunto sul passo on No. 1748, on Victor as in the Trovatore miserere with Merrilees, soprano(!) both as 4092 and 31311 and on other labels, some of his accompaniments, as noted above, being provided by his own Royal Marine Band.

GIGLI, Beniamino (Tenor)

IMPORTED VICTOR RED SEAL 1920

64854	Mefistofele: Giunto sul passo.	
64855	Tosca: E lucevan le stelle.	
64867	Iris: Apri la tua finestra.	
64868	O surdato nnamurato (Cannio).	
64881	Tosca: Recondita armonia.	
64882	Mefistofele: Se tu mi doni (w. Scattola).	(926)
74605	Faust: Salve dimora.	
74606	Gioconda: Enzo Grimaldo (w. Zani).	(6382)
74614	Favorita: Vieni, ah vien (w. Casazza).	(6381)
74615	Lodoletta: Ah rivederla.	(6382)
74619	Gioconda: Laggiu nelle nebbie (w. Casazza).	(6381)
74620	Favorita: Spirto gentil.	

VICTOR RED SEAL 1921-1925

64933	Mefistofele: Dai campi.		(644)
64938	Gioconda: Cielo e mar.		(643)
64942	Mefistofele: Giunto sul passo.		(644)
64943	Tosca: E lucevan le stelle.	(926)	(942)
64944	Tosca: Recondita armonia.		(646)
64959	Iris: Apri la tua finestra.		(646)
64975	Santa Lucia Luntana (Mario).		(645)
66010	Tu Sola (de Curtis).		(906)
66070	Roi d' Ys: Vainement.		(906)
66095	Pagliacci: Vesti la giubba.		(643)
66102	Serenata (Toselli).		(645)

66170	Tosca: O dolci mani.	(942)
66207	Loreley: Nel verde maggio.	(975)
66208	Andrea Chernier: Come un bel di.	(975)
66274	Il Canto del Cigno (Saint-Saens).	(1025)
66275	Paquita (Buzzi-Peccia).	(1025)
	Povero Pulcinella (Buzzi-Peccia).	(1064)
	Funiculi-Funicula (Denza).	(1064)
87581	Romeo: Ah ne fuis pas (w. Bori).	(3027)
74687	Faust: Salve dimora.	(6138)
74688	Favorita: Spirto gentil.	(6139)
74742	Notturno d'Amor (Drigo).	(6446)
74793	Andrea Chernier: Improvviso.	(6139)
74804	Africana: O Paradiso.	(6138)
74876	Martha: M'appari.	(6446)

Note: Over half a dozen other Italian duets were not imported here, also solos such as a twelve-inch Gioconda on Gr. 2-052142.

GILIBERT, Charles (Baritone)

Gilibert died in 1910, a universally loved and admired artist. Noted for his distinctive interpretations of character parts, his beautiful legato, evidenced in the often mutilated Plaisir d'amour, could well serve as model to more glorified singers.

COLUMBIA RECORDS 1903

1234	La Vierge a la creche (Perilliou).
1235	L'Adieu (Tosti).
1236	Obstination (Fontenailles).
1239	Menuet d'Exaudet (Coote).
1251	Les Rameaux (Faure).
1254	Colinette (Alary) (w. Mme. Gilibert).

COLUMBIA RECORDS 1907-1908

30088	La Vierge a la creche (Perilliou).	
30089	Les Rameaux (Faure).	
30095	Plaisir d'amour (att: Martini).	(A5070)
30096	Don Giovanni: Serenade; Margoton.	(A5008)
30107	Lakme: Lakme, ton doux regard.	(A5004)
30108	Jolie Fille de Perth: Quand la flamme.	(A5007)
30121	Don Giovanni: Serenade.	(A5003)
30123	Madrigal (Lemaire).	(A5078)

VICTOR RED SEAL 1907-1910

74155	Serse: Largo.	(6140)
74208	Jolie Fille de Perth: Quand la flamme.	(6140)
81090	Malgre Moi (Pfeiffer).	
85118	Plaisir d'amour (att: Martini).	
85120	Bergerette (Weckerlin):`Margoton.	
88237	Carmen: Nous avons (w. Mme. Gilibert-Duchene-Dumesnil-Leroux).	
89011	Per valli per boschi (Blangini) (w. Melba).	
89012	Un ange est venue (Bemberg) (w. Melba).	

GILIBERT, Mme. Charles (Mezzo-Soprano)

See CARUSO, GILIBERT.

Note: Under her own name of Gabrielle Lejeune, she appears on Victor purple label, her duet with Devries from Fille de Mme. Angot being No. 70025.

GILLY, Dinh (Baritone)

For duets, see DESTINN.

Note: Regrettably, Victor did not make greater use of Gilly as did other companies including its own European affiliates, who presented him in out of the way works such as Coupe du Roi de Thule on DA 558 at the end of the acoustic period.

GIORGINI, Aristodemo (Tenor)

In a long recording career which included a complete electrical Boheme, this tenor enjoyed celebrity rank at an uncustomarily youthful age.

IMPORTED VICTOR RED SEAL 1910-1911

76010	Don Pasquale: Com'e gentil (w. Cho.).		
76011	Traviata: De' miei bollenti spiriti.		
87083	Manon: O dolor (w. Santoro-Nicolicchia-Cho.).		
88255	Sonnambula: D'un pensiero (w. Huguet-Cho.).	(89146)	(8057)
88319	Pearl Fishers: Del tempio (w. Federici).		

GIRALDONI, Eugenio (Baritone)

IMPORTED VICTOR RED SEAL 1903

5042	Demon: Deh non plorar.	(91034)

Note: Other of his early Milan issue were probably brought over here but his slightly later Fonotipias are even more interesting musically and include Lohengrin: Vendetta avro with Petri No. 92953 a selection not often recorded even in the original German.

GLUCK, Alma (Soprano)

That Reba Fierson from Bucharest would grow up to be America's favorite singer of Carry Me Back To Old Virginy is a wonderful testament to our melting-pot and, of course, her own great talents, notably that purity of voice and style which especially endeared her to audiences of the English speaking world.

VICTOR RED SEAL 1911-1915

64182	Tu-Habanera (Fuentes).	(658)
64183	My Laddie (Thayer).	(655)
64190	From the Land of the Sky Blue Water (Cadman).	(659)
64192	Will o' the wisp (Spross).	(659)
64209	Snow Maiden: Song of the Shepherd Lehl.	(647)
64213	Hubicka: Cradle Song.	(652)
64225	Boheme: Addio.	(649)
64267	Lo, Here the Gentle Lark (Bishop).	(654)
64268	Long Ago; A Maid Sings Light (MacDowell).	
64269	Sadko: Chanson Indoue.	(658)
64277	La Colomba (arr: Schindler).	(662)
64320	Have you seen but a whyte Lillie grow.	
64321	Red, Red Rose (Cottenet).	(665)
64322	Song of Chimes (Worrell).	(652)
64324	The Brook (Dolores).	(664)
64325	When Love is Kind (Moore).	(663)
64346	Irish Love Song (Lang).	(648)
64392	The Swallows (Cowen).	(665)
64398	Lass with the Delicate Air (Arne).	(663)
64399	Serenata (Tosti).	(662)
64400	Carmena (Wilson).	(661)
64412	Little Grey Home (Lohr).	(656)
64413	Sylvelin (Sinding).	

64415	As a beam o'er the face of the water.		(648)
64416	Braes o' Balquhidder (Tannahill).		
64421	Snow Maiden: Aller au bois.		(647)
64422	Comin' thro' the Rye.		(650)
64560	Boheme: Vals.		(649)
64564	I'se gwine back to Dixie (White) (w. Cho.).		(651)
74238	Pagliacci: Ballatella.		(6148)
74245	Carmen: Je dis que rien.		(6145)
74249	Hippolyte: Rossignols Amoureux.		
74251	Home Sweet Home (Bishop).		(6142)
74252	Louise: Depuis le jour.		(6145)
74263	Sonnambula: Ah non credea.		
74274	Natoma: Spring Song.		(6147)
74334	Parla (Arditi).		
74369	Jocelyn: Berceuse.		(6148)
74383	Czar's Bride: Liuba's Air (in Ger.).		
74386	My Old Kentucky Home (Foster).		
74420	Carry Me Back to Old Virginny (Bland) (w. Cho.).		(6141)
74423	Semele: Oh, Sleep.		(6144)
74442	Old Black Joe (Foster) (w. Cho.).		(6141)
87101	Elegie (Massenet) (w. Zimbalist).	(87513)	(3004)
87107	Whispering Hope (Hawthorne) (w. Homer).	(87524)	(3000)
87110	Oh, That We Two Were Maying (Nevin) (w. Homer).	(87525)	(3001)
87131	Hansel: Hexenritt (w. Homer).	(87526)	
87132	Abide With Me (Monk) (w. Homer).	(87527)	(3008)
87182	Du, du liegst mir (Pax) (w. Reimers).	(87536)	(3011)
87183	Hans und Liesel (w. Reimers).	(87537)	(3012)
87184	Der Jager lang (Pax) (w. Reimers).		
87185	Au clair de la lune (Lully) (w. Reimers).	(87538)	
87196	Old Folks at Home (Foster) (w. Zimbalist).	(87514)	(3006)
87198	Rock of Ages (Hastings) (w. Homer).	(87528)	(3009)
87199	Passage Bird's Farewell (Hildach) (w. Homer).	(87529)	
87200	Jesus, Lover of My Soul (Holbrook) (w. Homer).	(87530)	(3009)
87201	Life's Dream is O'er (Asher) (w. Homer).	(87531)	(3010)
87202	Tales of Hoffmann: Barcarolle (w. Homer).	(87532)	(3010)
87203	I Need Thee Every Hour (Lowry) (w. Homer).	(87533)	(3008)
87208	Monotone (Cornelius) (w. Zimbalist).		
87209	Le Bonheur (Saint-Saens) (w. Zimbalist).	(87515)	
87212	One Sweetly Solemn Thought (Ambrose) (w. Homer).	(87534)	(3000)
87224	Drunten im Unterland (Weigle) (w Reimers).	(87539)	(3013)
87226	Treue Liebe (Kucken) (w. Reimers).	(87540)	(3011)
87227	Das Steierland (Seidel) (w. Reimers).	(87541)	(3013)
87228	Es steht ein' Lind' (Berger) (w. Reimers).	(87542)	(3012)
87229	Der Tannenbaum (w. Reimers).	(87543)	(3014)
87236	When the Swallows (Abt) (w. Zimbalist).	(87516)	(3007)
87237	The Rosary (Nevin) (w. Zimbalist).	(87517)	(3006)
87244	Nur wer die Sehnsucht kennst (Tschaikowsky) (w. Zimbalist).		
		(87518)	(3007)
87511	Traviata: Brindisi (w. Caruso).		(3031)
88358	Le Nil (Leroux) (w. Zimbalist).	(89090)	(8028)
88375	Hymn of Praise: I Waited (w. Homer).	(89097)	
88380	Stabat Mater: Quis est homo (w. Homer).	(89098)	(8029)
88418	Hansel: Suse, liebe Suse (w. Homer).	(89099)	(8030)
88419	Hansel: Der kleine Sandmann (w. Homer).	(89100)	(8030)
88433	Ave Maria (Gounod) (w. Zimbalist).	(89091)	(8026)
88434	Angel's Serenade (Braga) (w. Zimbalist).	(89092)	(8026)
88539	Fiddle and I (Goodeve) (w. Zimbalist).	(89093)	(8027)

VICTOR RED SEAL 1916-1919

64566	Vogelhandler: Nightingale Song.	(654)
64588	Bonnie Sweet Bessie (Gilbert).	(650)

64589 Still wie die Nacht (Bohm). (657)
64590 Cradle Song (Mozart). (660)
64591 Bird of the Wilderness (Horsman). (660)
64592 Samson: Mon coeur.
64607 A Perfect Day (Bond) (w. Qt.). (656)
64625 Such a Li'l Fellow (Dichmont). (655)
64626 Canzonetta (Loewe). (657)
64627 Hark Hark the Lark (Schubert). (664)
64713 Prayer Perfect (Stenson).
64727 Two Folk Songs of Little Russia. (666)
64728 Dawn (Coleridge-Taylor).
64729 Darling Nelly Gray (Hanby) (w. Qt.). (653)
64750 L'Heure Exquise (Hahn). (666)
64793 Bring Back My Bonnie to Me (w. Qt.). (661)
64809 Little Old Log Cabin (Hays) (w. Qt.). (651)
64828 Nelly was a Lady (Foster) (w. Qt.). (653)
74465 Listen to the Mocking Bird (Winner). (6142)
74468 My Old Kentucky Home (Foster) (w. Cho). (6143)
74475 The Mother's Prayer (Thomas). (6146)
74503 She Wandered Down the Mountain Side (Clay). (6146)
74504 Atalanta: Come Beloved. (6147)
74534 Aloha Oe (Liliuokalani) (w. Qt). (6143)
74559 Theodora: Angels Ever Bright. (6144)
87267 Long, Long Ago (Bayly) (w. Homer). (87535) (3001)
87276 Chanson Hebraique (Ravel) (w. Zimbalist). (87519) (3003)
87278 God Be With'You (Tomer) (w. Zimbalist). (87520) (3005)
87284 Silent Night (Gruber) (w. Reimers). (87544) (3014)
87287 Romance Orientale (Rimsky-Korsakoff) (w. Zimbalist). (87521)
87296 Hatikva (Imber) (w. Zimbalist). (87522) (3003)
87300 In the Hour of Trial (Lane) (w. Zimbalist). (87523) (3005)
87566 Sweedish Cradle Song (w. Zimbalist). (3004)
88573 Sing Me to Sleep (Greene) (w. Zimbalist). (89094) (8027)
88576 Norma: Mira o Norma (w. Homer). (89101)
88577 Crucifix (Faure) (w. Homer). (89102) (8029)
88583 Der Spielmann (Hildach) (w. Zimbalist). (89095) (8046)
88593 Lost Chord (Sullivan) (w. Zimbalist). (89096) (8028)

Note: Several other Gluck recordings were assigned catalogue numbers including Der Sandmann (64517), Robin Adair (64593), A Rose Softly Blooming (74543) and, with violin obbligato by her husband, Zimbalist, selections such as Irish Love Song (87144), Oriental Romance (87146) and Sweet and Low (87283).

GODOWSKY, Leopold (Pianist)

COLUMBIA RECORDS 1913-1918

La Campanella (Paganini-Liszt). (A5484)
Hark Hark the Lark (Schubert-Liszt). (A5484)
Nocturne in E Flat (Chopin). (A5485)
Preludes in B Flat; F (Chopin). (A5485)
Gnomenreigen (Liszt). (A5550)
Polonaise in A Flat (Chopin). (A5550)
Berceuse in D Flat Op. 57 (Chopin). (A5597)
Waltz in G Flat (Chopin). (A5597)
Gondoliera (Liszt); If I Were A Bird (Henselt). (A5791) (7024M)
Waltz in A Flat (Chopin). (A5791)
Concert Etude No. 2 in D Flat (Liszt). (A5800)
Nocturne in E Flat (Chopin). (A5800)
Serenata (Moszkowski); Valse in E Minor (Chopin). (A5858)
Berceuse (Chopin). (A5858)
Rigoletto Paraphrase (Verdi-Liszt). (A5896)
Cradle Song (Henselt). (A5896)

Etude in F Minor Op. 25 (Chopin); Arabesque in A Flat
(Leschetizky)   **(A6013)**
Serenade in D Minor (Rubenstein); Vienna Waltz in F
(Poldini).   **(A6013)**

Note: In England, Chopin Preludes in B Flat and F listed above were coupled
with two Mendelssohn Songs Without Words on English Columbia D17713,
later L1088. Also issued June 1914 was a coupling of the Prelude in D Flat
and Waltz in C Sharp Minor, both by Chopin, on D17722, later L1095.

BRUNSWICK RECORDS 1920-1925

10022	Rustle of Spring (Sinding).	(15017)
10027	Witches' Dance (MacDowell).	(15017)
10031	Waltz in C Sharp Minor Op. 64 No. 2 (Chopin).	(15018)
10050	Melody in F (Rubenstein).	(15018)
30004	Marche Militaire (Schubert-Taussig).	(50008)
30016	Impromptu in A Flat (Chopin).	(50009)
30017	Fantasie Impromptu (Chopin).	(50008)
30019	Liebestraum (Liszt).	(50024)
30025	Kamennoi Ostrow (Rubenstein).	(50009)
	The Flatterer (Chaminade).	(15001)
	Spring Song (Mendelssohn).	(15001)
	Etudes Op. 10 No. 5; Op. 25 No. 9 (Chopin).	(15026)
	Prelude in C Sharp Minor (Rachmaninoff).	(15026)
	Maiden's Wish (Chopin-Liszt).	(15042)
	My Joys (Chopin-Liszt).	(15042)
	Capriccio in F Minor (Dohnanyi).	(15049)
	A la Bien Aimee (Schutt).	(15049)
	Music Box (Liadow).	(15081)
	Playera (Granados).	(15081)
	Polonaise Militaire Op. 40 No. 1 (Chopin).	(50015)
	Waltz in E Flat (Chopin).	(50015)
	On Wings of Song (Mendelssohn-Liszt).	(50016)
	Venezia e Napoli-Tarantella (Liszt).	(50016)
	Polonaise in A Flat Op. 53 (Chopin).	(50024)
	Ballade in A Flat (Chopin).	(50042)
	Nocturne in D Flat (Chopin).	(50042)

GORDON, Jeanne (Contralto)
COLUMBIA RECORDS 1920-1922

49740	Samson: Amour veins aider.	(68035D)	
49747	Masked Ball: Re dell' abisso.	(68051D)	
49752	Samson: Mon coeur.	(68035D)	(5011M)
49858	Carmen: Habanera.	(68051D)	(5011M)
78977	Madrigal of May (Nitke).		
79373	Silent Night (Gruber).		
80185	Gioconda: Voce di donna.	(33022D)	(86M)
80186	Mignon: Connais-tu le pays.	(33022D)	(86M)

For other records, see BARRIENTOS

GORITZ, OTTO (Baritone)
VICTOR RED SEAL 1911-1913

64163	Magic Flute: Ein Vogelfanger.	
64164	Hansel: Eine Hex' steinalt.	
64165	Fidelio: Welch' ein Augenblick.	
64184	Konigskinder: O du liebheilige.	
64203	Rheingold: Bin ich nun frei.	
64215	Siegfried: Wohin schleichst du (w. Reiss).	
74212	Trompeter von Sakkingen: Es hat nicht.	
74215	Tannhauser: Blick ich umher.	(15-1030)

74230 Flying Dutchman: Wie oft in Meeres.
74287 Konigskinder: Ihr Kindlein.
74288 Zar und Zimmermann: So spielt ich.
74289 Marriage of Figaro: Ach offnet.
74322 Flying Dutchman: Wie aus der Ferne.
74342 Goldene Kreuz: Wie anders war.					(15-1030)
74343 An der Weser (Pressel).

For other Victor records, see GADSKI.

COLUMBIA RECORDS 1916-1917

43928 Spielmannsleben (Lorelberg) (part I).			(A2066)
43929 Spielmannsleben (Lorelberg) (part IV).			(A2076)
43941 Spielmannsleben (Lorelberg) (part II).			(A2066)
43943 Spielmannsleben (Lorelberg) (part III).			(A2076)
43950 Roslein rot (w. Sembach-Bloch-Braun).			(E3515)
44533 Ich wand're nicht (Schumann).				(E3271)
44560 Ich grolle nicht (Schumann).				(E3271)
58305 Susser Papa: Ach das erfreut.				(E3464)
58306 Susser Papa: Schnuteken, Komm.				(E3464)
59418 Der Sturme auf Luttich (Loewe).				(E5124)
59420 Wenn du Kein Spielmann (Hofmann).			(E5130)
59422 Fridericus Rex (Loewe).					(E5124)
59423 Spielmann Lied (Nicolai).				(E5130)

Note: Goritz partiality toward the lighter German works for which he even acted as arranger and impressario, was evidenced in earliest Odeon imports which included a Goldene Kreuz item on No. 50156. Other examples exist throughout his career, though it cannot be said that his voice ever reflects much of a light touch.

GRAINGER, Percy (Pianist)

COLUMBIA RECORDS 1919-1925

Gum-Suckers March (Grainger).			(A3381) (2002M)
Turkey in the Straw (Guion).			(A3381) (2002M)
Cradle Song (Brahms-Grainger).			(A3685) (2000M)
Spoon River (Masters-Grainger).			(A3685) (2000M)
Golliwogg's Cake Walk (Debussy).	(33001D) (30002D) (2001M)
Gavotte (Gluck-Brahms).			(33001D) (30002D) (2001M)
Rustle of Spring (Sinding).		(33026D) (30006D) (2003M)
To a Water-Lily (MacDowell).		(33026D) (30006D) (2003M)
Water Music-Hornpipe (Handel-Grainger).	(30010D) (2004M)
Warum (Schumann).				(30010D) (2004M)
Scherzo Op. 31 No. 2 (part I) (Chopin).		(30019D) (2025M)
Scherzo Op. 31 No. 2 (part II) (Chopin).	(30019D) (2025M)
Hungarian Rhapsody No. 2 (part I) (Liszt).	(A6000) (8914M)
Hungarian Rhapsody No. 2 (part II) (Liszt).	(A6000) (8914M)
Valse in A Flat Op. 42 (Chopin).			(A6027)
Polonaise in A Flat Op. 53 (Chopin).			(A6027)
Country Gardens; Shepherd's Hey (Grainger).	(A6060) (7001M)
Prelude in A Flat Op. 28 No. 17 (Chopin).	(A6060) (7000M)
Hungarian Fantasy (part I) (Liszt).		(A6115) (8915M)
Hungarian Fantasy (part II) (Liszt).		(A6115) (8915M)
Polish Dance Op. 3 No. 1 (Scharwenka).		(A6128)
To Spring (Grieg); One More Day (Grainger).	(A6128)
Valse in A Flat (Brahms); Juba Dance (Dett).	(A6145) (7000M)
Molly on the Shore (Grainger).			(A6145)
Hungarian Rhapsody No. 12 (part I) (Liszt).	(A6161) (8916M)
Hungarian Rhapsody No. 12 (part II) (Liszt).	(A6161) (8916M)
Wedding Day at Troldhaugen (Grieg).		(A6192) (7002M)
Paraphrase on Tschaikowsky's Waltz (Grainger).	(A6192) (7002M)

Polonaise in E (part I) (Liszt).	(A6205)	(7003M)
Polonaise in E (part II) (Liszt).	(A6205)	(7003M)
Liebestraum (Liszt).	(A6217)	
Norwegian Bridal Procession (Grieg).	(A6217)	(7001M)

Note: No. 2001M was much later changed to 183M.

GRANFORTE, Apollo (Baritone)

IMPORTED VICTOR RED SEAL 1925

La Paloma (Yradier).	(1114)
Alma Llanera (Gutierrez).	(1114)
Barber of Seville: Largo al factotum.	(6541)
Otello: Credo.	(6541)
Rigoletto: Pari siamo.	(6542)
Rigoletto: Cortigiani.	(6542)

GRAYVILL, Jose (Soprano)

COLUMBIA RECORDS 1907-1908

30066	Diamants de la Couronne: Air.	(C1043)
30067	Mireille: Valse.	(C1057)
30101	Dinorah: Ombra leggiera.	(A5005)
30102	The Bird Carol (Knapp).	(A5000)
30114	Hugenots: Nobles Seigneurs.	(A5007)
30119	Pearl of Brazil: Charmant oiseau.	(A5004)
30130	Valse (Venzano).	

Note: In South America, where some of these recordings were originally released, several couplings of them were later made differing from those noted above.

HACKETT, Charles (Tenor)

COLUMBIA RECORDS 1919-1925

49604	Barber of Seville: Ecco ridente.	(68043D)	(9016M)
49623	Africana: O Paradiso.	(68054D)	(9008M)
49645	Boheme: Che gelida manina.	(68045D)	(9017M)
49666	Forza del Destino: Solenne (w. Stracciari).		(9009M)
49734	Aida: O terra addio (w. Ponselle).	(71000D)	(9010M)
49895	Elisir d'Amore: Una furtiva lagrima.	(68045D)	(9017M)
49936	Could I (Tosti).	(68069D)	(9019M)
49947	Carmen: Canzone del fior.	(68044D)	(9018M)
98003	Parted (Tosti).	(68069D)	(9019M)
98038	Snowy Breasted Pearl (Robinson).	(68083D)	(9021M)
98040	Gioconda: Cielo e mar.	(68054D)	(9008M)
98045	Romeo: Ah leve-toi, soleil.	(68043D)	(9016M)
98047	Don Giovanni: Il mio tesoro.	(68044D)	(9018M)
98094	Favorita: Spirto gentil.	(68002D)	(9020M)
98095	Manon: Ah fuyez.	(68002D)	(9020M)
98116	Asthore (Trotere).	(68083D)	(9021M)
98159	Aida: Celeste Aida.		(9022M)
98160	Pearl Fishers: Je crois entendre.		(9022M)
78929	I'd Build A World (Nicholls).	(33016D)	
78930	There Is No Death (O'Hara).	(33035D)	(4015M)
79060	Mother, I Love You (Rice).	(33034D)	
79099	Tosca: E lucevan le stelle.	(33014D)	(4016M)
79196	Dear Old Pal of Mine (Rice).		(4006M)
79282	Song of Songs (Moya).	(33016D)	(4003M)
79283	Je sais que vous etes gentil (Christine).		

79287	A Dream (Bartlett).	(33017D)	(4013M)
79518	Love Sends a Little Gift of Roses (Openshaw).	(33015D)	(4005M)
79521	Duna (McGill).	(33033D)	(4014M)
79704	There's Sunlight in Your Eyes (Harling).	(33015D)	
79879	Because (d'Hardelot).	(33017D)	(4013M)
79885	Martha: Ah so pure.	(33023D)	(4004M)
79891	Bohemian Girl: Then You'll Remember Me.	(33045D)	(4004M)
79896	Drink To Me Only With Thine Eyes.	(33045D)	(4003M)
80080	Cavalleria Rusticana: Siciliana.	(33023D)	
80097	Mother Machree (Ball).	(33034D)	(4005M)
80562	Heaven At The End Of The Road (Osgood).	(33033D)	(4014M)
80599	The Living God (O'Hara).	(33035D)	(4015M)
80604	Mefistofele: Dai campi.	(33014D)	(4016M)
80673	I Shall Know (Manna-Zucca).		(4006M)
64384	Serenade (Schubert) (w. Seidel).	(1S)	
	I Hear A Thrush At Eve (Cadman).	(33006D)	(4017M)
	Thank God For A Garden (Del Riego).	(33006D)	(4017M)
140087	Marcheta (Schertzinger).	(33050D)	(4024M)
140107	Memory Lane (De Sylva).	(33050D)	(4024M)
140367	Old Pal (Van Alstyne).	(33051D)	(4025M)
140366	All Alone (Berlin).	(33051D)	(4025M)
140346	Where Are You Tonight (Christy).	(33053D)	(4026M)
140347	One Little Dream Of Love (Simpson).	(33053D)	(4026M)
AX369	Serenade (Schubert).		(9005M)
AX370	Who Is Sylvia (Schubert).		(9005M)

For other records, see BARRIENTOS

Note: The AX matrix numbers above indicate recordings made in England, where several other selections were also released, especially of songs and arias in English.

HAMBOURG, Mark (Pianist)

Note: A two-part rendition of Beethoven's Moonlight Sonata, issued abroad as Gramophone Nos. 05544 and 05520, was assigned Red Seal Nos. 74193 and 74194, possibly for the Canadian trade, though a listing of this selection there later bore the number 177000.

HAMLIN, George (Tenor)

Hamlin's records are marked by a warm, almost lush quality, usually associated with Italian tenors, but possessed by no means all of them.

VICTOR RED SEAL 1908-1915

64089	Dear Little Shamrock (Cherry).	
64144	Sally In Our Alley (Carey).	
64245	Cavalleria Rusticana: Brindisi.	
64246	Summer Day (Nevin); Row Gently (Jensen).	
64247	Minnelied (Brahms).	
64248	Im Kahne (Grieg).	
64270	Saw Ye My Saviour (Brackett).	(667)
64282	Dispettosi Amanti (Parelli).	
64295	Shepard, Show Me (Brackett).	(667)
64296	Lehn' deine Wang (Jensen).	
64348	Under The Rose (Fisher).	
64387	Cavalleria Rusticana: Siciliana.	
64531	Santa Lucia.	(615)
74111	Walkure: Siegmunds Liebeslied.	
74113	Lord is My Light (Allitson).	
74139	Faust: All Hail, Thou Dwelling.	
74140	Dear Heart (Mattei).	
74143	The Penitent (Vanderwater).	

74185 Boheme: Che gelida manina.
74200 O'er Waiting Harpstrings (Root).
74201 Turn Ye to Me (Lawson).
74248 Lolita (Buzzi-Peccia) (in English).
74250 Creation: In Native Worth.
74306 Onaway, Awake (Coleridge-Taylor).
74310 Good Night, Little Girl (Macy).   (6149)
74378 Love's Sorrow (Shelley).
74457 Love's Nocturne (Temple).
88161 Hymn of Praise: Sorrows of Death.   (74133)
88162 Bohemian Girl: Then you'll remember me.   (74134)   (6149)

Note: Unreleased recordings include two of Reimann's "Lindenlaub" (64155), (64462), Oh I'm Not Myself At All (64323) and Povenzalisches Lied (64337).

HANSEN, Cecilia (Violinist)

VICTOR RED SEAL 1924

Berceuse (Jarnefelt).   (1035)
Berceuse (Cui).   (1035)
74877 Hungarian Dance No. 4 (Brahms-Auer).   (6447)
74878 Rondino (Vieuxtemps).   (6447)

HARROLD, Orville (Tenor)

The Harrold recording of Rudolph's Narrative is considered one of the best on discs and reveals, as do all his others, his manly voice and bearing.

COLUMBIA RECORDS 1913-1916

36422 Snowy Breasted Pearl (Robinson).   (A5439)
36423 *I Hear You Calling Me (Marshall).   (D17716) (L1091)
36424 Elisir d'Amore: Una furtiva lagrima.   (A5432)
36425 Martha: Ah so pure.   (A5432)
36483 Jocelyn: Lullaby.   (A5439)
38384 *For You Alone (Geehl).   (D9708) (D1366)
38668 *Absent (Metcalf).   (D9708) (D1366)
46869 My Wonderful Love For Thee (Ball).   (A2056)
46870 You're the Best Little Mother (Ball).   (A2056)
48514 Awake Dearest One (Ball) (w. Locke).   (A5813)
48711 Sunshine of Your Smile (Ray) (w. Locke).   (A5813)

* These were issued in England on double face English Columbia records with numbers noted. Lydia Locke was Mrs. Harrold.

VICTOR RED SEAL 1920-1924

64892 Values (Vanderpool).
64909 When Your Ship Comes In (Strickland).
64916 Life (Speaks).   (668)
66017 Saltimbanques: C'est l'amour.
66052 Great Awakening (Kramer).   (668)
66071 My Mother (White).   (669)
66100 Tell Her I Love Her (De Faye).   (669)
66051 Fleurette (Wood).   (980)
66212 That is Why (Krahmer).   (980)
66257 On the Banks of the Wabash (Dresser).   (1014)
66258 Way Down in Old Indiana (Dresser).   (1014)
74624 Boheme: Che gelida manina.   (6151)
74716 Louise: Depuis longtemps (w. Gauthier).   (6151)
74737 The Living God (O'Hara).   (6150)
74795 Ride On (Eville).   (6150)
74813 Lohengrin: Mein lieber Schwan.

HAYES, Roland (Tenor)

Note: Among the earliest singers in this century to popularize the justly
celebrated sp.rituals of his race was Roland Hayes, whose artistic interpretations of them included a moving "Bye and Bye" to be found both on a privately
issued Columbia No. 91012 and a Vocalion impor.ation from England released
as No. 21002.

HEIFETZ, Jascha (Violinist)

VICTOR RED SEAL 1918-1925

64758	Valse Bluette (Drigo).	(673)
64759	Ruins of Athens-Chorus of Dervishes-(Beethoven).	(671)
64760	Capricieuse Op. 17 (Elgar).	(672)
64769	Meditation Op. 32 (Glazounow).	(676)
64770	Ruins of Athens-Turkish March-(Beethoven).	(671)
64823	Guitarre Op. 45 No. 2 (Mozkowski-Sarasate).	(672)
64833	Caprice No. 20 (Paganini-Kreisler).	(670)
64856	Minuet (Porpora-Kreisler).	(673)
64917	Sicilienne and Rigaudon (Francoeur-Kreisler).	(674)
66022	Serenade Op. 4 (d'Ambrosio).	(676)
66037	Caprice No. 13 (Paganini-Kreisler).	(670)
66097	Zapateado Op. 23 No. 6 (Sarasate).	
66110	Spanish Dance (Granados-Kreisler).	(674)
66123	Hungarian Dance No. 1 in G Minor (Brahms).	(675)
66139	Slavonic Dance No. 1 in G Minor (Dvorak-Kreisler).	(675)
66200	Raymonda-Grand Adagio-(Glazounow).	(970)
66201	Hebrew Lullaby (Achron).	(970)
66233	Minuet in D (Mozart).	(997)
66234	Widmung (Schumann-Auer).	(997)
66273	Quartet in D No. 35-Vivace-(Haydn-Auer).	(1024)
66191	Scherzo Op. 42 No. 2 (Tschaikowsky).	(1024)
	Stimmung (Achron).	(1048)
	Waltz in D (Godowsky).	(1048)
	Gentle Maiden (Scott); Cortege (Boulanger).	(1082)
	Nocturne (Boulanger).	(1082)
74562	Scherzo Tarantelle Op. 16 (Wieniawski).	(6159)
74563	Ave Maria (Schubert-Wilhelmj).	(6152)
74568	Hebrew Melody (Achron).	(6160)
74569	Spanish Dance Op. 21 No. 1 (Sarasate).	(6154)
74570	Ronde des Lutins (Bazzini).	(6159)
74581	Moto Perpetuo (Paganini).	
74583	On Wings of Song (Mendelssohn).	(6152)
74600	Concerto Op. 22-Romance-(Wieniawski).	(6160)
74616	Nocturne in E Flat Op. 9 No. 2 (Chopin-Sarasate).	(6156)
74626	Introduction and Tarantelle Op. 43 (Sarasate).	(6154)
74635	Serenade Op. 48-Valse-(Tschaikowsky).	(6155)
74646	Symphonie Espagnole-Andante (Lalo).	(6156)
74660	Berceuse (Juon); Raymonda—Valse (Glazounow).	(6158)
74678	Violin Concerto—Canzonetta (Tschaikowsky).	(6158)
74689	Zigeunerweisen No. 1 (Sarasate).	(6153)
74694	Zigeunerweisen No. 2 (Sarasate).	(6153)
74711	Serenade Melancolique Op. 26 (Tschaikowsky).	(6155)
74721	Concerto in E Minor-Finale (Mendelssohn).	(6157)
74750	Rondo in G (Mozart-Kreisler).	(6161)
74764	Concerto in A Minor Op. 28—Andante (Goldmark).	(6157)
74811	Nocturne Op. 27 No. 2 (Chopin).	(6161)
74820	Slavonic Dance No. 2 in E Minor (Dvorak-Kreisler).	(6376)
74821	Slavonic Dance No. 3 in G (Dvorak-Kreisler).	(6376)
	Hebrew Dance (Achron).	(6491)
	Habanera (Sarasate).	(6491)
	Carmen; Fantasie (arr: Sarasate).	(6510)
	Havanaise (Saint-Saens).	(6510)

HEINEMANN, Alexander (Baritone)
COLUMBIA RECORDS 1911-1912
30630	Am Neckar, Am Rhein (Abt).	(A5268)
30631	In einem Kuhlen Grunde.	(A5269)
30632	Standchen (Schubert).	(A5268)
30633	Beiden Grenadiere (Schumann).	(A5269)
30982	Serse: Largo.	(A5415)

Note: Other recordings of this noted lieder singer with an unusually vibrant quality include folk songs like Hans und Liese and Och, Moder on Columbia A982 as well as more substantial items in a fairly large group of imports on Victor black seal, among which Beethoven's Ich liebe dich Gr. 4-42468 appeared as No. 63780.

HELENA, Editha (Soprano)

Note: In addition to violin imitations and the like, this popular member of the Aborn Opera Company with her phenomenal high notes, was heard in more impressive fashion in arias sung both in the original tongue as on the twelve-inch 1908 coupling of Rigoletto and Sonnambula Victor No. 35067, and in English as in her 1913 Mme. Butterfly selections on No. 17346.

HEMPEL, Frieda (Soprano)
VICTOR RED SEAL 1912-1917
76017	Variations on Mozart Air (Adam)	(88404)	(6364)
87179	Puritani: Qui la voce.		
87234	Wiegenlied (Mozart).		
87235	Masked Ball: Volta la terrea.		
87250	Melody in F (Rubenstein).		
87261	Just You (Burleigh).		
87268	Bird Song (Soderberg).		
87270	When I Was Seventeen (Lilljebjorn).		
88382	Hugenots: O beau pays.		
88383	Ernani: Ernani involami.	(6163)	
88410	Villanelle (Dell'Acqua).		
88450	Marriage of Figaro: Deh vieni.		
88463	Parla (Arditi).	(6364)	
88470	Puritani: Vien, diletto.		
88471	Traviata: Ah fors e lui.	(6163)	
88476	Il Bacio (Arditi).		
88540	Blue Danube (Strauss).	(88664)	(6162)
88541	Ben Bolt (Kneass).		
88543	Ma Curley-Headed Babby (Clutsam).		
88567	Martha: Last Rose of Summer.		
88588	Wine, Women and Song (Strauss).	(6162)	
89079	Traviata: Dite alla giovine (w. Amato).	(15-1020)	
89081	Traviata: Imponete (w. Amato).	(15-1020)	
89082	Rigoletto: Figlia Mio Padre (w. Amato).		

For other records, see CARUSO

Note: The first item above was originally introduced in Toreador, though Hempel interpolated it into Daughter of the Regiment. This and other earliest releases were from imported masters, some of which were soon replaced with domestic recordings under the same number. Other numbers assigned include Efenlied (87279), Charmant oiseau from Pearl of Brazil (88435) and a twelve-inch Mozart Wiegenlied-Schlafe mein Prinzchen (88446), these last two, at least, probably being imports as they do occur on 1911/2 Gramophone recordings as Nos. 033126 and 043193 respectively with matrices 608m and 2227c. Her earlier Odeons, some of which came out on Okeh after a lapse of well over a decade, include a 1908 issue of a two-part Lucia mad scene, in German, on Nos. 76032/3.

HERBERT, Victor (Cellist)

VICTOR RED SEAL 1912

64239	Low Back'd Car (Lover).	
64240	Angel's Whisper (Lover).	(677)
64297	Petite Valse (Herbert).	(677)
64298	Scherzo Op. 12 No. 2 (Van Goens).	
74286	Pensee Amoureuse (Herbert).	
74300	Simple Aveu (Thome).	

Note: The above, of course, present the affable Herbert at his original music stand. His more famous locations at the podium and composer's desk are well entrenched on a host of early discs of several makes, both ~oles being often combined as on Victor No. 70049 (55113; 55200) which is the Natoma: Dagger Dance played by Herbert's Orchestra.

HERTZ, Alfred (Conductor)

See SAN FRANCISCO SYMPHONY ORCHESTRA.

HOFMANN, Josef (Pianist)

COLUMBIA RECORDS 1912-1922

Spring Song (Mendelssohn).	(A1178)	
Warum (Schumann).	(A1178)	
Papillon (Grieg).	(A2434)	
Spinning Song (Mendelssohn).	(A2434)	
Prelude in C Sharp Minor (Rachmaninoff).	(A5302)	
Marche Militaire (Schubert-Taussig).	(A5302)	
Polonaise in A Op. 40 No. 1 (Chopin).	(A5419)	
Valse Caprice (Rubenstein).	(A5419)	
Liebestraum (Liszt).	(A5443)	
Waltz in E Minor (Chopin).	(A5443)	
Etude in C Minor (Sternberg).	(A5755)	
Prelude in G Minor (Rachmaninoff).	(A5755)	
Venezia e Napoli (Liszt).	(A5915)	(7024M)
Minuet in G (Paderewski).	(A5915)	(8900M)
Erlkonig (Schubert-Liszt).	(A5942)	(8911M)
Caprice Espagnole (Moszkowski).	(A5942)	(8911M)
Valse Brilliante Op. 34 No. 1 (Chopin).	(A6045)	(7079M)
Hunting Song (Mendelssohn); La Jongleuse (Moszkowski).		
	(A6045)	(7079M)
Rondo Capriccioso (Mendelssohn).	(A6078)	(8900M)
Berceuse (Chopin).	(A6078)	
Valse Gracile (Parker); Birds at Dawn (Dillon).	(A6125)	
Prelude in C Sharp Minor (Rachmaninoff).	(A6125)	(7005M)
Fantasie Impromptu (Chopin).	(A6174)	(7004M)
Rustling of the Woods (Liszt).	(A6174)	
Papillon (Grieg); Spinning Song (Mendelssohn).	(A6211)	(7004M)
Maiden's Wish (Chopin-Liszt).	(A6211)	(7005M)

Note: Rubenstein's Valse Caprice appeared in England coupled with the Chopin E Flat Nocturne on English Columbia D17714, later L1089.

BRUNSWICK RECORDS 1923-1925

Gavotte (Gluck-Brahms).	(15046)
Murmurs of the Forest (Liszt).	(15046)
Nocturne (Hofmann).	(15053)
Prelude in C Sharp Minor (Rachmaninoff).	(15053)
Ruins of Athens—Turkish March (Beethoven).	(15057)
Waltz in C Sharp Minor (Chopin).	(15057)
Melody in F (Rubenstein).	(15098)
Polonaise Militaire (Chopin).	(15098)

Hungarian Rhapsody No. 2 (part I) (Liszt).		(50023)
Hungarian Rhapsody No. 2 (part II) (Liszt).		(50023)
Walkure: Magic Fire Music.		(50035)
Pastorale and Capriccio (Scarlatti).		(50035)
Nocturne in F Sharp Op. 15 No. 2 (Chopin).		(50044)
Scherzo in B Minor Op. 20 No. 1 (Chopin).		(50044)
Prelude in G Minor (Rachmaninoff).		(50045)
My Joys (Chopin-Liszt).		(50045)

HOLLMAN, Josef (Cello)

VICTOR RED SEAL 1905-1906

64001	Ave Maria (Schubert).	(922)
64046	Le Cygne (Saint-Saens).	(922)
74001	Petite Valse (Hollman).	
74002	Andante (Hollman).	
74044	Traumerei (Schumann).	
74045	Serenade (Blockx).	

For other records, see EAMES.

Note: This Dutch musician was especially favored in England, where Edward VII awarded him the gold medal for music just about the time the above records appeared. It is doubtful, however, that they had anything to do with it any more than did his earlier European discs.

HOMER, Louise (Contralto)

What a big voice Homer's was and how well she managed it in the simplest and most complex of her diversified undertakings.

VICTOR RED SEAL 1903-1905

81013	Faust: Le parlate d'amor.		(64019)
81014	Annie Laurie (Scott).		(64021)
81020	May Day (Walthew).		(64024)
81036	Sing Me a Song (Homer).		(64026)
81055	Gioconda: Stella del marinar.		(64020)
81077	Old Folks at Home (Foster).		(64025)
81078	Carmen: Habanera.		(64022)
81079	Filles de Cadiz (Delibes).		(64023)
85004	Prophete: Scene de la prison.		
85005	Hugenots: Nobil Signori.	(74021)	(15-1011)
85006	Messiah: He Shall Feed His Flock.		(74018)
85014	Samson: Mon coeur.		(74020)
85015	Orfeo: Away with crying.		(74017)
85043	Don Carlos: O don fatale.		(74023)
85069	Turn Ye to Me (Lawson).		(74024)
85083	Elijah: O Rest in the Lord.		(74022)
85084	Filles de Cadiz (Delibes).		(74019)
85085	Prophete: Ah mon fils.		(74016)

VICTOR RED SEAL 1906-1911

81084	Trovatore: Stride la vampa.
85102	Elijah: O Rest in the Lord.
85103	Messiah: He Shall Feed His Flock.
85104	Gioconda: Voce di donna.
85105	Martha: Esser mesto.
85106	Faust: Quando a te lieta.
85107	Hugenots: Nobil Signori.
85108	Samson: Mon coeur.
85109	Faust: Le parlate d'amor.
85110	Adriana Lecouvreur: Acerba voluta.
85111	Trovatore: Stride la vampa.

87008	Filles de Cadiz (Delibes).	
87009	At Parting (Rogers).	
87033	Trovatore: Stride la vampa.	(678)
87074	Banjo Song (Homer).	(680)
87075	Faust: Le parlate d'amor.	(678)
87501	Samson: Vengeance at last (w. De Gogorza).	
88088	Lost Chord (Sullivan).	(6418)
88128	Old Black Joe (Foster).	(6170)
88132	Stabat Mater: Fac ut portem.	(6167)
88199	Samson: Mon coeur.	(6164)
88200	Faust: Quando a te lieta.	
88201	Samson: Amour, viens aider.	(6165)
88204	Die Lorelei (Liszt).	(6171)
88231	Die Allmacht (Schubert).	(15-1011)
88284	Prophete: Ah mon fils.	
88285	Orfeo: Che faro senza Euridice.	(6165)
88286	Alceste: Fatal Divinita.	
88288	Elijah: O Rest in the Lord.	(6168)
88309	There is a Green Hill (Gounod).	(6169)
89009	Martha: Mesta ognor (w. Abott).	
89020	Lakme: Dome epais (w. Eames).	
89021	Lohengrin: Du Aermste (w. Eames).	

VICTOR RED SEAL 1912-1918

87204	I Cannot Sing the Old Songs (Claribel).	(685)
87205	Boats sail (Homer); Sing to Me (Mendelssohn).	
87206	Annie Laurie (Scott).	(686)
87255	Robin Hood: Oh Promise Me.	(680)
87259	Last Night (Kjerulf).	(685)
87260	Flee as a Bird (Dana).	(684)
87262	Janet's Choice (Claribel).	
87263	Don't Ceare (Carpenter).	
87264	Where is My Boy Tonight (Lowry).	(681)
87265	Nur wer die Sehnsucht kennst (Tschaikowsky).	(682)
87277	Star Spangled Banner (Smith).	
88384	Come Unto Me (Coenen).	
88407	Requiem; Dearest (Homer).	
88414	Babylon (Watson).	
88574	Messiah: He Was Despised.	(6166)
88575	My Heart Ever Faithful (Bach).	(6171)
88584	Serse: Largo.	(6167)
88585	Love's Old Sweet Song (Molloy).	(6170)

VICTOR RED SEAL 1919-1925

87301	I Love to Tell the Story (Fischer) (w. Cho.).	(681)
87303	Hard Times (Foster).	(679)
87309	Oh, Boys, Carry Me 'Long (Foster) (w. Cho.).	(679)
87327	When the Roses Bloom (Reichardt).	(682)
87329	Just for To-day (Abbott).	(684)
87334	My Ain Folk (Lemon).	(683)
87345	My Ain Countrie (Hanna).	(683)
87354	Christ the Lord (Wesley).	(971)
87359	Lane to Ballybree (Speaks).	(686)
87375	Ring Out Wild Bells (Gounod).	(971)
87376	Sheep and Lambs (Homer).	(979)
87377	Auld Scotch Sangs (Leeson).	(979)
	Barnyard Song (Brockway).	(1028)
	Little Orphant Annie (Krull).	(1028)
	Mignon: Connais-tu le pays.	(1052)
	Mignon: Gavotte.	(1052)
	Battle Hymn of the Republic (Howe).	(1074)
	America the Beautiful (Ward).	(1074)

87570	Last Night (Kjerulf) (w. Stires).	(3015)
87572	Banjo Song (Homer) (w. Stires).	(3016)
87575	Oh Morning Land (Phelps) (w. Stires).	(3028)
87578	Venetian Song (Tosti) (w. Stires).	(3016)
87580	Go Pretty Rose (Marzials) (w. Stires).	(3015)
87582	Hark the Herald Angels (Mendelssohn) (w. Stires).	(3028)
88613	Messiah: He Shall Feed His Flock.	(6166)
88614	Messiah: O Thou That Tellest.	(6169)
88627	Samson: Printemps qui commence.	(6164)
88640	Mother Goose Songs (Homer).	
88658	St. Paul: But the Lord.	(6168)
88667	Calvary (Rodney).	(6418)
89158	Stabat Mater: Quis est Homo (w. Stires).	(8031)
89159	My Sweet Repose (Schubert) (w. Stires).	(8031)

For other records, see CARUSO, FARRAR, GADSKI, GLUCK.

Note: No. 87109 was assigned to a recording of Nancy Lou. Louise Homer Stires was a daughter.

HUBERMAN, Bronislaw (Violinist)

BRUNSWICK RECORDS 1921-1925

30023	Nocturne in E Flat Op. 9 No. 2 (Chopin).	
30024	La Capricieuse (Elgar).	
30027	Suite in D—Air for G String (Bach).	
	Melodie Op. 42 No. 3 (Tschaikowsky).	(15002)
	Second Mazurka Op. 19 (Wieniawski).	(15002)
	Hungarian Dance No. 1 (Brahms-Joachim).	(15022)
	Ronde des Lutins (Bazzini).	(15022)
	Hungarian Dance No. 7 (Brahms).	(15063)
	Orfeo: Melodie.	(15063)
	Ballade (Vieuxtemps).	(50019)
	Polonaise (Vieuxtemps).	(50019)
	Mazurka (Zarazycke).	(50022)
	Kol Nidre (Bruch).	(50022)
	Concerto No. 2—La Campanella (Paganini).	(50026)
	Violin Concerto—Canzonetta (Tschaikowsky).	(50026)
	Concerto No. 2—Romance (Wieniawski).	(50031)
	Capriccio Valse (Wieniawski).	(50031)
	Symphonie Espagnole—Andante (Lalo).	(50041)
	Symphonie Espagnole—Rondo (Lalo).	(50041)
	Violin Concerto—Andante (Mendelssohn).	(50049)
	Violin Concerto—Finale (Mendelssohn).	(50049)
	Jota Navarra (Sarasate).	(50051)
	Romanza Andaluza (Sarasate).	(50051)
	Kreutzer Sonata (Beethoven) (w. Schultze) (parts 1 to 6).	(50062/3/4)

HUGUET, Giuseppina (Soprano)

For duets, see DE LUCIA, DE TURA, GIORGINI, PAOLI.

Note: Singing both at La Scala and the Academy of Music before the turn of the century, this full-voiced Spanish coloratura made hundreds of recordings both in solo and concerted pieces, selected partners among the latter accounting for their occasional Red Seal status. Beginning October 1903, however, domestic catalogues contained many imports on black and later blue labels by Josefina or Giuseppina Huguet, the name changing with the language of the selection. Bearing various single and double-face numbers, these include many examples of her wonderful singing, among them the Linda di Chamounix: O luce issued as No. 52529 (62090).

IVOGUN, Maria (Soprano)

BRUNSWICK RECORDS 1923-1925

Il Bacio (Arditi).	(50029)	(30101)
Pearl of Brazil: Charmant oiseau.	(50029)	(30101)
Liebesfreud (Kreisler).	(50050)	(30105)
O Schoner Mai (Strauss).	(50050)	(30105)
Schweizer Echolied (Eckert).		(30107)
Blue Danube Waltz (Strauss).		(30107)
Manon: Je marche sur tous les chemins.	(50081)	
Rigoletto: Caro Nome.	(50081)	
Die Post (Schubert).	(15075)	(10119)
Horch, Horch, Die Lerch (Schubert).	(15075)	(10119)
Lo Here the Gentle Lark (Bishop).		(10174)
Tales from the Vienna Woods (Strauss).		(10174)

Note: Among Ivogun's many German Odeon recordings, one brought here by Okeh was the last act duet from Don Pasquale No. 76998 and was issued as Am. Od. 45014, later Ok. 50302, the tenor on it being her high-voiced husband, Karl Erb, himself a recorder of many excellent Odeons including couplings of the lesser known arias from Mignon, frequently omitted because of their high tessitura.

JACOBY, Josephine (Contralto)

See CARUSO, FARRAR, McCORMACK.

Note: Along with Knote, Dippel, Rappold, Burgstaller and others, Jacoby was included in solo arias in Edison's 1906 inaugural group of B series cylinders.

JADLOWKER, Herman (Tenor)

VICTOR RED SEAL 1912

76023	Boheme: Che gelida manina.	
76024	Traviata: De' miei bollenti spiriti.	
76025	Romeo: Ah leve-toi, soleil.	
76026	Lohengrin: In fernem Land.	
76027	Carmen: Air de la fleur.	
88359	Donne Curiose: Il cor nel contento (w. Farrar).	(89115)

Note: Jadlowker made a tremendous number of discs covering his very extensive repertoire, including Bartered Bride on Odeon No. 99099, released November 1908, and Parsifal, from which duets with the bass, Paul Knupfer, Gramophone Nos. 044252/3, were issued December 1913. Representations of the former make appeared here much later on Okeh while Opera Disc brought over seventy of the latter, the duets mentioned appearing as Nos. 72560/1, these, at least, having something in common with his later cantorial days.

JEFFERSON, Joseph (Actor)

COLUMBIA RECORDS 1903

1468	Rip Van Winkle—Scene in the Mountain.	(A385)
1469	Rip Van Winkle—Rip meets Meenie.	(A390)

Note: Jefferson also appeared on Berliner Gramophone discs among others of the 1890s. Other speech items included such notable names as Ada Rehan, Maggie Mitchell and Robert Ingersoll.

JERITZA, Maria (Soprano)

VICTOR RED SEAL 1922-1925

66057	Tote Stadt: Lautenlied.	(688)
66111	Tosca: Vissi d'arte.	(687)
66124	Tannhauser: Dich teure Halle.	(688)
66147	Cavalleria Rusticana: Voi lo sapete.	(687)
66224	Fedora: Son gente risoluta.	(990)
66225	Fedora: Dio di giustizia.	(990)
66271	Widmung (Schumann).	(1022)
66272	Dein blaues Auge (Brahms).	(1022)
	Walkure: Du bist der Lenz.	(1037)
	Lohengrin: Euch Luften.	(1037)
	Libestreu (Brahms).	(1077)
	Allerseelen (Strauss).	(1077)
74749	Lohengrin: Elsas Traum.	(6172)
74760	Tannhauser: Elisabeths Gebet.	(6172)
74776	Flying Dutchman: Traft ihr das Schiff.	
74818	Gioconda: Suicidio.	(6375)
74819	Alceste: Divinites du Styx.	(6375)
	Arioso (Delibes).	(6536)
	Cid: Pleurez mes yeux.	(6536)

Note: No. 66156 was assigned to "L'amour est une vertu rare" from Thais. Among earlier Odeons, the Ariadne Auf Naxos: Es gibt ein Reich, No. 79201, was issued here as Okeh No. 50602.

JOHNSON, Edward (Tenor)

IMPORTED COLUMBIA RECORDS 1915

42187	Mother o' Mine (Tours).	(A1673)
42198	O Come with Me (van der Stucken).	(A1673)
74741	Parsifal: Il Santo Gral.	(A5630)
74742	Parsifal: Soltanto un arma val.	(A5630)

VICTOR RED SEAL 1920-1924

64839	Her Bright Smile (Wrighton).	
64840	Pagliacci: Vesti la giubba.	
64864	Sunrise and You (Penn).	(692)
64886	Girl of the Golden West: Ch' ella mi creda.	(689)
64895	Land of the Long Ago (Ray).	(694)
64905	Fedora: Amor ti vieta.	(689)
64930	Lassie o' Mine (Walt).	(692)
64946	Just That One Hour (Eville).	(694)
64970	Because You're Here (Rice).	(690)
64985	Want of You (Vanderpool).	(691)
64998	Heart to Heart (Vanderpool).	(690)
66029	Someone Worth While (Stephens).	(693)
66060	I Love You More (Lee).	(691)
66061	I Had a Flower (Kellie).	(693)
66210	Colleen o' Mine (Strickland).	(978)
66211	Tho' Shadows Fall (MacDermid).	(978)
74654	Elijah: If With All Your Hearts.	

Note: Under the name of Edoardo di Giovanni, which he had used in creating leading roles in La Nave and others at La Scala, other Columbia imports were issued in South America including Manon Lescaut: Ah Manon (42153) and Pagliacci: Vesti la giubba (42154) coupled on S61. In England, likewise, his Italianized name was used, even for songs like de Lara's Garden of Sleep and Lehmann's Ah Moon of My Delight, issued February 1915 as No. 502.

JORN, Karl (Tenor)

COLUMBIA RECORDS 1915-1917

37237	Abschied (Altniederlandisches Volkslied).	(A5735)
37309	Der Rattenfanger von Hammeln (Nuendorff).	(A5735)
45600	Das Herz am Rhein.	(A1776)
45607	Ungeduld (Schubert).	(A1777)
45608	Das Wandern (Schubert).	(A1777)
45614	Schlummerliedchen.	(A1840)
45615	Morgen Hymne.	(A1840)
45716	Der Tiroler und Sein Kind.	(A1794)
45717	Rheinlied.	(A1776)
45718	Wenn die Schwalben Heimwarts Ziehn.	(A1841)
45719	Der Verschwender: Hobellied.	(A1795)
45720	Jagerleben.	(A1841)
45721	Annchen von Tharau.	(A1862)
45730	Madle Ruck. Ruck. Ruck.	(A1795)
45731	Auf Der Alm Da Gibt's Koa Sund.	(A1794)
45732	Die Lorelei.	(A1862)
45753	Du du liegst mir im Herzen (w. De Marion).	(A1778)
45754	Freut euch des Lebens (w. De Marion).	(A1778)
58538	Schwarzwaldmadel: Tanz Madel mit mir.	(E3560)
58539	Schwarzwaldmadel: Was wir ertraumt.	(E3560)

Note: Like so many other German singers, Jorn, who died recently in Denver, left behind a horde of recorded material, for the most part more substantial than what is listed above as an example of Columbia's bid for the German language trade. It is doubtful if even these customers could always tell from the titles which are reproduced exactly as they were printed, just who wrote the music on these and like records in this series, which seemingly featured texts rather than composers, often unknown or lesser figures who had set beloved stanzas to their own tunes. Meanwhile, his Victor blue seal imports were more easily distinguishable even in titles like Fruhlingslied on No. 45077, since the composer's name is included; in this case a decoy, Gounod.

JOURNET, Marcel (Bass)

Faust, as can be seen below, was an early favorite of Journet and when he dominated the complete recording of that opera a quarter of a century later, he set a standard that is unlikely to be matched for a long time.

COLUMBIA RECORDS 1905

3109	Ernani: Infelice.	(A533)
3133	Sonnambula: Vi ravviso.	(C131)
3134	Chanson des peupliers (Doria).	(E619)
3135	Lakme: Lakme. ton doux regard.	(A545)
3136	Chalet: Vallons de l'Helvetie.	(A542)

VICTOR RED SEAL 1905-1908

81053	Chanson des peupliers (Doria).	(64011)	
81059	Lohengrin: Konigs Gebet.	(64013)	(915)
81060	Martha: Canzone del porter.	(64014)	(698)
81061	Joconde: Dans un delire.	(64012)	
85046	Ernani: Infelice.	(74008)	
85047	Lakme: Lakme. ton doux regard.	(74009)	
85050	Les Boeufs (Dupont).	(74010)	
85051	Don Carlos: Ella giammai m'amo.	(74011)	(8047)
85114	Carmen: Je suis Escamillo (w. Dalmores).		
85115	Faust: O Merveille (w. Dalmores).		
88500	Puritani: Suoni la tromba (w. Ancona).		
64035	Boheme: Vecchia zimarra.	(698)	

64036	Faust: Le veau d'or.	(695)
64052	Damnation of Faust: Chanson de la puce.	
64053	Damnation of Faust: Voici des roses.	
64054	Damnation of Faust: Serenade.	
64077	Ernani: Infelice.	
74003	Faust: O Merveille (w. Van Hoose).	
74004	Faust: Que voulez-vous (w. Van Hoose-De Gogorza).	
74006	Tannhauser: O du mein holder Abendstern.	(6365)
74036	Faust: Serenade.	(6174)
74037	Les Rameaux (Faure).	(6175)
74038	Deux Grenadiers (Schumann).	(6177)
74039	La Marseillaise (de Lisle).	(6177)
74103	Tales of Hoffmann: Scintille diamant.	
74104	Barber of Seville: La calunnia.	(6174)
74123	Jongleur de Notre Dame: Legende.	(6180)
95201	Meistersinger: Quintet (w. Gadski-Mattfield-Van Hoose-Reiss).	

VICTOR RED SEAL 1909-1912

64119	Faust: Invocation.		(695)
64126	Mefistofele: Ave Signor.		(915)
64137	Faust: Serenade.		
64150	Don Giovanni: Madamina.		
64157	Sigurd: Au nom de Roi Gunther.		
64235	Magic Flute: Isis, c'est l'heure.		(699)
64236	Freischutz: Neou qu'il ne m'echappe pas.		
64237	Le Voyageur (Godard).		
64238	Messe de Minuet (Fontenailles).		
74152	Herodiade: Astres etincelants.		
74153	Chalet: Dans le service de l'Autriche.		
74154	Philemon: Que les songes.		
74156	Hugenots: Piff, Paff.	(6173)	(15-1003)
74191	Don Giovanni: Nella bionda.		(6180)
74195	Philemon: Au bruit des lourds.		(15-1003)
74210	Mefistofele: Son lo spirito.		
74265	Sur les Cimes (Hue).		
74266	Magic Flute: La Haine et la colere.		
74267	La Procession (Franck).		
74268	Rheingold: Abendlich strahlt.		
74269	Queen of Sheba: Sous les pieds.		
74270	Mignon: Ninna-Nanna.		(6365)
74271	Charite (Faure).		
74272	Le Soir (Gounod).		
74273	Favorita: Splendon piu belle (w. Cho.).		
74275	Hugenots: D'un sacro zel (w. Cho.).		(6173)
74276	Gotterdammerung: Hier sitz' ich.		
74281	Chalet: Dans le service de l'Autriche.		(15-1026)
74282	Robert: Valse infernale (w. Cho.).		(6176)
89055	Faust: Scene des Epees (w. Amato-Cho.).		(8003)
89056	Puritani: Suoni la tromba (w. Amato).		(8061)

VICTOR RED SEAL 1916-1922

64557	Le Pere de la Victoire (Ganne).	(697)
64558	La Brabanconne (Campenhout).	(696)
64567	Fratelli d'Italia (Novaro).	(700)
64582	Requiem (Faure): Pie Jesu.	
64585	Chant de Guerre Cosaque (Massenet).	(696)
64586	Marche Lorraine (Ganne).	(697)
64587	Cleopatre: Air de la lettre.	(699)
64647	Les Boeufs (Dupont).	(701)
64648	Himno Nacional Argentino (Conradi).	(700)
64651	Chant Patriotique Belge (18th Cent.)	

64656	Le Filibustier (Georges).	(701)
74464	Bozhe Tsarya khrani (Lvoff).	
74466	Srpska Himna (Jenko).	
74472	O Salutaris (Luce).	(6179)
74473	Le Clarion (Andre).	(6178)
74474	Trovatore: Abietta Zingara.	(6176)
74508	Le Cor (Flegier).	(6178)
74519	Noel (Adam).	(6179)
74735	Hosanna (Granier).	(6175)
76032	Wm. Tell: Ah Matilde (w. Martinelli).	(10009)

IMPORTED VICTOR RED SEAL 1925

Nerone: Ecco il magico specchio. (6483)

For other records, see CARUSO, CLEMENT, FARRAR.

Note: A host of other Journet recordings were assigned numbers including another Infelice from Ernani (64055), Pauvre martyr from Patrie (64084), the Hymne Imperial Russe (64579), Le Regiment de Sambre et Meuse (64580), Dalle stanze from Lucia (64581) and again on (66054), Le Chant du Depart (64583), La Troussaint (64646), Credo d'Amour (64649), Priere (64657), Le Cure de Varreddes (64659), Madamina from Don Giovanni (64691), and on twelve-inch Pro peccatis from Stabat Mater (74471), Anatheme de Balthazar from Favorita (74520), also on (74748), Hosanna (74521), Au Morte Pour La Patrie (74524). Several of these look as though they might well have appeared in the French or French-Canadian catalogues at least, but when the Favorita excerpt was finally issued on Heritage Series as No. 15-1026, it was labelled a first edition.

JUCH, Emma (Soprano)

The close of her career found Emma Juch most noted as a concert and oratorio singer, though it was her participation that had earlier given impetus to the American Opera Company under Theodore Thomas and to the troupe which bore her own name.

VICTOR RED SEAL 1904

81046	Messiah: Come unto Him.	(64018)
85033	Lohengrin: Elsas Traum.	(74014)
85034	Serenata (Tosti).	(74015)

KINDLER, Hans (Cellist)

VICTOR RED SEAL 1920-1923

64841	Minuet (Handel).	(705)
64861	Fond Recollections Op. 64 No. 1 (Popper).	
64896	Orientale (Cui).	(702)
64932	Nina (att: Pergolesi).	(705)
66011	Simple Aveu (Thome).	(704)
66026	Arabian Melody (Glazounow).	(702)
66049	Reverie (Dunkler).	(703)
66053	Wiegenlied (Schubert); Gavotte (Mehul-Burmester).	(703)
66120	Killarney (Balfe).	(704)
74682	Song Without Words (Van Goens).	

Note: Four years prior to his entrance into Red Seal ranks, Kindler made several double-face Blue Seal records, most interesting of which, the Gavotte Op. 23 by Popper and Valensin's Minuet appeared on No. 45116.

KING, Roxy (Soprano)

Settling in Brazil after a career in Germany and elsewhere, this American soprano became an ardent partisan of the considerable musical heritage of that country.

VICTOR RED SEAL 1908-1909

64087	Trovas (Portugese).
64095	The Long Ago.
64097	Home Sweet Home (Bishop).
64129	Salvator Rosa: Mia piccirella.
74112	Schiavo: O Ciel di Parahyba.
74125	Mamma dice (Gomes).
74169	Pelo amor (Madrugara).
74170	Guarany: C'era una volta.
74171	Gioconda: Suicidio.

KINGSTON, Morgan (Tenor)

In addition to his duties at the Metropolitan Opera House itself, Kingston is remembered for the work he did in that company's Century Theatre performances in English, the language of his records as well.

IMPORTED COLUMBIA RECORDS 1913-1915

6141	When Shadows Gather (Marshall).	(A5652)
6148	Songs My Mother Taught Me (Dvorak).	(A5495)
6171	Ianthe (Halkett).	(A5474)
6194	An Evening Song (Blumenthal).	(A5495)
6207	Onaway Awake Beloved (Cowen).	(A5476)
6208	Asthore (Trotere).	(A5539)
6209	The Kerry Dance (Molloy).	(A5474)
6212	Eleanore (Coleridge-Taylor).	(A5476)
6217	For You Alone (Geehl).	(A5527)
6254	My Message (d'Hardelot).	(A5551)
6295	Nada (Mott).	(A5551)
6302	Make New Friends (Parry).	(A5652)
6339	Where My Caravan Has Rested (Lohr).	(A5539)
6351	The Rosary (Nevin).	(A5527)
	Parted (Tosti).	(A5624)
	Come into the Garden, Maud (Balfe).	(A5624)
	Avourneen (King).	(A5692)
	Love's Garden of Roses (Wood).	(A5692)

COLUMBIA RECORDS 1914-1917

36857	Boheme: Mimi's so fickle (w. Kreidler).	(A5546)
36870	The Last Watch (Pinsuti).	(A5564)
36912	Forza del Destino: In this solemn hour (w. Kreidler).	(A5577)
36913	Samson: Look down, O Lord.	(A5577)
36918	Bohemian Girl: Then You'll Remember Me.	(A5604)
36919	Roses (Adams).	(A5767)
36926	Lily of Killarney: The moon has raised (w. Kreidler).	(A5564)
36927	Once Again (Sullivan).	(A5767)
36932	Lohengrin: From distant shore.	(A5604)
37328	Wonderful Garden (Foster).	(A5934)
39241	Samson: Israel Burst Your Bonds.	(A1575)
39268	Cavalleria Rusticana: Siciliana (Eng.).	(A1575)
48643	Onaway Awake Beloved (Coleridge-Taylor).	(A5863)
48644	Judas Maccabaeus: Sound An Alarm.	(A5863)
48656	My Little Love (Hawley).	(A5934)
48821	Sun-Down Sea (Steckel).	(A5909)
48827	Kiss Me Love (Tosti).	(A5909)

48833 Yeoman of the Guard: Strange Adventure (w. Macbeth-Keyes-
Croxton). (A5861)
48834 Mikado: Madrigal (w. Macbeth-Keyes-Croxton). (A5861)
48837 Gondoliers: In contemplative (w. Macbeth-Keyes-Croxton). (A5891)

KIRKBY-LUNN, Louise (Contralto)

Although she sang here both before and after these recordings were released, it is her native England that really exploited this excellent vocalist.

COLUMBIA RECORDS 1905

3278 For a dream's sake (Cowen).
3279 Willow Song (Sullivan).

KOSHETZ, Nina (Soprano)

BRUNSWICK RECORDS 1922-1923

At the Ball (Tschaikowsky).	(15029)	(10137)
None But the Lonely Heart (Tschaikowsky).	(15029)	(10137)
Eastern Romance (Rimsky-Korsakoff).	(15031)	(10138)
Humoresque (Moussorgsky).	(15031)	(10138)
Over the Steppe (Gretchaninoff).	(15043)	(10139)
To the Sun (Koshetz).	(15043)	(10139)
Oi' Mamo (Ukranian).	(15055)	(10140)
Winds are Blowing (Ukranian).	(15055)	(10140)
Pique Dame: Lisa's Air.	(50036)	(30106)
Reverie and Dance (Moussorgsky).	(50036)	(30106)

KREIDLER, Louis (Baritone)

The influence at the time of the organization called "Society for the Pro-
motion of Opera in English" can be seen in the items below and elsewhere.

COLUMBIA RECORDS 1914

36858 Faust: Even Bravest Heart. (A5546)
36871 Trovatore: Tempest of the Heart. (A5570)
36928 Masked Ball: Is It Thou. (A5570)

For other records, see **KINGSTON.**

KREISLER, Fritz (Violinist)

VICTOR RED SEAL 1910-1916

64130 Old Folks at Home (Foster). (722)
64131 Hungarian Dance in G Minor (Brahms-Joachim). (712)
64132 Gavotte in E (Bach). (712)
64142 Chanson sans paroles (Tschaikowsky). (716)
64156 Variations (Tartini-Kreisler). (710)
64202 Aubade Provencale (Couperin-Kreisler). (713)
64292 Chanson Louis XIII (Couperin-Kreisler). (713)
64313 Orfeo: Melodie.
64314 Schon Rosmarin (Kreisler). (721)
64315 Andantino (Martini-Kreisler). (710)
64319 Berceuse (Townsend). (711)
64406 Viennese Melody (Gaertner-Kreisler). (910)
64408 Austrian Hymn (Haydn-Kreisler). (910)
64488 Slavonic Dance No. 1 (Dvorak-Kreisler). (723)
64502 The Rosary (Nevin). (720)
64503 Serenade Espagnole (Chaminade-Kreisler). (724)
64504 Mazurka in A Minor Op. 67 No. 4 (Chopin-Kreisler). (726)

64529	Old Refrain (Kreisler).	(720)
64542	Song Without Words No. 25—May Breeze (Mendelssohn).	
64556	Spanish Dance (Granados-Kreisler).	(724)
64563	Songs My Mother Taught Me (Dvorak-Kreisler).	(727)
64565	Berceuse Romantique (Kreisler).	(711)
64600	Rondino on a theme by Beethoven (Kreisler).	(715)
64601	Arlesienne Suite: Adagietto (Bizet).	(715)
64614	Minuet (Boccherini).	(718)
74172	Bohemian Fantasie (Smetana).	(6188)
74180	Humoresque (Dvorak).	(6181)
74182	Thais: Meditation.	(6186)
74196	Liebesfreud (Kreisler).	(6182)
74197	Caprice Viennois (Kreisler).	(6181)
74202	Moment Musical (Schubert); Tambourin (Rameau-Kreisler).	(6185)
74203	Tambourin Chinois (Kreisler).	(6185)
74294	Scherzo (Dittersdorf).	(6187)
74330	Chanson (Cottenet).	(6188)
74332	Praeludium (Bach).	
74333	Liebeslied (Kreisler).	(6182)
74384	Serse: Largo (arr. Kreisler).	(6184)
74387	Indian Lament (Dvorak-Kreisler).	(6186)
74437	Slavonic Dance No. 2 in E Minor (Dvorak-Kreisler).	(6183)
74463	Wienerisch (Godowsky).	(6187)
74487	Quartet Op. 11: Andante Cantabile (Tschaikowsky). (6184)	(8041)
76028	Concerto for Two Violins (pt. I) (Bach) (w. Zimbalist).	(8040)
76029	Concerto for Two Violins (pt. II) (Bach) (w. Zimbalist).	(8040)
76030	Concerto for Two Violins (pt. III) (Bach) (w. Zimbalist).	(8041)

VICTOR RED SEAL 1917-1925

64655	Poor Butterfly (Hubbell).	(714)
64660	Underneath the Stars (Spencer-Pasternack).	(719)
64670	Rosamunde Ballet (Schubert-Kreisler).	(723)
64709	Paraphrase on Minuet (Paderewski-Kreisler).	(718)
64730	Dream of Youth (Winternitz).	(708)
64731	Polichinelle Serenade (Kreisler).	(721)
64817	Beautiful Ohio (Earl).	(707)
64824	Nobody Knows the Trouble I See (arr: White).	(722)
64857	Gypsy Serenade (Valdez).	(709)
64873	Forsaken (Koschat-Winternitz).	(708)
64890	Sadko: Chanson Indoue (arr. Kreisler).	(706)
64902	Who Can Tell (Kreisler).	(719)
64924	Love Nest (Hirsch).	(714)
64947	On Miami Shore (Jacobi).	(707)
64961	Melody in A (Dawes).	(725)
64974	Souvenir (Drdla).	(716)
64993	To Spring Op. 43 No. 6 (Grieg).	(727)
64842	La Gitana (arr. Kreisler).	(709)
66023	Paradise (Krakauer-Kreisler).	(725)
66041	Waltz Op. 39 No. 15 (Brahms-Hochstein).	(726)
66079	Scheherazade—Chanson Arabe (Rimsky-Korsakoff-Kreisler).	(706)
66104	Aucassin and Nicolette (Kreisler).	(717)
66127	Pale Moon (Logan-Kreisler).	(728)
66137	Toy Soldier's March (Kreisler).	(728)
66149	Midnight Bells (Heuberger-Kreisler).	(717)
66157	Mazurka Op. 33 No. 2 (Chopin-Kreisler).	(947)
66176	Melodie Op. 16 No. 2 (Paderewski-Kreisler).	(947)
66196	Cherry Ripe (Scott).	(966)
66197	Entr'acte (Kramer).	(966)
66231	Love Sends A Little Gift of Roses (Openshaw).	(994)
66232	The World is Waiting for the Sunrise (Seitz).	(994)
66250	Minuet (Haydn-Friedberg).	(1010)
66251	Old French Gavotte (Friedberg).	(1010)

66269	From the Land of the Sky Blue Water (Cadman).	(1021)
66270	Negro Spiritual Melody.	(1021)
	Poupee Valsante (Poldini-Kreisler).	(1029)
	Orange Blossoms: Kiss in the Dark (arr. Kreisler).	(1029)
	Slavonic Lament (Schuett-Friedberg).	(1043)
	Dirge of the North (Balogh-Kreisler).	(1043)
	Chansonnette (Bass).	(1062)
	Tote Stadt: Pierrot's Dance Song (arr. Kreisler).	(1062)
	Dance Orientale (Rimsky-Krosakow).	(1075)
	Molly on the Shore (Grainger-Kreisler).	(1075)
	Legend of the Canyon (Cadman).	(1093)
	Caprice Antique (Balogh-Kreisler).	(1093)
87577	Farewell to Cucullain (trans. Kreisler) (w. H. Kreisler).	(3017)
87579	Serenade (Jeral-Kreisler) (w. H. Kreisler).	(3017)
	Miniature Viennese March (Kreisler) (w. H. Kreisler).	(3035)
	Syncopation (Kreisler) (w. H. Kreisler).	(3035)
	Abendlied (Schumann) (w. H. Kreisler).	(3036)
	Nina (att. Pergolesi) (w. H. Kreisler).	(3036)
	Andante in F (Beethoven-Kreisler) (w. H. Kreisler).	(3037)
	Minuet in G (Beethoven-Kreisler) (w. H. Kreisler).	(3037)
74720	Coq d'Or: Hymn to the Sun (arr. Kreisler).	(6183)
	Concerto No. 4 in D (Mozart) (w. Orch.).	(6520/1/2/3)

For other records, see **FARRAR, McCORMACK.**

Note: Some of the last listed solos as well as duets with his brother and the Mozart concerto are imported recordings. Other Kreisler recordings to which numbers were assigned include Moment Musical (64555), Scherzo (64568) and Rondino (64575).

KREISLER, Hugo (Cellist)

IMPORTED VICTOR RED SEAL 1922-1924

66040	Serenade Espagnole (Chaminade-Kreisler).	(729)
66082	Viennese Folk Song Fantasy (arr. H. Kreisler).	(729)
66116	Apple Blossoms: I'm in Love.	(956)
66185	Apple Blossoms: Letter Song.	(956)
66218	Liebeslied (Kreisler).	(987)
66219	Serenade (Drigo).	(987)
	La Cinquantaine (Gabriel-Marie).	(1039)
	Melody in F (Rubenstein).	(1039)

For other records, see **F. KREISLER.**

KRISTMANN, Emilia (Soprano)

IMPORTED VICTOR RED SEAL 1903

5044	Ave Maria (Gounod).	(91035)
91064	Sancta Maria (Faure).	
91065	Doubt (Glinka).	

Note: Also imported early from St. Petersburg was a group of Columbia discs which appeared on a light blue seal with black lettering.

KRUSZELNICKA, Salomea (Soprano)

IMPORTED VICTOR RED SEAL 1903

61078	Tosca: Vissi d'arte.	(66005)

Note: This record appeared first as a black seal, was withdrawn July 1907 and re-instated as a Red Seal number four years later for Latin-American catalogues. Meanwhile, her much more extensive issue for Fonotipia under the Italianized form of her name, Krusceniski, had included one of her favorite roles, Adriana Lecouvreur, from which the Poveri fiori, recorded in 1907, bore No. 92089 (C-F29).

KUBELIK, Jan (Violinist)

IMPORTED VICTOR RED SEAL 1903

5029	Serenade (Drdla).	(91024)
5030	Lucia: Sextet (arr. St. Lubin).	(91025)

IMPORTED VICTOR RED SEAL 1911-1914

64390	Suite in D—Air for G String (Bach).
74255	Zapateado (Sarasate).
74256	Pierrot's Serenade (Randegger).
74257	Perpetuum Mobile (Ries).
74365	Romance in E Flat (Rubenstein-Wilhelmj).
74366	Spanish Dance No. 8 (Sarasate).
74367	Romanza Andaluza (Sarasate).
74368	Sonata No. 6—Adagio; Allegro (Handel).
74370	Concerto Op. 22—Finale (Wieniawski).

For other records, see MELBA.

Note: Also assigned numbers in 1925 were the following 1912 imports of Kubelik: the Canzonetta from the Tschaikowsky concerto as No. 88672, a Mozart romance as No. 88673, Drdla's Serenade as No. 88674 and Sarasate's Zigeunerweisen as No. 88675. After recording the very earliest group above, at wh.ch time he also essayed the technical difficulties of the Sauret cadenza to the Paganini concerto, Kubelik also made a large number of Fono.pias including Wieniawski's Scherzo Tarantelle on No. 39884 (C-F29).

KURT, Melanie (Soprano)

COLUMBIA RECORDS 1917

44444	Herber Abschied.	(E3274)
44558	Mignon: Kennst du das land.	(E3274)
59450	Tannhauser: Dich teure Halle.	(E5139)
59456	Siegfried: Ewig war ich.	(E5139)

Note: On Victor, Kurt appeared on black label imports, among which the duet with Feinhals, Versank ich jetzt, from Flying Dutchman was No. 68374. It is unfortunate that a subsequent recording with Friedrich Schorr in the memorable baritone part, Gr. Bz5007, was not the one thus made available to us.

LA FORGE, Frank (Pianist)

In addition to being accompanist for several of the singers, La Forge appeared on Red Seal label briefly as a soloist. Later, solo work was issued in purple and blue seal categories.

VICTOR RED SEAL 1908

64083	Gavotte (La Forge); Papillon (Lavallee).
74101	Etude de Concert (MacDowell).

LA GOYA (Canzonetista)

IMPORTED VICTOR RED SEAL 1913-1920

64349	Balance.	(45222)
64350	Ven y ven (Gomez).	(45228)
64351	La Reina del Cortijo.	(45227)
64352	Chulona, dale, dale.	(45221)
64353	Tirana del Tripili (Chapi).	(45226)
64354	Stornelli Montagnoli.	(45231)
64355	Camarona (Gimenez).	(45223)

64356	Seguidillas (Calleja).	(45229)
64357	El Guiro.	(45229)
64595	Cigarrona (Valverde).	(45224)
64436	Ay Benito (Valverde).	(45221)
64452	Tapame (Yust).	(45225)
64453	El Apache (Krier).	(45227)
64507	Serenata Apache (Cadenas).	(45226)
64508	Cara Morena (Faixa).	(45222)
64509	Zagala (Faixa).	(45225)
64523	Baiada de los Pastores (Mediavilla).	(45220)
64678	Esencia Chula (Zamacios).	(45232)
64679	Fea (Abades).	(45232)
64680	Agua que no hay (Abades).	(45220)
64681	Di mi Holanda (Larruga).	(45230)
64682	Del Iris Bar (Abades).	(45231)
64701	Chulapa soy (Larruga).	(45224)
64702	El daie, daie (Alonso).	(45223)
64703	La gitana celosa (Orejon).	(45230)
64704	Serenata de Pierrot (Mediavilla).	(45228)
64848	Modistilla (Teres).	(45233)
64849	Cantinera (Teres).	(45234)
64850	El Monaguillo (Teres).	(45235)
64851	La Munequita (Teres).	(45235)
64852	Mi Tirana (Larruga).	(45233)
64853	Inglesita (Teres).	(45234)
64869	El amor es fragil (Faixa).	(45236)
64870	Campanela (Padilla).	(45237)
64871	Cancion del Rhin (Cadenas).	(45237)
64872	Jacara (Teres).	(45236)

Note: Later Victor issues were in the blue seal classification to which the above had by then been transferred.

LAMONT, Forrest (Tenor)

A list of the many American operas in which Lamont was first protagonist of leading parts would include Azora, Daughter of the Forest, Light from St. Agnes and others attesting to his ready musicianship and the persistent encouragement of native composers by the Chicago Opera.

OKEH RECORDS 1919-1920

Trovatore: Di quella pira.	(6001)
Tosca: E lucevan le stelle.	(6001)
Love Here is My Heart (Silesu).	(6002)
A Dream (Bartlett).	(6002)
I m Dreaming My Life Away (Chiafarelli).	(6003)
Somewhere A Voice is Calling (Tate).	(6003)
Cavalleria Rusticana: Siciliana.	(6007)
Cavalleria Rusticana: Brindisi.	(6007)
Rigoletto: Questa o quella.	(6009)
Rigoletto: E il sol (w. Marina Campanari).	(6009)

LANDOWSKA, Wanda (Harpsichordist)

VICTOR RED SEAL 1924

66203	Harmonious Blacksmith (Handel).	(973)
66204	Sonata in A—Turkish March (Mozart).	(973)
	Bourree d'Auvergne (Landowska).	(1038)
	La Chasse (Scarlatti).	(1038)

LASHANSKA, Hulda, (Soprano)

COLUMBIA RECORDS 1917-1921

49338	Annie Laurie (Scott).	(68066D)	
49339	Home Sweet Home (Bishop).	(68028D)	
49364	Louise: Depuis le jour.	(68056D)	(5021M)
49443	Bonnie Sweet Bessie (Gilbert).	(68066D)	
49516	Carmen: Je dis que rien.	(68056D)	(5021M)
49963	Long, Long Ago (Bayly).	(68028D)	(5005M)
77719	Songs My Mother Taught Me (Dvorak).	(33038D)	
77744	My Curly-Headed Babby (Clutsam).	(33010D)	
77843	Mlle. Modiste: Kiss Me Again.	(33009D)	(33M)
77878	Pirate Dreams (Huerter).	(33037D)	(34M)
77989	Mighty Lak' a Rose (Nevin).	(33047D)	(24M)
78355	Thy Beaming Eyes (MacDowell).	(33036D)	(35M)
78356	Erminie: Lullaby.	(33047D)	
78392	Fiddle and I (Goodeve).	(33037D)	(34M)
79114	Lullaby (Brahms).	(33010D)	
79115	Sweetest Story Ever Told (Stults).	(33029D)	
79209	Hatikvah (Russotto).		
79212	Sing Me to Sleep (Greene).	(33029D)	(24M)
79213	Happy Days (Strelezski).	(33038D)	
79840	Last Night (Kjeruif).	(33009D)	(33M)
79856	Just a-Wearyin' for You (Bond).	(33036D)	(35M)

VICTOR RED SEAL 1922-1924

66020	Sweet and Low (Barnby) (w. Qt.).	(730)
66021	Canzonetta (Loewe-Martens).	(730)
66194	Paride e Elena: Spiagge amate.	(964)
66195	Lungi dal caro bene (Secchi).	(964)
66276	Bird of Love Divine (Wood).	(1023)
66277	Love Came Calling (Zamecnik).	(1023)
	My Curly-Headed Babby (Clutsam).	(1044)
	Sweetest Story Ever Told (Stults).	(1044)

LAURI-VOLPI, Giacomo (Tenor)

BRUNSWICK RECORDS 1923-1925

Cavalleria Rusticana: Addio alla madre.	(50038)	
Andrea Chernier: Improvviso.	(50038)	
Boheme: Che gelida manina.	(50073)	
Schiavo: Quando nascesti tu.	(50073)	
Rigoletto: La donna e mobile.	(15047)	
Rigoletto: Questa o quella.	(15047)	
Carme (de Curtis).	(15050)	(10131)
Mamma Mia (Nutile).	(15050)	(10131)
Ideale (Tosti).	(15067)	(10133)
La Mia Canzone (Tosti).	(15067)	(10133)
Luna d'Estate (Tosti).	(15072)	(10136)
Serenata (Mascagni).	(15072)	(10136)
Pagliacci: Vesti la giubba.	(15085)	
Cavalleria Rusticana: Brindisi.	(15085)	
Trovatore: Di quella pira.	(15095)	
Trovatore: Ah si ben mio.	(15095)	
Manella Mia (Valente).		(10172)
Cielo Turchino (Ciociano).		(10172)

Note: Prior to the release of his domestic discs, several of Lauri-Volpi's Fono-tipia recordings were imported by Okeh including, of course, selections which showed off his brilliant high tones like Favorita: Spirto gentil, No. 74910, Ok 53304.

LAZARO, Hipolito (Tenor)

IMPORTED VICTOR RED SEAL 1916

74495	Africana: O Paradiso.	
74496	Favorita: Spirto gentil.	

Note: These two imports appeared as Black Seal Records Nos. 68542, 68539 respectively in Latin-American catalogues, which also listed other selections including Recondita armonia from Tosca on 68538.

COLUMBIA RECORDS 1916-1920

46736	Rigoletto: La donna e mobile.	(33025D)	(2022M)
46737	Rigoletto: Questa o quella.	(33025D)	(2022M)
46752	Puritani: Vieni fra questa braccia.		(3911M)
47211	Trovatore: Di quella pira.	(2013M)	(3911M)
48740	Tosca: E lucevan le stelle.		
48741	Boheme: Che gelida manina.	(68063D)	(7103M)
48747	Africana: O Paradiso.	(68032D)	
48748	Favorita: Spirto gentil.	(68055D)	(8938M)
48749	Favorita: Una vergine.	(68055D)	
48750	Tosca: Recondita armonia.	(68033D)	(7103M)
48762	Aida: Celeste Aida.	(68034D)	(7054M)
48782	Faust: Salve dimora.		(8938M)
48783	Puritani: A te o cara.	(68034D)	(7054M)
48787	Manon: Il sogno.		(8939M)
48788	Martha: M'appari.	(68032D)	(8931M)
48792	Manon: Ah dispar.	(68063D)	(8939M)
49020	Pagliacci: Vesti la giubba.	(68033D)	(7028M)
49350	Ave Maria (Gounod) (w. Jacobsen).		(8931M)
49354	Traviata: Parigi o cara (w. Barrientos)	(71001D)	(8928M)
49914	Eili Eili.		(7025M)
83016	Marina: Costa la de levante.		

IMPORTED COLUMBIA RECORDS 1925

Chiquita (Lacalle).	(3912M)
Te Quiero (Serrano).	(3912M)
Ojas Tapatios (Velasco).	(3913M)
La Espanolita (Penella).	(3913M)
La Guinda (Delfin).	(3914M)
Mi Jota (Fornells).	(3914M)
Ay Ay Ay (Perez).	(8932M)
Emigrantes: Granadinas.	(8932M)
Ay Del Ay (Osma).	(8933M)
Carmen: Canzone del fior.	(8933M)
Tosca: E lucevan le stelle.	(8934M)
Boheme: Che gelida manina.	(8934M)
Aida: Celeste Aida.	(8935M)
Gioconda: Cielo e mar.	(8935M)
Hugenots: Bianca al par.	(8936M)
Africana: O Paradiso.	(8936M)

Note: The imports from Spain listed above bore matrix numbers between K451 and K467 for the ten inch and KX24 and KX36 for the twelves.

LAZZARI, Virgilio (Bass)

VOCALION RECORDS 1922-1924

30171	Boheme: Vecchia zimarra.	(60040)
30173	Faust: Dio dell'or.	
52088	Barber of Seville: La calunnia.	(70040)
	Simon Boccanegra: Il lacerato spirito.	(70040)

LEHMANN, Lilli (Soprano)

Note: Of such enduring fame is the name of Lilli Lehmann that mention of her records here is not amiss though they were never incorporated into domestic series and those that reached the imported Columbia-Fonotipia B series numbered less than a dozen. Of these, four of the most thrilling have just recently been re-recorded by the Collectors Record Shop. Imagine almost any Wagnerian soprano today doing the florid Traviata aria or "O hatt'ich Jubals Harf" from Joshua at an age of sixty with impeccable coloratura, trills and full-bodied notes two and more lines above the staff. Even then, you would not begin to realize the impact of these justly celebrated recordings made for Odeon well over forty years ago.

LELIWA, Tadeusz (Tenor)

Note: Under the above name, Columbia released some early Polish imports including a serenade from the Mazepa of Muncheimer (not Tschaikowsky) the Miserere from Trovatore and Halka: Dumka. These were numbered 35246/47/48 and were followed, several years later, by his appearance in like listing on imported Victor black seal which also included his version of the Halka selection on No. 69518. Meanwhile, among the many Fonotipia discs released in I aly under the name of Enzo Leliva was Juive: Rachele allor che Iddio on No. 92410.

LEONHARDT, Robert (Baritone)

Note: If Leonhardt did not make the most records of any singer of the acoustic era, he was not far behind and the leader was probably another German who could cater to the apparently insatiable taste for standard lighter works in that tongue. In addition to imports on these and other labels, Leonhardt made both Victor and Columbia popular-priced domestic discs, the second group being the larger and including the Loblied der Polin from Beggar Student (44071) E3271.

LEVITZKI, Mischa (Pianist)

COLUMBIA RECORDS 1923-1925

Marche Militaire Op. 51 No. 1 (part I) (Schubert)	(A3949)	
Marche Militaire Op. 51 No. 1 (part II) (Schubert).	(A3949)	
Hungarian Rhapsody No. 6 (part I) (Liszt).	(A6232)	(7007M)
Hungarian Rhapsody No. 6 (part II) (Liszt).	(A6232)	(7007M)
Etude Op. 25 No. 1 (Chopin); La Jongleuse (Moszkowski).	(65000D)	(7008M)
Waltz in G Flat; Etude on Black Keys (Chopin).	(65000D)	(7008M)
Valse de Concert (Levitzki).	(65024D)	(7009M)
Waltz in A (Levitzki); Troika (Tschaikowsky).	(65024D)	(7009M)
Waltz in E Minor (Chopin).	(65030D)	(7098M)
Orfeo: Air (arr. Sgambati).	(65030D)	(7098M)

Note: No. 7007M was later changed to 5088M.

LIPKOWSKA, Lydia (Soprano)

Lipkowska was gifted with considerable personal charm as well as musical talent but these are very hard to refine from the harsh, indistinct recording under which she labored.

COLUMBIA RECORDS 1911

30623	Rigoletto: Figlia, Mio Padre (w. Baklanoff).	(A5296)
30711	Romeo: Valse.	(A5294)
30712	Rigoletto: Caro nome.	(A5295)

80713	Manon: Je marche sur tous les chemins.	(H1059)
80714	Manon: Adieu notre petite table.	(H1059)
80717	Lucia: Mad scene.	(A5295)
80718	Don Giovanni: La ci darem (w. Blanchart).	(A5297)
80719	Traviata: Pura siccome (w. Blanchart).	(A5296)
80720	Barber of Seville: Dunque io son (w. Blanchart).	(A5297)
80723	Lipkowska Waltz (Triolin) (in Russian).	(A5294)

LITVINNE, Felia (Soprano)

IMPORTED VICTOR RED SEAL 1903

5111	Cid: Pleurez mes yeux.	(91052)

Note: Though she had been singing here well over a decade as Mlle. Litvinov, and was sister-in-law to the ever popular De Reszkes, this Russian born soprano was all but overlooked domestically while Paris recorded her numerous times for Fonotipia-Odeon and others.

LLOYD, Edward (Tenor)

Note: Early London recordings of this venerable tenor were assigned Red Seal numbers in 1925, though they never had general release in this country. These included Elijah: If With All Your Hearts (87399). Elijah: Then shall the Righteous (87400). Come into the Garden, Maud (88690). Queen of Sheba: Lend me your aid (88691), I'll sing thee Songs of Araby (88692) and Judas Maccabaeus: Sound an Alarm (88693).

LYNE, Felice (Soprano)

In Hammerstein's London operatic venture, this American soprano, at least, met considerable success and was participant in Don Quichotte, Children of the Don and other novelties.

COLUMBIA RECORDS 1915

37154	Rigoletto: Caro nome.	(A5686)
37155	Spring's Awakening (Sanderson).	(A5656)
37156	A Dream Fancy (Marshall).	(A5656)
37160	Voci di Primavera (Strauss).	(A5686)

MAETERLINCK, Georgette Leblanc (Soprano)

COLUMBIA RECORDS 1912-1913

Carmen: Air des cartes.	(A1153)
Thais: L'amour est une vertu.	(A1153)
Amadis: Bois epais.	(A1243)
Elle Avait Trois Couronnes (Febrier).	(A1243)

Note: After mentioning her author-husband's name five times in a short blurb about her, it is unfortunate that Columbia did not further celebrate this well publicized marriage by offering this singer in something from Pelleas, Monna Vanna or Ariane et Barbe-bleue.

MANTELLI, Eugenia (Contralto)

Note: Mantelli was, by far, the outstanding singer of Zonophone's popular-priced classical series of mixed origin. On it, she repeated the familiar contralto arias from Favorita, Hugenots, Mignon, Carmen, etc., she had done on Bettini cylinders the previous decade and added such beautiful songs as Lotti's Pur dicesti on No. 12588 as well as several duets with Parvis.

MARAK, Otokar (Tenor)

Note: Another prolific recorder, Marak's work was divided between the usual operatic repertoire and songs of his native Bohemia. Some of the latter appeared here as imports like Bendl's May Song, which was an early single-face Victor black seal No. 52805, later doubled on No. 16635. Others were domestic recordings like the Prapor Slavy (86082) issued by Columbia as E4663.

MARCEL, Lucille (Soprano)

IMPORTED VICTOR RED SEAL 1911
76018 Tosca: Vissi d'arte.

COLUMBIA RECORDS 1913

Otello: Ave Maria.	(A5482)
Thou Art A Child (Weingartner).	(A5482)

Note: By birth Wasself, by marriage Weingartner, this native of New York recorded abroad items in French, such as Obstination on Gr. 33804 and in German, in which she sings the Faust jewel song on Gr. 043165 as well as in Italian.

MARCONI, Francesco (Tenor)

IMPORTED VICTOR RED SEAL 1910

88226	Lucrezia Borgia: Di pescatore.	(76004)
89046	Puritani: Vieni fra questa (w. Galvany).	

Note: Marconi's Italian recordings ranged from operetta upwards and included a duet with the venerable Cotogni.

MARDONES, Jose (Bass)

Possessor of a stentorian organ, which was amenable, at the same time, to the most delicate lyricism, Mardones never made a really poor recording.

COLUMBIA RECORDS 1910-1914

4427	Boheme: Vecchia zimarra.		(A846)	
4428	Faust: Rammenta i lieti di.		(A847)	
4429	Faust: Dio dell'or.		(A847)	
4430	Ernani: Infelice.		(A846)	
4432	Meus Amores (Baldomir).		(H34)	(1918M)
21584	Dame Mas (Ochoa).		(S11)	(1915M)
21585	La Perjura (Tejada).		(S11)	(1915M)
21586	Nostalgia (Ochoa).		(S12)	
21587	El Tamborilero (Ochoa).		(S12)	
21713	Plegaria (Anglada).		(S54)	
21715	Mascotte: Balada de Pipo.		(S55)	
21716	Dos Princesas: Vals.		(S55)	
21717	Chimes of Normandy: Vals.		(S54)	
30409	Puritani: Suoni la tromba (w. Blanchart).		(A5184)	
30414	Mefistofele: Ave Signor.		(A5192)	(6916M)
30415	Mefistofele: Son lo spirito.		(A5216)	
30417	Mef'stofele: Ecco il mondo.		(A5216)	
30423	Barber of Seville: La calunnia.	(A5200)	(7055M)	(5054M)
30425	Hugenots: Piff, Paff.		(A5192)	
30432	Simon Boccanegra: Il lacerato spirito.		(A5201)	
30449	Guitarrico: Jota.		(A5202)	(6913M)
30458	Faust: Serenata.	(A5200)	(7055M)	(5054M)
30459	Stabat Mater: Pro peccatis.		(A5201)	

30469	Juive: Se oppressi ognor.	(A5202)	
30470	Tempestad: Romanza.	(H1043)	(6913M)
30474	Juramento: Romanza.	(H1052)	
30560	Robert: Suore che riposate.	(H1094)	
36366	Aida: Nume custode (w. Zenatello. Cho.).	(A5426)	(7032M)

COLUMBIA RECORDS 1919-1923

49419	Ernani: Infelice.	(A6095)	(7056M)	(5058M)
49420	Brindo a tu Salud (Anglada).	(65026D)	(7071M)	(5063M)
49427	Salvatore Rosa: E quanto.	(65026D)	(7071M)	(5063M)
49430	Simon Boccanegra: Il lacerato spirito.	(S5101)		(6916M)
49438	Carmen: Canzone del Toreador (w. Cho.).	(A6095)	(7056M)	(5058M)
49563	Maruxa: Goldoron.	(A6225)	(7060M)	(5062M)
49591	Robert: Suore che riposate.	(A6200)	(7058M)	(5060M)
49602	Magic Flute: Possente Numi.	(A6220)	(7059M)	(5061M)
49628	Nabucco: Del futuro nel bujo.	(A6220)	(7059M)	(5061M)
49629	Mefistofele: Ave Signor.	(A6225)	(7060M)	(5062M)
49632	Hugenots: Piff Paff.	(A6200)	(7058M)	(5060M)
49635	Rocked in the Cradle (Gooch).	(A6134)	(7057M)	(5059M)
49671	Asleep in the Deep (Petrie).	(A6134)	(7057M)	(5059M)
56008	El Artillero (Anglada).	(S5124)		(6915M)
77832	O Pallide Mammole (Trimarchi).	(S84)		(1919M)
78145	Saeta y Praviana (Cancion Asturiana).	(S78)		(1917M)
78149	El Arriero (Di Nogero).	(A3309)	(2023M)	(122M)
78213	Tango de las Frutas (Anglada).	(S79)		(1921M)
79012	Ay Ay Ay (Perez).	(A3309)	(2023M)	(122M)
79031	Satisfaccion (Anglada).			(1920M)
79038	Vizcaya (Anglada).			(1920M)
82229	Non te olvido (Cancion Vasca).	(S77)		(1916M)
82230	Clavelitos (Valverde).	(S77)		(1916M)
82233	Os Teus Ollos (Cancion Gallega).	(S78)		(1917M)
82413	La Reja (Larruga).	(S83)		(1918M)
82414	Mefisto (Carelli).	(S84)		(1919M)
82420	Alborado (Alvarez).			(1921M)
83018	Unha Noite (Cancion Gallega).	(S5123)		(6914M)
83019	Nostalgia (Anglada).	(S5193)		(6915M)

For other Columbia Records, see BARRIENTOS, BRONSKAJA, CONSTANTINO.

VICTOR RED SEAL 1923-1925

66141	Alegria del Batallon: Cancion del soldado	(921)
66159	Tristes Amores (Muguerza).	(921)
74808	Vespri Siciliani: O tu Palermo.	(6434)
74832	Requiem (Verdi): Confutatis.	(6420)
74833	Stabat Mater: Pro peccatis.	(6420)
74854	Nabucco: Tu sul labbro.	(6434)
74890	Lucrezia Borgia: Vieni la mia vendetta.	(6456)
74891	Pipele (Ferrari): Questa notte.	(6456)
	Norma: Ite sul colle.	(6537)
	Star of the North: Beati i di.	(6537)

For other Victor Records, see MARTINELLI

MARLOWE, Julia (Actress)

See SOTHERN and MARLOWE.

MARSH, Lucy Isabelle (Soprano)

VICTOR RED SEAL 1913-1914

74345	Carmen: Parle-moi de ma mere (w. McCormack).	(8034)
74398	Aida: O terra addio (w. McCormack).	(8034)

Note: Although her association with McCormack advanced her to the only Red Seal status she enjoyed before the orthophonic period, Marsh made many worthy items over a fifteen year period for lesser categories. Belieing their price classification were such pieces as Theodora: Angels ever bright on No. 35075; Intorno all'idol mio (Cesti) on No. 45069; Serva Padrona: S.izzoso on No. 55051; Stabat Mater: Inflammatus (w. Cho.) on No. 70037 [55162]. Previously, she also appeared on Columbia in selections such as Lincke's Glow Worm on No. 3791 [A435].

MARTIN, Riccardo (Tenor)

Martin's recordings represent some of his diverse roles but nothing of native works in which he participated such as Mona and Pipe of Desire.

VICTOR RED SEAL 1910-1911

87050	Tosca: E lucevan le stelle.	
87051	Als die alte Mutter (Dvorak).	
87081	Mme. Butterfly: Amore o grillo.	
87503	Mme. Butterfly: Lo so che (w. Fornia-Scotti).	
88276	Walkure: Siegmunds Liebeslied.	
88277	Cavalleria Rusticana: Addio alla madre.	(15-1029)
88316	Cid: O Souverain.	(15-1029)

MARTINELLI, Giovanni (Tenor)

VICTOR RED SEAL 1914-1918

64286	Rigoletto: Questa o quella.	(731)
64382	Rigoletto: La donna e mobile.	(733)
64393	Tosca: E lucevan le stelle.	(733)
64409	Gioconda: Cielo e mar.	(738)
64410	Manon Lescaut: Donna non vidi mai.	(738)
64420	Tosca: Recondita armonia.	(731)
64484	Pagliacci: Vesti la giubba.	(736)
64486	Ideale (Tosti).	(739)
64487	Masked Ball: Barcarola.	(732)
64505	Trovatore: Di quella pira.	(732)
64514	Ernani: Come rugiada.	(737)
64544	Cavalleria Rusticana; Siciliana.	(734)
64574	Ouvre ton coeur (Bizet).	(735)
64595	Mattinata (Leoncavallo).	(739)
64652	Iris: Apri la tua finestra.	(737)
64700	Don Pasquale: Com' e gentil (w. Cho.).	734)
64772	O ben tornato, amore (Roxas).	
74381	Boheme: Che gelida manina.	(6192)
74391	Carmen: Air de la fleur.	(6191)
74424	Aida: Celeste Aida.	(6192)
74426	Serenata (Mascagni).	(6194)
74439	Trovatore: Ah si ben mio.	(6190)
74440	Africana: O Paradiso.	(6193)
74469	Martha: M'appari.	(6193)
74483	Lucia: Fra poco a me.	(6189)
74517	L'Ultima Canzone (Tosti).	(6195)
74518	Traviata: De' miei bollenti spiriti.	(6212)
74537	Lucia: Tu che a Dio.	(6189)
76032	Wm. Tell: Ah Matilde (w. Journet).	(10009)
88530	Trovatore: Miserere (w. Destinn-Cho.)	(89119) (6190)

VICTOR RED SEAL 1919-1923

64774	Werther: Pourquoi me reveiller.	(735)
66062	Zaza: E un riso gentil.	(736)

74573	Faust: Salut demeure.	(6191)
74683	Zaza: O mio piccolo tavolo.	(6194)
74712	Eugen Onegin: Eco lontano.	(6195)
74800	Wm. Tell: O muto asil.	(6212)
74809	Fascisti Hymn (Gasteldo).	
89160	Don Carlos: Dio che nell'alma (w. De Luca).	(8047)
95213	Wm. Tell: Troncar suoi di (w. De Luca-Mardones).	(10009)

For other records, see **ALDA, FARRAR.**

Note: One of the items assigned a catalogue number as belonging to Martinelli is a Fruhlingslied or Spring Song (64287). This would seem to belong more properly to Fornia who has the subsequent number. The recordings of La mia canzone (64485) and the Faust trio with Alda-Mardones (95214) seem more likely to be correctly ascribed.

MASON, Edith (Soprano)

BRUNSWICK RECORDS 1924-1925

Mme. Butterfly: Ancora un passo.	(15096)
Faust: Air des bijoux.	(15096)
From the Land of Sky Blue Water (Cadman).	(10177)
Dreamin' Time (Strickland).	(10177)
Martha: Last Rose of Summer.	(30108)
Good Bye (Tosti).	(30108)

MATZENAUER, Margarete (Contralto)

Contraltos are the most eclectic of singers and Matzenauer was particularly noted for her prodigious knowledge of a multitude of scores. In some, she even essayed roles which pushed almost beyond the natural limits of her extensive range, but always with consummate musicianship.

VICTOR RED SEAL 1912-1913

87102	Walkure: Fort denn eile.	(904)
87103	Carmen: Seguidilla.	
88360	Africana: In grembo a me.	
88363	Favorita: O mio Fernando.	
88364	Parsifal: Ich sah' das Kind.	(6327)
88365	Robert: Roberto tu che adoro.	
88430	Cavalleria Rusticana: Voi lo sapete.	(6327)
88431	Aida: Ritorna vincitor.	
89061	Carmen: Si tu m'aimes (w. Amato-Cho.).	
89062	Favorita: Ah l'alto ardor (w. Amato).	(8003)

COLUMBIA RECORDS 1915

37068	The Rosary (Nevin).	(A5641)	
37069	Stille Nacht (Gruber).	(A5641)	
37264	Kiss Me, Love (Tosti).	(A5698)	(5005M)
37265	Aprile (Tosti).	(A5698)	

VICTOR RED SEAL 1924

87387	Trovatore: Stride la vampa.	(999)
87388	Lucrezia Borgia: Brindisi.	(999)
	Gioconda: Voce di donna.	(6471)
	Hugenots: Nobil signori salute.	(6471)

Note: A Pathe Silent Night was re-recorded onto Actuelle No. 025089, Perfect 11539. A two-part Fidelio: Komm' o Hoffnung, listed Nov. 1913 as Gr. 043235 and 2-43424, was later offered for sale here on Opera Disc Nos. 76282, 74602.

MAUREL, Victor (Baritone)

Note: The creator of Verdi's Iago and Falstaff is too important to leave out of consideration though his interesting recording of "Quand'ero paggio" from the later opera was never a part of any domestic series other than its most recent re-issues and re-recordings. That it much delighted the Fonotipia studio audience of 1907 is evident by their warm response to the verses sung in both Italian and French. Earlier discs, particularly those of his other great Shakespearean characterization, are likewise noteworthy.

McCORMACK, John (Tenor)

Of John McCormack, much has been written and will continue to be, both by his proud fellow Irishmen and others. Those who lament the time he devoted to trifles, when he could sing Mozart or Handel to perfection, are apt to overlook the many fine compositions in between these extremes, songs which needed an art such as his to raise them from the lower realms if not quite to enroll them among the highest.

VICTOR RED SEAL 1910-1912

64117	The Minstrel Boy (Moore).				(763)
64120	I Hear You Calling Me (Marshall).			(754)	(10-1436)
64127	When Shadows Gather (Marshall).				
64138	Annie Laurie (Scott).				(740)
64153	Dear Little Shamrock (Cherry).				(753)
64154	My Lagen Love (English).				
64174	Naughty Marietta: I'm falling in love.				(765)
64180	Believe Me if All Those Endearing Young Charms.				(746)
64181	Mother Machree (Ball).				(768)
64205	Macushla (MacMurrough).			(759)	(10-1436)
64250	Happy Morning Waits (Parelli).				
64252	Take, Oh Take Those Lips Away (Bennett).				(749)
64253	A Child's Song (Marshall).				
64254	A Farewell (Liddle).				
64255	I Know of Two Bright Eyes (Clutsam).				
64256	Eileen Aroon (MacMurrough).				
64257	The Rosary (Nevin).				(776)
64258	Wearing of the Green.				(788)
64259	Harp That Once Thro' Tara's Halls (Moore).				(746)
64260	Silver Threads Among the Gold (Danks).				(781)
74157	Killarney (Balfe).				(6199)
74158	Come Back to Erin (Claribel).				(6201)
74166	Snowy Breasted Pearl (Robinson).				(6201)
74175	Molly Bawn (Lover).				(6206)
74184	Has Sorrow Thy Young Days Shaded (Moore).				(6206)
74204	Drink to me only with thine eyes.				(6197)
74232	Ah Moon of My Delight (Lehmann).				(6197)
74236	Kathleen Mavourneen (Crouch).				(6199)
74237	Irish Emigrant (Baker).				(6207)
74242	She is Far from the Land (Moore).				(6207)
74243	An Evening Song (Blumenthal).				(6205)
74295	Natoma: Paul's Address.				
74296	Like Stars Above (Squire).				
74298	Maire, My Girl (Aitken).				
74299	Asthore (Trotere).				(6198)
87063	Lakme: Vieni al contento.	(64171)	(775)	(3029)	(10-1438)
87078	Li Marinari (Rossini) (w. Sammarco).	(87563)			
87082	Pearl Fishers: Del tempio (w. Sammarco).	(87553)			(10-1439)
88215	Lucia: Fra poco a me.	(74223)			(6196)
88216	Carmen: Canzone del fior.	(74218)			(6200)
88217	Elisir d'Amore: Una furtiva lagrima.	(74219)			(6204)
88218	Boheme: Che gelida manina.	(74222)			(6200)

88230	Faust: Salve dimora.	(74220)	(6203)
88245	Daughter of the Regiment: Per viver vicino.	(74221) (6203)	(15-1015)
88249	Lucia: Tu che a Dio.	(74224)	(6196)
89044	Boheme: Ah Mimi (w. Sammarco).		(15-1009)

VICTOR RED SEAL 1913-1915

64302	At Dawning (Cadman).	(742)
64303	Mefistofele: Dai campi.	(10-1438)
64304	Mefistofele: Giunto sul passo.	(923)
64305	Pearl Fishers: Mi par d'udire.	(923)
64307	Maritana: There is a flower.	(775) (10-1437)
64309	Sweet Genevieve (Tucker).	(780)
64310	My Dreams (Tosti).	(745)
64311	Where the River Shannon Flows (Russell).	(758)
64312	Manon: Il sogno.	(767)
64316	Molly Brannigan.	(743)
64317	Within the Garden of My Heart (Scott).	(764)
64318	Dear Love, Remember Me (Marshall).	(754)
64326	Foggy Dew (Clay).	(763)
64328	Say Au Revoir (Kennedy).	(780)
64329	Low Back'd Car (Lover).	(753)
64331	Down in the Forest (Ronald).	
64332	Mother o' Mine (Tours).	(776)
64333	Sospiri Miei (Bimboni).	
64340	I Hear a Thrush at Eve (Cadman).	(742)
64341	Eileen Allanna (Thomas).	(758)
64342	Good Bye, Sweetheart (Hatton).	(764) (10-1437)
64343	A Little Love (Silesu).	(771)
64344	Rigoletto: Questa o quella.	(767)
64345	Nearer, My God to Thee (Mason).	(773)
64374	Le Portrait (Parkyn).	
64375	I'll sing thee Songs of Araby (Clay).	(760)
64405	Somewhere a Voice is Calling (Tate).	(783)
64407	Mavis (Craxton).	(770)
64423	Come Where My Love Lies (Foster) (w. Cho.).	(751)
64424	Who Knows (Ball).	(789)
64425	Little Grey Home (Lohr).	(770)
64426	My Wild Irish Rose (Olcott).	(895)
64427	Bonnie Wee Thing (Lehmann).	(895)
64428	Beautiful Isle of Somewhere (Fearis).	(744)
64429	Golden Love (Wellings).	
64430	Because (d'Hardelot).	(745)
64431	Avourneen (King).	
64432	Mary of Argyle (Nelson).	(740)
64433	Ben Bolt (Kneass).	(747)
64434	A Dream (Bartlett).	(759)
64437	Funiculi Funicula (Denza) (w. Cho.).	(751)
64440	Lily of Killarney: The Moon (w. Werrenrath).	(3024)
64476	It's a Long, Long Way (Williams) (w. Cho.).	(896)
64495	Until (Sanderson).	(750)
64496	Evening Song (Hadley).	(760)
64497	When the Dew is Falling (Schneider).	(789)
64498	Morning (Speaks).	
64499	Vacant Chair (Washburn) (w. Cho.).	(896)
74328	Traviata: De' miei bollenti spiriti.	
74329	Nirvana (Adams).	
74345	Carmen: Parle-moi de ma mere (w. Marsh).	(8034)
74346	Good Bye (Tosti).	(6198)
74398	Aida: O terra addio (w. Marsh).	(8034)
74428	When My Ships Come Sailing Home (Dorel).	(6205)
74432	The Trumpeter (Dix).	(6209)
74434	Come into the Garden, Maud (Balfe).	(6202)

74435	Turn Ye to Me (Wilson).		
74436	Adeste Fideles (w. Cho).		(6208)
87191	Serenade (Schubert) (w. Kreisler).	(87545)	(3021)
87192	Ave Maria (Mascagni) (w. Kreisler).	(87546)	(3021)
87230	Serenata (Moszkowski) (w. Kreisler).	(87547)	(3018)
87231	Carme (de Curtis) (w. Kreisler).	(87548)	(3018)
87232	Flirtation (Meyer-Helmund) (w. Kreisler).	(87549)	(3022)
87233	Calm as the Night (Bohm) (w. Kreisler).	(87550)	(3023)
87512	Boheme: O soave fanciulla (w. Bori).	(3029)	(10-1439)
88453	Traviata: Parigi o cara (w. Bori). (89126)	(10006)	(15-1009)
88479	Angel's Serenade (Braga) (w. Kriesler).	(89103)	(8033)
88481	Ave Maria (Gounod) (w. Kreisler).	(89104)	(8032)
88482	Le Nil (Leroux) (w. Kreisler).	(89105)	
88483	Jocelyn: Berceuse (w. Kreisler).	(89106)	(8032)
88484	Ave Maria (Schubert) (w. Kreisler).	(89107)	(8033)
89080	Rigoletto: Quartet (w. Bori-Jacoby-Werrenrath).		(10006)

VICTOR RED SEAL 1916-1919

64532	Sing, Sing Birds on the Wing (Nutting).	(782)
64543	A Little Bit of Heaven (Ball).	(768)
64546	Forgotten (Cowles).	(761)
64549	Venetian Song (Tosti).	(786)
64559	Old Refrain (Kreisler).	(752)
64578	Parted (Tosti).	(757)
64599	Bohemian Girl: Then you'll remember me.	(747)
64603	Dreams (Strelezki).	(761)
64604	Your Eyes (Schneider).	(777)
64605	Little Boy Blue (Nevin).	(769)
64606	Cradle Song 1915 (Kreisler).	(752)
64622	Sunshine of Your Smile (Ray).	(783)
64623	Love Here is My Heart (Silesu).	(771)
64630	Tommy Lad (Margetson).	(769)
64631	When Irish Eyes are Smiling (Ball).	(788)
64664	Star Spangled Banner (Smith) (w. Cho.).	
64665	Eileen: Ireland My Sireland.	(756)
64666	Eileen: Eileen Alanna Asthore.	(756)
64694	There's a Long, Long Trail (Elliott).	(766)
64696	Keep the Home Fires Burning (Novello).	(766)
64699	Any Place is Heaven (Lohr).	(741)
64712	Crucifix (Faure) (w. Werrenrath).	(3024)
64726	Lord is My Light (Allitsen).	(744)
64732	Rainbow of Love (Ferrari).	(778)
64733	Trumpet Call (Sanderson).	
64741	Send Me Away With A Smile (Piantadosi).	
64773	God Be With Our Boys (Sanderson).	
64778	Little Mother of Mine (Burleigh).	(755)
64785	Dear Old Pal of Mine (Rice).	(755)
64787	Love's Garden of Roses (Wood).	(774)
64791	When You Come Back (Cohan).	
64796	My Irish Song of Songs (Sullivan).	(772)
64803	Calling Me Home to You (Dorel).	(750)
64814	When You Look in the Heart of a Rose (Methven).	(778)
64818	First Rose of Summer (Kern).	(762)
64825	Roses of Picardy (Wood).	(748)
74479	Meistersinger: Prize Song.	(6209)
74484	Don Giovanni: Il mio tesoro. (6204)	(15-1015)
74485	Kerry Dance (Molloy).	(6202)
74486	Non e ver (Mattei).	
74564	Joseph: Champs paternels.	
87245	Tales of Hoffmann: Barcarolle (w. Kreisler). (87551)	(3019)
87258	Serenade (Raff) (w. Kreisler). (87552)	(3019)

VICTOR RED SEAL 1920-1925

64837	That Tumble-Down Shack (Sanders).	(785)
64838	Only You (Schneider).	(777)
64860	Your Eyes Have Told Me So (Blaufuss).	(787)
64878	Barefoot Trail (Wiggers).	(741)
64900	Thank God for a Garden (Del Riego).	(786)
64901	Monsieur Beaucaire: Honour and Love.	(765)
64913	When You and I Were Young (Butterfield).	(781)
64925	'Tis an Irish Girl (Ball).	(784)
64926	Next Market Day; Ballynure Ballad (arr. Hughes).	(743)
64962	Beneath the Moon of Lombardy (Craxton).	(748)
64976	Somewhere (Waters).	(782)
64982	Learn to Smile (Hirsch).	(762)
64994	Little Town in Ould County Down (Sanders).	(772)
66012	Rose of My Heart (Lohr).	(779)
66024	Road That Brought You (Hamblen).	(779)
66028	Sweet Peggy O'Neil (Waldrop).	(784)
66080	Wonderful World of Romance (Wood).	(774)
66096	Semele: O Sleep.	(749)
66109	Three O'Clock in the Morning (Robledo).	(787)
66112	Mother in Ireland (Lyman).	(785)
66122	Jesus, My Lord.	(773)
66146	Kingdom Within Your Eyes (Nichols).	(757)
66162	Remember the Rose (Simons).	(918)
66163	Sometime You'll Remember (Head).	(918)
66189	Love Sends a Little Gift of Roses (Openshaw).	(961)
66190	Wonderful One (Grofe).	(961)
66198	Somewhere in the World (Ayer).	(968)
66199	Where the Rainbow Ends (Ayer).	(968)
66155	Bard of Armagh (Hughes).	(983)
66215	Would God I Were the Tender Apple Blossom (Page).	(983)
66242	Take a Look at Molly (Lockwood).	(1003)
66243	Sometime (Lockwood).	(1003)
66252	Marcheta (Schertzinger).	(1011)
66253	Indiana Moon (Jones).	(1011)
66267	A Love Song (Levey).	(1020)
66268	Little Yvette (Wood).	(1020)
	Bridal Dawn (Martin).	(1040)
	When (Benham).	(1040)
	Thanks Be to God (Dickson).	(1059)
	Dream Once Again (Squire).	(1059)
	All Alone (Berlin).	(1067)
	Rose-Marie (Friml).	(1067)
	Pur dicesti (Lotti).	(1081) (10-1435)
	Swans (Kramer).	(1081)
74791	Lost Chord (Sullivan).	(6208)
87571	When Night Descends (Rachmaninoff) (w. Kreisler).	(3020)
87573	Since You Went Away (Johnson) (w. Kreisler).	(3022)
87574	O Cease Thy Singing (Rachmaninoff) (w. Kreisler).	(3020)
87576	The Last Hour (Kramer) (w. Kreisler).	(3023)

Note: Also assigned numbers were recordings that included God's Hand (64548), Berceuse (64777), Flow Gently (w. Werrenrath) (74544). Recent issues of Heritage Series and a memorial album included the items noted above as 10- and 15- and others not previously released here on Victor including Atalanta: Come beloved and Mozart's Ridente la calma on 10-1434, Brahms' Feldeinsamkeit on 10-1435 and the Faust final trio (w. Melba-Sammarco) on 15-1019. Among the numerous Odeons of the 1906-1908 period, some of which appeared on Columbia-Fonotipia, were McCormack recordings of a typically wide variety, including Irish songs like The Croppy Boy on No. 57522 (Am. 33014).

MELBA, Nellie (Soprano)

Melba is the nearest thing to perfection in vocal technique and critics who
hail nothing but glissando and parlando in singing might do well to listen to her
recordings made at forty-five, fifty-five, even sixty-five and learn how Italian
arias, French art-songs and English ballads benefit alike from proper production.

IMPORTED VICTOR MAUVE LABEL 1904-1905

94001	Les Anges Pleurent (Bemberg).
94002	Chant Venetien (Bemberg).
94003	Come Back to Erin (Claribel).
94004	Auld Lang Syne.
94005	Old Folks at Home (Foster) (w. Trio).
94006	Good Night (Gatty) (w. Trio).
94007	Away on the Hill (Ronald).
95012	Good Bye (Tosti).
95013	Lucia: Mad scene.
95014	Traviata: Ah fors e lui.
95015	Traviata: Sempre libera.
95016	Penseroso: Sweet Bird.
95017	Three Green Bonnets (D'Hardelot).
95018	Rigoletto: Caro nome.
95019	Se Saran Rose (Arditi).
95020	Hamlet: A vos jeux.
95021	Hamlet: Pale et blonde.
95022	Mattinata (Tosti).
95023	Nymphes et Sylvains (Bemberg).
95024	Si Mes Vers (Hahn).
95025	Marriage of Figaro: Porgi amor.
95026	Home, Sweet Home (Bishop).
95027	Lo, Here the Gentle Lark (Bishop).
95028	Sur le lac (Bemberg).

VICTOR RED SEAL 1907-1909

88064	Traviata: Ah fors e lui.	
88065	Good Bye (Tosti).	
88066	Faust: Air des bijoux.	
88067	Marriage of Figaro: Voi che sapete.	
88068	Penseroso: Sweet Bird (flute by North).	
88069	Hamlet: A vos jeux.	
88070	Hamlet: Pale et blonde.	
88071	Lucia: Mad scene (flute by North).	
88072	Boheme: Addio.	
88073	Lo, Here the Gentle Lark (Bishop) (flute by North).	
88074	Boheme: Mi chiamano Mimi.	
88075	Tosca: Vissi d'arte.	
88076	Se Saran Rose (Arditi).	
88077	Mattinata (Tosti).	(6221)
88078	Rigoletto: Caro nome.	(6213)
88079	Serenata (Tosti).	(6221)
88080	Si Mes Vers (Hahn).	
88148	Otello: Salce, salce.	
88149	Otello: Ave Maria.	
88150	Ye Banks and Braes o' Bonnie Doon.	(6218)
88151	D'une prison (Hahn).	
88156	Believe Me If All Those Endearing Young Charms.	
88182	Oh Lovely Night (Ronald).	
89011	Per Valli (Blangini) (w. Gilibert).	
89012	Une Ange (Bemberg) (w. Gilibert).	
95200	Boheme: O soave fanciulla (w. Caruso).	

VICTOR RED SEAL 1910-1916

88064	Traviata: Ah fors e lui.		(6213)
88065	Good Bye (Tosti).		(6222)
88066	Faust: Air des bijoux.		(6215)
88067	Marriage of Figaro: Voi che sapete.		(6219)
88068	Penseroso: Sweet Bird (fl.-Lemmone).		(6214)
88071	Lucia: Mad Scene (fl.-Lemmone).	(6219)	(18143)
88072	Boheme: Addio.		(6210)
88073	Lo, Here the Gentle Lark (Bishop) (fl.-Lemmone).		(6214)
88074	Boheme: Mi chiamano Mimi.		(6210)
88075	Tosca: Vissi d'arte.		(6220)
88076	Se Saran Rose (Arditi).		(6220)
88148	Otello: Salce, salce.		(6211)
88149	Otello: Ave Maria.		(6211)
88182	Oh Lovely Night (Ronald).		(6222)
88250	Roi d' Ys: Vainement.		
88251	Hamlet: Des larmes de la nuit.		(6215)
88252	Don Cesar: Sevillana.	(88662)	(6216)
88449	Comin' thro' the Rye.		(6218)
88452	Magdalen at Michael's Gate (Lehmann).		
88454	Old Folks at Home (Foster).		(6217)
88455	John Anderson, My Jo (White).		
88456	Romance (Bourget); Mandoline (Debussy).		
88477	Louise: Depuis le jour.		(6216)
88485	Songs My Mother Taught Me (Dvorak).		
88551	Annie Laurie (Scott).		(6217)
89073	Ave Maria (Gounod) (w. Kubelik).		
89074	Re Pastore: L'Amero (w. Kubelik).		

Note: Few artists received such detailed announcements as Melba whose re-takes of previous recordings were openly heralded, as in the 1910 group above which are thus re-listed in exception to our general rule though the catalogue numbers remained unchanged. Other recordings given different numbers be-speaking re-takes in two instances include Oh Lovely Night (88157), Les Anges Fleurent and Chant Venetien (88457) and Songs My Mother Taught Me (88553). A reversal of usual roles is accomplished on purple seal Victor No. 70023 later blue seal No. 55111, where the prima donna sits at the piano to accompany her occasional obbl.gatist, John Lemmone, in a flute solo, By the Brook, by Wetzger.

MELCHIOR, Lauritz (Tenor)

Note: Danish catalogues of pre-World War I days carry this famous name among the baritone ranks. Later acoustics extended to his more customary range and included German recordings for several makes, his early Walkure: Siegmunds Liebeslied (2-7742) being imported here on Odeon No. 1011 and soon remade by him on electrical Brunswick and ever so many subsequent masters.

MENGELBERG, Willem (Conductor)

See NEW YORK PHILHARMONIC.

METZGER, Ottilie (Contralto)

COLUMBIA RECORDS 1914

Prophete: Ah mon fils.	(A5565)
Samson: Mon coeur.	(A5565)

Note: In contrast to her sparse representation here, Metzger made a great number of German recordings for various companies including Odeon, which released in 1908 familiar contralto items like the Carmen card song as No. 64905 and Gioconda: Voce di donna as No. 64913.

MICHAILOWA, Marie (Soprano)

IMPORTED VICTOR RED SEAL 1903

5045	Lucia: Mad Scene.		(91036)
5046	Serenade (Gounod).	(91037)	(61144)
5121	See'st Thou the Moon (Rubenstein) (w. Davidow).		(91060)
5126	Crucifix (Faure) (w. Orlow).		(91061)
91063	Pearl of Brazil: Charmant oiseau (in French).		

IMPORTED VICTOR RED SEAL 1905-1909

61126	Stormy Breezes (Edlichko).	(790)
61127	Birds are Gaily Singing (Rubenstein) (w. Turgarinoff).	
61128	The Handkerchief.	
61129	Lucia: Mad Scene.	
61130	Pearl of Brazil: Charmant oiseau.	
61131	Ave Maria (Gounod).	(790)
61132	Harold: Cradle Song.	
61133	Fateful Moment (Tschaikowsky).	
61134	Freischutz: Annie's Air.	
61135	In Silence (Gurilow) (w. Turgarinoff).	
61136	Pique Dame: O viens (w. Turgarinoff).	
61137	Doubt (Glinka) (w. Turgarinoff).	
61138	Traviata: Un di felice (w. Davidow).	
61139	Jocelyn: Berceuse.	
61140	Oh Sing to Me (Dlusski).	
61141	Rigoletto: Caro nome.	
61142	Russian Folk Song (Dargomischsky) (w. Turgarinoff).	
61143	Sea Gull's Cry (Grodski) (w. Turgarinoff).	
61178	Traviata: Addio del passato.	(901)
61179	Demon: The night is calm.	
61181	Let Joy Abide (Trojansky).	

Note: Although she recorded for other makes, it was Russian Gramophone
which presented Michailowa in a great galaxy of parts, sung, as are those above,
almost exclusively in Russian. Among the hundreds of her early recordings are
many from native works with such exotic titles as Boyarinya Vera Shiloga on
No. 2-23439 and Zabava Putiatishna on No. 2-23451.

MIURA, Tamaki (Soprano)

COLUMBIA RECORDS 1917

49260	Mme. Butterfly: Un bel di.	(60005D)
49265	Mme. Butterfly: O quanti occhi (w. Kittay).	(60005D)

Note: Further capitalizing on the Japanese background, which also impelled
the writing of an opera "Namiko San", Columbia issued songs in her native
language, one of which, when translated, read: Don't tie the pony to the cherry
tree (77496) (E4222).

MOORE, Grace (Soprano)

Note: Before shifting to Brunswick for electrical recordings, Moore made some
mementos of her pre-Metropolitan days on Victor black seal records. These
acoustic releases of 1925 were from the Music Box Revue in which she starred
at the time and include Tell Her in the Springtime and Listening on No. 19613
and Rock-a-bye Baby on one side of No. 19668.

MORESCHI, Alessandro (Soprano)
See SISTINE CHOIR.

Note: Moreschi was one of the last castrati and, as such, sings on several of
the early records made in the Sistine Chapel. On others, he appears in a directing
role.

MORINI, Erika (Violinist)

VICTOR RED SEAL 1921-1924

64979	Faust: Waltz (arr. Sarasate).	(791)
66038	Canzonetta (Godard).	(792)
66074	Am Springbrunnen (Cchumann).	(791)
66086	Valse Sentimentale (Schubert-Franko).	(792)
66153	Serenade (Toselli).	(957)
66186	June—Barcarolle (Tschaikowsky).	(957)
74686	Capriccio Valse (Wieniawski).	(6227)
74692	Romanza Andaluza (Sarasate).	(6226)
74717	Concerto Op. 22—Romance (Wieniawski).	(6227)
74727	Mazurka Op. 26 (Zarzycki).	(6445)
74797	Romance in G (Svendsen).	(6226)
74869	Carmen: Fantasie (arr. Sarasate).	(6445)
74888	Flower Song (Lange).	(6454)
74889	Hearts and Flowers (att. Tobani).	(6454)

MUCK, Karl (Conductor)
See BOSTON SYMPHONY ORCHESTRA.

MUZIO, Claudia (Soprano)
Note: Muzio was a great celebrity and won her largest audience toward the
end of her all too brief career when her electrical Columbia imports showed the
record buyers of this period what a prior era had been like. Her earliest appearance on discs here was likewise through import when Victor issued her 1911
Milan recording of Mi chiamano Mimi from Boheme as one side of Blue Seal
No. 55028. During the many years she sang in New York and Chicago, she re-
corded hill-and-dale discs for Edison and Pathe. The latter company, did, in
the 1920-1925 period, issue several of these as dubbings on Actuelle and later
Perfect records. Included among them were: Ernani: Ernani involami and Mme.
Butterfly: Ancora un passo on No. 025072 (11511); Trovatore: D'amor sull'ali
and Tosca: Vissi d'arte on No. 025087 (11523); Wm. Tell: Selva opaca and
Masked Ball: Ma dall'arido on No. 025104 (11540); Aida: O patria mia and
Gianni Schicchi: O mio babbino on No. 025106; Manon Lescaut; In quelle trine
and Trovatore: Tacea la notte on No. 025109.

NAVARRO, Inocencio (Baritone)

IMPORTED VICTOR RED SEAL 1916-1920

64573	Maruxa: Golondron.	(45239)
64738	La Adoracion (Gilabert) (w. Cho.).	(45238)
64739	Caminito de Belen (Monterde) (w. Cho.).	(45238)
64740	Crucifix (Faure).	(45239)
64865	La Mantilla (Alvarez).	(45240)
64866	Los Ojos Negros (Alvarez).	(45240)
74604	Goldene Kreuz: Brindis (w. Cho.).	(55137)

Note: Many other imports appeared on blue and black seal exclusively.

NEW YORK OPERA CHORUS
VICTOR RED SEAL 1906-1911

64047	Faust: Deponiam il brando.
64048	Cavalleria Rusticana: Gli aranci olezzano.
64049	Rigoletto: Scorrendo unite.
64050	Trovatore: Squilli e cheggi.
74213	Faust: Kermesse Scene.
74214	Faust: Deposons les armes.

Note: Choruses were usually relegated to lesser labels, even the name Metropolitan Opera, failing to raise slightly later issues above blue seal rank.

NEW YORK PHILHARMONIC ORCHESTRA (cond. Mengelberg)
VICTOR RED SEAL 1923-1925

66131	Les Preludes (part IV) (Liszt).	
66222	Le Rouet d'Omphale (part I) (Saint-Saens).	(989)
66223	Le Rouet d'Omphale (part II) (Saint-Saens).	(989)
	Symphony No. 5—Allegro (part I) (Beethoven).	(1069)
	Symphony No. 5—Allegro (part II) (Beethoven).	(1069)
74756	Coriolan Overture (part I) (Beethoven).	(6223)
74757	Coriolan Overture (part II) (Beethoven).	(6223)
74766	Oberon: Overture (part I).	(6224)
74767	Oberon: Overture (part II).	(6224)
74780	Les Preludes (part I) (Liszt).	(6225)
74781	Les Preludes (part II) (Liszt).	(6225)
74782	Les Preludes (part III) (Liszt).	(6373)
74838	Les Preludes (part IV) (Liszt).	(6373)
74816	Symphonie Pathetique (2d movement) (Tschaikowsky).	(6374)
74817	Symphonie Pathetique (4th movement) (Tschaikowsky).	(6374)
74844	Serenade Op. 48—Waltz (Tscnaikowsky).	(6427)
74845	Tales from the Vienna Woods (Strauss).	(6427)
74904	Athalia—War March (Mendelssohn).	(6464)
74905	Festival March (Halvorsen).	(6464)
	Rosamunde Overture (Schubert).	(6479)
	Rosamunde Entr'acte (Schubert).	(6479)

Note: Philharmonic recordings prior to the above were made on Columbia under Stransky's direction. The coming of Toscanini as conductor coincided with earliest Brunswick electrics.

NEY, Elly (Pianist)
BRUNSWICK RECORDS 1922-1925

Hungarian Dance No. 2 (Brahms).	(15021)
Nocturne in F Sharp Op. 15 No. 2 (Chopin).	(15021)
Soirees de Vienne (Schubert-Liszt).	(15024)
Hark Hark the Lark (Schubert-Liszt).	(15024)
Spinning Song (Mendelssohn); Moment Musical (Schubert).	(15036)
Ecossaises (Beethoven-d'Albert).	(15036)
Valse Petite (Carreno).	(15094)
Feux d'Artifice (Debussy).	(15094)
Etude Op. 10 No. 3 (Chopin).	(50032)
Hungarian Rhapsody No. 8 (Liszt).	(50032)

NIELSEN, Alice (Soprano)

From the opening of the Fortune Teller in 1898 right through her many successes in grand opera, Nielsen's work was marked by great sincerity and an outstanding ability for sustained song.

VICTOR RED SEAL 1907-1908

64068	Traviata: Addio del passato.	
64091	Romeo: Ne fuis pas (w. Constantino).	
74062	Boheme: Mi chiamano Mimi.	
74063	Rigoletto: E il sol (w. Constantino).	
74064	Lucia: Verranno a te (w. Constantino).	
74074	Barber of Seville: Una voce poco fa.	
74075	Traviata: Parigi o cara (w. Constantino).	(8035)
74076	Faust: Dammi ancor (w. Constantino).	(8035)
74087	Don Pasquale: Quel guardo.	
74107	Il Bacio (Arditi).	(6228)
74108	Romeo: Ange adorable (w. Constantino).	
74117	Daughter of the Regiment: Convien partir.	
74121	Martha: Last Rose of Summer.	(6228)

COLUMBIA RECORDS 1911-1915

19734	Sweet Adeline (Armstrong).	(A1143)	(54M)
19735	Darling Nelly Gray (Hanby).	(A1143)	(54M)
30579	Martha: Last Rose of Summer.		(A5283)
30580	Old Folks at Home (Foster).		(A5299)
30581	Marriage of Figaro: Voi che sapete.		(H1085)
30582	Bonnie Sweet Bessie (Gilbert).		(A5299)
30583	Don Giovanni: Batti, Batti.		(A5249)
30585	My Laddie (Thayer).		(A5401)
30586	Marriage of Figaro: Deh vieni.		(A5249)
30587	Faust: Le Roi de Thule.		(A5247)
30588	Annie Laurie (Scott).	(A5245)	(A6201)
30589	Kathleen Mavourneen (Crouch).	(A5245)	(A6201)
	From the Land of the Sky-Blue Water (Cadman).		(A5298)
	Sacrifice: Chonita's Prayer.		(A5298)
30591	Home, Sweet Home (Bishop).		(A5283)
30592	Il Bacio (Arditi).		(A5246)
30593	Mme. Butterfly: Ancora un passo.		(A5250)
30594	Mme. Butterfly: Piccolo Iddio.		(A5300)
30595	Mme. Butterfly: Un bel di.		(A5250)
30596	Boheme: Addio.		(A5246)
30597	Mefistofele: L'altra notte.		(A5248)
30598	Tosca: Vissi d'arte.		(A5248)
30599	Carmen: Je dis que rien.		(A5247)
30728	Mme. Butterfly: Ieri son salita.		(A5300)
30729	Good Bye (Tosti).		(A5401)
30737	Rigoletto: Si vendetta (w. Blanchart).		(A5301)
30738	Rigoletto: Tutte le feste (w. Blanchart).		(A5301)
30924	Faust: Tardi si fa (w. Zenatello).		(H1073)
30927	Sweet Genevieve (Cooper).		(A5425)
30941	In the Gloaming (Harrison).		(A5425)
37172	Oh, I'm not Myself (Lover).		(A5669)
37173	Believe Me If All Those Endearing Young Charms.		(A5678)
37174	Love's Old Sweet Song (Molloy).		(A5670)
37178	Bendemeer's Stream (Gatty).		(A5670)
37179	Day is Done (Spross).		(A5717)
37180	Spirit Flower (Tipton).		(A5717)
37184	Old Black Joe (Foster).		(A5678)
37202	Low Back'd Car (Lover).		(A5669)
37203	Killarney (Balfe).		(A5711)
37206	Barney O'Hea (Lover).		(A5711)
39874	By the Waters of Minnetonka (Lieurance).		(A1732)
39875	From the Land of the Sky-Blue Water (Cadman).		(A1732)

COLUMBIA RECORDS 1924

81648	A Little Coon's Prayer (Hope) (w. Qt.).	(30007D)
81649	Nebber Min' Mah Honey (Riker) (w. Qt.).	(30007D)

NIGHTINGALE (Bird)

IMPORTED VICTOR RED SEAL 1911

64161   Song of a Captive Nightingale.

Note: So effective was Herr Reich in his aviary at Bremen that Respighi included the results in his score for "The Pines of Rome."

NORDICA, Lillian (Soprano)

COLUMBIA RECORDS 1907-1911

30133	Gioconda: Suicidio.	(68082D)
30144	Hunyadi Laszlo: Ah regebes.	(68080D)
30483	Damon (Stange).	
30486	From the Land of the Sky-Blue Water (Cadman);	
	Mighty Lak' a Rose (Nevin).	(68081D)
30652	Tristan: Liebestod.	(68082D)
30653	Annie Laurie (Scott).	(68081D)
30657	Mandoline (Debussy).	
30661	Mignon: Io son Titania.	(68080D)
30677	Serenade (Strauss).	

Note: A host of unreleased Nordica items occasionally turn up in test pressings. Few of these or the recordings which actually were published here or abroad show her tremendous voice to advantage, a notable exception being her thrilling rendition of a very popular Hungarian aria in the original tongue.

NOTE, Jean (Baritone)

IMPORTED VICTOR RED SEAL 1903

5075	Herodiade: Vision fugitive.	(91045)
5084	Hamlet: Brindisi.	(91051)

Note: Among France's many highly prolific recorders, Note appeared here, on different occasions, in a variety of discs, too often of the sentimental and quasi-religious songs which seemed to have a ready market. His Credo du paysan, for instance, imported here as Victor black seal No. 98408 (63130) had been done for many labels of the 1900-1908 period, being also No. 1-5037 among his fifteen early Favorites.

NOVAES, Guiomar (Pianist)

VICTOR RED SEAL 1919-1924

64826	Feux-Follets (Philipp).	(793)
64879	Brazilian Tango (Levy).	(793)
64880	Guitarre (Moszkowski).	(794)
64939	Ruins of Athens—Turkish March (Beethoven).	(795)
64940	Spring Song (Mendelssohn).	(795)
64941	Mazurka in D Op. 33 No. 2 (Chopin).	(794)
66237	Dance of the Gnomes (Liszt).	(1000)
66238	Witches Dance (MacDowell).	(1000)
66130	La Jongleuse (Moszkowski).	(1001)
66239	Orfeo: Ballet des Ombres.	(1001)
74618	Gavotte (Gluck-Brahms).	(6229)
74675	Brazilian National Hymn Fantasie (part I) (Gottschalk).	(6372)
74676	Nocturne (Paderewski).	(6229)
74826	Brazilian National Hymn Fantasie (part II) (Gottschalk).	(6372)
74874	Murmuring Woods (Liszt).	(6444)
74875	Nocturne in G (Rubenstein).	(6444)

NUIBO, Francisco (Tenor)

VICTOR RED SEAL 1905

81057	Martha: Air des larmes.	(64015)
81058	Mignon: Elle ne croyait pas.	(64017)
81072	Mireille: Anges du Paradis.	(64016)
85041	Carmen: Air de la fleur.	(74012)
85075	Romeo: Ah, leve-toi, soleil.	(74013)

COLUMBIA RECORDS 1905

3127	Martha: Air des larmes.	(A545)
3128	Carmen: Air de la fleur.	
3129	Romeo: Ah, leve-toi, soleil.	
3130	Je ne pleurais (Queille).	
3138	Werther: Air de Werther.	

Note: Whether Spanish or French, as is variously claimed, Nuibo made good use of his short American stay and some of his Columbia discs remained long after his departure, in foreign series couplings.

OBER, Margarete (Contralto)

VICTOR RED SEAL 1914-1917

64442	Gioconda: Stella del marinar.
64443	Gioconda: Voce di donna.
64444	Heimweh (Wolf).
64445	An die Musik (Schubert).
64446	Ich liebe dich (Beethoven).
64447	Mit deinen blauen Augen (Brahms).
64448	Widmung (Schumann).
64449	Wiegenlied (Humperdinck).
64500	Liebestreu (Brahms).
64506	Trovatore: Stride la vampa.
64635	Fruhlingsglaube (Schubert).
74396	Rheingold: Weiche, Wotan (w. Werrenrath).
74397	Prophete: Ach, Mein Sohn.
74441	Dem Unendlichen (Schubert).
76031	Boris Godounow: Garden Scene (Ital.) (w. Althouse).

Note: No. 64612 was assigned to Allerseelen. Amid many German recordings were several duets with tenors, her partners in the familiar fourth act scene from Aida being changed from time to time. It was Jadlowker who opposed her on Odeon 99594 (Am. 35007), Jorn on Gr. 044265 (65478), Melchior on B25035 (72936).

OLITZKA, Rosa (Contralto)

COLUMBIA RECORDS 1912-1913

30834	Gioconda: Voce di donna.	(A5341)
30835	Samson: Printemps qui commence.	(A5369)
30836	Samson: Mon coeur.	(A5369)
30837	Agnus Dei (Bizet).	(A5428)
30838	Prophete: Ah mon fils.	(A5340)
30839	Cid: Pleurez mes yeux.	(A5379)
30840	Serse: Largo.	(A5341)
30847	Orfeo: Che faro senza Euridice.	(A5379)
30849	Tannhauser: Frau Holda.	(A5340)
30995	Sapho: O ma lyre immortelle.	(A5428)
38438	Ich liebe dich (Grieg).	(A1344)
38439	Pique Dame: O jeunes filles.	(A1344)

Note: Olitzka was quite an itinerant as well as an internationalist in the early days of recording and shows up in various capitals on several labels and in a variety of languages including English in which she sang Kathleen Mavourneen for Zonophone in 1904.

ONEGIN, Sigrid (Contralto)

BRUNSWICK RECORDS 1922-1925

Lucrezia Borgia: Brindisi.	(15039)	
Trovatore: Stride la vampa.	(15039)	
Auf dem Kirchhofe (Brahms).	(15048)	
Sapphische Ode (Brahms).	(15048)	
Es ist Bestimmt (Mendelssohn).	(15062)	(10132)
Der Lindenbaum (Schubert).	(15062)	(10132)
Exultate Jubilate: Alleluja (Mozart).	(15070)	(10135)
Wiegenlied (Mozart).	(15070)	(10135)
Vaggvisa (arr. Raucheissen).	(15073)	(10118)
Herdegossen (Berg).	(15073)	(10118)
The Blind Ploughman (Clarke).	(15083)	(10125)
The Fairy Pipers (Brewer).	(15083)	(10125)
Trovatore: Ai nostri monti (w. Chamlee).	(15093)	
Trovatore: Mal reggendo (w. Chamlee).	(15093)	
Caro Mio Ben (Giordani).		(10161)
Dormi pure (Scuderi).		(10161)
Carmen: Chanson Boheme.	(50018)	
Samson: Mon coeur.	(50018)	
Samson: Amour viens aider.	(50028)	
Prophete: Ah mon fils.	(50028)	
Orfeo: Che faro senza Euridice.	(50039)	
Gioconda: Voce di donna.	(50039)	

Note: Onegin's fluent vocalization enhanced a variety of schools and included among many imported acoustics, Evangelimann: O schone Jugendtage on Gr. 043372 (72720).

PADEREWSKI, Ignace Jan (Pianist)

Though he lived and recorded well into the electrical age, Paderewski's best pianism is to be found on these acoustics.

IMPORTED VICTOR RED SEAL 1912-1914

88321 Minuet in G (Paderewski).
88322 Valse Brilliante Op. 34 No. 1 (Chopin).
88357 Hark Hark the Lark (Schubert-Liszt).
88401 La Campanella (Paganini-Liszt).
88402 Etude in F Minor (Liszt).
88408 Maiden's Wish Op. 74 No. 1 (Chopin-Liszt).
88436 Chant d'Amour (Stojowski).
88444 Berceuse (Chopin).
88445 Aufschwung (Schumann).
88491 La Bandoline (Couperin).
88492 Carrillon de Cythere (Couperin).
88494 Warum (Schumann).

VICTOR RED SEAL 1917-1925

64706	Etude in G Flat Op. 25 No. 9 (Chopin).	(914)
66150	Spinning Song (Mendelssohn).	(914)
66160	Chant du Voyageur (Paderewski).	(917)
66161	Etude in G Sharp Minor Op. 25 No. 6 (Chopin).	(917)
	Mazurka in A Flat Op. 59 No. 2 (Chopin).	(1027)
	Mazurka in F Sharp Minor Op. 59 No. 3 (Chopin).	(1027)

74529	Nocturne in F Sharp Op. 15 No. 2 (Chopin).	(6233)
74530	Polonaise Militaire Op. 40 No. 1 (Chopin).	(6234)
74533	Minuet in G (Paderewski).	(6232)
74535	Cracovienne Fantastique (Paderewski).	(6230)
74539	Waltz in C Sharp Minor Op. 64 No. 2 (Chopin).	(6234)
74545	Nocturne in F Op. 15 No. 1 (Chopin).	(6233)
74655	Valse Brilliante Op. 34 No. 1 (Chopin).	(6389)
74656	Hark Hark the Lark (Schubert-Liszt).	
74657	La Bandoline (Couperin).	(6388)
74658	Warum (Schumann).	(6388)
74674	La Campanella (Paganini-Liszt).	(6389)
74765	Nocturne in B Flat (Paderewski).	(6232)
74777	Maiden's Wish Op. 74 No. 1 (Chopin-Liszt).	(6231)
74788	Hungarian Rhapsody No. 10 (Liszt).	(6231)
74796	Valse in A Flat Op. 42 (Chopin).	(6230)
74805	Hungarian Rhapsody No. 2 (part I) (Liszt).	(6235)
74806	Hungarian Rhapsody No. 2 (part II) (Liszt).	(6235)
74802	Berceuse Op. 57 (Chopin).	(6428)
74843	My Joys: Chant Polonais Op. 74 No. 5 (Chopin-Liszt).	(6428)
74862	Etude in A Minor Op. 25 No. 11 (Chopin).	(6438)
74863	Etude de Concert in F Minor (Liszt).	(6438)
74879	Etude in C Sharp Minor Op. 25 No. 7 (Chopin).	(6448)
74880	Mazurka in A Minor Op. 17 No. 4 (Chopin).	(6448)
	Funeral March (Chopin).	(6470)
	Hark Hark the Lark (Schubert-Liszt).	(6470)
	Impromptu in B Flat Op. 142 No. 3 (part I) (Schubert).	(6482)
	Impromptu in B Flat Op. 142 No. 3 (part II) (Schubert).	(6482)
	Reflets dans l'eau (Debussy).	(6538)
	Flying Dutchman—Spinning Song (arr. Liszt).	(6538)

PALET, Jose (Tenor)

IMPORTED VICTOR RED SEAL 1920-1923

64992	Dolores: Di que es verdad.	(927)
66015	Lucrezia Borgia: Di pescatore.	(927)
66088	Marina: Costa la de levante (part I) (w. Cho.).	(928)
66089	Marina: Costa la de levante (part II) (w. Cabrera-Rabazo-Cho.).	(928)
66113	Wm. Tell: Andiam, corriam (w. Cho.).	(919)
66114	Masked Ball: La rivedro (w. Cho.).	(919)
74637	Dolores: Jota (w. Cho.).	(6384)
74638	Marina: Duo Marina y Jorge (w. Farry).	(6384)
74731	Bruja: Jota (w. Cho.).	(6390)
74761	Gigantes y Cabezudos: Coro de repatriados.	(6390)
74773	Tempestad: Salve.	(6393)
74790	Meistersinger: Canto del examen.	(6393)

Note: Palet's early Fonotipia recordings were of a more Italianate complexion.

PAOLI, Antonio (Tenor)

Much admired by his fellow Puerto Ricans, Paoli was also the choice of Leoncavallo for the leading role in the recorded Pagliacci which he directed.

IMPORTED VICTOR RED SEAL 1908-1910

91073	Pagliacci: Versa il filtro (w. Huguet-Cigada-Pini-Corsi).	
91078	Samson: Figli miei.	
91080	Prophete: Re del ciel (w. Cho.).	
91081	Mlle. de Belle Isle: Si io t'amo.	
91082	Trovatore: Di geloso amor (w. Joanna-Cigada).	
92009	Pagliacci: Un grande spettacolo (w. Cigada-Pini-Corsi-Rosci-Cho.).	(89136) (8050)

92010	Pagliacci: Un tal gioco.		
92011	Pagliacci: Aitalo Signor (w. Huguet-Cigada-Pini-Corsi).		
92012	Pagliacci: No Pagliaccio.		
92013	Pagliacci: Finale (w. Huguet-Cigada-Pini-Corsi-Badini-Cho.).	(89137)	(8050)
92030	Africana: O Paradiso.		
92032	Trovatore: Di quella pira (w. Cho.).		
92035	Carmen: Mia tu sei (w. Salvador-Huguet-Cigada).	(89138)	
92048	Wm. Tell: Che finger tanto (w. Cigada).	(89148)	(8051)
92049	Trovatore: Miserere (w. Joanna-Cho.).		
92050	Carmen: Io t'amo ancor (w. Passeri-Cho.).	(89139)	
92051	Wm. Tell: Troncar suoi di (w. Cigada-Sillich).	(89149)	(8051)
88240	Otello: Dio mi potevi.		
88268	Aida: Nume custode (w. De Segurola-Cho.).	(89120)	(8037)

PARETO, Graziella (Soprano)

IMPORTED VICTOR RED SEAL 1909-1911

88224	Sonnambula: Ah non credea.	(76003)	(88607)
76006	Lucia: Mad Scene.		(88604)
76007	Rigoletto: Caro nome.		(88606)
76008	Voci di primavera (Strauss).		(88608) (6400)
76009	Lucia: Quando rapita.		(88605)
92505	Don Giovanni: La ci darem (w. Ruffo).		(8053)
92506	Rigoletto: Lassu in ciel (w. Ruffo).		(8053)

IMPORTED VICTOR RED SEAL 1921

88630	Don Pasquale: Quel guardo.	(6401)
88631	Pearl Fishers: Siccome un di.	(6401)
88632	Il Bacio (Arditi).	(6400)
88641	Marriage of Figaro: Deh vieni.	(6402)
88642	O Bimba Bimbetta (Sibella).	(6402)

Note: Other imports exist from both early and late periods and include Catalonian songs like L'Hereu Riera and others.

PARVIS, Taurino (Baritone)

COLUMBIA RECORDS 1905-1906

3079	Pagliacci: Prologo.		(A531)
3080	Occhi di fata (Denza).		(A527)
3113	Ernani: O de verd' anni miei.		(A540)
3114	Giulia (Denza).		
3115	Amore (Tirindelli).	(A529)	(A868)
3123	Falstaff: Quand'ero paggio.		
3124	Carmen: Canzone del Toreador.		
3125	Traviata: Pura siccome un angelo.		
3126	Rigoletto: Deh non parlare.		
3139	Trovatore: Il balen.		
3140	Carmen: Canzone del Toreador.		(A543)
3141	Pagliacci: Prologo.	(30000)	(A5011)
3159	Mattinata (Leoncavallo).	(A530)	(A868)
3168	Barber of Seville: Largo al factotum.	(A537)	(A860)

For other records, see CIAPARELLI

Note: Aside from Nos. 3123-26 which were issued only in seven-inch form, most of the above appeared in various foreign series couplings, as did the scores of imported Columbias including Musica Pro'bita on No. 10814 (C737). His work for many other companies, especially Zonophone, ran the gamut of the customary baritone repertoire both in opera like Forza del Destino on No. 12598 and Italian canzone like Mascagni's Serenata on No. 12560.

PATTI, Adelina (Soprano)

As early as 1890, cylinders by Patti, her tenor-husband Niccolini and other members of her own company were sold by the Metropolitan Phonograph Company of New York. Though fifteen years later found her well past sixty when she recorded the items below among others, the loveliness of quality and beauty of style that had always marked her long, triumphant career is still apparent.

IMPORTED VICTOR PATTI RED SEAL RECORDS 1906

95029	Home, Sweet Home (Bishop).
95030	Martha: Last Rose of Summer.
95031	Robin Adair (Keppel).
95032	Comin' thro' the Rye.
95033	Old Folks at Home (Foster).
95034	Within a Mile of Edinboro' (Hook).
95035	Kathleen Mavourneen (Crouch).
95036	Si vous n'avez rien (Rothschild).
95037	Faust: Air des bijoux.
95038	Serenata (Tosti).
95039	Don Giovanni: Batti, batti.
95040	Pur dicesti (Lotti).
95041	Marriage of Figaro: Voi che sapete.
95042	On Parting (Patti).

PATTIERA, Tino (Tenor)

BRUNSWICK RECORDS 1921-1925

10048	Tosca: Recondita armonia.	
	Trovatore: Di quella pira.	(15019)
	Gioconda: Cielo e mar.	(15019)
	Pagliacci: Vesti la giubba.	(15044)
	Tosca: E lucevan le stelle.	(15044)

PHILADELPHIA SYMPHONY ORCHESTRA, (cond. Stokowski)

VICTOR RED SEAL 1917-1925

64752	Hungarian Dance No. 5 (Brahms).	(797)
64753	Hungarian Dance No. 6 (Brahms).	(797)
64768	Peer Gynt—Anitra's Dance (Grieg).	(799)
64822	Carmen: Prelude to Act I.	(796)
66058	Minuet (Boccherini).	(798)
66098	Moment Musical Op. 94 No. 3 (Schubert).	(799)
66106	March of the Cauccasian Chief (Ippolitow-Ivanow).	(796)
66128	Nutcracker Suite—Dance of the Flutes (Tschaikowsky).	(798)
66171	Faust: Waltz from Kermesse.	(944)
66172	Mignon: Gavotte.	(944)
66263	Carmen: Soldiers Changing the Guard.	(1017)
66264	Carmen: March of the Smugglers.	(1017)
	Prelude in E Minor Op. 28 No. 4 (Chopin).	(1111)
	Song Without Words Op. 40 No. 6 (Tschaikowsky).	(1111)
	Dance of the Amazon (Liadow).	(1112)
	Fireworks (Stravinsky).	(1112)
	Hungarian Dance No. 1 (Brahms).	(1113)
	L'Arlesienne Suite No. 2—Spanish Dance (Bizet).	(1113)
74560	Midsummer Night's Dream—Scherzo (Mendelssohn).	(6238)
74567	Orfeo: Dance of the Spirits.	(6238)
74593	Scheherazade—Festival at Bagdad (Rimsky-Korsakoff).	(6246)
74598	Invitation to the Waltz (Weber).	(6237)
74602	Rienzi: Overture (part I).	(6239)
74603	Rienzi: Overture (part II).	(6239)

74609	Symphony No. 40—Menuetto (Mozart).	(6243)
74621	Espana (Chabrier).	(6241)
74627	Blue Danube (Strauss).	(6237)
74631	'New World' Symphony—Largo (Dvorak).	(6236)
74647	Hungarian Rhapsody No. 2 (Liszt).	(6236)
74661	Eighth Symphony—Allegretto (Beethoven).	(6243)
74671	Samson: Bacchanale.	(6241)
74684	Walkure: Ride of the Valkyres.	(6245)
74691	Scheherazade—Young Prince (Rimsky-Korsakoff).	(6246)
74698	Finlandia (Sibelius).	(6366)
74713	Symphony Pathetique—March; Scherzo (Tschaikowsky).	(6242)
74722	Symphony No. 3—Poco allegretto (Brahms).	(6242)
74729	Salome: Salome's Dance (part I).	(6240)
74730	Salome: Salome's Dance (part II).	(6240)
74736	Walkure: Magic Fire Music.	(6245)
74758	Tannhauser: Overture (part I).	(6244)
74759	Tannhauser: Overture (part II).	(6244)
74768	Tannhauser: Overture (part III).	(6478)
74803	Khowantchina: Entr'acte.	(6366)
74814	Viennese Dances (Schubert).	
74846	Symphony No. 5—Andante (part I) (Tschaikowsky).	(6430)
74847	Symphony No. 5—Andante (part II) (Tschaikowsky).	(6430)
74848	Symphony No. 5—Andante (part III) (Tschaikowsky).	(6431)
74849	Snow Maiden: Dance of Tumblers.	(6431)
74894-99	Unfinished Symphony (Schubert).	(6459/60/61)
	Tannhauser: Fest March.	(6478)
	Afternoon of a Faun (part I) (Debussy).	(6481)
	Afternoon of a Faun (part II) (Debussy).	(6481)
	Lohengrin: Prelude (part I).	(6490)
	Lohengrin: Prelude (part II).	(6490)
	Firebird Suite (Stravinsky).	(6492/93)

For other records, see RACHMANINOFF

Note: Catalogue numbers were also assigned to Tschaikowsky's Nutcracker Suite (64767), and Symphonie Pathetique (74565) (74566).

PIETRACEWSKA, Carolina (Contralto)

IMPORTED VICTOR RED SEAL 1910-1911

88225	Masked Ball: Re dell'abisso.	(76005)
88269	Aida: Gia i sacerdoti (w. Barrera).	

Note: Another typical role found her joined by chorus in Gioconda: Voce di donna on Gr. No. 053238.

PIMAZZONI, Giuseppe (Baritone)

COLUMBIA RECORDS 1909-1910

4133	Pagliacci: Prologo.	(H24)
4134	Masked Ball: Eri tu.	(A857)
4135	Carmen: Canzone del Toreador.	(A765)
4139	Don Giovanni: Serenata.	(H24)
4140	Gioconda: Ah Pescator.	(H25)
4141	Traviata: Di Provenza.	(A857)
4143	Trovatore: Il balen.	(A764)
4144	Ernani: O de' verd' anni miei.	(H26)
4145	Dinorah: Sei vendicata assai.	(A765)
4146	Faust: Dio possente.	(A764)
4147	Stabat Mater: Pro peccatis.	(A763)
4148	Ave Maria (Luzzi).	(A763)

Note: Where domestic couplings were not made at the time, the H series numbers are given above.

PINZA, Ezio (Bass)

IMPORTED VICTOR RED SEAL 1925

Mignon: Ninna-Nanna.	(1103)
Favorita: Splendon piu belle (w. Cho.).	(1103)
Favorita: Non sai tu (w. D'Alessio).	(1130)
Mefistofele: Son lo spirito.	(1130)
Forza del Destino: Il santo speco (w. Cho.).	(1131)
Norma: Ah del tebro (w. Cho.).	(1131)
Trovatore: Di due figli.	(6515)
Juive: Voi che del Dio.	(6515)

PLANCON, Pol (Bass)

The most cultivated inhabitant of the lower bass clef on records was undoubtedly the great Pol Plancon. When he runs up and down the scales of the drum-major air from Le Caid, one would think that all bassos were supposed to have beauty of tone, agility of movement and refinement of taste.

IMPORTED VICTOR RED SEAL 1903

5017	Caid: Air du Tambour-Major.	(91015)
5018	Philemon: Au bruit.	
5019	Deux Grenadiers (Schumann).	(91016)
5021	Faust: Le Veau d'or.	(91017)
5022	Faust: Serenade.	(91018)

VICTOR RED SEAL 1904-1905

81023	Noel (Adam).	
81033	Stabat Mater: Pro peccatis.	
81034	Damnation of Faust: Serenade.	
81035	Romeo: Couplets de Capulet.	
81037	Chalet: Vallons de l'Helvetie.	
81038	Faust: Le Veau d'or.	
81039	Embarquez-vous (Godard).	
81040	Faust: Serenade.	(800)
81056	Philemon: Au bruit.	
81065	Dinorah: Chant du Chasseur.	
81066	Credo (Faure).	
81073	Le Soupir (Bemberg).	
81076	Si tu veux (Massenet).	
85018	Sonnambula: Vi ravviso.	
85019	Caid: Air du Tambour-Major.	
85020	Les Rameaux (Faure).	
85023	Le Lac (Neidermeyer).	
85024	Deux Grenadiers (Schumann).	
85042	Magic Flute: O Isis.	(6371) (15-1007)
85064	Le Vallon (Gounod).	
85065	Jesus de Nazareth (Gounod).	(6248)
85066	Lazzarone (Ferrari); Filibustier (Georges).	(15-1007)
85076	Le Cor (Flegier).	
85077	Magic Flute: Qui sdegno.	
85082	Seasons: Air du Laboureur.	

VICTOR RED SEAL 1906-1908 (orch. acc.)

88034	Caid: Air du Tambour-Major.	(85019) (18143)
81034	Damnation of Faust: Serenade.	(800)
81038	Faust: Le Veau d'or.	
81086	Martha: Canzone del porter.	
81087	Damnation of Faust: Chanson de la puce.	
85020	Les Rameaux (Faure).	(6347)

85024	Deux Grenadiers (Schumann).	(6247)	
85099	Noel (Adam).	(6248)	
85100	Faust: Serenade.		
85116	Don Carlos: Elle ne m'aime pas.		
85117	Damnation of Faust: Voici des roses.		
85119	Caid: Air du Tambour-Major.	(6247)	
85124	Etoile du Nord: O jours heureux.		
85125	Robert: Nonnes qui reposez.	(6371)	
85126	Mignon: Ninna-Nanna.		
95300	Faust: Alerte (w. Eames-Dalmores).		

PONSELLE, Rosa (Soprano)

No more lush outpouring of sound has been heard in our times than the Ponselle voice at its prime. You held your breath lest it break in its consistency but it never did, and that constitutes the amazing achievement which separates true greatness from occasional merit, such greatness as has all but vanished in less than two decades.

COLUMBIA RECORDS 1919-1923

49557	Aida: O patria mia.	(68036D)	(8910M)
49558	Forza del Destino: La vergine (w. Cho.).	(68038D)	(8910M)
49559	Trovatore: D'amor sull'ali.	(68058D)	(8909M)
49560	Good Bye (Tosti).	(68064D)	(7038M)
49569	Tosca: Vissi d'arte.	(68059D)	(7065M)
49570	Cavalleria Rusticana: Voi lo sapete.	(68039D)	(8909M)
49571	Mme. Butterfly: Un bel di.	(68059D)	(7065M)
49585	Keep the Home Fires Burning (Novello) (w. Cho.).		(7038M)
49686	Vespri Siciliani: Bolero.	(68037D)	
49720	Norma: Casta diva.	(68060D)	(7063M)
49734	Aida: O terra addio (w. Hackett).	(71000D)	(9010M)
49735	Gioconda: Suicidio.	(63039D)	(7034M)
49859	Forza del Destino: Pace, Pace.	(68038D)	(7033M)
49869	Mlle. Modiste: Kiss Me Again.	(68077D)	(7061M)
49870	Maria Mari (di Capua).	(68064D)	(7035M)
49920	Sadko: Song of India.	(68077D)	(7061M)
49922	Trovatore: Mira d'acerbe (w. Stracciari).	(71000D)	(9010M)
49925	Rachem (Manna-Zucca).		(7025M)
49934	Old Folks at Home (Foster).	(68065D)	(7064M)
49935	Home Sweet Home (Bishop).	(68065D)	(7064M)
49982	Maritana: Scenes that are brightest.	(68078D)	(7062M)
49983	O Sole Mio (di Capua) (w. C. Ponselle).		(9007M)
49988	Blue Danube (Strauss).	(68078D)	(7062M)
78325	Whispering Hope (Hawthorne) (w. B. Maurel).	(36000D)	(2019M)
78557	Abide With Me (Monk) (w. B. Maurel).	(36000D)	
78846	Tales of Hoffmann: Barcarolle (w. C. Ponselle).	(36001D)	
78847	Comin' thro' the Rye (w. cadenza) (w. C. Ponselle).	(36002D)	
78920	Values (Vanderpool).		
79971	Manon Lescaut: In quelle trine.	(36001D)	(2014M)
79980	Little Alabama Coon (Starr) (w. Qt.).	(33003D)	(2024M)
80307	Rose of My Heart (Lohr).	(33003D)	(2024M)
80392	Where My Caravan Has Rested (Lohr) (w. C. Ponselle).	(36002D)	(2019M)
98028	Ernani: Ernani involami.	(68037D)	(7034M)
98029	Otello: Ave Maria.	(68060D)	(7063M)
98051	Trovatore: Tacea la notte.	(68036D)	(7033M)
98058	Wm. Tell: Selva opaca.	(68058D)	(7026M)
98059	Africana: In grembo a me.	(68000D)	
98062	Boheme: Mi chiamano Mimi.	(68000D)	(7035M)
98063	Pagliacci: Ballatella.	(68084D)	(7066M)
98092	Aida: Ritorna vincitor.	(68084D)	(7066M)

VICTOR RED SEAL 1924-1925

66240	Cradle Song (Brahms).	(1002)
66241	Lullaby (Scott).	(1002)
66255	Maria, Mari (di Capua).	(1013)
66256	Carme (de Curtis).	(1013)
	Love's Sorrow (Shelley).	(1057)
	My Lovely Celia (Higgins).	(1057)
74860	Aida: Ritorna vincitor.	(6437)
74861	Aida: O patria mia.	(6437)
74866	Forza del Destino: Pace, Pace.	(6440)
74867	Ernani: Ernani involami.	(6440)
74886	Goodbye (Tosti).	(6453)
74887	Serenade (Tosti).	(6453)
	Otello: Ave Maria.	(6474)
	Otello: Salce, salce.	(6474)
	Africana: In grembo a me.	(6496)
	Gioconda: Suicidio.	(6496)

Note: **Columbia No. 7065M was later changed to 5095M. There is more than one "take" on some of the items above and, of course, several selections like Oberon which remained unpublished.**

POWELL, Maud (Violinist)

Lady violinists were common even in Maud Powell's day but, like most, she asked no special indulgence, nor did the many composers who dedicated difficult and important compositions to her.

VICTOR RED SEAL 1905-1912

81051	Slavonic Cradle Song (Neruda).	(64027)	(809)
81052	Polonaise (Vieuxtemps).	(64028)	(809)
64073	Minuet in D (Mozart).		(805)
64074	Souvenir (Drdla).		(808)
64075	Orfeo: Melodie.		(807)
64076	The Bee (Schubert); Minute Waltz (Chopin).		(810)
64103	At the Brook (Boisdeffre).		(801)
64104	Mazurka (Zarzycki).		(805)
64134	Traumerei (Schumann).		
64143	Dixie (Emmett).		
64227	Serse: Largo.		(804)
64262	Zigeunerweisen (Sarasate).		(811)
64264	To Spring (Grieg).		(810)
64265	Le Cygne (Saint-Saens).		(801)
64281	Serenata (Moszkowski).		(807)
64300	Marionettes (Gilbert).		
64301	Caprice (Ogarew).		(806)
85039	St. Patrick's Day (Vieuxtemps).	(74025)	(6254)
85040	Concerto in E Minor—Finale (Mendelssohn).	(74026)	(6252)
74135	Thais: Meditation.		(6255)
74173	Capriccio Valse (Wieniawski).		(6250)
74177	Ave Maria (Schubert).		(6249)
74179	Concerto Op. 22—Romance (Wieniawski).		(6252)
74183	Will-o'-the-Wisp (Sauret).		(6258)
74188	Zephyr (Hubay).		
74246	Deep River (Coleridge-Taylor).		(6253)
74259	Spanish Dance Op. 26 No. 8 (Sarasate).		(6254)
74283	Cavatina (Raff).		(6251)
74324	Hejre Kati (Hubay).		(6258)
74325	Have Pity, Sweet Eyes (Tenaglia).		(6378)
74326	Kujawik (Wieniawski).		(6250)

VICTOR RED SEAL 1913-1917

64373	Salut d'amour (Elgar).	(802)
64454	Mignon: Gavotte (arr. Sarasate).	(803)
64457	Tales of Hoffmann: Barcarolle.	(802)
64458	Chanson a Bercer (Schmitt).	
64459	Silver Threads Among the Gold (Danks).	(808)
64520	Tambourin (Leclair).	
64521	Gondoliers (Saar).	
64611	Molly on the Shore (Grainger).	(811)
64615	Love's Delight (Martini).	
64617	Petite Valse (Herbert).	
64618	Sonata in E—Second Movement (Bach).	
64619	Sonata in E—Fourth Movement (Bach).	
64620	Minuet in G (Beethoven).	(804)
64621	Guitarrero (Drdla).	(803)
64705	Little Firefly (Cadman).	
64734	Poupee Valsante (Poldini-Hartmann).	(806)
74354	Minuet (Boccherini).	
74355	Kol Nidre (Bruch).	(6256)
74357	Bourree (Bach); Menuetto (Gluck).	
74402	Valse Triste (Sibelius).	(6256)
74408	Twilight (Massenet); Musette (Sibelius).	
74412	Serse: Largo.	(6249)
74446	Concerto in G—Allegro Maestoso (de Beriot).	(6378)
74447	Rosamunde—Entr'acte (Schubert).	
74492	Concerto in G—Andante Tranquillo (de Beriot).	
74493	Concerto in G—Allegro Moderato (de Beriot).	(6257)
74494	Humoresque (Dvorak).	(6255)
74531	Fifth Nocturne (Leybach).	(6251)
74547	Four American Folk Songs.	(6253)
74548	Elegie (Massenet); Maiden's Wish (Chopin).	(6257)

Note: **Other selections also assigned catalogue numbers include Little Red Lark (64208), Arkansaw Traveler (64211), Berceuse from Jocelyn (64435), Gems from La Boheme (74546).**

RACHMANINOFF, Sergei (Pianist)

The true greatness of musical giants is often one of personal integrity and Rachmaninoff reveals this in all his work even amid the technical dexterity, so brilliant yet unforced and so clear and even in all voices.

VICTOR RED SEAL 1920-1925

64906	Lilacs (Rachmaninoff).	(1051)
64919	Le Coucou (Daquin).	(812)
64921	Spinning Song (Mendelssohn).	(814)
64935	Dr. Gradus ad Parnassum (Debussy).	(813)
64963	Prelude in G Sharp Minor Op. 32 No. 12 (Rachmaninoff).	(812)
64971	Waltz in D Flat Op.. 64 No. 1 (Chopin).	(815)
64980	Golliwogg's Cake-Walk (Debussy).	(813)
66007	Waltz in G Flat Major (Chopin).	
66016	Prelude in C Sharp Minor Op. 3 No. 2 (Rachmaninoff).	(814)
66059	Etude in F Minor (Dohnanyi).	(943)
66085	L'Arlesienne Suite—Minuet (Bizet).	(316)
66105	Waltz and Elfin Dance (Grieg).	(815)
66129	Serenade Op. 3 No. 5 (Rachmaninoff).	(816)
66154	La Jongleuse (Moszkowski).	(943)
66138	Waltz in A Flat Op. 40 No. 8 (Tschaikowsky).	(972)
66202	Waltz in B Minor Op. 69 No. 2 (Chopin).	(972)
66248	Mazurka in C Sharp Minor Op. 63 No. 3 (Chopin).	(1008)
66249	If I Were a Bird (Henselt).	(1008)
	Humoresque (Tschaikowsky).	(1051)

74628	Prelude in G Minor Op. 23 No. 5 (Rachmaninoff).	(6261)
74630	Troika en traineaux (Tschaikowsky).	(6260)
74645	Prelude in G Major Op. 32 No. 5 (Rachmaninoff).	(6261)
74679	Waltz in E Flat Op. 18 (Chopin).	(6259)
74723	Liebeslied (Kreisler-Rachmaninoff).	(6259)
74728	Polka de W. R. (Rachmaninoff).	(6260)
74807	Polichinelle (Rachmaninoff).	(6452)
74885	Nocturne in F Sharp Minor Op. 15 No. 2 (Chopin).	(6452)
89166-71	Concerto No. 2—Second and Third Movements (Rachmaninoff)	
	(w. Philadelphia Symphony) (6 parts).	(8064/5/6)

RAISA, Rosa (Soprano)

During a career which received its first great acclaim when she appeared as Rosa Raisa Burstein at the Parma festival in 1913, its longest in Chicago and its most noteworthy the night she created Turandot under Toscanini, this dramatic singer spent little time in recording studios and that to exceedingly poor advantage. Only a spot or two of the records below, as in the plaintive air from Mefistofele, give a just indication of a huge voice of tremendous power with great range and flexibility.

VOCALION RECORDS 1920-1924

30101	Eili Eili.	
30108	Don Giovanni: La ci darem (w. Rimini).	(60019)
30115	Vespri Siciliani: Bolero.	(60047)
30134	Ye Who Have Yearned Alone (Tschaikowsky).	
30155	Tosca: Vissi d'arte.	(60047)
30160	Kalinka (Russian).	(60036)
30165	Night (Russian).	(60036)
52007	Otello: Ave Maria.	(70018)
52013	Forza del Destino: Pace, Pace.	(70018)
52023	Aida: La fatal pietra (w. Crimi).	
52031	Crucifix (Faure) (w. Rimini).	(70032)
52043	Aida: O terra addio (w. Crimi).	(70034)
52048	Cavalleria Rusticana: Voi lo sapete.	(70031)
52051	La Paloma (Yradier).	(70031)
55001	Norma: Casta diva.	
55007	Trovatore: Miserere (w. Crimi-Cho.).	
55010	Trovatore: Miserere (w. Tokatyan-Cho.).	(70032)
	Aida: Ritorna vincitor.	(70007)
	Aida: O patria mia.	(70007)
	Gioconda: Suicidio.	(70034)
	Mefistofele: L'altra notte.	(70036)
	Mme. Butterfly: Un bel di.	(70036)
	Ernani: Ernani involami.	(70039)
	Trovatore: Mira d'acerbe (w. Rimini).	(70039)

REGIS, Georges (Tenor)
IMPORTED VICTOR RED SEAL 1909-1910

61192	Wm. Tell: Barcarolle.	(45026)
61193	Mignon: Elle ne croyait pas.	(45023)
64145	Villanelle (Reber).	(45024)
64146	Dragons de Villars: Ne parle pas.	(45024)
64147	Mignon: Adieu Mignon.	(45023)
64148	Parais a ta fenetre (Gregh).	(45025)
64149	Illusion (Barbirolli).	(45025)

Note: Other imports were issued directly on black and blue seal Victors, none, however, from L'Attaque du Moulin, in which Regis sang Le Sentinelle at the Metropolitan Opera, advancing Clement, the creator of this role, to that of Dominique.

REIMERS, Paul (Tenor)

As soloist on Blue Seal records, Reimers gave his intimate and delightful interpretations of such songs as Schumann's Du bist wie eine Blume on No. 45060; Phyllis und die Mutter and To Mary (White) on No. 45062; Coeur de ma mie (Dalcroze) and Dimanche a l'aube (Ducourdray) on No. 45063; Wohin (Schubert) and Auf Flugeln des Gesanges (Mendelssohn) on No. 45065; I Wonder How the Old Folks are at Home and Memories (Van Alstyne) on No. 45134; and Schubert's Standchen on No. 55045. His art at duet singing was earlier evidenced in European Odeon recordings with Culp.

For duets, see GLUCK.

REISS, Albert (Tenor)

VICTOR RED SEAL 1911

64187 Gasparone: Er soll dein Herr.
64188 Hansel: Hexenritt.
64214 Schon war's doch: Nord-Express.
64215 Siegfried: Wohin schleichst (w. Goritz).
74235 Siegfried: Zwangvolle Plage.

For other records, see GADSKI.

Note: While he set a standard for Mime, which is matched only by his own electrical recordings from the Ring, Reiss made a number of unpublished items from other works. As a manager, he was gratefully remembered for performances of neglected Mozart works such as Bastien et Bastienne and Impressario.

RENAUD, Maurice (Baritone)

The rich vibrance of Renaud's voice makes phonographs rattle; his characterizations made critics rejoice.

IMPORTED VICTOR RED SEAL 1903

5031 Roi de Lahore: Promesse de mon avenir. (91026)
5035 Favorita: Pour tant amour. (91027)
5036 Tannhauser: O douce etoile. (91028)

IMPORTED VICTOR RED SEAL 1907

91066 Hamlet: Comme une pale fleur.
91067 Tannhauser: O douce etoile. (614)
91068 Wm. Tell: Sois immobile.
91069 Rondel de l'adieu (de Lara).
91070 Noel Paien (Massenet).
91072 Le Soir (Gounod). (614)
92002 Roi de Lahore: Promesse de mon avenir. (15-1021)
92003 Herodiade: Vision fugitive. (15-1021)

RENNYSON, Gertrude (Soprano)

COLUMBIA RECORDS 1912

30987 Tannhauser: Dich teure Halle. (A5427)
30988 Lohengrin: Elsas Traum. (A5427)
30989 Elijah: Hear Ye Israel (part I). (A5407)
30990 Elijah: Hear Ye Israel (part II). (A5407)

Note: This alumna of Bayreuth also appeared on several minor labels, particularly of the "hill-and-dale" variety.

RETHBERG, Elisabeth (Soprano)

So many stars of today have momentary excellence, marred by uncontrollable lapses into bad singing. When Rethberg was at the height of her vocal powers, no tones were unlovely, no notes slighted, no words shrieked. No musicians were then offended, no audiences apathetic.

BRUNSWICK RECORDS 1924-1925

Standchen (Schubert).	(15069)	(10134)
Solvejgs Gesang (Grieg).	(15069)	(10134)
Ich liebe dich (Grieg).	(15082)	(10124)
Canzonetta (Loewe).	(15082)	(10124)
Ave Maria (Gounod).		(10163)
Auf Flugeln des Gesanges (Mendelssohn).		(10163)
Au Printemps (Gounod).		(10166)
Nur Wer Die Sehnsucht Kennst (Tschaikowsky) (cello. Willeke)		(10166)
Angel's Serenade (Braga) (viol. Fradkin).		(10189)
Elegy (Massenet) (viol. Fradkin).		(10189)
Aida: O patria mia.	(50043)	
Aida: Ritorna vincitor.	(50043)	
Andrea Chernier: La mamma morta.	(50054)	
Boheme: Mi chiamano Mimi.	(50054)	
Tosca: Vissi d'arte.	(50065)	
Mme. Butterfly: Un bel di.	(50065)	

Note: Among Rethberg's acoustic Odeons were a number of duets with Tauber including Mme. Butterfly: Die prunkende on No. 80732.

RIMINI, Giacomo (Baritone)

VOCALION RECORDS 1920-1924

30149	Otello: Brindisi.		(60046)
30167	Allegro: Come and Trip It.		
30177	Martha: Canzone del porter.		(60046)
45001	Pagliacci: Prologo.	(52036)	(70024)
52002	Otello: Credo.		
52008	Carmen: Canzone del Toreador.		(70028)
52033	Traviata: Di Provenza.		(70024)
52039	Due Granatieri (Schumann).		(70029)
52047	Masked Ball: Eri tu.		(70033)
52049	Danza (Rossini).		(70029)
52050	Africana: Adamastor.		(70033)
55009	Barber of Seville: Largo al factotum.		(70028)
	Jewels of Madonna: Serenata (w. Cho.).		(60012)
	El Relicario (Padilla).		(60012)
	Fedora: La donna russa.		(60051)
	Masked Ball: Alla vita.		(60051)

For other records, see RAISA, SCOTNEY.

Note: For Fonotipia-Odeon, Rimini had made a number of recordings including the standard duets from Rigoletto on Nos. 82485-88, the soprano being Alessandrowich, who, on her own, had done such things as Don Pasquale: Quel guardo on No. 37200.

ROSING, Vladimir (Tenor)

VOCALION RECORDS 1921-1925

30141	Spring Waters (Rachmaninoff).	
30172	In the Silence of the Night (Rachmaninoff).	(60048)
30178	Sadko: Song of India.	(60048)

	The Clock (Sachnowsky).	(60052)
	Yeremoushka's Cradle Song (Moussorgsky).	(60052)
52021	Song of the Flea (Moussorgsky).	(70022)
52022	Prince Igor: Vladimir's Cavatina.	(70022)
52029	Faust: Salut demeure.	(70021)
52034	Carmen: Air de la fleur.	(70021)
	Song of the Volga Boatmen (arr. Koenemann).	(38018)
	Volga Lullaby (Arensky).	(38018)

Note: The later releases above were recorded by Vocalion in England.

ROTHIER, Leon (Bass)

COLUMBIA RECORDS 1916-1918

48632	Magic Flute: O Isis et Osiris.	(A5812)	
48633	La Marseillaise (de l'Isle).	(A5823)	(7027M)
48634	Caid: Air du Tambour-Major.	(A5876)	
48645	Le Cor (Flegier).	(A5999)	
48647	Hugenots: Piff Paff.	(A5876)	
48659	Don Carlos: Ella giammai m'amo.	(A5812)	
48791	Pere de la Victoire (Ganne).	(A5823)	
49169	Deux Grenadiers (Schumann).	(A5999)	(7027M)
58545	Star Spangled Banner (Smith) (French).	(E3558)	
58546	America (Carey) (French).	(E3558)	

For other records, see CARUSO.

Note: One of the proudest Collectors Record Shop releases, No. 51, couples an unpublished Damnation of Faust: Serenade with part of a 1939 radio broadcast on which this excellent artist announces and sings the Louise: Berceuse.

RUFFO, Titta (Baritone)

IMPORTED VICTOR RED SEAL 1907-1909

91500	Rigoletto: Veglia o donna (w. Galvany).	(3033)
91501	Rigoletto: Si vendetta (w. Galvany).	(3033)
92037	Hamlet: Brindisi (w. Cho.).	
92038	Don Carlos: Per me giunto.	(15-1028)
92039	Barber of Seville: Largo al factotum.	(6405)
92040	Pagliacci: Prologo.	(6405)
92041	Rigoletto: Pari siamo.	
92042	Hamlet: Monologo—Essere o non essere.	(6403)
92043	Faust: Dio possente.	(6406)
92064	Hamlet: Come il romito fior.	(6403)
92065	Carmen: Canzone del Toreador (w. Cho.).	(6406)
92066	Rigoletto: Cortigiani (w. Cho.).	(8054)
92500	Hamlet: Nega se puoi la luce (w. Galvany).	(8055)
92501	Barber of Seville: Dunque io son (w. Galvany).	(8054)
92502	Rigoletto: Piangi fanciulla (w. Galvany).	(8059)
92503	Traviata: Dite alla giovine (w. Galvany).	(8055)
92504	Forza del Destino: Le minaccie (w. Ischierdo).	
92505	Don Giovanni: La ci darem (w. Pareto).	(8053)
92506	Rigoletto: Lassu in cielo (w. Pareto).	(8053)

VICTOR RED SEAL 1912-1916

87112	Don Giovanni: Serenata.	(818)
87113	Masked Ball: Alla vita.	(937)
87114	Zaza: Buona Zaza.	(824)
87121	Non penso a lei (Ferradini).	(933)
87123	Suonno 'e fantasia (Capolongo).	(823)
87125	Zaza: Zaza, piccola zingara.	(824)

87133	Visione Veneziana (Brogi).	(823)
87137	Thais: Ahime fanciullo ancora.	(934)
87138	E suonan le Campane (Titta).	(933)
87139	Torna a Surriento (de Curtis).	(932)
87140	Maria, Mari (di Capua).	(932)
87141	Traviata: Di Provenza.	(936)
87142	Malena: Disse il saggio.	
87143	Thais: Ecco dunque l'orribil citta.	(934)
87145	E canta il grillo (Billi).	
87147	E la mia dama (Ferradini).	
87148	Trovatore: Il balen.	(936)
87149	Malena: Ma tu sfiorata.	
87150	Meriggiata (Leoncavallo).	
87151	Rigoletto: Miei signori.	(937)
87152	Non penso a lei (Ferradini) (mat. 9229e).	
87153	Hamlet: Spettro Infernal.	(935)
87154	Hamlet: Spettro Santo.	(935)
87155	Chatterton: Tu sola a me.	
87156	Trovatore: Per me ora fatale.	
87157	Trovatore: Di geloso (w. Fosca-Ischierdo).	
87158	Puritani: Suoni la tromba (w. De Segurola).	(87564)
87166	Faust: Rammenta i lieti di.	(819)
87174	Don Giovanni: Fin ch'han dal vino.	(938)
87177	Guitarrico: Jota de Perico.	(820)
87194	Nabucco: Tremin gl'insani.	
87195	Oh che m' importa (Titta).	
87220	Tosca: Gia mi dicon venal.	(938)
87222	Faust: Serenata.	(819)
87223	Africana: All'erta Marinar.	(817)
88366	Dinorah: Sei vendicata assai.	(6398)
88391	Barber of Seville: Largo al factotum.	
88392	Pagliacci: Prologo (part I).	(6268)
88393	Pagliacci: Prologo (part II).	(6268)
88394	Gioconda: Ah Pescator.	(6265)
88395	Dai Canti d'Amore (Titta).	(15-1028)
88396	Gioconda: O Monumento.	(6398)
88466	Otello: Credo.	(6267) (8045)
88486	Cristoforo Colombo: Aman lassu le stelle.	
88527	Due Granatieri (Schumann).	
88528	Faust: Dio possente.	(6429)
88544	Masked Ball: Eri tu.	(6266)
89058	Rigoletto: Deh non parlare (w. Finzi-Magrini).	(8059)
89075	Otello: Si per ciel (w. Caruso).	(8045)

VICTOR RED SEAL 1920-1925

87323	Munasterio (Costa).	(821)
87325	Andrea Chernier: Son sessant' anni.	(817)
87331	Querida (Doda).	(822)
87336	Ernani: Lo vedremo.	(818)
87341	El Relicario (Padilla).	(822)
87342	Sei morta nella vita mia (Costa).	(821)
87343	Novembre (Tremisot).	(820)
87352	Martha: Canzone del porter.	(876)
87360	Falstaff: Quand' ero paggio.	(876)
87369	Damnation of Faust: Serenata.	(963)
87370	Demon: Do not weep (in Russian).	(963)
87381	Hamlet (Shakespeare): Apparizione.	(985)
87382	Hamlet (Shakespeare): Essere o non.	(985)
87383	Santa Lucia.	(995)
87384	Marechiare (Tosti).	(995)
87393	Lolita (Buzzi-Peccia).	(1019)
87394	Perjura (Tejada).	(1019)

	Lakme: Lakme ton doux regard.		(1070)	
	Credo du Paysan (Goublier).		(1070)	
	Chitarrata Abruzzese (Tosti).		(1076)	
	Mia sposa sara la mia bandiera (Rotoli).		(1076)	
88391	Barber of Seville: Largo al factotum.		(6263)	
88618	Rigoletto: Pari siamo.		(6263)	
88619	Hamlet: Brindisi.	(6266)	(18140)	
88621	Otello: Era la notte.		(6267)	
88622	Africana: Adamastor.		(6262)	
88626	Andrea Chernier: Nemico della patria.		(6262)	
88637	Falstaff: L'Onore Ladri.		(6264)	
88639	Roi de Lahore: O casto fior.		(6265)	
88643	Patrie: Pauvre martyr obscur.			
88660	Ernani: O de' verd' anni miei.		(6264)	
88668	Cristoforo Colombo: Dunque ho sognato.		(6429)	

Note: Nos. 87139-42, 87145-58, 87381-82 and 88391-96 are also imported recordings and since Ruffo's immense popularity warranted the inclusion by Victor of all but a few of his available European selections, it is too bad they did not see fit to publish as well his Gioconda duet with Caruso or other unreleased American masters.

RUNGE, Gertrude (Soprano)

IMPORTED VICTOR RED SEAL 1905

71027 Mignon: Ich bin Titania.

Note: Runge could be found on German Gramophone releases as early as 1900, her "Ich liebe dich" being No. 43045; many subsequent ones appeared here as Victor black seal records.

RUSZCOWSKA, Elena (Soprano)'

IMPORTED VICTOR RED SEAL 1910-1912

76016	Stabat Mater: Inflammatus.		
87069	Tosca: Trionfa di nuova (w. Cunego).	(87558)	
88261	Aida: Ohime di guerra (w. De Casas-Cunego-Cho.).		
88262	Aida: Fu la sorte (w. De Casas).		
88263	Aida: Ebben qual nuovo (w. De Casas).	(89150)	
88265	Aida: Su dunque (w. Badini).		
88266	Aida: Su del Nilo (w. Cappiello-Tapergi-Davi-Cho.).	(89155)	(8056)
88267	Aida: Rivedrai le foreste (w. Maggi).	(89152)	(8052)
88271	Gioconda: L'amo come (w. De Casas).	(89151)	
88272	Tosca: Non la sospiri (w. Cunego).	(89153)	(8049)
88273	Tosca: Qual occhio al mondo (w. Cunego).	(89154)	(8049)
88274	Tosca: Amaro sol per te (w. Cunego).	(89121)	
88373	Aida: Pieta ti prenda (w. De Casas).		

Note: The first item above was Gr. No. 053250 in Italy, source of many other recordings not released here.

SAGI-BARBA Emilio (Baritone)

IMPORTED VICTOR RED SEAL 1909-1911

61186	Juramento: Romanza.	(45278)
61187	Guerra Santa: Romanza.	(45278)
61188	Dos Princesas: Vals.	(45273)
61189	Chimes of Normandy: Vals.	(45273)
61190	Diablo en el Poder: Romanza.	(45276)
61191	Guitarrico: Serenata.	(45280)

61194	Alma de Dios: Coro de Hungaros (w. Cho.).	(45272)
61195	Grumete: Romanza.	(45276)
61196	Hijas de Eva: Romanza.	
61197	Tempestad: Monologo.	(45301)
61198	Mousquetaires au Couvent: Romanza.	(45283)
61199	Mascotte: Duo (w. Vela).	(45296)
61200	Conquista de Madrid: Romanza.	(45274)
61208	Miss Helyett: Romanza de Ricardo.	(45283)
61209	Bohemios: Coro de Bohemios (w. Cho.).	(45272)
61210	Gran Via: Caballero de gracia.	(45285)
61211	Jugar con Fuego: Coro de Locos (w. Cho.).	(45279)
61212	Plegaria (Alvarez).	(45286)
61214	Merry Widow: Marcha (w. Lopez-Meana-Gamero-Moreno).	(45297)
61215	Merry Widow: Vals (w. Vela).	(45295)
61216	Juramento: Duo de la Diana (w. Vela).	(45296)
64118	Mujer y Reina: Serenata (w. Cho.).	(45279)
64124	Bohemios: Duo (w. Vela).	(45291)
64125	Entre mi Mujer y el Negro: Tango.	(45277)
64152	Duo de la Africana: Duo (w. Vela).	(45291)
64175	Dollar Princess: Duo del Examen (w. Vela).	(45293)
64176	Dollar Princess: Duo de la Maquina (w. Vela).	(45293)
64177	Dollar Princess: Entrada de Freddy.	(45287)
64178	Waltz Dream: Duo (w. Alarcon).	(45289)
64179	Lolita (Buzzi-Peccia) (Span.).	(45280)
71047	Campanone: Salida de Campanone.	(55146)
71048	Campanone: Duo (w. Vela).	(55148)
71049	Saltimbanques: Arieta.	
71050	Marina: (Arrieta) Duo (w. Vela).	
71051	Saltimbanques: Duo (w. Vela).	
71052	Juramento: Duo del piano (w. Vela).	
74161	Rigoletto: Cortigiani (w. Cho.) (Span.).	(55147)
74162	Mascotte: Balada de Pipo (w. Cho.).	(55146)
74226	Dollar Princess: Duo final (w. Vela).	(55151)

IMPORTED VICTOR RED SEAL 1913-1916

64358	Gracia Espanola (Alvarez).	(45277)
64362	Rosary (Nevin) (Span.).	(45282)
64363	Molinos de Viento: Serenata.	(45288)
64364	Tempestad: Monologo.	
64365	Nazareth (Titto).	(45284)
64366	Mis Amores (Alfonso).	(45281)
64367	Voreta la Mar (Palau).	(45288)
64368	Rey de las Montanas: Consejos.	(45287)
64369	Celos Cubanos (Sagi-Barba).	(45275)
64370	Romanza (Schumann) (Span.).	(45283)
64371	Count of Luxembourg: Duo (part I) (w. Vela).	(45290)
64376	Cadetes de la Reina: Septimino (w. Vela-Vinas-Altes-Conto).	(45298)
64377	Cadetes de la Reina: Duo de la Carta (w. Vinas).	(45294)
64378	Cadetes de la Reina: Marcha (w. Vela-Vinas-Altes-Conto).	(45298)
64379	Count of Luxembourg: Duo (part II) (w. Vela).	(45290)
64380	Count of Luxembourg: Duo final (w. Vela).	(45294)
64381	Canto de Primavera: Romanza.	(45274)
64461	Golondrinas: Duo final (w. Vela).	(45292)
64463	Golondrinas: Se reia.	(45285)
64464	Golondrinas: Juanito (w. Gonzales-Garcia-Revilla-Asensio).	(45297)
64466	Golondrinas: Risa infernal (w. Vela).	(45292)
64510	Alborada (Alvarez).	(45271)
64511	Granada (Alvarez).	(45271)
64524	Mi pobre reja (Tabuyo).	(45281)
64525	Mi serrana (Alvarez).	(45282)
64526	En Calesa (Alvarez).	(45275)

64527	Plegaria a la Santisima Virgen (Agueral).	(45284)
64570	Rey que Rabio: Cancion del Rey (w. Vela).	(45295)
64572	Duo de la Africana: Duo (w. Lopez).	(45289)
74344	Molinos de Viento: Duo (w. Vela).	(55151)
74350	A tus Ojos (Fuster).	(55143)
74351	Merry Widow: Cuento.	(55147)
74352	Patria (Cancion espanola).	(55144)
74361	Cadetes de la Reina: Duo final (part I) (w. Vela).	(55149)
74362	Cadetes de la Reina: Duo final (part II) (w. Vela).	(55149)
74363	Cadetes de la Reina: Balada (w. Vela).	(55148)
74382	Marina: Cuarteto (w. Vela-etc.).	
74389	Canto del Presidiario (Alvarez).	(55143)
74390	La Partida (Alvarez).	(55144)
74411	Golondrinas: Oh Puck (w. Vela).	(55150)
74413	Golondrinas: Caminar.	(55145)
74414	Golondrinas: Serenata de Pierrot.	(55145)
74415	Golondrinas: Final del Acto I (w. Vela).	(55150)
74470	Rey que Rabio: Cuarteto (w. Vela-Haro-Lopez).	

Note: In 1922, the above were coupled on blue seal records in which category subsequent Sagi-Barba items were released. The Lehar operetta on No. 64368 is probably Das Furstenkind.

SAMAROFF, Olga (Pianist)

VICTOR RED SEAL 1921-1925

64965	Ruins of Athens—Turkish March (Beethoven).	(825)
64995	Sparks Op. 36 No. 6 (Moszkowski).	(825)
66075	Spring Song (Mendelssohn).	(826)
66148	Naiads at the Spring (Juon).	(826)
74696	Liebestraum (Liszt).	(6269)
74772	Walkure: Ride of Valkyries (arr. Hutcheson).	(6270)
74785	Nocturne Op. 54 No. 4 (Grieg).	(6419)
74794	La Campanella (Paganini-Liszt).	(6270)
74799	Nocturne in E Flat Op. 9 No. 2 (Chopin).	(6269)
74831	Sonata in B Minor Op. 58—Finale (Chopin).	(6419)
74852	Ballade in A Flat Op. 47 (part I) (Chopin).	(6433)
74853	Ballade in A Flat Op. 47 (part II) (Chopin).	(6433)
74881	Hungarian Rhapsody No. 12 (part I) (Liszt).	(6450)
74882	Hungarian Rhapsody No. 12 (part II) (Liszt).	(6450)
	Aufschwung (Schumann).	(6475)
	Romance (Schumann).	(6475)
	Clair de Lune (Debussy).	(6540)
	Intermezzo in E Flat Op. 117 No. 1 (Brahms).	(6540)

SAMMARCO, Mário (Baritone)

VICTOR RED SEAL 1910-1911

87077	Uocchie de suonno (Costa).	
88257	Africana: Adamastor.	
88258	L'Ultima Canzone (Tosti).	
88259	Otello: Era la notte.	
88260	Otello: Credo.	
88310	Africana: Adamastor.	(15-1018)
88312	Hamlet: Brindisi.	(15-1013)
88314	Traviata: Di Provenza.	
88315	Rigoletto: Cortigiani.	
88320	Rigoletto: Pari siamo.	
89042	Rigoletto: Tutte le feste (w. Sembrich).	

For other records, see McCORMACK.

Note: Nos. 88257-60 are from imported masters, unfortunately but a few of the many that might have been chosen. Other European items include a great number of Fonotipias, among which Andrea Chernier: Un dì m'era on No. 92172 (C-F91) was released a dozen years after he had created the baritone part in 1896.

SAN FRANCISCO SYMPHONY ORCHESTRA (conductor: Hertz)

VICTOR RED SEAL 1925

Parsifal: Prelude (part I).	(6498)
Parsifal: Prelude (part II).	(6498)
Parsifal: Prelude (part III).	(6499)
Parsifal: Good Friday Music (part I).	(6499)
Parsifal: Good Friday Music (part II).	(6500)
Parsifal: Good Friday Music (part III).	(6500)
Fra Diavolo: Overture (part I).	(6506)
Fra Diavolo: Overture (part II).	(6506)
Phedre Overture (Massenet) (part I).	(6539)
Phedre Overture (Massenet) (part II).	(6539)

SCAMPINI, Augusto (Tenor)

IMPORTED VICTOR RED SEAL 1911

76014 Ricordanze (Vittadini).

Note: A solitary import though many more were available.

SCHARWENKA, Xaver (Pianist)

COLUMBIA RECORDS 1911-1913

Valse Brilliante Op. 34 No. 1 (Chopin).	(A5260)
Polish Dance Op. 3 No. 1 (Scharwenka).	(A5260)
Fantasie Impromptu Op. 66 (Chopin).	(A5261)
Spanish Serenade Op. 63 No. 1 (Scharwenka).	(A5261)
Rondo Capriccioso (Mendelssohn).	(A5467)
Liebestraum (Liszt).	(A5467)

Note: Rondo Capriccioso was coupled in England with Weber's Invitation to the Waltz on English Columbia No. 401, issued September 1913.

SCHIPA, Tito (Tenor)

IMPORTED VICTOR RED SEAL 1919-1920

64804	Rigoletto: Ella mi fu rapita.	(925)
64805	Rigoletto: Parmi veder le lagrime.	(925)
64806	Lucia: Tu che a Dio.	
74629	Manon: Ah dispar vision.	

VICTOR RED SEAL 1922-1925

66039	Emigrantes: Granadinas.	(827)
66045	Pagliacci: Serenata d'Arlecchino.	(828)
66067	Princesita (Padilla).	(827)
66077	Manon: Il sogno.	(828)
66117	Chi se nne scorda cchiu (Barthelemy).	(952)
66121	Napulitanata (Costa).	(952)
66142	Quiereme Mucho (Roig).	(929)
66143	A la orilla de un Palmar (Ponce).	(929)
66192	Barber of Seville: Ecco ridente.	(965)
66193	Barber of Seville: Se il mio nome.	(965)

	Mi Viejo Amor (Oteo).	**(1030)**
	Rosalinda (Fuentes).	**(1030)**
	A Cuba (Schipa).	**(1031)**
	Jota (de Falla).	**(1031)**
	Pesca d' Ammore (Barthelemy).	**(1063)**
	Serenata (Silvestri).	**(1063)**
74753	Ay Ay Ay (Perez).	**(6423)**
74839	A Granada (Palacios).	**(6423)**
	Mignon: Ah non credevi tu.	**(6465)**
	Mignon: Addio, Mignon.	**(6465)**

For other records, see GALLI-CURCI.

Note: The youthful Schipa Milan recordings were issued on lowest price label abroad as they were in Latin American catalogues, where, among 1916 releases, his Faust: Salve dimora (Gr. 252147, later 7-52122) was listed as Victor No. 67661. Several of his Pathe items were re-recorded in the Actuelle series, among them Falstaff: Dal labbro il canto on No. 025083 (Perfect 11505).

SCHORR, Friedrich (Baritone)

BRUNSWICK RECORDS 1924-1925

Zar und Zimmermann: Sonst spielt' ich.	**(15088)**
Don Giovanni: Standchen.	**(15088)**
Der Lindenbaum (Schubert).	**(10160)**
Die Ehre Gottes (Beethoven).	**(10160)**
Forgotten (Cowles).	**(10173)**
The Old Road (Scott).	**(10173)**

Note: Just prior to the above, Vocalion had released a Wotans Abschied from Walkure as No. 21007, this being the Deutsche Grammophon coupling No. 62392 (B 2050/1).

SCHUMANN-HEINK, Ernestine (Contralto)

Those who fondly remember Schumann-Heink singing lullabies to a brood twice or more removed are due for a startling revelation when they hear her earlier command of coloratura. At all times, however, she was one of those great few who could make a C major scale sound like a masterpiece.

COLUMBIA RECORDS 1903

1378	Prophete: Ah mon fils.
1379	Lucrezia Borgia: Trinklied.
1380	Samson: Mein Herz.
1381	Bolero (Arditi).
1382	Tod und das Madchen (Schubert).

VICTOR RED SEAL 1906-1910

81085	Wiegenlied (Brahms).	
85092	Love's Lottery: Sweet Thoughts of Home.	
85093	St. Paul: But the Lord.	
85094	Samson: Mein Herz.	
85095	Prophete: Ach, mein Sohn.	
85096	Lucrezia Borgia: Trinklied.	**(15-1012)**
85112	Rinaldo: Lascia ch' io pianga.	
85113	Nur wer die Sehnsucht kennst (Tschaikowsky).	
87012	Fruhlingszeit (Becker).	**(830)**
87013	Tod und das Madchen (Schubert).	
87020	Danza (Chadwick).	
87021	Treue Liebe (Kucken).	**(836)**
87022	Irish Love Song (Lang).	

87032	Children's Prayer (Reger); Liebesfeier (Weingartner).	
88090	Mignon: Kennst du das Land.	(6367)
88091	Orfeo: Ach ich habe sie verloren.	
88092	Rheingold: Weiche, Wotan (w. Witherspoon).	
88093	Bolero (Arditi).	(6367) (15-1012)
88094	Prophete: Scene de la prison (part I).	
88095	Prophete: Scene de la prison (part II).	(6279)
88108	The Rosary (Nevin).	(6277)
88118	His Lullaby (Bond).	(6274)
88138	Stille Nacht (Gruber).	(6281)
88139	I und mei Bua (Millocker).	(6278)
88140	Rienzi: Gretcher Gott.	
88155	Es ist bestimmt (Mendelssohn).	
88187	Prophete: Ah mon fils.	(6279)
88188	Lucrezia Borgia: Trinklied.	(6278)
88189	Rinaldo: Lascia ch' io pianga.	
88190	Samson: Mein Herz.	(6280)
88191	St. Paul: But the Lord.	(6271)
88196	Clemenza di Tito: Parto, parto.	
88197	Mondnacht (Schumann).	
88212	Sapho: O ma lyre.	

VICTOR RED SEAL 1912-1916

87094	A Child's Prayer (Harold).	(911)
87104	Die Forelle (Schubert).	
87124	Spinnerliedchen (Reimann).	(830)
87129	When the Roses Bloom (Reichardt).	(837)
87168	Good Morning, Sue (Delibes).	
87170	Im Kahne (Grieg).	
87171	The Robin Sings (MacDowell).	
87172	Allah (Chadwick).	
87221	The Rosary (Nevin).	(833)
87239	Sapphische Ode (Brahms).	
87240	Mother Sings (Grieg).	
87241	Wiegenlied (Brahms).	
87504	Wanderers Nachtlied (Rubenstein) (w. Farrar).	
88336	Cry of Rachel (Salter).	(6275)
88337	Sei still (Raff).	
88342	Erlkonig (Schubert).	(6273)
88343	Traume (Wagner).	(6272)
88381	Von Himmel hoch (Luther).	(6281)
88400	Barbchen; Schlafliedchen (Hermann).	
88416	Agnus Dei (Bizet).	(6271)
88417	Samson: Der Fruhling erwachte.	(6280)
88448	My Heart Ever Faithful (Bach).	
88451	Kerry Dance (Molloy).	(6276)
88547	Lorelei (Silcher).	(6273)
88548	Before the Crucifix (La Forge).	(6275)
88549	One Sweetly Solemn Thought (Ambrose).	(6274)
88550	Das Erkennen (Loewe).	(6272)
89060	Trovatore: Ai nostri monti (w. Caruso).	(8042)

VICTOR RED SEAL 1917-1925

87280	Nearer My God to Thee (Mason).	(829)
87282	Just before the battle, Mother (Root).	
87286	Cradle Song (MacFayden).	(837)
87288	Thy Beaming Eyes (MacDowell).	(833)
87295	When the Boys Come Home (Speaks).	(835)
87298	Onward Christian Soldiers (Sullivan).	(834)
87299	Taps (Pasternack).	(835)
87302	Sun of My Soul (Ritter).	(834)

87307	In the Sweet Bye and Bye (Webster).	(832)
87320	The Home Road (Carpenter).	(831)
87326	Sometime We'll Understand (McGranahan).	(832)
87330	Adeste Fideles (Portugal).	(829)
87332	Still wie die Nacht (Bohm).	(836)
87337	If I Forget (Thompson).	(831)
87340	Lead Kindly Light (Dykes).	(911)
87353	Wiegenlied (Brahms).	(838)
87363	Rock Me to Sleep, Mother (Leslie).	(838)
87373	Sweetheart (Stewart).	(969)
87374	Dreamin' Time (Strickland).	(969)
87385	Mondnacht (Schumann).	(996)
87386	Tod und das Madchen (Schubert).	(996)
	Traum durch die Dammerung (Strauss).	(1045)
	Sapphische Ode (Brahms).	(1045)
	Du du liegst mir im Herzen.	(1049)
	Der Tannenbaum.	(1049)
88592	Danny Boy (Weatherly).	(6276)
88620	Old Folks at Home (Foster).	(6277)

Note: Also assigned numbers were other recordings of Brahms' Wiegenlied (81083) and Tschaikowsky's Nur wer die Sehnsucht kennst (85101) as well as Down in the Forest (87130) and The War (87238).

SCOTNEY, Evelyn (Soprano)
VOCALION RECORDS 1920-1924

30146	Rigoletto: Si vendetta (w. Rimini).	(60019)
30157	Lo Here the Gentle Lark (Bishop).	(60041)
30159	Love's Old Sweet Song (Molloy).	(60042)
30161	I Passed By Your Window (Brahe).	(60041)
30163	Your Voice (MacDermid).	(60042)
	The Robin's Song (Perkins).	(60004)
	Si mes vers (Hahn).	(60004)
	Blue Bells of Scotland (Grant).	(60013)
	Home Sweet Home (Bishop).	(60013)
52001	Traviata: Ah fors e lui.	(70011)
52005	Voci di primavera (Strauss).	(70014)
52009	Faust: Air des bijoux.	(70015)
52016	Rigoletto: Piangi fanciulla (w. Rimini).	(70011)
52027	Pearl of Brazil: Charmant oiseau.	(70015)
52040	Mignon: Je suis Titania.	(70014)
55002	Rigoletto: Caro nome.	(70002)
55004	Lucia: Mad scene.	(70002)
	Romeo: Valse.	(70000)
	Blue Danube Waltz (Strauss).	(70000)
	Barber of Seville: Una voce poco fa.	(70004)
	Theme and Variations (Proch).	(70004)

Note: Scotney's very appealing coloratura was well represented on English recordings too.

SCOTT, Henri (Bass)

Concert companion of Caruso on his tour of 1908, Scott sang many parts in many places after that, even an open-air Mephistopheles at Ebbets Field.

COLUMBIA RECORDS 1913-1916

36451	Caid: Air du Tambour Major.	(A5450)
36452	Requiem (Verdi): Confutatis.	(A5442)
36453	Gloria (Buzzi-Peccia).	(A5442)

36454	Vespri Siciliani: O tu Palermo.	(A5450)
36761	Maritana: In Happy Moments.	(A5500)
36762	Bohemian Girl: Heart Bow'd Down.	(A5500)
36763	Don Giovanni: Madamina.	(A5504)
36764	Sonnambula: Vi ravviso.	(A5504)
36879	Magic Flute: In diesen Heil'gen Hallen.	(A5552)
36880	Puritani: Suoni la tromba (w. Dufranne).	(A5558) (7032M)
36881	Ernani: Infelice.	(A5552)
37138	Bedouin Love Song (Pinsuti).	(A5651)
37139	Martha: Drinking Song.	(A5651)
48569	Faust: Even Bravest Heart.	(A5877)
48570	Gypsy John (Clay).	(A5877)
48571	Thy Sentinel Am I (Watson).	(A5799)
48572	I Fear No Foe (Pinsuti).	(A5799)

SCOTTI, Antonio (Baritone)

Scotti's records reveal a very appealing quality if limited range, but long after even this was gone, he commanded a leading place on the operatic stage by dint of a poise and acting ability matched by few baritones and much fewer tenors.

COLUMBIA RECORDS 1903

1205	Carmen: Canzone del Toreador.	(A620)
1206	Pagliacci: Prologo.	
1207	Don Giovanni: Serenata; Fin ch'han dal vino.	

VICTOR RED SEAL 1903-1905

5023	Faust: Dio possente (Imported Recording).	(91019)
81021	Pagliacci: Prologo.	
81022	Faust: Dio possente.	
81041	Sonnambula: Vi ravviso.	
81042	Aida: Suo padre.	
81043	Don Pasquale: Bella siccome un angelo.	
81054	Otello: Brindisi.	
81063	Mandolinata (Paladilhe).	
81064	Roi de Lahore: O casto fior.	
81070	Masked Ball: Alla vita.	
85016	Don Giovanni: Serenata; Falstaff: Quand'ero paggio.	
85017	Faust: Dio possente.	
85030	Rigoletto: Pari siamo.	
85031	Rigoletto: Deh non parlare; Don Giovanni: Fin ch'han dal vino.	
85044	Masked Ball: Eri tu.	
85045	Otello: Credo.	
85067	Don Carlos: Per me giunto.	
85068	Elisir d'Amore: Come Paride vezzoso.	
85071	Pagliacci: Prologo.	
85072	Triste Aprile (de Lava).	

VICTOR RED SEAL 1906-1911

87034	Sonnambula: Vi ravviso.	
87040	Otello: Brindisi.	
87084	Scetate (Costa).	
87503	Mme. Butterfly: Lo so che (w. Martin-Fornia).	
88028	Sonnambula: Vi ravviso.	
88029	Pagliacci: Prologo.	(6282)
88030	Otello: Credo.	
88032	Rigoletto: Pari siamo.	
88082	Otello: Brindisi.	(6283)
88083	Maria, Mari (di Capua).	(6282)

88122	Tosca: Gia mi dicon venal.	(6284)	(18142)
88194	Don Giovanni: Serenata; Falstaff: Quand'ero paggio.		(6283)
88195	Falstaff: L'Onore Ladri.		
88203	Faust: Dio possente.		(6284)
88282	Faust: Morte di Valentino (w. Cho.).		
88290	Luna Nova (Costa) (w. Cho.).		
89002	Don Pasquale: Vado corro (w. Sembrich).		(6356)

For other records, see CARUSO, FARRAR.

SEIDEL, Toscha (Violinist)

COLUMBIA RECORDS 1918-1925

49447	Concerto Op. 22—Romance (Wieniawski).	(68073D)	
49448	Nocturne in E Minor Op. 72 (Chopin-Auer).	(68074D)	(9900M)
49449	Caprice Viennois (Kreisler).	(68029D)	
49453	Serenade (Schubert-Elman).	(68075D)	(9027M)
49454	Humoresque (Dvorak-Kreisler).	(68031D)	(9003M)
49526	Eili Eili.		
49564	Zigeunerweisen (Sarasate).	(68030D)	(9900M)
49624	Quartet Op. 11—Andante cantabile (Tschaikowsky).	(68074D)	
49630	Hejre Kati (Hubay).	(68076D)	
49685	Meditation (Morrison).	(68075D)	
49689	Canzonetta (d'Ambrosio).	(68072D)	(9003M)
49690	Hungarian Dance No. 1 (Brahms-Joachim).	(68030D)	(9001M)
49771	Concerto Op. 35—Canzonetta (Tschaikowsky).	(68073D)	(9002M)
49904	Liebesfreud (Kreisler).	(68072D)	(9002M)
49950	Paraphrase on Paderewski's Minuet (Kreisler).	(68029D)	
77899	Traumerei (Schumann).	(33013D)	
78138	Orientale (Cui).	(33027D)	(4001M)
78746	Madrigale (Simonetti).	(33042D)	(4000M)
78747	Polish Dance (Scharwenka).	(33043D)	
78760	Valse Bleue (Margis).	(33041D)	
78798	I'm Forever Blowing Bubbles (Kellette).		
79488	Serenade Espagnole (Kreisler).	(33027D)	
79788	Gavotte in F (Beethoven-Kramer).	(33043D)	
79835	Peer Gynt—Anitra's Dance (Grieg).	(33042D)	(4000M)
80623	Schon Rosmarin (Kreisler).	(33041D)	(4002M)
81006	Valse Sentimentale (Schubert-Franko).	(33013D)	
98046	Angel's Serenade (Braga-Pollitzer).	(68031D)	
	Symphonie Espagnole—Andante (Lalo).	(68021D)	(9000M)
	Concerto in E Minor—Finale (Mendlessohn).	(68021D)	(9000M)
	Slavonic Dance No. 2 (Dvorak-Kreisler).	(68076D)	(9001M)
	Hebrew Melody (Achron).		(9027M)
	Indian Snake Dance (Burleigh).	(33002D)	(4001M)
	Chanson Arabe (Rimsky-Korsakoff-Kreisler).	(33002D)	
	Souvenir Poetique (Fibich).	(33028D)	
	Rondino on a theme of Beethoven (Kreisler).	(33028D)	(4002M)
	Valse Triste (Sibelius).	(33049D)	(4023M)
	Pastorale (Scarlatti).	(33049D)	(4023M)
	Turkish March (Beethoven-Auer).		(4033M)
	Polichinelle (Kreisler).		(4033M)

Also see HACKETT.

SEMBACH, Johannes (Tenor)

COLUMBIA RECORDS 1916-1917

43935	Fruhlingszeit (Becker).	(E3096)
43938	Winterlied (Koss).	(E3096)
43939	Der Lenz (Hildach).	(E3139)
43950	Roslein rot (w. Bloch-Goritz-Braun).	(E3515)

43962	Gute Nacht (Abt).	(E3270)
43963	Du bist wie eine Blume (Schumann).	(E3270)
44620	Der Asra (Rubenstein).	(E3139)
48725	Meistersinger: Preislied.	(A5889)
48726	Walkure: Siegmunds Liebeslied.	(A5835)
48727	Freischutz: Durch Die Walder.	(A5842)
48729	Siegfried: Nothung Nothung.	(A5842)
48730	Lohengrin: Mein lieber Schwan.	(A5889)
48731	Lohengrin: In fernem Land.	(A5835)
59461	Am Meer (Schubert).	(E5141)
59462	Sehnsucht (Rubenstein).	(E5141)

Note: Like some of his domestic Columbias, Sembach's Victor imports were put into lesser categories, his Germanized Trovatore: Di quella pira being black seal No. 63198 and that coupled Lohengrin: Telramunds Klage as sung by Leopold Demuth, a fine baritone whose very early records included a seven-inch Tempelscene from Goldmark's Queen of Sheba on No. 42780.

SEMBRICH, Marcella (Soprano)

Sembrich's records do not do justice to her great renown. While they reveal much of her highly esteemed musicianship, the voice itself is often hooted and too vibrant for the limited intensity of early acoustics. She is one singer who would have benefited much from the electrical process.

COLUMBIA RECORDS 1903

1364	Ernani: Ernani involami.	(A618)
1365	Voci di primavera (Strauss).	
1366	Traviata: Ah fors e lui.	(A618)

VICTOR RED SEAL 1905

81047	Sonnambula: Ah non giunge.	
81048	Standchen (Strauss).	
81049	Der Nussbaum (Schumann).	
81050	Maiden's Wish (Chopin).	
85035	Traviata: Ah fors e lui.	
85036	Voci di primavera (Strauss).	
85037	Faust: Aria dei gioelli.	
85038	Don Giovanni: Batti batti.	

VICTOR RED SEAL 1906-1910

88017	Rigoletto: Caro nome.	(6292)
88018	Traviata: Ah fors e lui.	(6292) (18140)
88019	Voci di primavera (Strauss).	(6291)
88020	Marriage of Figaro: Deh vieni.	
88021	Lucia: Mad scene.	(6285)
88022	Ernani: Ernani involami.	(15-1027)
88023	Parla (Arditi).	(6291)
88024	Faust: Air des bijoux.	(6289)
88026	Don Giovanni: Batti batti.	(6288)
88027	Sonnambula: Ah non giunge.	(6288)
88046	Martha: Last Rose of Summer.	
88047	Home Sweet Home (Bishop).	(6287)
88096	Lass with the Delicate Air (Arne).	(6286)
88097	Barber of Seville: Una voce poco fa.	(6285)
88098	Mignon: Connais-tu le pays.	(6289)
88099	Love Me—Mazurka (Chopin).	
88100	Maiden's Wish (Chopin).	
88101	Halka: Gydyby rannem.	
88102	Martha: Last Rose of Summer.	(6287)
88103	Nightingale (Alabieff) (in Russian).	(6293)

88104	Norma: Casta diva.	(6290)
88105	Puritani: Qui la voce.	(6290)
88107	Merry Widow: Dolce amor.	(6293)
88141	Semiramide: Bel raggio.	(6356)
88142	Linda di Chamounix: O luce.	(15-1027)
88143	Vespri Siciliani: Bolero.	
89002	Don Pasquale: Vado corro (w. Scotti).	(6356)
89010	Hamlet: Doute de la lumiere (w. De Gogorza).	
89042	Rigoletto: Tutte le feste (w. Sammarco).	
95202	Marriage of Figaro: Che soave (w. Eames).	(8043)

VICTOR RED SEAL 1912-1913

88387	Dollar Princess: Vals (arr. La Forge).	
88388	Tales from Vienna Woods (Strauss-La Forge).	
88389	Waltz Dream: Non sai (arr. La Forge).	
88390	Comin' thro' the Rye.	(6286)

For other records, see CARUSO

SIROTA, Gerson (Cantor)

IMPORTED VICTOR RED SEAL 1904

61074	Wehosor Schotan.	
61082	Schlochs Esrei Midoisch.	
61100	Humze lona.	(17738)
61101	Rezei.	(17740)
61102	Jaale.	(17739)
61103	Mi Scheosso nissim.	(17738)
61104	Veseorei olecho.	(17740)
61105	Mimkoimoi hu jifen.	
61106	Jisgadal wejiskadasch.	(17739)
61107	Umipnei chatoenu.	
71025	Adoin Oilom.	(35450)
71026	Odom yasoido meator.	(35450)

IMPORTED VICTOR RED SEAL 1912-1913

64228	Birchas Kohanim.	(17771)
64229	Veseorei olecho.	(17744)
64230	Halbein Chatoeinu.	
64231	Kawakors Roe Adroi.	(17745)
64272	Habein Jakir li.	(17746)
64273	Hajajm horas oilom.	
64274	Usanen Teikef.	(17741)
64275	Broisch haschono.	(17741)
64276	El Mole rachmim.	(17745)
64383	Aw Horachmim.	(17771)
64384	W'nemor loi hibit oven.	(17744)
64385	Iru Eineinu.	(17746)
64386	Mo oischu.	

Note: It is hoped that the orthodox reader will not take amiss the above means of suggesting the Hebrew texts which Sirota repeated likewise on early imported Favorite records such as 1-75597 Jaale, issued with 1-75606 Wehosor as Columbia E6004. At a much later date, he sang more easily recognized items from Aida, Tosca, Trovatore, etc.

SISTINE CHAPEL Recordings

IMPORTED VICTOR RED SEAL 1903

5064	MORESCHI: Messe Solennelle (Rossini): Crucifixus.	(91039)
5065	COMANDINI: Laudate pueri dominum (Capocci).	(91040)
5067	CHOIR: Intonuit de Coelo (Capocci).	(91041)

IMPORTED VICTOR RED SEAL 1904-1905

61108	CHOIR, (Rella): Offertorio e Communione—M. di S. Gregorio.
61109	FRE. SEMINARY: Alleluja "Pascha Nostrum".
61110	FRE. SEMINARY: Haec Dies Col Versetto.
61111	AUGUSTINIAN: Introito—Messa dell' Assunzione.
61112	AUGUSTINIAN: Puer Natus in Bethlehem.
61113	AUGUSTINIAN: Sequenza—Messa di Pentecoste.
61114	AUGUSTINIAN: Tractus et Antiphona—Messa pro Defunctis.
61115	MORESCHI: Pie Jesu (Leybach).
61116	MORESCHI, BOEZI, DADO, CHO.: Laudamus Te (Capocci). (893)
61117	MORESCHI: Messe Solennelle (Rossini): Crucifixus.
61118	MORESCHI: Hostias et Preces (Terziani).
61119	MORESCHI: Preghiera—Romanza (Tosti).
61120	VATICAN ORCH.: Inno Pontifico.
61121	VATICAN ORCH.: Trombe d'Argento.
61122	POTHIER: Carattere Fondamentale.
61123	CHOIR, (Perosi): Esultate Justi (Viadana). (893)
61124	CHOIR, (Kanzler): La Cruda Mia Nemica (Palestrina).
61125	CHOIR, (Kanzler): Improperia (Vittoria).
71001	CHOIR, (Rella): Kyrie Eleison.
71002	CHOIR, (Rella): Gloria in Excelsis Deo. (6334)
71003	CHOIR, (Rella): I due Alleluja.
71004	CHOIR, (Rella): Credo (part I).
71005	CHOIR, (Rella): Credo (part II).
71006	CHOIR, (Rella): Sanctus et Agnus Dei.
71007	CHOIR, (Rella): Sequentia della M. di S. Gregorio.
71008	BENEDICTINES: Introitus in Assunzione B. M. V.
71009	FRE. SEMINARY: Introito di Pasqua.
71010	FRE. SEMINARY: Introito—Messa "Sacerdotes Dei."
71011	BENEDICTINES: Introito—Messa "Sacerdotes Dei"
71012	BENEDICTINES: I Due Alleluja—M. di S. Gregorio.
71013	AUGUSTINIAN: Primo Responsorio—Io Notturno dell'uffico di Natale.
71014	BENEDICTINES: Offertorio e Communione—Messa Gregoriana
71015	MORESCHI, CHO.: Oremus Pro Pontefice (Calzanera). (6334)
71016	BOEZI, CHO.: Gratias Agimus Tibi (Capocci).
71017	BIANCHINI, CHO.: Domine Deus (Capocci).
71018	RELLA: Prolusione al Corso Pratico.
71019	BARON KANZLER: Communicazione fatta al Congresso.
71020	MOCQUEREAU: L'Ecole Gregorienne.
71021	DE SANTI: Discorso d'Apertura.
71022	POTHIER: Carattere Fondomentale.
71023	CHOIR, (Perosi): Filiae Jerusalem (Gabrielli).
71024	CHOIR, (Kanzler): Sicut Cervus (Palestrina).

IMPORTED VICTOR RED SEAL 1924

	CHOIR, (Rella): Adeste Fidelis (Portugal). (1046)
	CHOIR, (Rella): Exultate Deo (Palestrina). (1046)
	CHOIR, (Rella): Ave Maria (Vittoria). (1071)
	CHOIR, (Rella): O Salutaris Hostia (Perosi). (1071)
74870	CHOIR, (Rella): Laudate Dominum (Palestrina). (6442)
74871	CHOIR, (Rella): Tenebrae factae sunt (Palestrina). (6442)

Note: In giving titles as they are listed in early catalogues, it is hoped that sufficient accuracy prevails to identify the wonderful Gregorian Chants. The artists will be recognized as soloists of the Sistine Chapel and the choral groups as those of the pupils of the French Seminary, the Augustinian Fathers and the Benedictines of St. Anselmo, directed by Rev. Father Janssens. Among the choirs, the earlier group under Mons. Rella comprised 1200 voices and executed these recordings in St. Peter's Church on the Centenary of St. Gregorius Magnus, April 11, 1904. Nos. 61122 and 71018-22 are discourses by the reverend fathers named.

SLEZAK, Leo (Tenor)

IMPORTED VICTOR RED SEAL 1909-1910

61201	Masaniello: Schlummerlied.	
61202	Cavalleria Rusticana: Siciliana (in German).	
61203	Lohengrin: Nun sei bedank.	(894)
61204	Romeo: Ach geh'auf.	
61205	Cavalleria Rusticana: Abschied von der Mutter.	
61206	Manon: Traum.	
61207	Die Lotosblume (Schumann).	(894)
64111	Der Lenz (Hildach).	
64112	Prophete: Pastorale.	
64113	Aida: Holde Aida.	
64115	Queen of Sheba (Goldmark): Magische Tone.	
64116	Manon: Flieh', o flieh'.	
74168	Carmen: Nur ein Wort (w. Kittel).	

COLUMBIA RECORDS 1912

30991	Otello: Ora e per sempre addio.	(A5385)
30992	Aida: Celeste Aida.	(A5396)
30993	Trovatore: Ah si ben mio.	(A5385)
30994	Lohengrin: Mein liebe Schwan.	(A5395)
36363	Meistersinger: Preislied.	(A5395)
36364	Gioconda: Cielo e mar.	(A5396)

Note: Of the absolutely top-notch singers Slezak probably leads in the number and variety of recordings made for many companies over a long span of years, several other imported items being released here as Opera Disc and Okeh-Odeon among others.

SMIRNOV, Dmitri (Tenor).

IMPORTED VICTOR RED SEAL 1922-1923

66042	Maria, Mari (di Capua).	(912)
66166	Werther: Pourquoi me reveiller.	(912)
74740	Sadko: Chanson Indoue.	(6105)
74741	Pearl Fishers: Mi par d'udir.	(6105)

Note: Other imports assigned catalogue numbers in 1925 were the 1911/2 recordings of At My Window by Rachmaninoff (87397), Gretchaninoff s Cradle Song (87398), Romance of the Young Gypsy from Aleko (88687), "O Give Me Oblivion" from Dubrovsky (88688).

SORO, Cristina (Soprano)

VICTOR RED SEAL 1918-1923

64762	Nueva Cancion "Copihue Rojo" (Barriga).	
64801	Manon: Romanza.	
66107	Estrellita (Ponce).	(920)
66108	Carro del Sol: Cancion Veneciana.	(920)
66182	Lejos de Ti (Ponce).	(954)
66183	Vida Mia (Fuentes).	(954)
74585	Wally: Ebben ne andro.	
74586	Vogando (Cancion Chilena).	
74789	Trovatore: D'amor sull' ali.	(6409)

SOTHERN, E. H.—JULIA MARLOWE (Actors)

VICTOR RED SEAL 1921-1922

74662	Romeo and Juliet: Balcony Scene (part I).	(6298)
74663	Romeo and Juliet: Balcony Scene (part II).	(6298)
74673	Merchant of Venice: Shylock's Speech; Mercy Speech.	(6297)
74699	Julius Caesar: Friends, Romans, Countrymen.	(6295)
74700	Julius Caesar: If you have tears.	(6295)
74701	As You Like It: All the world's a stage.	
74702	Hamlet: To be or not to be.	(6294)
74703	Hamlet: Speech to the players.	(6294)
74704	Taming of the Shrew: Good Morrow, Kate.	(6299)
74705	Taming of the Shrew: What is your will.	(6299)
74706	Julius Caesar: Brutus and Portia.	(6296)
74707	Twelfth Night: The Duke and Viola.	(6296)
74708	Merchant of Venice: The Casket Scene.	(6297)

SPENCER, Janet (Contralto)

Spencer was much admired as a concert singer both in New York and her native Boston.

VICTOR RED SEAL 1911-1912

64186	Bolero (Arditi).	
64189	Good Bye, Sweet Day (Vannah).	(913)
64200	Moon Drops Low (Cadman).	
64249	White Dawn is Stealing (Cadman).	(913)
74231	Gae to Sleep (Fisher).	
74253	Don Carlos: O don fatale.	(15-1022)
74290	Elijah: O Rest in the Lord.	
74291	Hills of Skye (Harris).	(15-1022)

STANLEY, Helen (Soprano)

COLUMBIA RECORDS 1916-1917

48582	Dreams (Strelezki).	(A5809)
48586	Kerry Dance (Molloy).	(A5958)
48642	Love's Sorrow (Shelley).	(A5809)
48863	Don Giovanni: In quali eccessi.	(A5912)
48876	Carmen: Io dico che non.	(A5912)
49128	Down by the Sally Gardens.	(A5958)

Note: A native of Cincinnati, Stanley made the usual trek to Europe and returned with the experience of several seasons at Wurzburg.

STILES, Vernon (Tenor)

Note: An early condensed version of Mme. Butterfly on Columbia records included Stiles' duet with Richards labeled "The whole world over" on No. 30152 and a love scene with Vivienne on three sides Nos. 30161-63. His later work, still in English, revolved about more customary titles such as Bartlett's Dream (47463) issued as A2264.

STOKOWSKI, Leopold

See Philadelphia Symphony Orchestra.

STRACCIARI, Riccardo (Baritone)

COLUMBIA RECORDS 1917-1921

49180	Pagliacci: Prologo.	(68049D)	(9901M)
49181	Barber of Seville: Largo al factotum.	(68048D)	(9011M)
49192	Rigoletto: Cortigiani.	(68048D)	(9011M)
49214	Faust: Dio possente.	(68049D)	(9006M)
49215	Traviata: Di Provenza.	(68046D)	(9901M)
49220	Trovatore: Il balen.	(68047D)	(9013M)
49221	Masked Ball: Eri tu.	(68046D)	(9006M)
49333	Elegie (Massenet) (viol. Jacobsen).	(68070D)	(9902M)
49517	There's a Long Long Trail (Elliott) (w. Qt.).	(68071D)	(9015M)
49522	Core 'ngrato (Cardillo).	(68070D)	(9007M)
49590	The Sunshine of Your Smile (Ray).	(68071D)	(9015M)
49666	Forza del Destino: Solenne (w. Hackett).		(9009M)
49694	'Cause of You (Waller).		
49758	La Paloma (Yradier).	(68050D)	(9012M)
49922	Trovatore: Mira d'acerbe (w. Ponselle).	(71000D)	(9010M)
49968	Carmen: Canzone del Toreador (w. Cho.).	(68047D)	(9013M)
49971	Ideale (Tosti).	(68050D)	(9012M)
77085	Masked Ball: Alla vita.	(33024D)	
77088	Ernani: O de' verd' anni miei.	(33021D)	(4019M)
77089	Rigoletto: Pari siamo.	(33021D)	(4019M)
77261	Elegie (Massenet) (viol. Zentay).		
78097	O Sole Mio (di Capua).	(33018D)	
78099	Until (Sanderson).	(33046D)	
78100	Santa Lucia.	(33019D)	(4022M)
78101	Canta pe' me (de Curtis).	(33040D)	(4018M)
78104	Funiculi Funicula (Denza) (w. Cho.).	(33019D)	(4022M)
78407	When the Evening Bells are Ringing (von Tilzer).	(33046D)	
78686	Dear Little Boy of Mine (Ball).		
79636	Gioconda: Ah Pescator (w. Cho.).	(33024D)	
79701	Mattinata (Tosti).	(33018D)	
79719	La Spagnuola (di Chiara).	(33039D)	(4020M)
79720	Mattinata (Leoncavallo).	(33020D)	(4021M)
79736	Tu Sola (de Curtis).	(33040D)	(4018M)
79737	Parlatemi d'amor (de Curtis).	(33020D)	(4021M)
79875	Nostalgia (de Curtis).	(33039D)	(4020M)

IMPORTED COLUMBIA RECORDS 1925

Zaza: Buona Zaza.	(4007M)
Zaza: Zaza, piccola zingara.	(4007M)
Damnation of Faust: Serenata.	(4008M)
Hamlet: Come il romito fior.	(4008M)
Tosca: Gia mi dicon venal.	(4009M)
Andrea Chernier: Son sessant' anni.	(4009M)
Wally: T'amo ben io.	(4010M)
Hamlet: Brindisi.	(4027M)
Tannhauser: Allor che tu.	(4027M)
Damnation of Faust: Canzone della puce.	(4028M)
Damnation of Faust: Su queste rose.	(4028M)
Otello: Era la notte.	(4029M)
Otello: Brindisi.	(4029M)
Pagliacci: Prologo (part I).	(4030M)
Pagliacci: Prologo (part II).	(4030M)
O Sole Mio (di Capua).	(4031M)
Lucia: Cruda funesta smania.	(4031M)
Nabucco: Chi mi toglie.	(4032M)
Nabucco: Dio di Giuda.	(4032M)
Tannhauser: O tu bel' astro.	(9023M)
Agnus Dei (Bizet).	(9023M)

Otello: Credo.   (9024M)
Tosca: Te Deum.   (9024M)
Dinorah: Sei vendicata assai.   (9025M)
Africana: All'erta; Adamastor.   (9025M)

For other records, see BARRIENTOS.

Note: Extending his recording career, which had begun in 1904, well into the electrical era, Stracciari made replacements for the Barber of Seville and Rigoletto coupling under the same number, 9011M, and later dominated the complete performances of these operas with his ability to express emotion through song, not shout or grimace or extraneous sound effects. How many of our American baritones never learned this.

STRAUSS, Richard (Conductor) and Symphony Orchestra

BRUNSWICK RECORDS 1922

Salome: Salome's Dance (part I).   (50002)
Salome: Salome's Dance (part II).   (50002)
Burger als Edelmann—Intermezzo (Strauss).   (50017)
Burger als Edelmann—Menuett (Strauss).   (50017)

SUNDELIUS, Marie (Soprano)

VOCALION RECORDS 1920-1922

30104	Ave Maria (Gounod).	(60016)
30113	Fagelins Visa (Soderberg).	(60045)
30120	Boheme: Vals di Musetta.	(60016)
30147	Elegie (Massenet).	(60024)
30150	The Rosary (Nevin).	(60024)
52012	Boheme: Mi chiamano Mimi.	(70025)
52014	Mme. Butterfly: O quanti occhi (w. Crimi).	(70027)
52017	Lohengrin: Elsa's Dream.	(70025)

Note: Columbia had earlier listed Sundelius among its standard and foreign language series including such items as Mary of Allendale (45926) on No. A1875 and Bland Fjallen (43813) on No. E2836.

SWARTZ, Jeska (Mezzo-Soprano)

COLUMBIA RECORDS 1913

| 36434 | Faust: Le parlate d'amor. | (A5438) |
| 36435 | Maid of Orleans: Farewell ye Hills. | (A5438) |

Note: The Tschaikowsky work is also known as Joan of Arc in English in which it is sung by this member of the Boston Opera Company.

TAMAGNO, Francesco (Tenor)

Earlier cylinders of Tamagno would reveal him as a younger Othello though hardly a more dramatic, brilliant or authentic one.

VICTOR RED SEAL 1904

95001	Otello: Esultate.
95002	Otello: Morte d'Otello.
95003	Otello: Ora e per sempre.
95004	Andrea Chernier: Improvviso.
95005	Prophete: Re del ciel.
95006	Trovatore: Di quella pira.
95007	Prophete: Sopra Berta.
95008	Samson: Figli miei.

95009 Wm. Tell: O muto asil.
95010 Wm. Tell: Corriam, corriamo.
95011 ,Herodiade: Quand nos jours.

TERRY, Ellen (Actress)

VICTOR RED SEAL 1911

64191 Much Ado About Nothing: I have brought Claudio.
64193 Winter's Tale: Act II, Scene 1.
64194 Merchant of Venice: Mercy Speech.
74239 Hamlet: Ophelia's Mad Scene.
74240 Romeo and Juliet: Potion Scene.

Note: Early Bettini cylinders listed Terry among its theatrical celebrities along with Bernhardt, Coquelin, Drew, Guilbert, Langtry, Nethersole, Nielson, Rejane Salvini and von Sonnenthal among others.

TETRAZZINI, Luisa (Soprano)

The one and only Tetrazzini sang so much in the Spanish-Portugese speaking world in her early days, it would not be surprising were it established that the Zonophone records listed below originated considerably south or east of New York or San Francisco to which they have been ascribed. Likewise the suggestion that her famous brother-in-law, Cleofonte Campanini, accompanied her on these early discs, makes one wonder if so great a musician on the podium could be so bad a one at the piano. When Tetrazzini finally came to the capitals of the English speaking world in her mid thirties, she revealed on the stage and in the recording studios what coloratura singing can be but rarely is.

ZONOPHONE RECORDS 1903

2500	Lucia: Mad scene.	(10000)
2501	Barber of Seville: Una voce poco fa.	(10002)
2502	Rigoletto: Caro nome.	(10001)
2503	Romeo: Vals.	(10003)
2504	Sonnambula: Ah non giunge.	(10004)

IMPORTED VICTOR RED SEAL 1908-1909

92014	Rigoletto: Caro nome.		
92015	Mignon: Io son Titania.	(15-1001)	
92016	Lakme: Dov' e l'Indiana bruna.		
92017	Dinorah: Ombra leggiera.	(88298)	
92018	Lucia: Mad scene.		
92019	Marriage of Figaro: Voi che sapete.	(88300)	(15-1001)
92020	Barber of Seville: Una voce poco fa.		
92021	Traviata: Sempre libera.		
92022	Don Giovanni: Batti, batti.		
92060	Traviata: Ah fors e lui.		
92061	Romeo: Vals.	(88302)	(6345)
92063	Serenata (Tosti).		
92067	Lucia: Regnava nel silenzio.	(88303)	(6396)
92068	Masked Ball: Saper vorreste.		
92069	Sonnambula: Ah non credea.		
92070	Aprile (Tosti).	(88306)	(6336)

VICTOR RED SEAL 1911-1915

88291	Carnival of Venice (Benedict) (part I).	(6339)
88292	Carnival of Venice (Benedict) (part II).	(6339)
88293	Traviata: Ah fors e lui; Sempre libera.	(6344)
88294	Hijas del Zebedeo: Carceleras.	
88295	Rigoletto: Caro nome.	(6344)
88296	Mignon: Io son Titania.	(6342)
88297	Lakme: Dov' e l'Indiana bruna.	(6340)
88298	Dinorah: Ombra leggiera.	(6340)
88299	Lucia: Mad scene.	(6337)
88301	Barber of Seville: Una voce poco fa.	(6337)
88304	Masked Ball: Saper vorreste.	(6341)
88305	Sonnambula: Ah non credea.	(6396)
88307	Air and Variations (Proch).	(6336)
88308	Martha: Last Rose of Summer.	(6343)
88311	Swiss Echo Song (Eckert) (Ital.).	(6342)
88313	Sonnambula: Ah non giunge.	(6345)
88318	Pearl of Brazil: Charmant oiseau.	(6343)
88349	The Swallows (Cowen).	(6338)
88420	Trovatore: Tacea la notte.	(6346)
88423	Vals (Venzano).	(6341)
88426	Trovatore: D'amor sull'ali.	(6346)
88427	Rhapsodie (de Koven); Vergebliches Standchen (Brahms) (Ital.).	
88428	Bonnie Sweet Bessie (Gilbert).	(6338)
88432	Rosalinda: Pastoral.	
88502	Forza del Destino: Pace, Pace.	(6397)
88503	Carmen: Io dico che non.	(6397)
88504	Vespri Siciliani: Bolero.	
88505	Nina (att: Pergolesi).	
88506	Linda di Chamounix: O luce.	
88508	Solvejg's Song (Grieg) (Ital.).	

For other records, see CARUSO.

TEYTE, Maggie (Soprano)

COLUMBIA RECORDS 1914-1916

39114	Down in the Forest (Ronald).		(A1555)
39116	When Love is Kind (Moore).		(A1472)
39118	Obstination (de Fontenailles).		(A1471)
39120	Mifawny (Foster).		(A1490)
39121	L' Heure Exquise (Hahn).		(A1490)
39122	An Open Secret (Woodman).		(A1471)
39123	Little Grey Home in the West (Lohr).	(A1472)	(A1938)
39271	Believe Me if All Those Endearing Young Charms.		(A1555)
46209	A Little Love (Silesu).		(A1957)
46210	Just You (Burleigh).		(A1957)
46211	Until (Sanderson).		(A1938)
48813	Oft in the Stilly Night (Stevenson).	(A5834)	(5031M)
48814	Home Sweet Home (Bishop).	(A5834)	(5031M)

Note: Collectors surprised to find Maggie Teyte's name so early in record history will be even more so to learn of a 1907 Gramophone Company recording of Because on No. 3729.

THIBAUD, Jacques (Violinist)

IMPORTED VICTOR RED SEAL 1922-1924

66064	Serenite (Vieuxtemps).	(976)
66065	Moment Musical (Schubert); Minuet Caprice (Rode).	(977)

66066	Tambourin (Rameau); Saltarelle (Wieniawski).	(977)
66209	Slavonic Dance No. 1 (Dvorak-Kreisler).	(976)

For other records, see CORTOT.

Note: Much earlier than the above were Thibaud's Fonotipia records including Scherzando by Marsich, No. 39222 (C-F115).

THOMAS, John Charles (Baritone)

Note: Thomas' early days in musical comedy were marked by recordings for smaller companies who featured him in current theatrical successes and songs of the lighter variety. Some five years after Imperial, a hill-and-dale outfit, had released items from Alone at Last, Thomas began a series of Vocalion records which numbered two score during the 1921-1925 period and included, in addition to the more usual fare, Pagliacci: Prologo on No. 52024 and Elijah: It is enough on No. 52028 (70019). When Brunswick bought out this company, it continued the recording of this very popular singer with ten acoustics followed by much more interesting electricals.

TOKATYAN, Armand (Tenor)

VOCALION RECORDS 1923-1925

55010	Trovatore: Miserere (w. Raisa-Cho.).	
	Tosca: E lucevan le stelle.	(60056)
	Tosca: Recondita armonia.	(60056)
	Gioconda: Cielo e mar.	(70006)
	Tarantella Sincera (di Crescenzo).	(70006)
	Faust: Salut demeure.	(70008)
	Manon: Ah fuyez.	(70008)
	Africana: O Paradiso.	(70041)
	Carmen: Canzone del fior.	(70041)
	Fedora: Amor ti vieta.	(60070)
	Cavalleria Rusticana: Siciliana.	(60070)

TOSCANINI, Arturo (Conductor) and La Scala Orchestra

VICTOR RED SEAL 1921-1922

64952	La Pisanella—Quai del Porto (Pizzetti).	(840)
64986	L'Arlesienne Suite No. 2—Farandole (Bizet).	(839)
64999	Carmen: Prelude to Act IV.	(839)
66030	Don Pasquale: Overture (part I).	(841)
66031	Don Pasquale: Overture (part II).	(841)
66081	Secret of Suzanne: Overture.	(840)
74668	Symphony No. 39—Menuetto (Mozart).	(6303)
74669	Symphony No. 39—Allegro (Mozart).	(6303)
74672	Gagliarda (Galilei).	(6301)
74690	Symphony No. 1—Finale (Beethoven).	(6300)
74695	Damnation of Faust: Rakoczy March.	(6300)
74725	Scenes Pittoresques—Fete Boheme (Massenet).	(6301)
74745	Midsummer Night's Dream—Wedding March (Mendelssohn).	(6302)
74769	Symphony No. 5—Finale (part I) (Beethoven).	(6304)
74770	Symphony No. 5—Finale (part II) (Beethoven).	(6304)
74779	Midsummer Night's Dream—Scherzo (Mendelssohn).	(6302)

TRENTINI, Emma (Soprano)

COLUMBIA RECORDS 1907-1908

30087	Boheme: Vals di Musetta.	
30122	Don Giovanni: Vedrai carino.	(A5026)

Note: A decade elapsed between her appearances in La Scala in 1902 and the opening of "The Firefly", and Trentini sang on many records in between. Among the several Gramophone imports which Victor incorporated into its black label series was the first act finale, Verranno a te, from Lucia with Martinez-Patti on No. 52570 (62106).

TURGARINOFF, Klavdila (Contralto)

For duets, see MICHAILOWA.

Note: The masculine spelling on Victor labels (the correct form would have Turgarinowa) might have been due to the wonderful low tones she had in common with other Russian contraltos. Her many Gramophone records included native operas as well as more westernly ones such as Faust on No. 23483.

TURNER, Alan (Baritone)

Note: Turner appeared on all makes of the 1908 period singing in English both operatic excerpts from diverse works like Trovatore on Victor 5564 and Veronique on American 031306 as well as standard pieces like Sweet Genevieve on Zonophone 411 and For All Eternity on Columbia 3948.

VAN HOOSE, Ellison (Tenor)

Both here and abroad, Van Hoose was soloist with leading organizations. With the New York Oratorio Society, he sang in its first performance of Dream of Gerontius, November 1902.

VICTOR RED SEAL 1906-1908

85089	O Come With Me (Van der Stucken).	(74033)
85090	Lohengrin: In fernem Land.	(74034)
85091	Am Rhein und beim Wein (Ries).	(74035)
74003	Faust: O Merveille (w. Journet).	
74004	Faust: Que voulez-vous (w. De Gogorza-Journet).	
74005	Martha: Solo profugo (w. De Gogorza).	
74007	Aida: Celeste Aida.	
95201	Meistersinger: Quintet (w. Gadski-Mattfield-Journet-Reiss).	

COLUMBIA RECORDS 1912

30884	When the Roses Bloom (Reichardt).	(A5352)
30885	Lass with the Delicate Air (Arne).	(A5352)

VANNI, Roberto (Tenor)

Note: Vanni, who sang mostly minor roles at the Metropolitan and Chicago Operas, after coming from La Scala, appears on Bettini and other cylinders as well as several brands of early discs. Of those he made for Columbia, some were issued abroad in more distinguished a category than they enjoyed here, including the Carmen Canzone del flor on No. 1363.

VAN ROOY, Anton (Baritone)

COLUMBIA RECORDS 1906-1909

30028	Das Muhlrad.	(A5017)
30029	Die Beiden Grenadiere (Schumann).	(A5015)
30086	Carmen: Chanson du Toreador.	
30097	Phyllis und die Mutter.	(A5000)
30098	Meistersinger: O Eva.	

30109	Les Rameaux (Faure).	(A5001)
30131	Der Lindenbaum (Schubert).	(A5087)
30164	Am Meer (Schubert).	(A5074)
30165	Der Asra (Rubenstein).	(A5074)
30167	Wanderlied (Schumann).	(A5087)

IMPORTED VICTOR RED SEAL 1909

92062 Lohengrin: Dank, Konig, dir.

Note: Van Rooy was included in the 1899 Bettini cylinder catalogue and was advertised, both by name and picture, in magazines of the year 1903 as having made Victor Red Seal records. That some of his London issue of the prior year were pressed as part of the 5000 series seems evident, as is also the case with the Russian gypsy singer, Vialtzeva.

VELA, Luisa (Soprano)

IMPORTED VICTOR RED SEAL 1909-1916

61213	Merry Widow: Cancion de Vilia.	(45301)
64465	Golondrinas: Cancion del Acto I.	(45299)
64467	Golondrinas: La Primavera.	(45299)
64569	Rey que Rabio: Ay di me.	(45300)
64571	Rey que Rabio: Duo (w. Haro).	(45300)

For other records, see SAGI-BARBA.

Note: Vela was wife of Sagi-Barba and a prominent member of his own company.

VIAFORA, Gina C. (Soprano)

See Ciaparelli-Viafora.

VILLANI, Luisa (Soprano)

Though not afforded celebrity classification by Columbia, Luisa Villani was important both for her creation of the part of Fiora in "L'Amore dei Tre Re" and her decided successes in other dramatic roles.

COLUMBIA RECORDS 1911-1912

30812	Trovatore: Miserere (w. Cartica-Cho.).	(A5325)
30814	Aida: O terra addio (w. Cartica-Cho.).	(A5331)
36382	Cavalleria Rusticana: Innegiamo (w. Cho.).	(A5404)

VINCENT, Ruth (Soprano)

Ruth Vincent was a pupil of Herman Klein who contributed so much to phonographic lore during a long and busy lifetime.

COLUMBIA RECORDS 1906

3358	Villanelle (Dell' Acqua).	(30001)	(A5014)
3377	Home Sweet Home (Bishop).	(30002)	(A5009)
30022	Killarney (Balfe).		(A5020)
30024	Comin' thro' the Rye.		(A5021)
30025	Nymphes et Sylvains (Bemberg).		(A5016)

IMPORTED COLUMBIA RECORDS 1908

6009	Tom Jones: Which is My Own True Self.	(A5086)
6016	Penseroso: Sweet Bird.	(A5086)
6017	Pearl of Brazil: Charmant oiseau.	(A5077)
6018	Lo, Here the Gentle Lark (Bishop).	(A5077)

WEIL, Herman (Baritone)

COLUMBIA RECORDS 1916-1917

43958	Swabischer Landler.	(E3172)
44001	Das Steierland (Seydler).	(E3172)
44753	Im Walde (Walbach).	(E3403)
44754	Matrosenlied (Ramrath).	(E3403)
59430	Beiden Grenadiere (Schumann).	(A5864)
59431	Wald Andacht (Abt).	(A5864)

Note: More in keeping with Weil's usual work than his Columbias issued on banner or lesser labels were a series of imports available here on Opera Disc, which included the Meistersinger: Fliedermonolog on No. 65137 (Gr. 043235).

WEINGARTNER, Felix (Conductor) and Columbia Symphony Orchestra

COLUMBIA RECORDS 1913-1914

Tristan: Liebestod.	(A5464)
Invitation to the Dance (Weber-Weingartner).	(A5464)
Carmen: Prelude and Intermezzo Act IV.	(A5559)
L'Arlesienne—Prelude and Adagietto (Bizet).	(A5559)
Walkure: Magic Fire Scene.	(A5594)
Symphonie Pathetique—First Movement (Tschaikowsky).	(A5594)

Note: The above are but faint harbingers of the huge quantity of excellent recordings Weingartner was to make for Columbia beginning a decade later. That he was composer of anything but smaller pieces and that his operas included an Orestes trilogy, a Cain and Abel and many others would never be guessed from his records. Unlike several of his contemporaries, he was not a self-publicist.

WERRENRATH, Reinald (Baritone)

VICTOR RED SEAL 1919-1925

64830	Molly (Herbert).	
64843	Dreaming Alone in the Twilight (Moore).	(843)
64863	Duna (McGill).	(844)
64897	Fortune Teller: Gypsy Love Song.	(844)
64914	Stein Song (Bullard).	(945)
64931	Colleen o' My Heart (Penn).	(842)
64950	Story of the Rose (Mack).	(846)
64964	Love Sends a Little Gift of Roses (Openshaw).	(843)
64987	There's Sunlight in Your Eyes (Harling).	(847)
66018	Where My Dear Lady Sleeps (Smith).	(848)
66032	Blossom Time: Tell Me Daisy.	(846)
66047	Moonrise (Samuels).	(842)
66087	Little Shawl of Blue (Hewitt).	(845)
66118	Little Man (Ball).	(845)
66132	Kashmiri Song (Woodforde-Finden).	(848)
66145	Heaven at the End of the Road (Osgood).	(847)
66173	Robin Hood: Brown October Ale.	(945)
66180	World is Waiting for the Sunrise (Seitz).	(951)
66181	Rose in the Bud (Forster).	(951)
66216	A Brown Bird Singing (Wood).	(984)
66217	Sittin', Thinkin' (Fisher).	(984)
66226	Can't You Hear Me Callin' Caroline (Roma) (w. Qt.).	(991)
66227	When You Were Sweet Sixteen (Thornton) (w. Qt.).	(991)
66278	Little Jessie James: I Love You.	(1026)
66279	Little Jessie James: Suppose I Had Never Met You.	(1026)
	Dream Girl: Broad Highway.	(1055)

	Heart o' Mine (Herbert).	(1055)
	Sun and Moon (Penn).	(1072)
	Drumadoon (Sanderson).	(1072)
	Dear Old Girl (Morse) (w. Qt.).	(1078)
	She was bred in Old Kentucky (Carter) (w. Qt.).	(1078)
74610	Herodiade: Vision fugitive.	
74719	Nazareth (Gounod).	(6426)
74783	On the Road to Mandalay (Speaks).	(6360)
74815	Goin' Home (Dvorak).	(6472)
74827	Danny Deever (Damrosch).	(6360)
74842	Holy Night (Adam).	(6426)
	Follow Me (Dett).	(6472)
87569	Don Giovanni: La ci darem (w. Garrison).	

For other records, see McCORMACK, OBER.

Note: For ten years prior to his inclusion in the Red Seal rank as a soloist, Werrenrath's voice could be heard on hundreds of Victor records of other categories including some of great musical importance like Allerseelen (Strauss) and Zur Ruh' (Wolf) on No. 17179; Euridice (Caccini): Non piango on No. 45069; Orfeo (Monteverdi): Tu se' morta on No. 45083; Indian Queen: I attempt from Love's sickness on No. 45092; Euridice (Peri): Funeste piaggie on No. 55051; Deux Journees: Guide Thou My Steps on No. 55075.

WHEATLEY, Walter (Tenor)

Though born in Missouri, Wheatley's prominence was greatest in England, where the following recordings originate and in Italy, where he was an original protagonist in Errisguola.

IMPORTED COLUMBIA RECORDS 1914-1915

6064	Carmen: Flower Song.	(A5510)
6065	Boheme: Your tiny hand.	(A5510)
27171	Maritana: There is a flower.	(A1422)
27172	Maritana: Yes let me like a soldier fall.	(A1422)
28486	Drink to me only with thine eyes.	(A1718)

WHITE, Carolina (Soprano)

During the period of her stay at the Chicago Opera, this youthful American singer enjoyed the lead in almost all initial presentations of contemporary Italian works.

COLUMBIA RECORDS 1912-1914

30869	Mme. Butterfly: Un bel di.	(A5354)
30870	Robert: Roberto tu che adoro.	(A5353)
30871	Louise: Depuis le jour.	(H1080)
30897	Pagliacci: Ballatella.	(A5353)
30898	Marriage of Figaro: Dove sono.	(A5354)
36717	Irish Love Song (Lang).	(A5488)
36719	Aida: Ritorna vincitor.	(A5499)
36720	Martha: Last Rose of Summer.	(A5488)
36722	Aida: O patria mia.	(A5499)
36938	Serenata (Tosti).	(A5571)
36941	L'Ultima Canzone (Tosti).	(A5571)
38348	O Sole Mio (di Capua).	(A1330)
38351	Natoma: Spring Song.	(A1432)
38352	Manon Lescaut: In quelle trine.	(A1330)
38837	At Parting (Rogers).	(A1376)
38838	Lass with the Delicate Air (Arne).	(A1376)
38839	Sweetest Story Ever Told (Stults).	(A1432)
39341	A Birthday (Woodman).	(A1591)
39342	I Hear a Thrush at Eve (Cadman).	(A1591)

WHITEHILL, Clarence (Baritone)

VICTOR RECORDS 1912-1918

64278	Walkure: Wotans Abschied (part I).	
64279	Bedouin Love Song (Pinsuti).	(853)
64359	Old Black Joe (Foster).	(850)
64360	In the Gloaming (Harrison) (w. Cho.).	(850)
64388	Uncle Rome (Homer).	
64519	Ich grolle nicht (Schumann).	
64602	Marching through Georgia (Work).	(849)
64608	Tramp, Tramp, Tramp (Root).	
64609	Some Day I'll Wander Back (Huntley) (w. Qt.).	(852)
64610	Take Me Back to Home (Huntley).	(852)
64613	Nancy Lee (Adams).	(851)
64677	America (Carey).	(849)
64707	'Tis but a Little Faded Flower (Thomas).	(853)
64719	My Homeland (Speaks).	(851)
64735	Panurge: Chanson de la Touraine.	
64789	Mate o' Mine (Elliot).	
74305	Walkure: Wotans Abschied (part II).	
74320	Elijah: Lord God of Abraham.	(6350)
74321	Love's Old Sweet Song (Molloy).	(6307)
74364	Thais: Voila donc la terrible cite.	
74380	Elijah: It is Enough.	(6350)
74405	Requiem (Verdi): Confutatis.	
74406	Parsifal: Amfortas Gebet.	
74407	Bohemian Girl: Heart Bow'd Down.	(6307)
74425	I'll Take You Home Again, Kathleen (Westendorf).	(6306)
74433	I Want to See the Old Home (Stewart) (w. Cho.).	(6306)
74451	Dream Faces (Hutchinson).	(6305)
74452	Some Day (Wellings).	(6305)
74556	Two Grenadiers (Schumann).	

IMPORTED VICTOR RED SEAL 1924

74855	Walkure: Wotan bids farewell.	(6435)
74856	Walkure: Wotan kisses Brunnhilde.	(6435)
74857	Walkure: The rock is surrounded by fire.	
74858	Siegfried: Wotan invokes Erda.	(6436)
74859	Siegfried: Siegfried's ascent.	(6436)

Note: **Recordings to wh'ch numbers were also assigned include: Es blink der Tau (64391), Juanita (64456), Mate o' Mine (64494), two trials of Massa's in the Cold, Cold Ground (64522) (64756), When the Great Red Dawn is Shining (64788) and Ring Out, Sweet Bells of Peace (64800). Examples of his pre-Wagnerian days and later work in that genre occur also on early Zonophone, Gramophone and other makes.**

WILLIAMS, Evan (Tenor)

VICTOR RED SEAL 1907-1910

64078	A Dream (Bartlett).	(854)
64080	Sweet Miss Mary (Neidlinger).	(860)
64086	Queen of Sheba: Lend Me Your Aid (part I).	
64088	Mary of Argyle (Nelson).	(864)
64092	Lead Kindly Light (Dykes).	(859)
64093	Serenade (Schubert).	(869)
64096	Queen of Sheba: Lend Me Your Aid (part II).	(868)
64100	The Lass of Richmond Hill (McNally).	(858)
64102	Little Boy Blue (Nevin).	(861)
64105	Auld Lang Syne.	(862)
64106	Holy Night (Adam).	(859)

64109	Absent (Metcalf).	(854)
64133	Because (d'Hardelot).	(871)
64139	Four-Leaf Clover (Brownell).	(855)
64141	Mentra Gwen.	(867)
74088	Elijah: If With All Your Hearts.	(6316)
74089	Love Abiding (Jordan).	
74093	Stabat Mater: Cuius animam.	(6324)
74094	Love Shall Be Lord (Corbett).	
74100	All Through the Night (Boulton).	(6318)
74109	Come into the Garden, Maud (Balfe).	(6310)
74115	Meistersinger: Prize Song.	(6314)
74119	Crossing the Bar (Willeby).	(6311)
74122	Carmen: Flower Song.	(6322)
74126	Messiah: Thy Rebuke; Behold and See.	(6316)
74127	Prodigal Son: How Many Hired Servants.	(6368)
74128	Martha: Like a Dream.	(6322)
74129	Boheme: Thy Hands are Frozen.	
74130	Lohengrin: In Distant Land.	(6314)
74131	Judas Maccabaeus: Sound An Alarm.	(6324)
74136	St. Paul: Be Thou Faithful.	(6323)
74141	Favorita: Spirit So Fair.	(6308)
74148	Africana: Oh Paradise.	(6308)
74150	Elisir d'Amore: A Furtive Tear.	
74160	Forgotten (Cowles).	(6309)
74181	O Na Byddai 'n Haf (Davies).	
74187	Star of Bethlehem (Adams).	(6320)
74189	Messiah: Ev'ry Valley.	(6315)
74190	Messiah: Comfort Ye.	(6315)

VICTOR RED SEAL 1911-1918

64158	A May Morning (Denza).	(863)
64199	Good Bye, Sweetheart (Hatton).	(858)
64210	Loch Lomond.	(862)
64216	Hedge Roses (Schubert).	
64217	Return of Spring (Schumann).	(863)
64218	Hark Hark the Lark (Schubert).	(869)
64219	Wynken, Blynken and Nod (Paissiello).	(866)
64220	The Sandman (Schaefer).	(866)
64221	Hearing (Miessner).	
64271	Alice Where Art Thou (Ascher).	(856)
64280	Jean (Burleigh).	
64306	A Perfect Day (Bond).	(857)
64327	Ah Love But a Day (Protheroe).	(855)
64389	Just a-Wearyin' for You (Bond).	(857)
64411	Beautiful Isle of Somewhere (Fearis).	(865)
64512	Spray of Roses (Sanderson).	
64513	Pipes of Gordon's Men (Hammond).	(867)
64516	From the Land of the Sky-Blue Water (Cadman).	(871)
64545	Ninety and Nine (Sankey).	(865)
64594	When the Boys Come Home (Speaks).	
64634	Chiming Bells of Long Ago (Shattuck).	(856)
64650	Elijah: Then Shall the Righteous.	(868)
64711	There Little Girl (Stephens).	(861)
64761	Tim Rooney's at the Fightin' (Flynn).	
64763	Yn iach i ti Gumbri.	(870)
64764	Y Deryn Pur.	(870)
64765	Mother My Dear (Treharne).	(864)
64771	A Little Bit o' Honey (Bond).	(860)
74198	Open the Gates of the Temple (Knapp).	(6320)
74199	Oh Dry Those Tears (del Riego).	(6313)
74205	Answer (Robyn).	(6309)
74254	My Pretty Jane (Bishop).	(6319)

74331	A Spirit Flower (Tipton).	(6319)
74356	Holy City (Adams).	(6312)
74403	Samson (Handel): Total Eclipse.	(6368)
74404	Beloved, It is Morn (Aylward).	(6310)
74409	My Ain Folk (Lemon).	(6318)
74410	The Cross (Ware).	
74419	Death of Nelson (Braham).	
74453	The Lost Chord (Sullivan).	(6311)
74476	Dreaming of Home (Ordway) (w. Cho.).	(6321)
74477	Face to Face (Johnson).	(6312)
74480	Mollie Darling (Hays) (w. Cho.).	(6317)
74490	When You and I Were Young (Butterfield) (w. Cho.).	(6317)
74498	Hymn of Praise: Sorrows of Death.	(6323)
74550	Good Bye (Tosti).	(6313)
74551	Her Beautiful Hands (Stephens).	
74571	Song That Reached My Heart (Jordan).	(6321)

Note: Other recordings assigned numbers include: Good Bye Sweet Day (Vannah) No. 64114; Yesterday and Today (Spross) No. 64460; The Moon Drops Low (Cadman) No. 64515; Seek Ye the Lord (Roberts) (w. Cho.) No. 74454; The Palms (Faure) No. 74549; of these No. 74454 was scheduled for release in Dec. 1915 though it does not appear in the catalogues. Early black seal records were disguised under such names as Henry Evans, etc. with a picture obviously not that of Williams in the supplements announcing them. However, the voice, as in Jordan's The song that reached my heart on No. 5643 is unmistakably that of this full-throated tenor who so well fulfilled a Handelian tradition of long standing.

WILSON, Margaret Woodrow (Soprano)

Presidents' daughters will take to song and Margaret Woodrow Wilson (the middle name, we suspect, was not originally there any more than it really began that of her illustrious father) did so with emphasis on Scotch lore and patriotic feelings.

COLUMBIA RECORDS 1914-1918

36860	Low Back'd Car (Lover).	
36883	Will Ye No Come Back (Nairne).	
39195	My Laddie (Thayer) (or.).	
39196	My Lovely Celia (Higgins).	
39267	Leezie Lindsay.	
39764	Star Spangled Banner (Smith) (w. Cho.).	(A1685)
77297	My Old Kentucky Home (Foster) (w. Qt.).	(A2416)
77302	My Laddie (Thayer) (p.).	(A2416)

WITHERSPOON, Herbert (Bass)

VICTOR RED SEAL 1907-1911

64071	Mother o' Mine (Tours).	
64108	Flow Gently Sweet Afton (Spillman).	(873)
64151	Rolling Down to Rio (German).	(874)
64185	Requiem; Dearest (Homer).	
64212	Muletier de Tarragone (Henrion).	
64222	In questa tomba (Beethoven).	
74070	Samson (Handel): Honor and Arms.	
74071	Meet Me by Moonlight (Wade).	(6329)
74072	Messiah: Why do the Nations.	(6326)
74078	Gypsy John (Clay).	
74079	By the Short Cut to the Roses; Black Sheelah.	
74080	Messiah: The Trumpet Shall Sound.	(6326)

74081	Elijah: Lord God of Abraham.	
74082	Elijah: It is Enough.	
74137	The Lost Chord (Sullivan).	(6325)
74138	Seasons: With Joy the Impatient Husbandman.	(6328)
74144	Parsifal: Charfreitags-Zauber.	(6330)
74145	Meistersinger: Was duftet doch.	
74192	Stabat Mater: Pro peccatis.	
74206	Caid: Air du Tambour-Major.	
74207	Vespri Sciliani: O tu Palermo.	
74233	Vittoria (Floridia).	
74241	Simon Boccanegra: Il lacerato spirito.	
88092	Rheingold: Weiche Wotan (w. Schumann-Heink).	

VICTOR RED SEAL 1912-1918

64243	Border Ballad (Cowen).	
64347	St. Matthew Passion: At Eventide.	
64471	A Memory (Huntley-Park).	
64472	Pirate Song (Gilbert).	
64473	Marriage of Figaro: Se vuol ballare.	
64474	Eyes of Blue (Orth).	
64528	A Warrior Bold (Adams).	(874)
64533	Rose Marie (Molloy).	
64534	Off to Philadelphia.	
64535	Just You (Burleigh).	(872)
64645	Old Black Mare (Squire).	
64743	Old Oaken Bucket (Woodworth).	(873)
64751	Bird and the Rose (Horrocks).	(872)
74277	Queen of Sheba: Sous les pieds.	
74278	Bendemeer's Stream (Moore).	
74279	Hosanna (Granier).	(6325)
74323	Der Wanderer (Schubert).	
74327	Mary of Allendale (Hook).	
74347	Simon the Cellarer (Hatton).	
74348	Der Lindenbaum (Schubert).	(6329)
74349	Auld Fisher (Elma).	
74416	All in the April Evening (Dick).	
74417	One Sweetly Solemn Thought (Ambrose).	(6328)
74418	Maria, Mari (di Capua).	
74450	Calvary (Rodney).	
74458	Three Fishers (Hullah).	
74497	Trompeter von Sakkingen: It Was Not So.	
74505	Judas Maccabaeus: Arm Arm Ye Brave.	(6330)
74513	Scipione: Hear Me Ye Winds and Waves.	

Note: Additional assigned numbers include In Old Madrid (64755), Foaming Billows (74228) and Call Me Back (74501), to which Witherspoon undoubtedly brought his customarily resolute approach and dignified bearing.

WRIGHT, Rosa Linde (Contralto)

COLUMBIA RECORDS 1906

| 3502 | La Paloma (Yradier). | (A509) |
| 30031 | Hugenots: Nobil Signori. | (A5015) |

Note: Columbia often enlisted the services of lesser known artists for a very limited number of recordings and then released only a part of these.

YAW, Ellen Beach (Soprano)

While her concert publicity mentioned the songs she composed and the Rose of Persia she inspired, it was Yaw's G in altissimo that was most calculated to bring in the customers.

VICTOR RED SEAL 1907

64079 Swiss Echo Song (Eckert).
74090 Lakme: Ou va la jeune Hindoue.
74091 Re Pastore: L'ameio saro constante.
74092 Marriage of Jeannette: Chanson du Rossignol.

YSAYE, Eugen (Violinist)

COLUMBIA RECORDS 1913-1914

36513 Meistersinger: Prize Song.
36514 Scherzo Valse (Chabrier).
36516 Lointain Passe (Ysaye).
36519 Beiceuse (Faure).
36520 Concerto in E Minor—Finale (Mendelssohn).
36521 Mazurkas (Wieniawski).
36523 Rondino Op. 32 (Vieuxtemps).
36524 Hungarian Dance No. 5 (Brahms).
36525 Capiice Viennois (Kreisler).
36526 Albumblatt (Wagner).
36907 Ave Maria (Schubert).
36908 Humoresque (Dvorak).

Note: Much respected by violinists as a performer and as a composer, Ysaye is also represented on discs as a conductor, his work wi.h the Cincinnati Symphony Orchestra including the Diagons de Villars Overture (49701) on No. A6159.

ZANELLI, Renato (Baritone)

Zanelli's was a fine baritone voice which later progressed upwards into the range suitable for a noteworthy Othello.

VICTOR RED SEAL 1919-1923

64831 Pagliacci: Prologo (part I). (881)
64832 Pagliacci: Prologo (part II). (881)
64834 La Spagnuola (di Chiara). (880)
64835 Zaza: Buona Zaza.
64858 Los Ojos Negros (Alvarez). (880)
64907 Zaza: Zaza, piccola zingara. (882)
64922 Wally: T amo ben io. (877)
64923 O Primavera (Tirindelli). (877)
64931 Ay Ay Ay (Perez). (878)
64954 El Relicario (Padilla). (878)
64972 Madrigal de Mai (Nitke). (879)
66013 Marianina (Ferri). (882)
66025 Chimes of Normandy: Dans mes voyages. (879)
66055 Il Sogno (Tosti). (916)
66167 Mamma (Gastaldon). (916)
74622 Rigoletto: Pari siamo. (6383)
74632 Favorita: A tanto amor. (6383)
74747 Ave Maria (Luzzi).

ZENATELLO, Giovanni (Tenor)

COLUMBIA RECORDS 1912-1913

19693 Cavalleria Rusticana: Brindisi. (A1142)
19694 Trovatore: Di quella pira. (A1142)
19851 Cavalleria Rusticana: Siciliana. (A1235)
19856 Pagliacci: Vesti la giubba. (A1235)

30890	Tosca: E lucevan le stelle.		(A5359)
30891	Otello: Morte d' Otello.		(A5359)
30922	Gioconda: Cielo e mar.		(A5400)
30924	Faust: Tardi si fa (w. Nielsen).		(H1073)
36366	Aida: Nume custode (w. Mardones-Cho.).	(A5426)	(7032M)
36372	Aida: Celeste Aida.		(A5400)

For other records, see DESTINN, GAY.

Note: Though he appeared on all major labels throughout a long recording career, Zena.ello's chief work was for the Fonotipia company which released a great number of pre-1909 items, including the Andrea Chern.er: Si fui soldato on No. 92213 (C-F96), as well as many of later date. On the stage Mme. Butterfly, Figlia di Jorio and Gloria were but some of the operas which utilized his services for premieres of varying success.

ZEPPILLI, Alice (Soprano)

If you are acquainted with the history of such works as Princesse d' Auberge and Quo Vadis in domestic performances, Zeppilli will be recalled as an important participant in both of them.

COLUMBIA RECORDS 1912

| 19805 | Manon: Gavotte. | (A1213) |
| 19806 | Tales of Hoffmann: Les oiseaux. | (A1213) |

ZEROLA, Nicola (Tenor)

VICTOR RED SEAL 1910-1911

87036	Masked Ball: Barcarola.	(64166)	
87037	Masked Ball: La rivedro.	(64167)	
87045	Trovatore: Di quella pira.	(64170)	(45218)
87046	Otello: Ora e per sempre addio.	(64168)	(45219)
87064	Pagliacci: Vesti la giubba.	(64169)	(45217)
88202	Otello: Morte d' Otello.	(74217)	(55133)
88243	Andrea Chernier: Improvviso.	(74216)	(55134)
64172	Trovatore: Deserto sulla terra.		(45218)
64173	Samson: Figli miei.		
64206	Pagliacci: Un tal gioco.		(45217)
64207	L'Alba Nascente (Parelli).		(45219)
74225	Aida: La fatal pietra; Morir si pura.		(55133)
74247	Pagliacci: No Pagliaccio.		(55134)

Note: As can be seen from the catalogue numbers, the Zerola records were twice reduced in price ending, after a decade, in the blue seal classification. He had been featured following the 1909 supplementary season at the Manhattan Opera House which had recruited him from an abandoned transient company.

ZIMBALIST, Efrem (Violinist)

VICTOR RED SEAL 1912-1924

64241	Humoresque (Tor Aulin).	(887)
64261	Orientale (Cui).	(886)
64266	Long Ago (MacDowell).	(885)
64335	Larghetto (Handel).	(883)
64455	Hebraisches Lied und Tanz (Zimbalist).	(887)
64518	Sonata Op. 42 No. 2—Andantino (Reger).	
64562	Polish Dance (Zimbalist).	(889)
64576	Serenata (Moszkowski).	(891)
64577	Chant d' Automne (Tschaikowsky).	(883)
64638	Massa's in de Cold, Cold Ground (Foster).	(888)

64640	Old Black Joe (Foster).	(888)
64710	Serenata (d 'Ambrosio).	(891)
64736	Chant Negre (Kramer).	(884)
64737	Chant de la Veslemoy (Halvorsen).	(884)
64813	Souvenir (Drdla).	(892)
64827	Le Deluge—Prelude (Saint-Saens).	(886)
64936	Serenade (Pierne).	(890)
64955	Russian Dance (Zimbalist).	(889)
66034	Spring Song (Mendelssohn).	(892)
66101	Salut d'amour (Elgar).	(890)
66119	Song Without Words (Tschaikowsky).	(885)
66220	Madrigale (Simonetti).	(988)
66221	Petite Serenade (Bethier).	(988)
	Improvisation (Zimbalist).	(1054)
	Entr' acte (Kramer).	(1054)
	Fortune Teller: Gypsy Love Song.	(1056)
	Guitarrero (Drdla).	(1056)
74280	Sicilienne; Minuet (Zimbalist).	(6369)
74303	Hungarian Dances Nos. 20, 21 (Brahms-Joachim).	(6333)
74337	Legende (Wieniawski).	(6369)
74338	Le Cygne (Saint-Saens); Waltz Op. 64 No. 1 (Chopin).	(6332)
74443	Alabama (Spalding).	
74444	Minuet in G (Beethoven); Gavotte in D (Gossec).	(6332)
74445	Broken Melody (van Biene).	(6331)
74467	Millions d' Arlequin (Drigo).	(6333)
74582	The Lark (Glinka-Auer).	(6331)
74883	Spanish Dance (Sarasate).	(6451)
74884	Humoresque (Bowen).	(6451)

For other records, see **GLUCK, KREISLER.**

Note: Also assigned numbers, if not released, were violin transcriptions of "I Hear You Calling Me" (64330) and "Serenade" (64561).

It will not astonish anyone that personages of great importance in political, theatrical and literary realms were less finicky than their musical brethren to expose their ideas or talents to the new-fangled talking machine. While contemporary confirmation of the records supposedly made by Brahms and Jenny Lind has not yet been forthcoming, journals of the last century tell in detail of the experiences before the horn of notables such as Browning and Tennyson. By the time commercial recording was ready to sell its wares in wholesale fashion, a veritable Who's Who was ready and willing to perpetuate their voices — all our presidents and their campaign rivals, authors of both utmost and no distinction and, of course, stage and screen stars ad infinitum.

The only element of surprise in the foregoing might come from finding out how very long ago it was that the phonograph was already capitalizing on the popularity of Al Jolson or Eddie Cantor or one Fred Allen, a saxophonist. However, it is outside the exclusively "celebrity issue" scope of this book to reveal the ancient facts on these figures. Rather do we confine ourselves, with three exceptions, to echoes of the Golden Age of Opera (and Concert) and hope that the timelessness of these will likewise belie their antiquity.

Columbia and Other Makes

As was pointed out in the introduction, Columbia had no distinctive numbering system to set apart its celebrity issues from those of a more transient value. At least up to 1924, any numerical catalogue of this company might show a Bonci or a Boninsegna in juxtaposition to a popular ditty. Such records as were contained in the top-price 33000D (ten-inch) and 68000D (twelve-inch) series, which existed for one brief year and the purple label 4000M (ten-inch) and 9000M (twelve-inch) series, which had just begun at the end of the acoustic era, will be found under Barrientos, Butt, Casals, Gordon, Hackett, Lashanska, Lazaro, Nordica, Ponselle, Seidel and Stracciari. From the foregoing double-face numbers, the size of most of the records listed under these artists can be determined; those released in single-face form only can be judged by the rule that most American records with five-digit numbers are of the same size if their first two numbers are similar.

During the most important period of Columbia's productivity, doublings were made in series with letter prefixes. Of these A 5000, C 1000, E 5000, H 1000, S 5000 are the most common twelve-inch while those with lower numbers in each letter group are mostly ten-inch. From this, and the willingness to indulge in a little numerical research within this book alone, it should be possible to calculate whether the Columbia records listed are large size or not. As for Vocalions, the leading 60000 (ten-inch) and 70000 (twelve-inch) double-face series will give the clue to the size of most of the corresponding single-face as well. The Brunswick records listed fall almost completely into the 10000 and 15000 groups for the ten-inch and the 30000 and 50000 for the twelve-inch. (Be careful, the first of these last two numbers is not the same size on Vocalion.)

With this springboard for individual initiative on the part of the collector, we jump to a more formidable task which he will now find completed.

Victor Red Seal
(Please refer to section on this label in the introduction.)

---

(500) *Ten-inch*   *Double-face* (615)

500	Caruso	529	Alda	558	Chaliapin	587	De Gogorza
501	Caruso	530	Alda	559	Clement	588	De Gogorza
502	Caruso	531	Alda	560	Cortot	589	De Gogorza
503	Caruso	532	Alda	561	Cortot	590	De Gogorza
504	Caruso	533	Alda	562	Cortot	591	De Gogorza
505	Caruso	534	Alda	563	Culp	592	De Luca
506	Caruso	535	Alda	564	Culp	593	De Luca
507	Caruso	536	Alda	565	Culp	594	De Luca
508	Caruso	537	Alda	566	Culp	595	De Luca
509	Caruso	538	Alda	567	Culp	596	De Luca
510	Caruso	539	Amato	568	Culp	597	Elman
511	Caruso	540	Battistini	569	Culp	598	Elman
512	Caruso	541	Besanzoni	570	Culp	599	Elman
513	Caruso	542	Bori	571	Dalmores	600	Elman
514	Caruso	543	Bori	572	De Gogorza	601	Elman
515	Caruso	544	Bori	573	De Gogorza	602	Elman
516	Caruso	545	Bori	574	De Gogorza	603	Elman
517	Caruso	546	Bori	575	De Gogorza	604	Elman
518	Caruso	547	Boston S. O.	576	De Gogorza	605	Elman
519	Caruso	548	Braslau	577	De Gogorza	606	Elman
520	Caruso	549	Braslau	578	De Gogorza	607	Elman
521	Caruso	550	Braslau	579	De Gogorza	608	Elman
522	Caruso	551	Braslau	580	De Gogorza	609	Elman
523	Caruso	552	Braslau	581	De Gogorza	610	Elman
524	Alda	553	Braslau	582	De Gogorza	611	Elman
525	Alda	554	Braslau	583	De Gogorza	612	Elman Qt.
526	Alda	555	Braslau	584	De Gogorza	613	Chemet
527	Alda	556	Braslau	585	De Gogorza	614	Renaud
528	Alda	557	Braslau	586	De Gogorza	615	Amato; Hamlin

616	Farrar	679	Homer	741	McCormack	804	Powell
617	Farrar	680	Homer	742	McCormack	805	Powell
618	Farrar	681	Homer	743	McCormack	806	Powell
619	Farrar	682	Homer	744	McCormack	807	Powell
620	Farrar	683	Homer	745	McCormack	808	Powell
621	Farrar	684	Homer	746	McCormack	809	Powell
622	Farrar	685	Homer	747	McCormack	810	Powell
623	Farrar	686	Homer	748	McCormack	811	Powell
624	Farrar	687	Jeritza	749	McCormack	812	Rachmaninoff
625	Farrar	688	Jeritza	750	McCormack	813	Rachmaninoff
626	Flonzaley Qt.	689	Johnson	751	McCormack	814	Rachmaninoff
627	Galli-Curci	690	Johnson	752	McCormack	815	Rachmaninoff
628	Galli-Curci	691	Johnson	753	McCormack	816	Rachmaninoff
629	Galli-Curci	692	Johnson	754	McCormack		
630	Galli-Curci	693	Johnson	755	McCormack	817	Ruffo
631	Gal'i-Curci	694	Johnson	756	McCormack	818	Ruffo
632	Galli-Curci	695	Journet	757	McCormack	819	Ruffo
633	Galli-Curci	696	Journet	758	McCormack	820	Ruffo
634	Galli-Curci	697	Journet	759	McCormack	821	Ruffo
635	Galli-Curci	698	Journet	760	McCormack	822	Ruffo
636	Garrison	699	Journet	761	McCormack	823	Ruffo
637	Garrison	700	Journet	762	McCormack	824	Ruffo
638	Garrison	701	Journet	763	McCormack	825	Samaroff
639	Garrison	702	Kindler	764	McCormack	826	Samaroff
640	Garrison	703	Kindler	765	McCormack	827	Schipa
641	Garrison	704	Kindler	766	McCormack	828	Schipa
642	Garrison	705	Kindler	767	McCormack	829	Schumann-Heink
643	Gigli	706	Kreisler	768	McCormack		
644	Gigli	707	Kreisler	769	McCormack	830	Schumann-Heink
645	Gigli	708	Kreisler	770	McCormack		
646	Gigli	709	Kreisler	771	McCormack	831	Schumann-Heink
647	Gluck	710	Kreisler	772	McCormack		
648	Gluck	711	Kreisler	773	McCormack	832	Schumann-Heink
649	Gluck	712	Kreisler	774	McCormack		
650	Gluck	713	Kreisler	775	McCormack	833	Schumann-Heink
651	Gluck	714	Kreisler	776	McCormack		
652	Gluck	715	Kreisler	777	McCormack	834	Schumann-Heink
653	Gluck	716	Kreisler	778	McCormack		
654	Gluck	717	Kreisler	779	McCormack	835	Schumann-Heink
655	Gluck	718	Kreisler	780	McCormack		
656	Gluck	719	Kreisler	781	McCormack	836	Schumann-Heink
657	Gluck	720	Kreisler	782	McCormack		
658	Gluck	721	Kreisler	783	McCormack	837	Schumann-Heink
659	Gluck	722	Kreisler	784	McCormack		
660	Gluck	723	Kreisler	785	McCormack	838	Schumann-Heink
661	Gluck	724	Kreisler	786	McCormack		
662	Gluck	725	Kreisler	787	McCormack	839	Toscanini
663	Gluck	726	Kreisler	788	McCormack	840	Toscanini
664	Gluck	727	Kreisler	789	McCormack	841	Toscanini
665	Gluck	728	Kreisler	790	Michailowa	842	Werrenrath
666	Gluck	729	H. Kreisler	791	Morini	843	Werrenrath
667	Hamlin	730	Lashanska	792	Morini	844	Werrenrath
668	Harrold	731	Martinelli	793	Novaes	845	Werrenrath
669	Harrold	732	Martinelli	794	Novaes	846	Werrenrath
670	Heifetz	733	Martinelli	795	Novaes	847	Werrenrath
671	Heifetz	734	Martinelli	796	Phila. S. O.	848	Werrenrath
672	Heifetz	735	Martinelli	797	Phila. S. O.	849	Whitehill
673	Heifetz	736	Martinelli	798	Phila. S. O.	850	Whitehill
674	Heifetz	737	Martinelli	799	Phila. S. O.	851	Whitehill
675	Heifetz	738	Martinelli	800	Plancon	852	Whitehill
676	Heifetz	739	Martinelli	801	Powell	853	Whitehill
677	Herbert	740	McCormack	802	Powell	854	Wil iams
678	Homer			803	Powell	855	Williams
						856	Williams

857	Williams	916	Zanelli	977	Thibaud	1038	Landowska
858	Williams	917	Paderewski	978	Johnson	1039	H. Kreisler
859	Wi'liams	918	McCormack	979	Homer	1040	McCormack
860	Will'ams	919	Palet	980	Harrold	1041	Culp
861	Williams	920	Soro	981	Chaliapin	1042	Gabrilowitsch
862	Williams	921	Mardones	982	Cortot	1043	Kreisler
863	Will'ams	922	Hollman	983	McCormack	1044	Lashanska
864	Wil iams	923	McCormack	984	Werrenrath	1045	Schumann-
865	Williams	924	De Gogorza	985	Ruffo		Heink
866	Williams	925	Schipa	986	Bori	1046	Sist'ne Choir
867	Williams	926	Gigli	987	H. Kreisler	1047	Galli-Curci
868	Williams	927	Palet	988	Zimbalist	1048	Heifetz
869	Williams	928	Palet	989	N.Y. Phi:har.	1049	Schumann-
870	Wi'l'ams	929	Schipa	990	Jeritza		Heink
871	Williams	930	Caruso	991	Werrenrath	1050	Chaliapin
872	Witherspoon	931	Galvany	992	De Gogorza	1051	Rachman-
873	Witherspoon	932	Ruffo	993	Fleta		inoff
874	Witherspoon	933	Ruffo	994	Kre'sler	1052	Homer
875	Braslau	934	Ruffo	995	Ruffo	1053	Bori
876	Ruffo	935	Ruffo	996	Schumann-	1054	Zimbal'st
877	Zanelli	936	Ruffo		Heink	1055	Werrenrath
878	Zanelli	937	Ruffo	997	Heifetz	1056	Z'mbalist
879	Zanelli	938	Ruffo	998	Galli-Curci	1057	Ponselle
880	Zanelli	939	Destinn	999	Matzenauer	1058	Bauer
881	Zanelli	940	Besanzoni;	1000	Novaes	1059	McCormack
882	Zanelli		Amato	1001	Novaes	1060	Elman
883	Zimbalist	941	Garrison	1002	Ponselle	1061	De Gogorza
884	Zimbalist	942	G'g'i	1003	McCormack	1062	Kreisler
885	Zimbal'st	943	Rachmaninoff	1004	Chaliapin	1063	Sch'pa
886	Zimbalist	944	Phila. S. O.	1005	Alda	1064	G'gli
887	Zimbalist	945	Werrenrath	1006	Garrison	1065	Fleta
888	Zimbalist	946	Alda	1007	Caruso	1066	Fleta
889	Zimbal'st	947	Kre'sler	1008	Rachman-	1067	McCormack
890	Zimbal'st	948	Fleta		inoff	1068	Galli-Curci
891	Zimbalist	949	De Muro	1009	Bori	1069	N.Y. Philhar.
892	Zimbal'st	950	Fleta	1010	Kreisler	1070	Ruffo
893	Sistine Choir	951	Werrenrath	1011	McCormack	1071	Sistine Choir
894	Slezak	952	Schipa	1012	Flonzaley Qt.	1072	Werrenrath
895	McCormack	953	Farrar	1013	Ponselle	1073	Fleta
896	McCormack	954	Soro	1014	Harrold	1074	Homer
897	Alda	955	De Luca	1015	Chemet	1075	Kre'sler
898	Bori	956	H. Kreisler	1016	Cortot	1076	Ruffo
899	De Gogorza	957	Morini	1017	Phila. S. O.	1077	Jeritza
900	Elman	958	Caruso	1018	Galli-Curci	1078	Werrenrath
901	Michailowa;	959	Galli-Curci	1019	Ruffo	1079	Elman
	Arral	960	Chaliapin	1020	McCormack	1081	McCormack
902	De Luca;	961	McCormack	1021	Kreisler	1082	Heifetz
	Clement	962	(unused)	1022	Jer.tza	1093	Kreisler
903	De Gogorza	963	Ruffo	1023	Lashanska	1097	Galli-Curci
904	Gadski;	964	Lashanska	1024	Heifetz	1103	Pinza
	Matzenauer	965	Schipa	1025	Gigli	1105	Chaliapin
905	Garrison	966	Kreisler	1026	Werrenrath	1106	Dal Monte
906	Gigli	967	Bori	1027	Paderewski	1107	De Gogorza
907	De Pachmann	968	McCormack	1028	Homer	1108	De Gogorza
908	Destinn	969	Schumann-	1029	Kreisler	1109	De Luca
909	Farrar		Heink	1030	Schipa	1110	De Pachmann
910	Kre'sler	970	Heifetz	1031	Schipa	1111	Phila. S. O.
911	Schumann-	971	Homer	1032	Alda	1112	Phila. S. O.
	Heink	972	Rachmaninoff	1033	Bori	1113	Phila. S. O.
912	Smirnov	973	Landowska	1034	Elman	1114	Granforte
913	Spencer	974	Elman	1035	Hansen	1117	Caruso
914	Paderewski	975	Gigli	1036	De Luca	1129	De Muro
915	Journet	976	Thibaud	1037	Jer.tza	1130	Pinza
						1131	Pinza

3000	Gluck	3010	Gluck	3020	McCormack	3029	McCormack
3001	Gluck	3011	Gluck	3021	McCormack	3030	Alda
3002	Dest'nn	3012	Gluck	3022	McCormack	3031	Caruso
3003	Gluck	3013	Gluck	3023	McCormack	3032	Bon'nsegna
3004	Gluck	3014	Gluck	3024	McCormack	3033	Ruffo
3005	Gluck	3015	Homer	3025	Farrar	3034	Ga'li-Curci
3006	Gluck	3016	Homer	3026	Fa~rar	3035	Kreisler
3007	G'uck	3017	Kreisler	3027	Gall'-Curci;	3036	Kreisler
3008	Gluck	3018	McCormack		Bori	3037	Kreisler
3009	Gluck	3019	McCormack	3028	Homer	3038	Galli-Curci

6000	Caruso	6050	Boston S. O.	6100	Elman	6140	Gilibert
6001	Caruso	6051	Braslau	6101	Elman	6141	Gluck
6002	Caruso	6052	Braslau	6102	Elman	6142	Gluck
6003	Caruso	6053	Calve		Quartet	6143	Gluck
6004	Caruso	6054	Calve	6103	Elman	6144	Gluck
6005	Caruso	6055	Calve		Quartet	6145	Gluck
6006	Caruso	6056	Calve	6104	Ansseau	6146	Gluck
6007	Caruso	6057	Chaliapin	6105	Smirnov	6147	Gluck
6008	Caruso	6058	Chaliapin	6106	Farrar	6148	Gluck
6009	Caruso	6059	Chaliapin	6107	Farrar	6149	Hamlin
6010	Caruso	6060	(unused)	6108	Farrar	6150	Harrold
6011	Caruso	6061	Chaliapin	6109	Farrar	6151	Harrold
6012	Caruso	6062	Clement	6110	Farrar	6152	Heifetz
6013	Caruso	6063	Cortot	6111	Farrar	6153	Heifetz
6014	Caruso	6064	Cortot	6112	Farrar	6154	Heifetz
6015	Caruso	6065	Cortot	6113	Farrar	6155	Heifetz
6016	Caruso	6066	Culp	6114	Flonzaley	6156	Heifetz
6017	Caruso	6067	Culp		Quartet	6157	Heifetz
6018	Caruso	6068	De Gogorza	6115	Flonzaley	6158	Heifetz
6019	Caruso	6069	De Gogorza		Quartet	6159	Heifetz
6020	Caruso	6070	De Gogorza	6116	Flonzaley	6160	Heifetz
6021	Caruso	6071	De Gogorza		Quartet	6161	Heifetz
6022	Caruso	6072	De Gogorza	6117	Flonzaley	6162	Hempel
6023	Caruso	6073	De Gogorza		Quartet	6163	Hempel
6024	Caruso	6074	De Gogorza	6118	Flonzaley	6164	Homer
6025	Caruso	6075	De Gogorza		Quartet	6165	Homer
6026	Caruso	6076	De Gogorza	6119	Flonzaley	6166	Homer
6027	Caruso	6077	De Luca		Quartet	6167	Homer
6028	Caruso	6078	De Luca	6120	Flonzaley	6168	Homer
6029	Caruso	6079	De Luca		Quartet	6169	Homer
6030	Caruso	6080	De Luca	6121	Flonzaley	6170	Homer
6031	Caruso	6081	De Luca		Quartet	6171	Homer
6032	Caruso	6082	De Pachmann	6122	Gadski	6172	Jeritza
6033	Caruso	6083	De Pachmann	6123	Galli-Curci	6173	Journet
6034	Caruso	6084	Dest'nn	6124	Gal'i-Curci	6174	Journet
6035	Caruso	6085	Des inn	6125	Gall'-Curci	6175	Journet
6036	Caruso	6086	Destinn	6126	Ga'li-Curci	6176	Journet
6037	Alda	6087	Destinn	6127	Galli-Curci	6177	Journet
6038	Alda	6088	Eames	6128	Galli-Curci	6178	Journet
6039	Amato	6089	Elman	6129	Gal'i-Curci	6179	Journet
6040	Amato	6090	Elman	6130	Galli-Curci	6180	Journet
6041	Amato	6091	Elman	6131	Gal'i-Curci	6181	Kreisler
6042	Amato	6092	Elman	6132	Gall'-Curci	6182	Kreisler
6043	Bat.istini	6093	Elman	6133	Gall'-Curci	6183	Kreisler
6044	Battistini	6094	Elman	6134	Galli-Curci	6184	Kreisler
6045	Battistini	6095	Elman	6135	Garrison	6185	Kreisler
6046	Battistini	6096	Elman	6136	Garrison	6186	Kreisler
6047	Besanzoni	6097	Elman	6137	Garrison	6187	Kreisler
6048	Bori	6098	Elman	6138	Gigli	6188	Kreisler
6049	Bori	6099	Elman	6139	Gigli	6189	Martinelli

6190	Martinelli	6253	Powell	6302	Toscanini	6362	De Gogorza
6191	Martinelli	6254	Powell	6303	Toscanini	6363	De Pachmann
6192	Martinelli	6255	Powell	6304	Toscanini	6364	Hempel
6193	Martinelli	6256	Powell	6305	Whitehill	6365	Journet
6194	Martinelli	6257	Powell	6306	Whitehill	6366	Phila. S. O.
6195	Martinelli	6258	Powell	6307	Whitehill	6367	Schumann-
6196	McCormack	6259	Rachman-	6308	Williams		Heink
6197	McCormack		inoff	6309	Williams	6368	Williams
6198	McCormack	6260	Rachman-	6310	Williams	6369	Zimbalist
6199	McCormack		inoff	6311	Williams	6370	Alda
6200	McCormack	6261	Rachman-	6312	Williams	6371	Plancon
6201	McCormack		inoff	6313	Williams	6372	Novaes
6202	McCormack	6262	Ruffo	6314	Williams	6373	N.Y. Philhar.
6203	McCormack	6263	Ruffo	6315	Williams	6374	N.Y. Philhar.
6204	McCormack	6264	Ruffo	6316	Williams	6375	Jeritza
6205	McCormack	6265	Ruffo	6317	Williams	6376	Heifetz
6206	McCormack	6266	Ruffo	6318	Williams	6377	De Pachmann
6207	McCormack	6267	Ruffo	6319	Williams	6378	Powell
6208	McCormack	6268	Ruffo	6320	Williams	6379	De Muro
6209	McCormack	6269	Samaroff	6321	Williams	6380	De Muro
6210	Melba	6270	Samaroff	6322	Williams	6381	Gigli
6211	Melba	6271	Schumann-	6323	Williams	6382	Gigli
6212	Martinelli		Heink	6324	Williams	6383	Zanelli
6213	Melba	6272	Schumann-	6325	Witherspoon	6384	Palet
6214	Melba		Heink	6326	Witherspoon	6385	De Muro
6215	Melba	6273	Schumann-	6327	Matzenauer	6386	De Muro
6216	Melba		Heink	6328	Witherspoon	6387	De Muro
6217	Melba	6274	Schumann-	6329	Witherspoon	6388	Paderewski
6218	Melba		Heink	6330	Witherspoon	6389	Paderewski
6219	Melba	6275	Schumann-	6331	Zimbalist	6390	Palet
6220	Melba		Heink	6332	Zimbalist	6391	Fleta
6221	Melba	6276	Schumann-	6333	Zimbalist	6392	Fleta
6222	Melba		Heink	6334	Sistine Choir	6393	Palet
6223	N.Y. Philhar.	6277	Schumann-	6335	Cortot	6394	Farrar
6224	N.Y. Philhar.		Heink	6336	Tetrazzini	6395	Boninsegna
6225	N.Y. Philhar.	6278	Schumann-	6337	Tetrazzini	6396	Tetrazzini
6226	Morini		Heink	6338	Tetrazzini	6397	Tetrazzini
6227	Morini	6279	Schumann-	6339	Tetrazzini	6398	Ruffo
6228	Nielsen		Heink	6340	Tetrazzini	6399	De Lucia
6229	Novaes	6280	Schumann-	6341	Tetrazzini	6400	Pareto
6230	Paderewski		Heink	6342	Tetrazzini	6401	Pareto
6231	Paderewski	6281	Schumann-	6343	Tetrazzini	6402	Pareto
6232	Paderewski		Heink	6344	Tetrazzini	6403	Ruffo
6233	Paderewski	6282	Scotti	6345	Tetrazzini	6404	Boninsegna
6234	Paderewski	6283	Scotti	6346	Tetrazzini	6405	Ruffo
6235	Paderewski	6284	Scotti	6347	Caruso;	6406	Ruffo
6236	Phila. S. O.	6285	Sembrich		Plancon	6407	Gay; Calve
6237	Phila. S. O.	6286	Sembrich	6348	Ansseau	6408	Battistini
6238	Phila. S. O.	6287	Sembrich	6349	Chemet	6409	Besanzoni;
6239	Phila. S. O.	6288	Sembrich	6350	Whitehill		Soro
6240	Phila. S. O.	6289	Sembrich	6351	Boninsegna;	6410	De Muro
6241	Phila. S. O.	6290	Sembrich		De Casas	6411	De Muro
6242	Phila. S. O.	6291	Sembrich	6352	De Gogorza	6412	De Muro
6243	Phila. S. O.	6292	Sembrich	6353	Alda	6413	Gadski;
6244	Phila. S. O.	6293	Sembrich	6354	Borl		Destinn
6245	Phila. S. O.	6294	Sothern	6355	Caruso	6414	Boninsegna;
6246	Phila. S. O.	6295	Sothern	6356	Sembrich		Galvany
6247	Plancon	6296	Sothern	6357	Galli-Curci	6415	Boninsegna;
6248	Plancon	6297	Sothern	6358	Cortot		Battistini
6249	Powell	6298	Sothern	6359	Culp	6416	Chaliapin
6250	Powell	6299	Sothern	6360	Werrenrath	6417	Cortot
6251	Powell	6300	Toscanini	6361	Flonzaley	6418	Homer
6252	Powell	6301	Toscanini		Quartet	6419	Samaroff

6420	Mardones	6451	Zimbalist	6483	Journet; Bertana	6518	Cortot
6421	De Muro	6452	Rachman-inoff	6484	Galeffi	6519	Cortot
6422	De Muro			6485	Galeffi	6520	Kreisler
6423	Schipa	6453	Ponselle	6486	Flonzaley Quartet	6521	Kreisler
6424	Elman	6454	Morini	6487	Dal Monte	6522	Kreisler
6425	Flonzaley Quartet	6455	Chaliapin	6488	Arabian	6523	Kreisler
6426	Werrenrath	6456	Mardones	6489	Chaliapin	6524	Cortot
6427	N.Y. Ph'lhar.	6457	Elman	6490	Phil'. S. O.	6525	Cortot
6428	Paderewski	6458	Caruso	6491	He'fetz	6526	Cortot
6429	Ruffo	6459	Phila S. O.	6492	Phila. S. O.	6527	Cortot
6430	Phila. S. O.	6460	Phila. S. O.	6493	Ph'la. S. O.	6528	De Muro
6431	Phila. S. O.	6461	Phila. S O.	6495	Dal Monte	6529	De Muro
6432	Gall'-Curci	6462	Gabrilowitsch	6496	Ponselle	6530	Arabian
6433	Samaroff	6463	Gabrilowitsch	6497	Chemet	6532	Chaliapin
6434	Mardones	6464	N.Y. Philhar.	6498	San Fran-c'sco S. O.	6533	Chaliapin
6435	Whitehill	6465	Sch'pa	6499	San Fran-c'sco S. O.	6534	Chaliapin
6436	Whitehill	6466	Dal Monte	6500	San Fran-cisco S. O.	6535	De Gogorza
6437	Ponselle	6467	Arabian			6536	Jeritza
6438	Paderewski	6468	Bauer	6501	Casals	6537	Mardones
6439	(unused)	6469	Galli-Curci	6503	Arabian	6538	Paderewski
6440	Ponselle	6470	Paderewski	6506	San Fran-cisco S. O.	6539	San Fran-cisco S. O.
6441	De Pachmann	6471	Matzenauer			6540	Samaroff
6442	S'stine Choir	6472	Werrenrath	6507	Arab'an	6541	Granforte
6443	De Luca	6473	Chemet	6510	Heifetz	6542	Granforte
6444	Novaes	6474	Ponselle	6512	Chaliapin	6548	Arab'an
6445	Morini	6475	Samaroff	6515	Pinza	6549	Fleta
6446	Gigli	6476	Arab'an	6516	Cortot	6551	De Muro
6447	Hansen	6477	Arab'an	6517	Cortot	6552	De Muro
6448	Paderewski	6478	Phila. S. O.			6553	De Muro
6449	Flonzaley Quartet	6479	N.Y. Ph lhar.				
6450	Samaroff	6480	De Pachmann				
		6481	Phila. S O.				
		6482	Paderewski				

8000	Caruso	8019	Farrar	8038	Caruso	8055	Ruffo
8001	Alda	8020	Farrar	8039	Farrar	8056	De Lucia; Ruszcowska
8002	Alda	8021	Farrar	8040	Kre'sler		
8003	Amato	8022	Farrar	8041	Kreisler	8057	De Lucia; Giorgini
8004	Borl	8023	Farrar	8042	Caruso		
8005	Caruso	8024	Farrar	8043	Eames	8058	De Lucia; Galvany
8006	Caruso	8025	Galli-Curci	8044	Alda		
8007	Caruso	8026	Gluck	8045	Caruso;Ruffo	8059	Ruffo
8008	Caruso	8027	Gluck	8046	Gluck; Destinn	8060	Gadski
8009	Caruso	8028	Gluck	8047	Martinelli; Journet	8061	Battistini; Amato
8010	Caruso	8029	Gluck				
8011	Caruso	8030	Gluck	8048	Gadski	8062	De Tura
8012	Caruso	8031	Homer	8049	Ruszcowska	8063	Fleta
8013	Caruso	8032	McCormack	8050	Paoli	8064	Rachman-inoff
8014	Caruso	8033	McCormack	8051	Paoli	8065	Rachman-inoff
8015	Caruso	8034	McCormack	8052	De Casas; Ruszcowska	8066	Rachman-inoff
8016	Caruso	8035	Nielsen	8053	Ruffo	8067	Galli-Curci
8017	Clement; Destinn	8036	Caruso	8054	Ruffo		
8018	Farrar	8037	Battistini; Paoli				

10000	Caruso	10003	Caruso	10006	McCormack	10009	Martinelli
10001	Caruso	10004	Caruso	10007	Caruso	10010	Caruso
10002	Caruso	10005	Caruso	10008	Caruso	10011	Caruso

No.	Name	No.	Name	No.	Name	No.	Name
64001	Hellman	64060	E. Cavalieri	64121	Elman	64183	Gluck
64002	De Lussan	64061	E. Caval eri	64122	Elman	64184	Goritz
64003	De Lussan	64062	E. Cavalieri	64123	Elman	64185	Witherspoon
64004	De Lussan	64063	E. Cavalieri	64124	Sagi-Barba		
64005	De Lussan	64064	E. Cavalieri	64125	Sagi-Barba	64186	Spencer
64006	De Lussan	64065	E. Cavalieri	64126	Journet	64187	Reiss
64007	Crossley	64066	E. Cavalieri	64127	McCormack	64188	Reiss
64008	Crossley	64067	E. Cavalieri	64128	Elman	64189	Spencer
64009	Crossley	64068	Nielsen	64129	King	64190	Gluck
64010	Crossley	64069	Constantino	64130	Kreisler	64191	Terry
64011	Journet	64070	Constantino	64131	Kreisler	64192	Gluck
64012	Journet	64071	Witherspoon	64132	Kreisler	64193	Terry
64013	Journet			64133	Williams	64194	Terry
64014	Journet	64072	Constantino	64134	Powell	64195	Beddoe
64015	Nuibo	64073	Powell	64135	Elman	64196	Beddoe
64016	Nuibo	64074	Powell	64136	De Gogorza	64197	Elman
64017	Nuibo	64075	Powell	64137	Journet	64198	Elman
64018	Juch	64076	Powell	64138	McCormack	64199	Williams
64019	Homer	64077	Journet	64139	Williams	64200	Spencer
64020	Homer	64078	Williams	64140	Elman	64201	Elman
64021	Homer	64079	Yaw	64141	Williams	64202	Kreisler
64022	Homer	64080	Williams	64142	Kreisler	64203	Goritz
64023	Homer	64081	Albani	64143	Powell	64204	Elman
64024	Homer	64082	Albani	64144	Hamlin	64205	McCormack
64025	Homer	64083	La Forge	64145	Regis	64206	Zerola
64026	Homer	64084	Journet	64146	Regis	64207	Zero'a
64027	Powell	64085	Ciaparelli	64147	Regis	64208	Powell
64028	Powell	64086	Williams	64148	Regis	64209	Gluck
64029	Blauvelt	64087	King	64149	Regis	64210	Williams
64030	Blauvelt	64088	Williams	64150	Journet	64211	Powell
64031	Blauvelt	64089	Hamlin	64151	Witherspoon	64212	Witherspoon
64032	Blass	64090	Constantino				
64033	Blass	64091	Nielsen	64152	Sagi-Barba	64213	Gluck
64034	Blass	64092	Williams	64153	McCormack	64214	Reiss
64035	Journet	64093	Williams	64154	McCormack	64215	Goritz
64036	Journet	64094	Ciaparelli	64155	Hamlin	64216	Williams
64037	De Gogorza	64095	King	64156	Kreisler	64217	Williams
64038	De Gogorza	64096	Williams	64157	Journet	64218	Williams
64039	De Gogorza	64097	King	64158	Williams	64219	Williams
64040	De Gogorza	64098	Arral	64159	De Gogorza	64220	Williams
64041	De Gogorza	64099	Arral	64160	De Gogorza	64221	Williams
64042	De Gogorza	64100	Williams	64161	Nightingale	64222	Witherspoon
64043	De Gogorza	64101	De Gogorza	64162	Forn'a		
64044	De Gogorza	64102	Williams	64163	Goritz	64223	Clement
64045	De Gogorza	64103	Powell	64164	Goritz	64224	De Pachmann
64046	Hollman	64104	Powell	64165	Goritz		
64047	N.Y. Opera Cho.	64105	Williams	64166	Zerola	64225	Gluck
64048	N.Y. Opera Cho.	64106	Williams	64167	Zerola	64226	Clement
64049	N.Y. Opera Cho.	64107	Arral	64168	Zerola	64227	Powell
64050	N.Y. Opera Cho.	64108	Witherspoon	64169	Zerola	64228	Sirota
64051	De Gogorza	64109	Williams	64170	Zerola	64229	Sirota
64052	Journet	64110	De Gogorza	64171	McCormack	64230	Sirota
64053	Journet	64111	Slezak	64172	Zero'a	64231	Sirota
64054	Journet	64112	Slezak	64173	Zerola	64232	Clement
64055	Journet	64113	Slezak	64174	McCormack	64233	Clement
64056	E. Cavalieri	64114	Williams	64175	Sagi-Barba	64234	Clement
64057	E. Cavalieri	64115	Slezak	64176	Sagi-Barba	64235	Journet
64058	E. Cavalieri	64116	Slezak	64177	Sagi-Barba	64236	Journet
64059	E. Cavalieri	64117	McCormack	64178	Sagi-Barba	64237	Journet
		64118	Sagi-Barba	64179	Sagi-Barba	64238	Journet
		64119	Journet	64180	McCormack	64239	Herbert
		64120	McCormack	64181	McCormack	64240	Herbert
				64182	Gluck	64241	Zimbalist

64242	De Gogorza	64302	McCormack	64364	Sagi-Barba	64427	McCormack
64243	Wither-	64303	McCormack	64365	Sagi-Barba	64428	McCormack
	spoon	64304	McCormack	64366	Sagi-Barba	64429	McCormack
64244	Fornia	64305	McCormack	64367	Sagi-Barba	64430	McCormack
64245	Hamlin	64306	W.lliams	64368	Sagi-Barba	64431	McCormack
64246	Hamlin	64307	McCormack	64369	Sagi-Barba	64432	McCormack
64247	Hamlin	64308	Alda	64370	Sagi-Barba	64433	McCormack
64248	Hamlin	64309	McCormack	64371	Sagi-Barba	64434	McCormack
64249	Spencer	64310	McCormack	64372	De Gogorza	64435	Powell
64250	McCormack	64311	McCormack	64373	Powell	64436	La Goya
64251	Campagno.a	64312	McCormack	64374	McCormack	64437	McCormack
64252	McCormack	64313	Kreisler	64375	McCormack	64438	Elman
64253	McCormack	64314	Kreisler	64376	Sagi-Barba	64439	Elman
64254	McCormack	64315	Keisler	64377	Sagi-Barba	64440	McCormack
64255	McCormack	64316	McCormack	64378	Sagi-Barba	64441	Culp
64256	McCormack	64317	McCormack	64379	Sagi-Barba	64442	Ober
64257	McCormack	64318	McCormack	64380	Sagi-Barba	64443	Ober
64258	McCormack	64319	Kreisler	64381	Sagi-Barba	64444	Ober
64259	McCormack	64320	Gluck	64382	Mart.nelli	64445	Ober
64260	McCormack	64321	Gluck	64383	Siro.a	64446	Ober
64261	Zimbalist	64322	Gluck	64384	Sirota	64447	Ober
64262	Powell	64323	Hamlin	64385	S.rota	64448	Ober
64263	De Pach-	64324	Gluck	64386	Sirota	64449	Ober
	mann	64325	Gluck	64387	Hamlin	64450	Alda
64264	Powell	64326	McCormack	64388	Whitehill	64451	Alda
64265	Powell	64327	Williams	64389	W.lliams	64452	La Goya
64266	Zimbalist	64328	McCormack	64390	Kubel.k	64453	La Goya
64267	Gluck	64329	McCormack	64391	Beddoe	64454	Powell
64268	Gluck	64330	Zimbal.st	64392	Gluck	64455	Zimbalist
64269	Gluck	64331	McCormack	64393	Martinelli	64456	Whitehill
64270	Hamlin	64332	McCormack	64394	Whitehill	64457	Powell
64271	Williams	64333	McCormack	64395	La Goya	64458	Powell
64272	Sirota	64334	Alda	64396	Culp	64459	Powell
64273	S.rota	64335	Zimbalist	64397	Cu.p	64460	Williams
64274	Sirota	64336	Elman	64398	Gluck	64461	Sagi-Barba
64275	Sirota	64337	Hamlin	64399	Gluck	64462	Hamlin
64276	S.rota	64338	Alda	64400	Gluck	64463	Sagi-Barba
64277	Gluck	64339	Alda	64401	Culp	64464	Sagi-Barba
64278	Whitehill	64340	McCormack	64402	Culp	64465	Vela
64279	Wh.t.h.ll	64341	McCormack	64403	Culp	64466	Sagi-Barba
64280	Wi.liams	64342	McCormack	64404	Culp	64467	Vela
64281	Powell	64343	McCormack	64405	McCormack	64468	Braslau
64282	Haml.n	64344	McCormack	64406	Kreisler	64469	Braslau
64283	Fornia	64345	McCormack	64407	McCormack	64470	Braslau
64284	Forn.a	64346	Gluck	64408	Kre.sler	64471	Wither-
64285	Fornia	64347	Wither-	64409	Martinelli		spoon
64286	Martinelli		spoon	64410	Martinelli	64472	Wither-
64287	Martinelli	64348	Haml.n	64411	Williams		spoon
64288	Fornia	64349	La Goya	64412	Gluck	64473	Wither-
64289	Forn.a	64350	La Goya	64413	Gluck		spoon
64290	Fornia	64351	La G.ya	64414	Culp	64474	Wither-
64291	De Pach-	64352	La Goya	64415	Gluck		spoon
	mann	64353	La Goya	64416	Gluck	64475	Braslau
64292	Kreisler	64354	La Goya	64417	Alda	64476	McCormack
64293	Garr.son	64355	La Goya	64418	Culp	64477	De Gogorza
64294	Clement	64356	La Goya	64419	Culp	64478	Braslau
64295	Hamlin	64357	La Goya	64420	Martinelli	64479	De Gogorza
64296	Hamlin	64358	Sagi-Barba	64421	Gluck	64480	De Gogorza
64297	Herbert	64359	Whitehill	64422	Gluck	64481	De Gogorza
64298	Herbert	64360	Wh.tehill	64423	McCormack	64482	De Gogorza
64299	Forn.a	64361	Beddoe	64424	McCormack	64483	(unused)
64300	Powell	64362	Sagi-Barba	64425	McCormack	64484	Martinelli
64301	Powell	64363	Sagi-Barba	64426	McCormack	64485	Martinelli

64486	Martinelli	64545	Williams	64608	Whitehill	64669	Galli-Curci
64487	Martinelli	64546	McCormack	64609	Wh tehill	64670	Kreisler
64488	Kreisler	64547	Elman	64610	Whitehill	64671	Elman Quartet
64489	Culp	64548	McCormack	64611	Powell		
64490	Culp	64549	McCormack	64612	Ober	64672	Culp
64491	Culp	64550	Culp	64613	Whitehill	64673	De Luca
64492	Culp	64551	Culp	64614	Kreisler	64674	Alda
64493	Culp	64552	Culp	64615	Powell	64675	Alda
64494	Whiteh'll	64553	Culp	64616	Garrison	64676	Culp
64495	McCormack	64554	Culp	64617	Powell	64677	Whiteh'll
64496	McCormack	64555	Kreisler	64618	Powell	64678	La Goya
64497	McCormack	64556	Kreisler	64619	Powell	64679	La Goya
64498	McCormack	64557	Journet	64620	Powell	64680	La Goya
64499	McCormack	64558	Journet	64621	Powell	64681	La Goya
64500	Ober	64559	McCormack	64622	McCormack	64682	La Goya
64501	De Gogorza	64560	Gluck	64623	McCormack	64683	Culp
64502	Kreisler	64561	Zimbalist	64624	De Gogorza	64684	De Luca
64503	Kreisler	64562	Zimbal.st	64625	Gluck	64685	De Luca
64504	Kreisler	64563	Kre.sler	64626	Gluck	64686	De Luca
64505	Martinelli	64564	Gluck	64627	Gluck	64687	Alda
64506	Ober	64565	Kreisler	64628	De Gogorza	64688	De Gogorza
64507	La Goya	64566	Gluck	64629	De Gogorza	64689	Alda
64508	La Goya	64567	Journet	64630	McCormack	64690	De Gogorza
64509	La Goya	64568	Kreisler	64631	McCormack	64691	Journet
64510	Sagi-Barba	64569	Vela	64632	De Gogorza	64692	Alda
64511	Sagi-Barba	64570	Sagi-Barba	64633	Braslau	64693	Alda
64512	Williams	64571	Vela	64634	Williams	64694	McCormack
64513	Williams	64572	Sagi-Barba	64635	Ober	64695	Garrison
64514	Martinelli	64573	Navarro	64636	Elman	64696	McCormack
64515	Williams	64574	Martinelli	64637	Garrison	64697	Garrison
64516	Williams	64575	Kreisler	64638	Zimbal.st	64698	De Gogorza
64517	Gluck	64576	Zimbal.st	64639	Elman	64699	McCormack
64518	Zimbalist	64577	Zimbal.st	64640	Zimbalist	64700	Martinelli
64519	Whiteh.ll	64578	McCormack	64641	Garrison	64701	La Goya
64520	Powell	64579	Journet	64642	Elman	64702	La Goya
64521	Powell	64580	Jou.net	64643	Elman	64703	La Goya
64522	Whitehill	64581	Journet	64644	Elman	64704	La Goya
64523	La Goya	64582	Journet	64645	Witherspoon	64705	Powell
64524	Sagi-Barba	64583	Journet			64706	Paderewski
64525	Sagi-Barba	64584	De Gogorza	64646	Journet	64707	Whitehill
64526	Sagi-Barba	64585	Journet	64647	Jou.net	64708	Braslau
64527	Sagi-Barba	64586	Jou.net	64648	Journet	64709	Kreisler
64528	Witherspoon	64587	Journet	64649	Journet	64710	Zimbalist
64529	Kreisler	64588	Gluck	64650	Williams	64711	Williams
64530	Elman	64589	Gluck	64651	Journet	64712	McCormack
64531	Hamlin	64590	Gluck	64652	Martinelli	64713	Gluck
64532	McCormack	64591	Gluck	64653	Alda	64714	Garrison
64533	Witherspoon	64592	Gluck	64654	Alda	64715	Alda
		64593	Gluck	64655	Kreisler	64716	Alda
64534	Witherspoon	64594	Williams	64656	Journet	64717	Alda
		64595	Martinelli	64657	Journet	64718	Braslau
64535	Witherspoon	64596	De Gogorza	64658	Alda	64719	Whitehill
		64597	De Gogorza	64659	Journet	64720	Culp
64536	Elman	64598	De Gogorza	64660	Kreisler	64721	Culp
64537	Elman	64599	McCormack	64661	Elman Quartet	64722	De Gogorza
64538	Elman	64600	Kreisler			64723	Galli-Curci
64539	Braslau	64601	Kreisler	64662	Alda	64724	Galli-Curci
64540	Braslau	64602	Whitehill	64663	De Gogorza	64725	Garrison
64541	Braslau	64603	McCormack	64664	McCormack	64726	McCormack
64542	Kreisler	64604	McCormack	64665	McCormack	64727	Gluck
64543	McCormack	64605	McCormack	64666	McCormack	64728	Gluck
64544	Martinelli	64606	McCormack	64667	Culp	64729	Gluck
		64607	Gluck	64668	De Luca	64730	Kreisler

64731 Kreisler	64790 Garrison	64853 La Goya	64913 McCormack
64732 McCormack	64791 McCormack	64854 Gigli	64914 Werrenrath
64733 McCormack	64792 Galli-Curci	64855 Gigli	64915 Elman
64734 Powell	64793 Gluck	64856 Heifetz	64916 Harrold
64735 Whitehill	64794 De Gogorza	64857 Kreisler	64917 Heifetz
64736 Zimbalist	64795 Garrison	64858 Zanelli	64918 Galli-Curci
64737 Zimbalist	64796 McCormack	64859 Alda	64919 Rachman-
64738 Navarro	64797 De Gogorza	64860 McCormack	inoff
64739 Navarro	64798 De Gogorza	64861 Kindler	64920 Garrison
64740 Navarro	64799 Braslau	64862 De Gogorza	64921 Rachman-
64741 McCormack	64800 Whitehill	64863 Werrenrath	inoff
64742 Braslau	64801 Soro	64864 Johnson	64922 Zanelli
64743 Wither-	64802 Alda	64865 Navarro	64923 Zanelli
spoon	64803 McCormack	64866 Navarro	64924 Kreisler
64744 Boston S. O.	64804 Sch.pa	64867 Gigli	64925 McCormack
64745 Boston S. O.	64805 Schipa	64868 Gigli	64926 McCormack
64746 Boston S. O.	64806 Schipa	64869 La Goya	64927 Alda
64747 Braslau	64807 Galli-Curci	64870 La Goya	64928 De Gogorza
64748 Gall.-Curci	64808 Garrison	64871 La Goya	64929 Galli-Curci
64749 Gall.-Curci	64809 Gluck	64872 La Goya	64930 Johnson
64750 Gluck	64810 Braslau	64873 Kreisler	64931 Werrenrath
64751 Wither-	64811 Garrison	64874 Flonzaley	64932 Kindler
spoon	64812 De Gogorza	Quartet	64933 Gigli
64752 Phila. S. O.	64813 Zimbalist	64875 Besanzoni	64934 De Luca
64753 Phila. S. O.	64814 McCormack	64876 Besanzoni	64935 Rachman-
64754 Boston S. O.	64815 Garrison	64877 Besanzoni	inoff
64755 Wither-	64816 De Gogorza	64878 McCormack	64936 Zimbalist
spoon	64817 Kreisler	64879 Novaes	64937 Braslau
64756 Whitehill	64818 McCormack	64880 Novaes	64938 Gigli
64757 Braslau	64819 Cortot	64881 G.gli	64939 Novaes
64758 Heifetz	64820 Galli-Curci	64882 G.gli	64940 Novaes
64759 Heifetz	64821 Elman	64883 Braslau	64941 Novaes
64760 Heifetz	64822 Phila. S. O.	64884 Elman	64942 Gigli
64761 Williams	64823 Heifetz	64885 Galli-Curci	64943 Gigli
64762 Soro	64824 Kreisler	64886 Johnson	64944 Gigli
64763 Williams	64825 McCormack	64887 Braslau	64945 Galli-Curci
64764 Williams	64826 Novaes	64888 De Gogorza	64946 Johnson
64765 Williams	64827 Zimbalist	64889 Flonzaley	64947 Kreisler
64766 Boston S. O.	64828 Gluck	Quartet	64948 Alda
64767 Phila. S. O.	64829 Elman	64890 Kreisler	64949 De Gogorza
64768 Phila. S. O.	64830 Werrenrath	64891 Garrison	64950 Werrenrath
64769 Heifetz	64831 Zanelli	64892 Harrold	64951 Zanelli
64770 Heifetz	64832 Zanelli	64893 Alda	64952 Toscanini
64771 Williams	64833 Heifetz	64894 Elman	64953 De Gogorza
64772 Martinelli	64834 Zanelli	64895 Johnson	64954 Zanelli
64773 McCormack	64835 Zanelli	64896 Kindler	64955 Zimbalist
64774 Martinelli	64836 De Gogorza	64897 Werrenrath	64956 Cortot
64775 De Luca	64837 McCormack	64898 De Gogorza	64957 De Luca
64776 De Luca	64838 McCormack	64899 Garrison	64958 Elman
64777 McCormack	64839 Johnson	64900 McCormack	64959 Gigli
64778 McCormack	64840 Johnson	64901 McCormack	64960 Alda
64779 Alda	64841 Kindler	64902 Kreisler	64961 Kreisler
64780 Alda	64842 Kreisler	64903 Elman	64962 McCormack
64781 Alda	64843 Werrenrath	64904 Galli-Curci	64963 Rachman-
64782 Alda	64844 Alda	64905 Johnson	inoff
64783 Garrison	64845 Braslau	64906 Rachman-	64964 Werrenrath
64784 Flonzaley	64846 Cortot	inoff	64965 Samaroff
Quartet	64847 De Gogorza	64907 Zanelli	64966 Garrison
64785 McCormack	64848 La Goya	64908 Alda	64967 Braslau
64786 De Gogorza	64849 La Goya	64909 Harrold	64968 Elman
64787 McCormack	64850 La Goya	64910 Cortot	64969 Garrison
64788 Whitehill	64851 La Goya	64911 De Gogorza	64970 Johnson
64789 Whitehill	64852 La Goya	64912 De Luca	

64971 Rachman-inoff	66028 McCormack	66089 Palet	66149 Kreisler
64972 Zanelli	66029 Johnson	66090 Fleta	66150 Paderewski
64973 Cortot	66030 Toscanini	66091 Fleta	66151 Elman
64974 Kreisler	66031 Toscanini	66092 Galli-Curci	66152 Alda
64975 Gigli	66032 Werrenrath	66093 Alda	66153 Morini
64976 McCormack	66033 De Gogorza	66094 De Gogorza	66154 Rachman-inoff
64977 Elman	66034 Zimbalist	66095 Gigli	
64978 Garrison	66035 Braslau	66096 McCormack	66155 McCormack
64979 Morini	66036 Alda	66097 Heifetz	66156 Jeritza
64980 Rachman-inoff	66037 Heifetz	66098 Phila. S. O.	66157 Kreisler
	66038 Morini	66099 Elman	66158 De Luca
64981 Alda	66039 Schipa	66100 Harrold	66159 Mardones
64982 McCormack	66040 H. Kreisler	66101 Zimbalist	66160 Paderewski
64983 Braslau	66041 Kreisler	66102 G.gli	66161 Paderewski
64984 De Gogorza	66042 Smirnov	66103 De Gogorza	66162 McCormack
64985 Johnson	66043 Chemet	66104 Kreisler	66163 McCormack
64986 Toscanini	66044 B. aslau	66105 Rachman-inoff	66164 De Gogorza
64987 Werrenrath	66045 Schipa		66165 Garrison
64988 Alda	66046 De Gogorza	66106 Phila. S. O.	66166 Smirnov
64989 Cortot	66047 Werrenrath	66107 Soro	66167 Zanelli
64990 De Luca	66048 Elman	66108 Soro	66168 Garrison
64991 Galli-Curci	66049 Kindler	66109 McCormack	66169 Garrison
64992 Palet	66050 De Luca	66110 Heifetz	66170 Gigli
64993 Kreisler	66051 Harrold	66111 Jeritza	66171 Ph.la. S. O.
64994 McCormack	66052 Harrold	66112 McCormack	66172 Phila. S. O.
64995 Samaroff	66053 Kindler	66113 Palet	66173 Werrenrath
64996 Braslau	66054 Journet	66114 Palet	66174 Alda
64997 De Gogorza	66055 Zanelli	66115 Braslau	66175 Alda
64998 Johnson	66056 Alda	66116 H. Kreisler	66176 Kreisler
64999 Toscanini	66057 Jeritza	66117 Schipa	66177 Fleta
66000 De Lucia	66058 Phila. S. O.	66118 Werrenrath	66178 Fleta
66001 De Lucia	66059 Rachman-inoff	66119 Zimbalist	66179 De Muro
66002 De Lucia		66120 Kindler	66180 Werrenrath
66003 De Lucia	66060 Johnson	66121 Schipa	66181 Werrenrath
66004 De Lucia	66061 Johnson	66122 McCormack	66182 Soro
66005 Kruszelnicka	66062 Marone.li	66123 Heifetz	66183 Soro
	66063 Chemet	66124 Jeritza	66184 De Luca
66006 De Lucia	66064 Thibaud	66125 Galli-Curci	66185 H. Kreisler
66007 Rachman-inoff	66065 Thibaud	66126 De Gogorza	66186 Morini
	66066 Thibaud	66127 Kreisler	66187 Galli-Curci
66008 Elman	66067 Schipa	66128 Phila. S. O.	66188 Galli-Curci
66009 Flonzaley Quartet	66068 De Luca	66129 Rachman-inoff	66189 McCormack
66010 Gigli	66069 Gall.-Curci		66190 McCormack
66011 Kindler	66070 Gigli	66130 Novaes	66191 Heifetz
66012 McCormack	66071 Harrold	66131 N. Y. Phil.	66192 Schipa
66013 Zanelli	66072 De Gogorza	66132 Werrenrath	66193 Schipa
66014 Galli-Curci	66073 Elman	66133 De Luca	66194 Lashanska
66015 Palet	66074 Morini	66134 Alda	66195 Lashanska
66016 Rachman-inoff	66075 Samaroff	66135 De Gogorza	66196 Kreisler
66017 Harrold	66076 Chemet	66136 Galli-Curci	66197 Kreisler
66018 Werrenrath	66077 Schipa	66137 Kreisler	66198 McCormack
66019 De Gogorza	66078 De Muro	66138 Rachman-inoff	66199 McCormack
66020 Lashanska	66079 Kreisler	66139 Heifetz	66200 Heifetz
66021 Lashanska	66080 McCormack	66140 Alda	66201 Heifetz
66022 Heifetz	66081 Toscanini	66141 Mardones	66202 Rachman-inoff
66023 Kreisler	66082 H. Kreisler	66142 Schipa	
66024 McCormack	66083 Braslau	66143 Sch pa	66203 Landowska
66025 Zanelli	66084 Braslau	66144 Elman	66204 Landowska
66026 Kindler	66085 Rachman-inoff	66145 Werrenrath	66205 Elman
66027 Alda	66086 Morini	66146 McCormack	66206 Elman
	66087 Werrenrath	66147 Jeritza	66207 Gigli
	66088 Palet	66148 Samaroff	66208 Gigli
			66209 Thibaud

66210	Johnson	66229	Fleta	66248	Rachman-	66264	Ph'la. S. O.
66211	Johnson	66230	Fleta		inoff	66265	Galli-Curci
66212	Harrold	66231	Kreisler	66249	Rachman-	66266	Galli-Curci
66213	Cortot	66232	Kreisler		inoff	66267	McCormack
66214	Cortot	66233	Heifetz	662~0	Kreisler	66268	McCormack
66215	McCormack	66234	Heifetz	66251	Kreisler	66269	Kreisler
66216	Werrenrath	66235	Gall'-Curci	66252	McCormack	66270	Kreisler
66217	Werrenrath	66236	Galli-Curci	66253	McCormack	66271	Jeritza
66218	H. Kreisler	66237	Novaes	66254	Flonza'ey	66272	Jeritza
66219	H. Kreisler	66238	Novaes		Quartet	66273	Heifetz
66220	Zimbalist	66239	Novaes	66255	Ponscl'e	66274	Gigli
66221	Zimbal'st	66240	Ponselle	66256	Ponselle	66275	Gigli
66222	N.Y. Phil.	66241	Ponselle	66257	Harrold	66276	Lashanska
66223	N.Y. Phil.	66242	McCormack	66258	Harrold	66277	Lashanska
66224	Jeritza	66243	McCormack	66259	Chemet	66278	Werrenrath
66225	Jeritza	66244	Alda	66260	Chemet	66279	Werrenrath
66226	Werrenrath	66245	Al'a	66261	Cortot		
66227	Werrenrath	66246	Garrison	66262	Cortot		*See note*
66228	De Gogorza	66247	Garrison	66263	Ph'la. S. O.		*on p. 187*

74001	Hollman	74042	De Gogorza	74079	Wither-	74116	Ciaparelli
74002	Hollman	74043	De Gogorza		spoon	74117	Nielsen
74003	Van Hoose	74044	Hollman	74080	Wither-	74118	De Gogorza
74004	Van Hoose	74045	Hollman		spoon	74119	Williams
74005	Van Hoose	74046	De Gogorza	74081	Wither-	74120	De Gogorza
74006	Journet	74047	De Gogorza		spoon	74121	Nielsen
74007	Van Hoose	74048	E. Cavalieri	74082	Wither-	74122	Will'ams
74008	Journet	74049	E. Caval'eri		spoon	74123	Journet
74009	Journet	74050	E. Caval'eri	74083	Constantino	74124	De Gogorza
74010	Journet	74051	Elman	74084	Constantino	74125	King
74011	Journet	74052	Elman	74085	Constantino	74126	Williams
74012	Nu'bo	74053	Elman	74086	De Gcgorza	74127	Williams
74013	Nuibo	74054	E. Cavalieri	74087	Nielsen	74128	Williams
74014	Juch	74055	E. Cavalieri	74088	Williams	74129	Williams
74015	Juch	74056	E. Cavalieri	74089	Williams	74130	Williams
74016	Homer	74057	E. Cavalieri	74090	Yaw	74131	Williams
74017	Homer	74058	E. Cavalieri	74091	Yaw	74132	Arral
74018	Homer	74059	E. Cavalieri	74092	Yaw	74133	Hamlin
74019	Homer	74060	E. Cavalieri	74093	Williams	74134	Hamlin
74020	Homer	74061	E. Cavalieri	74094	Will'ams	74135	Powell
74021	Homer	74062	Nielsen	74095	Albani	74136	W'll'ams
74022	Homer	74063	Nielsen	74096	Albani	74137	Wither-
74023	Homer	74064	Nielsen	74097	Albani		spoon
74024	Homer	74065	Constantino	74098	Albani	74138	Wither-
74025	Powell	74066	Constantino	74099	Albani		spoon
74026	Powell	74067	Constantino	74100	Williams	74139	Hamlin
74027	Blauvelt	74068	De Gogorza	74101	La Forge	74140	Hamlin
74028	Blass	74069	De Gogorza	74102	De Gogorza	74141	Will'ams
74029	Blass	74070	Wither-	74103	Journet	74142	Arral
74030	Blass		spoon	74104	Journet	74143	Hamlin
74031	Blass	74071	Wither-	74105	De Gogorza	74144	Wither-
74032	Blass		spoon	74106	Constantino		spoon
74033	Van Hoose	74072	Wither-	74107	Nielsen	74145	Wither-
74034	Van Hoose		spoon	74108	Nielsen		spoon
74035	Van Hoose	74073	Constantino	74109	Williams	74146	Arral
74036	Journet	74074	Nielsen	74110	De Gogorza	74147	Arral
74037	Journet	74075	Nielsen	74111	Hamlin	74148	Williams
74038	Journet	74076	Nielsen	74112	King	74149	De Gogorza
74039	Journet	74077	De Gogorza	74113	Hamlin	74150	Williams
74040	De Gogorza	74078	Wither-	74114	De Gogorza	74151	Arral
74041	De Gogorza		spoon	74115	Williams	74152	Journet

74153	Journet	74213	N.Y. Opera	74269	Journet	74317	De Pach-
74154	Journet		Cho.	74270	Journet		mann
74155	Gilibert	74214	N.Y. Opera	74271	Journet	74318	De Pach-
74156	Journet		Cho.	74272	Journet		mann
74157	McCormack	74215	Goritz	74273	Journet	74319	Clement
74158	McCormack	74216	Zerola	74274	Gluck	74320	Whitehill
74159	Bachaus	74217	Zerola	74275	Journet	74321	Wh'tehill
74160	Williams	74218	McCormack	74276	Journet	74322	Goritz
74161	Sagi-Barba	74219	McCormack	74277	Wither-	74323	Wither-
74162	Sagi-Barba	74220	McCormack		spoon		spoon
74163	Elman	74221	McCormack	74278	Wither-	74324	Powell
74164	Elman	74222	McCormack		spoon	74325	Powell
74165	Elman	74223	McCormack	74279	Wither-	74326	Powell
74166	McCormack	74224	McCormack		spoon	74327	Wither-
74167	Elman	74225	Zerola	74280	Zimbalist		spoon
74168	Slezak	74226	Sagi-Barba	74281	Journet	74328	McCormack
74169	King	74227	Fornia	74282	Journet	74329	McCormack
74170	King	74228	Wither-	74283	Powell	74330	Kreisler
74171	King		spoon	74284	De Pach-	74331	Williams
74172	Kreisler	74229	De Gogorza		mann	74332	Kreisler
74173	Powell	74230	Goritz	74285	De Pach-	74333	Kreisler
74174	Constantino	74231	Spencer		mann	74334	Gluck
74175	McCormack	74232	McCormack	74286	Herbert	74335	Alda
74176	Elman	74233	Wither-	74287	Goritz	74336	Elman
74177	Powell		spoon	74288	Goritz	74337	Zimbalist
74178	Elman	74234	De Gogorza	74289	Goritz	74338	Zimbalist
74179	Powell	74235	Reiss	74290	Spencer	74339	Elman
74180	Kreisler	74236	McCormack	74291	Spencer	74340	Elman
74181	Williams	74237	McCormack	74292	Elman	74341	Elman
74182	Kreisler	74238	Gluck	74293	De Pach-	74342	Goritz
74183	Powell	74239	Terry		mann	74343	Goritz
74184	McCormack	74240	Terry	74294	Kreisler	74344	Sagi-Barba
74185	Hamlin	74241	Wither-	74295	McCormack	74345	McCormack
74186	Elman		spoon	74296	McCormack	74346	McCormack
74187	Williams	74242	McCormack	74297	Campagnola	74347	Wither-
74188	Powell	74243	McCormack	74298	McCormack		spoon
74189	Williams	74244	Beddoe	74299	McCormack	74348	Wither-
74190	Williams	74245	Gluck	74300	Herbert		spoon
74191	Journet	74246	Powell	74301	De Pach-	74349	Wither-
74192	Wither-	74247	Zerola		mann		spoon
	spoon	74248	Hamlin	74302	De Pach-	74350	Sagi-Barba
74193	Hambourg	74249	Gluck		mann	74351	Sagi-Barba
74194	Hambourg	74250	Hamlin	74303	Zimbalist	74352	Sagi-Barba
74195	Journet	74251	Gluck	74304	De Pach-	74353	Alda
74196	Kreisler	74252	Gluck		mann	74354	Powell
74197	Kreisler	74253	Spencer	74305	Whitehill	74355	Powell
74198	Williams	74254	Williams	74306	Hamlin	74356	Williams
74199	Williams	74255	Kubelik	74307	(unused)	74357	Powell
74200	Hamlin	74256	Kubelik	74308	Elman	74358	Culp
74201	Hamlin	74257	Kubelik	74309	De Pach-	74359	De Gogorza
74202	Kreisler	74258	Clement		mann	74360	De Gogorza
74203	Kreisler	74259	Powell	74310	Hamlin	74361	Sagi-Barba
74204	McCormack	74260	De Pach-	74311	De Pach-	74362	Sagi-Barba
74205	Williams		mann		mann	74363	Sagi-Barba
74206	Wither-	74261	De Pach-	74312	De Pach-	74364	Whitehill
	spoon		mann		mann	74365	Kubelik
74207	Wither-	74262	De Gogorza	74313	De Pach-	74366	Kubelik
	spoon	74263	Gluck		mann	74367	Kubelik
74208	Gilibert	74264	Clement	74314	De Pach-	74368	Kubelik
74209	De Gogorza	74265	Journet		mann	74369	Gluck
74210	Journet	74266	Journet	74315	De Pach-	74370	Kubelik
74211	Fornia	74267	Journet		mann	74371	De Muro
74212	Goritz	74268	Journet	74316	De Pach-	74372	De Muro
					mann		

74373	De Muro	74433	Whitehill	74494	Powell	74553	Boston S. O.
74374	De Muro	74434	McCormack	74495	Lazaro	74554	Boston S. O.
74375	De Muro	74435	McCormack	74496	Lazaro	74555	Boston S. O.
74376	De Muro	74436	McCormack	74497	Wither-	74556	Whitehill
74377	De Muro	74437	Kreisler		spoon	74557	Galli-Curci
74378	Hamlin	74438	De Gogorza	74498	Williams	74558	Galli-Curci
74379	De Gogorza	74439	Martinelli	74499	Galli-Curci	74559	Gluck
74380	Whitehill	74440	Martinelli	74500	Galli-Curci	74560	Phila. S. O.
74381	Martinelli	74441	Ober	74501	Wither-	74561	Boston S. O.
74382	Sagi-Barba	74442	Gluck		spoon	74562	Heifetz
74383	Gluck	74443	Zimbalist	74502	De Gogorza	74563	Heifetz
74384	Kreisler	74444	Zimbalist	74503	Gluck	74564	McCormack
74385	Alda	74445	Zimbalist	74504	Gluck	74565	Phila. S. O.
74386	Gluck	74446	Powell	74505	Wither-	74566	Phila. S. O.
74387	Kreisler	74447	Powell		spoon	74567	Phila. S. O.
74388	Alda	74448	Alda	74506	De Luca	74568	Heifetz
74389	Sagi-Barba	74449	Alda	74507	Alda	74569	Heifetz
74390	Sagi-Barba	74450	Wither-	74508	Journet	74570	Heifetz
74391	Martinelli		spoon	74509	Galli-Curci	74571	Williams
74392	Elman	74451	Whitehill	74510	Galli-Curci	74572	De Luca
74393	Elman	74452	Whitehill	74511	Galli-Curci	74573	Martinelli
74394	Elman	74453	Williams	74512	Galli-Curci	74574	Elman Qrt.
74395	Elman	74454	Williams	74513	Wither-	74575	Elman Qrt.
74396	Ober	74455	Elman		spoon	74576	Elman Qrt.
74397	Ober	74456	Braslau	74514	De Luca	74577	Braslau
74398	McCormack	74457	Hamlin	74515	Elman	74578	Flonzaley
74399	Alda	74458	Wither-	74516	Elman Qrt.		Quartet
74400	Alda		spoon	74517	Martinelli	74579	Flonzaley
74401	Alda	74459	Elman	74518	Martinelli		Quartet
74402	Powell	74460	Culp	74519	Journet	74580	Flonzaley
74403	Williams	74461	Culp	74520	Journet		Quartet
74404	Williams	74462	Culp	74521	Journet	74581	Heifetz
74405	Whitehill	74463	Kreisler	74522	Galli-Curci	74582	Zimbalist
74406	Whitehill	74464	Journet	74523	Culp	74583	Heifetz
74407	Whitehill	74465	Gluck	74524	Journet	74584	Cortot
74408	Powell	74466	Journet	74525	Elman Qrt.	74585	Soro
74409	Williams	74467	Zimbalist	74526	De Luca	74586	Soro
74410	Williams	74468	Gluck	74527	Culp	74587	Cortot
74411	Sagi-Barba	74469	Martinelli	74528	De Luca	74588	Cortot
74412	Powell	74470	Sagi-Barba	74529	Paderewski	74589	Cortot
74413	Sagi-Barba	74471	Journet	74530	Paderewski	74590	Elman
74414	Sagi-Barba	74472	Journet	74531	Powell	74591	De Luca
74415	Sagi-Barba	74473	Journet	74532	Galli-Curci	74592	Flonzaley
74416	Wither-	74474	Journet	74533	Paderewski		Quartet
	spoon	74475	Gluck	74534	Gluck	74593	Phila. S. O.
74417	Wither-	74476	Williams	74535	Paderewski	74594	Galli-Curci
	spoon	74477	Williams	74536	Galli-Curci	74595	Braslau
74418	Wither-	74478	De Gogorza	74537	Martinelli	74596	Flonzaley
	spoon	74479	McCormack	74538	Galli-Curci		Quartet
74419	Williams	74480	Williams	74539	Paderewski	74597	Elman
74420	Gluck	74481	Garrison	74540	Culp	74598	Phila. S. O.
74421	De Gogorza	74482	Garrison	74541	Galli-Curci	74599	Galli-Curci
74422	De Gogorza	74483	Martinelli	74542	Garrison	74600	Heifetz
74423	Gluck	74484	McCormack	74543	Gluck	74601	Elman
74424	Martinelli	74485	McCormack	74544	McCormack	74602	Phila. S. O.
74425	Whitehill	74486	McCormack	74545	Paderewski	74603	Phila. S. O.
74426	Martinelli	74487	Kreisler	74546	Powell	74604	Navarro
74427	Culp	74488	Garrison	74547	Powell	74605	Gigli
74428	McCormack	74489	Garrison	74548	Powell	74606	Gigli
74429	Culp	74490	Williams	74549	Williams	74607	Elman
74430	Culp	74491	Garrison	74550	Williams	74608	Galli-Curci
74431	Culp	74492	Powell	74551	Williams	74609	Phila. S. O.
74432	McCormack	74493	Powell	74552	Galli-Curci	74610	Werrenrath

74611	Flonzaley Quartet	74667	Flonzaley Quartet	74725	Toscanini	74782	N.Y. Ph'l.
74612	Garrison	74668	Toscanini	74726	Flonzaley Quartet	74783	Werrenrath
74613	Besanzoni	74669	Toscanini			74784	Galli-Curci
74614	Gigli	74670	Cortot	74727	Morini	74785	Samaroff
74615	Gigli	74671	Phila. S. O.	74728	Rachman-inoff	74786	Galli-Curci
74616	Heifetz	74672	Toscanini			74787	De Luca
74617	Besanzoni	74673	Sothern	74729	Ph'la. S. O.	74788	Paderewski
74618	Novaes	74674	Paderewski	74730	Phila. S. O.	74789	Soro
74619	Gigli	74675	Novaes	74731	Palet	74790	Palet
74620	Gigli	74676	Novaes	74732	E'man	74791	McCormack
74621	Phila. S. O.	74677	Besanzoni	74733	Flonzaley Quartet	74792	Flonzaley Quartet
74622	Zanelli	74678	Heifetz	74734	Gal'i-Curci	74793	Gigli
74623	Cortot	74679	Rachman-inoff	74735	Journet	74794	Samaroff
74624	Harrold			74736	Phila. S. O.	74795	Harrold
74625	Garrison	74680	Besanzoni	74737	Harrold	74796	Paderewski
74626	Heifetz	74681	Braslau	74738	Ansseau	74797	Mor'ni
74627	Phila. S. O.	74682	Kindler	74739	Ansseau	74798	Cortot
74628	Rachman-inoff	74683	Martinelli	74740	Smirnov	74799	Samaroff
		74684	Phila. S. O.	74741	Smirnov	74800	Martinelli
74629	Schipa	74685	Flonzaley Quartet	74742	Gigli	74801	Flonzaley Quartet
74630	Rachman-inoff	74686	Morini	74743	Galli-Curci		
		74687	Gigli	74744	De Luca	74802	Paderewski
74631	Phila. S. O.	74688	Gigli	74745	Toscanini	74803	Phila. S. O.
74632	Zanelli	74689	Heifetz	74746	Flonzaley Quartet	74804	Gigli
74633	De Luca	74690	Toscanini			74805	Paderewski
74634	Flonzaley Quartet	74691	Phila. S. O.	74747	Zanelli	74806	Paderewski
		74692	Morini	74748	Journet	74807	Rachman-inoff
74635	Heifetz	74693	Flonzaley Quartet	74749	Jeritza		
74636	Cortot			74750	Heifetz	74808	Mardones
74637	Palet	74694	Heifetz	74751	Chemet	74809	Martinelli
74638	Palet	74695	Toscanini	74752	Chemet	74810	Cortot
74639	Galli-Curci	74696	Samaroff	74753	Schipa	74811	Heifetz
74640	De Muro	74697	De Luca	74754	Flonzaley Quartet	74812	Galli-Curci
74641	De Muro	74698	Phila. S. O.			74813	Harrold
74642	De Muro	74699	Sothern	74755	Flonzaley Quartet	74814	Phila. S. O.
74643	Elman	74700	Sothern			74815	Werrenrath
74644	Galli-Curci	74701	Sothern	74756	N.Y. Phil.	74816	N.Y. Phil.
74645	Rachman-inoff	74702	Sothern	74757	N.Y. Phil.	74817	N.Y. Phil.
		74703	Sothern	74758	Phila. S. O.	74818	Jeritza
74646	Heifetz	74704	Sothern	74759	Phila. S. O.	74819	Jeri'za
74647	Phila. S. O.	74705	Sothern	74760	Jer'tza	74820	Heifetz
74648	De Muro	74706	Sothern	74761	Palet	74821	Heifetz
74649	De Muro	74707	Sothern	74762	De Muro	74822	Cortot
74650	De Muro	74708	Sothern	74763	Ansseau	74823	Ansseaeu
74651	Alda	74709	De Muro	74764	Heifetz	74824	Cortot
74652	Flonzaley Quartet	74710	Flonzaley Quartet	74765	Paderewski	74825	Flonzaley Quartet
74653	Galli-Curci	74711	Heifetz	74766	N.Y. Phil.	74826	Novaes
74654	Johnson	74712	Martinelli	74767	N.Y. Phil.	74827	Werrenrath
74655	Paderewski	74713	Phila. S. O.	74768	Phila. S. O.	74828	Fleta
74656	Paderewski	74714	De Muro	74769	Toscanini	74829	Cortot
74657	Paderewski	74715	De Muro	74770	Toscanini	74830	Cortot
74658	Paderewski	74716	Harrold	74771	Elman	74831	Samaroff
74659	Cortot	74717	Morini	74772	Samaroff	74832	Mardones
74660	Heifetz	74718	Galli-Curci	74773	Palet	74833	Mardones
74661	Phila. S. O.	74719	Werrenrath	74774	Fleta	74834	De Muro
74662	Sothern	74720	Kreisler	74775	Fleta	74835	De Muro
74663	Sothern	74721	Heifetz	74776	Jeritza	74836	De Muro
74664	De Muro	74722	Phila. S. O.	74777	Paderewski	74837	Elman
74665	De Muro	74723	Rachman-inoff	74778	Fleta	74838	N.Y. Phil.
74666	De Muro	74724	Elman	74779	Toscanini	74839	Schipa
				74780	N.Y. Phil.		
				74781	N.Y. Phil.		

74840	Fionzaley Quartet	74865	De Pach-mann	74888	Morini	76006	Pareto
74841	Fionzaley Quartet	74866	Ponselle	74889	Morini	76007	Pareto
		74867	Ponselle	74890	Mardones	76008	Pareto
74842	Werrenrath	74868	De Pach-	74891	Mardones	76009	Pareto
74843	Paderewski		mann	74892	Elman	76010	Giorgini
74844	N.Y. Phil.	74869	Morini	74893	Elman	76011	Giorgini
74845	N.Y. Phil.	74870	Sistine Choir	74894	Phila. S. O.	76012	De Tura
74846	Phila. S. O.			74895	Phila. S. O.	76013	Della Torre
74847	Phila. S. O.	74871	Sistine Choir	74896	Phila. S. O.	76014	Scampini
74848	Phila. S. O.			74897	Phila. S. O.	76015	De Tura
74849	Phila. S. O.	74872	De Luca	74898	Phila. S. O.	76016	Ruszcowska
74850	Galli-Curci	74873	De Luca	74899	Phila. S. O.	76017	Hempel
74851	Galli-Curci	74874	Novaes	74900	Gabrilo-witsch	76018	Marcel
74852	Samaroff	74875	Novaes	74901	Gabrilo-witsch	76019	De Tura
74853	Samaroff	74876	Gigli			76020	Clement
74854	Mardones	74877	Hansen	74902	Gabrilo-witsch	76021	Clement
74855	Whitehill	74878	Hansen	74903	Gabrilo-witsch	76022	Clement
74856	Wh:tehill	74879	Paderewski			76023	Jadlowker
74857	Whitehill	74880	Paderewski	74904	N.Y. Phil.	76024	Jadlowker
74858	Whitehill	74881	Samaroff	74905	N.Y. Phil.	76025	Jadlowker
74859	Whitehill	74882	Samaroff	76000	De Lucia	76026	Jadlowker
74860	Ponselle	74883	Zimbalist	76001	De Lucia	76027	Jadlowker
74861	Ponselle	74884	Zimbalist	76002	De Lucia	76028	Kreisler
74862	Paderewski	74885	Rachman-inoff	76003	Pareto	76029	Kreisler
74863	Paderewski			76004	Marconi	76030	Kreisler
74864	De Pach-mann	74886	Ponselle	76005	Pietra-cewska	76031	Ober
		74887	Ponselle			76032	Martinelli

Note: Nos. 76000-32 actually belong to a different series, as do Nos. 66000-6; those in the ten-inch series, however, beginning with No. 66007 are a continuation of the 64000 group. The 61000 and 71000 series were mixed red and black. The records among them which appeared, at one time or another, on Red Seal, are included in the artists' section under Bachaus, Elman, Michailowa, Regis, Runge, Sagi-Barba, Sirota, Sistine Chapel, Slezak, Vela.

Likewise, records of celebrity category from the 2000 series will be found among artists in the early 81000 group; those from the 5000 series among artists in the 91000 group.

81001	Crossley	81025	Caruso	81049	Sembr:ch	81073	Plancon
81002	De Lussan	81026	Caruso	81050	Sembrich	81074	Campanari
81003	De Lussan	81027	Caruso	81051	Powell	81075	Campanari
81004	Crossley	81028	Caruso	81052	Powell	81076	Plancon
81005	Crossley	81029	Caruso	81053	Journet	81077	Homer
81006	Crossley	81030	Caruso	81054	Scotti	81078	Homer
81007	De Lussan	81031	Caruso	81055	Homer	81079	Homer
81008	De Lussan	81032	Caruso	81056	Plancon	81080	Campanari
81009	De Lussan	81033	Plancon	81057	Nuibo	81081	Campanari
81010	Campanari	81034	Plancon	81058	Nuibo	81082	Campanari
81011	Campanari	81035	Plancon	81059	Journet	81083	Schumann-Heink
81012	Campanari	81036	Homer	81060	Journet		
81013	Homer	81037	Plancon	81061	Journet	81084	Homer
81014	Homer	81038	Plancon	81062	Caruso	81085	Schumann-Heink
81015	Blass	81039	Plancon	81063	Scotti		
81016	Blass	81040	Plancon	81064	Scotti	81086	Plancon
81017	Blass	81041	Scotti	81065	Plancon	81087	Plancon
81018	Gadski	81042	Scotti	81066	Plancon	81088	Dalmores
81019	Gadski	81043	Scotti	81067	Blauvelt	81089	Gadski
81020	Homer	81044	Campanari	81068	Blauvelt	81090	Gilibert
81021	Scotti	81045	Gadski	81069	Blauvelt	81091	Gerville-Reache
81022	Scotti	81046	Juch	81070	Scotti		
81023	Plancon	81047	Sembrich	81071	Campanari	81092	De Gogorza
81024	Gadski	81048	Sembrich	81072	Nuibo		

85001	Campanari	85035	Sembrich	85069	Homer	85098	Eames
85002	Campanari	85036	Sembrich	85070	Blauvelt	85099	Plancon
85003	Campanari	85037	Sembrich	85071	Scotti	85100	Plancon
85004	Homer	85038	Sembrich	85072	Scotti	85101	Schumann-Heink
85005	Homer	85039	Powell	85073	Campanari		
85006	Homer	85040	Powell	85074	Campanari	85102	Homer
85007	Blass	85041	Nuibo	85075	Nuibo	85103	Homer
85008	Blass	85042	Plancon	85076	Plancon	85104	Homer
85009	Blass	85043	Homer	85077	Plancon	85105	Homer
85010	Blass	85044	Scotti	85078	Campanari	85106	Homer
85011	Blass	85045	Scotti	85079	Campanari	85107	Homer
85012	Gadski	85046	Journet	85080	Campanari	85108	Homer
85013	Gadski	85047	Journet	85081	Campanari	85109	Homer
85014	Homer	85048	Caruso	85082	Plancon	85110	Homer
85015	Homer	85049	Caruso	85083	Homer	85111	Homer
85016	Scotti	85050	Journet	85084	Homer	85112	Schuman-Heink
85017	Scotti	85051	Journet	85085	Homer		
85018	Plancon	85052	Eames	85086	Campanari	85113	Schumann-Heink
85019	Plancon	85053	Eames	85087	Campanari		
85020	Plancon	85054	Eames	85088	Campanari	85114	Dalmores
85021	Caruso	85055	Caruso	85089	Van Hoose	85115	Dalmores
85022	Caruso	85056	Caruso	85090	Van Hoose	85116	Plancon
85023	Plancon	85057	Eames	85091	Van Hoose	85117	Plancon
85024	Plancon	85058	Eames	85092	Schumann-Heink	85118	Gilibert
85025	Gadski	85059	Eames			85119	Plancon
85026	Campanari	85060	Eames	85093	Schumann-Heink	85120	Gilibert
85027	Campanari	85061	Eames			85121	Dalmores
85028	Campanari	85062	Eames	85094	Schumann-Heink	85122	Dalmores
85029	Gadski	85063	Eames			85123	Dalmores
85030	Scotti	85064	Plancon	85095	Schumann-Heink	85124	Plancon
85031	Scotti	85065	Plancon			85125	Plancon
85032	Gadski	85066	Plancon	85096	Schumann-Heink	85126	Plancon
85033	Juch	85067	Scotti				
85034	Juch	85068	Scotti	85097	Eames		

87001	Caruso	87022	Schumann-Heink	87042	Caruso	87067	De Tura
87002	Gadski			87043	Caruso	87068	De Casas
87003	Abott	87023	Farrar	87044	Caruso	87069	Ruszcowska
87004	Farrar	87024	Farrar	87045	Zerola	87070	Caruso
87005	Farrar	87025	Farrar	87046	Zerola	87071	Caruso
87006	Ancona	87026	Gadski	87047	De Lucia	87072	Caruso
87007	Abott	87027	Gerville-Reache	87048	De Lucia	87073	Farrar
87008	Homer			87049	De Lucia	87074	Homer
87009	Homer	87028	Gadski	87050	Martin	87075	Homer
87010	Ancona	87029	Farrar	87051	Martin	87076	Farrar
87011	Ancona	87030	Farrar	87052	Gadski	87077	Sammarco
87012	Schumann-Heink	87031	Farrar	87053	Caruso	87078	McCormack
		87032	Schumann-Heink	87054	Caruso	87079	Alda
87013	Schumann-Heink			87055	Farrar	87080	Gerville-Reache
		87033	Homer	87056	De Tura		
87014	Ancona	87034	Scotti	87057	Galvany	87081	Martin
87015	Ancona	87035	Gerville-Reache	87058	Galvany	87082	McCormack
87016	Gadski			87059	Galvany	87083	Giorgini
87017	Caruso	87036	Zerola	87060	Galvany	87084	Scotti
87018	Caruso	87037	Zerola	87061	Galvany	87085	Gerville-Reache
87019	Gadski	87038	Gerville-Reache	87062	Farrar		
87020	Schumann-Heink			87063	McCormack	87086	Alda
		87039	Gerville-Reache	87064	Zerola	87087	Dalmores
87021	Schumann-Heink	87040	Scotti	87065	Gerville-Reache	87088	Dalmores
		87041	Caruso	87066	Alda	87089	Dalmores
						87090	Alda

87091	Caruso	87149	Ruffo	87208	Gluck	87266	Caruso
87092	Caruso	87150	Ruffo	87209	Gluck	87267	Gluck
87093	Amato	87151	Ruffo	87210	Farrar	87268	Hempel
87094	Schumann-Heink	87152	Ruffo	87211	Caruso	87269	Caruso
		87153	Ruffo	87212	Gluck	87270	Hempel
87095	Caruso	87154	Ruffo	87213	Caruso	87271	Caruso
87096	Alda	87155	Ruffo	87214	Destinn	87272	Caruso
87097	Amato	87156	Ruffo	87215	Destinn	87273	Gadski
87098	Gadski	87157	Ruffo	87216	Alda	87274	Gadski
87099	Gadski	87158	Ruffo	87217	Bori	87275	Gadski
87100	Gadski	87159	Caruso	87218	Caruso	87276	Gluck
87101	Gluck	87160	Farrar	87219	Bori	87277	Homer
87102	Matzenauer	87161	Caruso	87220	Ruffo	87278	Gluck
87103	Matzenauer	87162	Caruso	87221	Schumann-	87279	Hempel
87104	Schumann-	87163	Farrar		Heink	87280	Schumann-
	Heink	87164	Farrar	87222	Ruffo		Heink
87105	Amato	87165	Farrar	87223	Ruffo	87281	Gadski
87106	Alda	87166	Ruffo	87224	Gluck	87282	Schumann-
87107	Gluck	87167	Gadski	87225	Bori		Heink
87108	Donalda	87168	Schumann-	87226	Gluck	87283	Gluck
87109	Homer		Heink	87227	Gluck	87284	Gluck
87110	Gluck	87169	Caruso	87228	Gluck	87285	(unused)
87111	Alda	87170	Schumann-	87229	Gluck	87286	Schumann-
87112	Ruffo		Heink	87230	McCormack		Heink
87113	Ruffo	87171	Schumann-	87231	McCormack	87287	Gluck
87114	Ruffo		Heink	87232	McCormack	87288	Schumann-
87115	Alda	87172	Schumann-	87233	McCormack		Heink
87116	Alda		Heink	87234	Hempel	87289	Farrar
87117	Alda	87173	Gadski	87235	Hempel	87290	Farrar
87118	Alda	87174	Ruffo	87236	Gluck	87291	Farrar
87119	Dalmores	87175	Caruso	87237	Gluck	87292	Farrar
87120	Dalmores	87176	Caruso	87238	Schumann-	87293	Caruso
87121	Ruffo	87177	Ruffo		Heink	87294	Caruso
87122	Caruso	87178	Bori	87239	Schumann-	87295	Schumann-
87123	Ruffo	87179	Hempel		Heink		Heink
87124	Schumann-	87180	Amato	87240	Schumann-	87296	Gluck
	Heink	87181	Bori		Heink	87297	Caruso
87125	Ruffo	87182	Gluck	87241	Schumann-	87298	Schumann-
87126	Farrar	87183	Gluck		Heink		Heink
87127	Farrar	87184	Gluck	87242	Caruso	87299	Schumann-
87128	Caruso	87185	Gluck	87243	Caruso		Heink
87129	Schumann-	87186	Caruso	87244	Gluck	87300	Gluck
	Heink	87187	Caruso	87245	McCormack	87301	Homer
87130	Schumann-	87188	Bori	87246	Destinn	87302	Schumann-
	Heink	87189	Bori	87247	Farrar		Heink
87131	Gluck	87190	Bori	87248	Farrar	87303	Homer
87132	Gluck	87191	McCormack	87249	Destinn	87304	Caruso
87133	Ruffo	87192	McCormack	87250	Hempel	87305	Caruso
87134	Farrar	87193	Amato	87251	Farrar	87306	Destinn
87135	Caruso	87194	Ruffo	87252	Gadski	87307	Schumann-
87136	Farrar	87195	Ruffo	87253	Farrar		Heink
87137	Ruffo	87196	Gluck	87254	Farrar	87308	Farrar
87138	Ruffo	87197	Destinn	87255	Homer	87309	Homer
87139	Ruffo	87198	Gluck	87256	Farrar	87310	Destinn
87140	Ruffo	87199	Gluck	87257	Farrar	87311	Farrar
87141	Ruffo	87200	Gluck	87258	McCormack	87312	Caruso
87142	Ruffo	87201	Gluck	87259	Homer	87313	Farrar
87143	Ruffo	87202	Gluck	87260	Homer	87314	Destinn
87144	Gluck	87203	Gluck	87261	Hempel	87315	Destinn
87145	Ruffo	87204	Homer	87262	Homer	87316	Destinn
87146	Gluck	87205	Homer	87263	Homer	87317	Destinn
87147	Ruffo	87206	Homer	87264	Homer	87318	Destinn
87148	Ruffo	87207	Destinn	87265	Homer	87319	Farrar

87320	Schumann-	87339	Battistini	87361	Chaliapin	87382	Ruffo
	Heink	87340	Schumann-	87362	Farrar	87383	Ruffo
87321	Caruso		Heink	87363	Schumann-	87384	Ruffo
87322	Farrar	87341	Ruffo		Heink	87385	Schumann-
87323	Ruffo	87342	Ruffo	87364	Farrar		Heink
87324	Destinn	87343	Ruffo	87365	Caruso	87386	Schumann-
87325	Ruffo	87344	Bori	87366	Caruso		Heink
87326	Schumann-	87345	Homer	87367	Chaliapin	87387	Matzenauer
	Heink	87346	Bori	87368	Chaliapin	87388	Matzenauer
87327	Homer	87347	Farrar	87369	Ruffo	87389	Chaliapin
87328	Bori	87348	Farrar	87370	Ruffo	87390	Chaliapin
87329	Homer	87349	Chaliapin	87371	Bori	87391	Bori
87330	Schumann-	87350	Farrar	87372	Bori	87392	Bori
	Heink	87351	Bori	87373	Schumann-	87393	Ruffo
87331	Ruffo	87352	Ruffo		Heink	87394	Ruffo
87332	Schumann-	87353	Schumann-	87374	Schumann-	87395	Caruso
	Heink		Heink		Heink	87396	Caruso
87333	Bori	87354	Homer	87375	Homer	87397	Smirnov
87334	Homer	87355	Chaliapin	87376	Homer	87398	Smirnov
87335	Caruso	87356	Bori	87377	Homer	87399	Lloyd
87336	Ruffo	87357	Farrar	87378	Chaliapin	87400	Lloyd
87337	Schumann-	87358	Caruso	87379	Bori		
	Heink	87359	Homer	87380	Bori		
87338	Battistini	87360	Ruffo	87381	Ruffo		

(87500) *Ten-inch*   *Single-face* (87582)

87500	Abott	87521	Gluck	87542	Gluck	87563	McCormack
87501	Homer	87522	Gluck	87543	Gluck	87564	Ruffo
87502	Farrar	87523	Gluck	87544	Gluck	87565	De Tura
87503	Fornia	87524	Gluck	87545	McCormack	87566	Gluck
87504	Farrar	87525	Gluck	87546	McCormack	87567	Galli-Curci
87505	Farrar	87526	Gluck	87547	McCormack	87568	Farrar
87506	Farrar	87527	Gluck	87548	McCormack	87569	Garrison
87507	Farrar	87528	Gluck	87549	McCormack	87570	Homer
87508	Farrar	87529	Gluck	87550	McCormack	87571	McCormack
87509	Farrar	87530	Gluck	87551	McCormack	87572	Homer
87510	Gadski	87531	Gluck	87552	McCormack	87573	McCormack
87511	Caruso	87532	Gluck	87553	McCormack	87574	McCormack
87512	McCormack	87533	Gluck	87554	Destinn	87575	Homer
87513	Gluck	87534	Gluck	87555	Destinn	87576	McCormack
87514	Gluck	87535	Gluck	87556	Alda	87577	Kreisler
87515	Gluck	87536	Gluck	87557	Bori	87578	Homer
87516	Gluck	87537	Gluck	87558	Ruszcowska	87579	Kreisler
87517	Gluck	87538	Gluck	87559	Boninsegna	87580	Homer
87518	Gluck	87539	Gluck	87560	Boninsegna	87581	Bori
87519	Gluck	87540	Gluck	87561	De Casas	87582	Homer
87520	Gluck	87541	Gluck	87562	De Lucia		

(88001) *Twelve-inch*   *Single-face* (88048)

88001	Caruso	88013	Eames	88025	Caruso	88037	Eames
88002	Caruso	88014	Eames	88026	Sembrich	88038	Gadski
88003	Caruso	88015	Eames	88027	Sembrich	88039	Gadski
88004	Caruso	88016	Eames	88028	Scotti	88040	Gadski
88005	Eames	88017	Sembrich	88029	Scotti	88041	Gadski
88006	Eames	88018	Sembrich	88030	Scotti	88042	Gadski
88007	Eames	88019	Sembrich	88031	(unused)	88043	Gadski
88008	Eames	88020	Sembrich	88032	Scotti	88044	Gadski
88009	Eames	88021	Sembrich	88033	(unused)	88045	Eames
88010	Eames	88022	Sembrich	88034	Plancon	88046	Sembrich
88011	Eames	88023	Sembrich	88035	Eames	88047	Sembrich
88012	Eames	88024	Sembrich	88036	Eames	88048	Caruso

88049	Caruso	88100	Sembrich	88151	Melba	88198	Gerville-
88050	Abott	88101	Sembrich	88152	Farrar		Reache
88051	Abott	88102	Sembrich	88153	De Gogorza	88199	Homer
88052	Farrar	88103	Sembrich	88154	De Gogorza	88200	Homer
88053	Farrar	88104	Sembrich	88155	Schumann-	88201	Homer
88054	Caruso	88105	Sembrich		Heink	88202	Zerola
88055	Ancona	88106	Caruso	88156	Melba	88203	Scotti
88056	Ancona	88107	Sembrich	88157	Melba	88204	Homer
88057	Gadski	88108	Schumann-	88158	Bachaus	88205	Gerville-
88058	Gadski		Heink	88159	(unused)		Reache
88059	Gadski	88109	Ancona	88160	Bachaus	88206	Caruso
88060	Caruso	88110	Abott	88161	Hamlin	88207	Caruso
88061	Caruso	88111	Gadski	88162	Hamlin	88208	Caruso
88062	Ancona	88112	Gadski	88163	Gadski	88209	Caruso
88063	Ancona	88113	Farrar	88164	Gadski	88210	Caruso
88064	Melba	88114	Farrar	88165	Gadski	88211	Farrar
88065	Melba	88115	Caruso	88166	Gerville-	88212	Schumann-
88066	Melba	88116	Gadski		Reache		Heink
88067	Melba	88117	Gadski	88167	Ancona	88213	Alda
88068	Melba	88118	Schumann-	88168	Ancona	88214	Alda
88069	Melba		Heink	88169	Ancona	88215	McCormack
88070	Melba	88119	Calve	88170	Ancona	88216	McCormack
88071	Melba	88120	Caruso	88171	Abott	88217	McCormack
88072	Melba	88121	Caruso	88172	De Gogorza	88218	McCormack
88073	Melba	88122	Scotti	88173	De Gogorza	88219	Galvany
88074	Melba	88123	Calve	88174	De Gogorza	88220	Galvany
88075	Melba	88124	Calve	88175	De Gogorza	88221	Galvany
88076	Melba	88125	Farrar	88176	De Gogorza	88222	Galvany
88077	Melba	88126	Farrar	88177	De Gogorza	88223	Boninsegna
88078	Melba	88127	Caruso	88178	De Gogorza	88224	Pareto
88079	Melba	88128	Homer	88179	De Gogorza	88225	Pietra-
88080	Melba	88129	Abott	88180	De Gogorza		cewska
88081	Ancona	88130	Calve	88181	De Gogorza	88226	Marconi
88082	Scotti	88131	Eames	88182	Melba	88227	De Tura
88083	Scotti	88132	Homer	88183	Gadski	88228	Domar
88084	Abott	88133	Eames	88184	Gerville-	88229	Farrar
88085	Calve	88134	Calve		Reache	88230	McCormack
88086	Calve	88135	Eames	88185	Gadski	88231	Homer
88087	Calve	88136	Gadski	88186	Gadski	88232	Battistini
88088	Homer	88137	Gadski	88187	Schumann-	88233	De Tura
88089	Calve	88138	Schumann-		Heink	88234	Galvany
88090	Schumann-		Heink	88188	Schumann-	88235	Galvany
	Heink	88139	Schumann-		Heink	88236	Galvany
88091	Schumann-		Heink	88189	Schumann-	88237	Gilibert
	Heink	88140	Schumann-		Heink	88238	Farrar
88092	Schumann-		Heink	88190	Schumann-	88239	Boninsegna
	Heink	88141	Sembrich		Heink	88240	Paoli
88093	Schumann-	88142	Sembrich	88191	Schumann-	88241	De Tura
	Heink	88143	Sembrich		Heink	88242	Boronat
88094	Schumann-	88144	Farrar	88192	Farrar	88243	Zerola
	Heink	88145	Farrar	88193	Farrar	88244	Gerville-
88095	Schumann-	88146	Farrar	88194	Scotti		Reache
	Heink	88147	Farrar	88195	Scotti	88245	McCormack
88096	Sembrich	88148	Melba	88196	Schumann-	88246	Caruso
88097	Sembrich	88149	Melba		Heink	88247	Alda
88098	Sembrich	88150	Melba	88197	Schumann-	88248	Alda
88099	Sembrich				Heink		

88249	McCormack	88309	Homer	88367	Eames	88425	Caruso
88250	Melba	88310	Sammarco	88368	Gerville-	88426	Tetrazzini
88251	Melba	88311	Tetrazzini		Reache	88427	Tetrazzini
88252	Melba	88312	Sammarco	88369	Gadski	88428	Tetrazzini
88253	Gadski	88313	Tetrazzini	88370	Gadski	88429	Caruso
88254	Gadski	88314	Sammarco	88371	Gadski	88430	Matzenauer
88255	Giorgini	88315	Sammarco	88372	Gadski	88431	Matzenauer
88256	Boninsegna	88316	Martin	88373	Ruszcowska	88432	Tetrazzini
88257	Sammarco	88317	Gerville-	88374	Battistini	88433	Gluck
88258	Sammarco		Reache	88375	Gluck	88434	Gluck
88259	Sammarco	88318	Tetrazzini	88376	Caruso	88435	Hempel
88260	Sammarco	88319	Giorgini	88377	Gadski	88436	Paderewski
88261	Ruszcowska	88320	Sammarco	88378	Caruso	88437	Amato
88262	Ruszcowska	88321	Paderewski	88379	Gadski	88438	Amato
88263	Ruszcowska	88322	Paderewski	88380	Gluck	88439	Caruso
88264	De Casas	88323	De Casas	88381	Schumann-	88440	Gadski
88265	Ruszcowska	88324	De Gogorza				Heink	88441	Gadski
88266	Ruszcowska	88325	Alda	88382	Hempel	88442	Gadski
88267	Ruszcowska	88326	Amato	88383	Hempel	88443	Gadski
88268	Paoli	88327	Amato	88384	Homer	88444	Paderewski
88269	Pietra-	88328	Amato	88385	Butt	88445	Paderewski
	cewska	88329	Amato	88386	Butt	88446	Hempel
88270	De Casas	88330	Dalmores	88387	Sembrich	88447	De Gogorza
88271	Ruszcowska	88331	Caruso	88388	Sembrich	88448	Schumann-
88272	Ruszcowska	88332	Caruso	88389	Sembrich		Heink
88273	Ruszcowska	88333	Caruso	88390	Sembrich	88449	Melba
88274	Ruszcowska	88334	Caruso	88391	Ruffo	88450	Hempel
88275	Gadski	88335	Caruso	88392	Ruffo	88451	Schumann-
88276	Martin	88336	Schumann-	88393	Ruffo		Heink
88277	Martin		Heink	88394	Ruffo	88452	Melba
88278	Gerville-	88337	Schumann-	88395	Ruffo	88453	McCormack
	Reache		Heink	88396	Ruffo	88454	Melba
88279	Caruso	88338	Amato	88397	Dalmores	88455	Melba
88280	Caruso	88339	Caruso	88398	Bori	88456	Melba
88281	Gerville-	88340	Amato	88399	Alda	88457	Melba
	Reache	88341	Amato	88400	Schumann-	88458	Caruso
88282	Scotti	88342	Schumann-		Heink	88459	Caruso
88283	Farrar		Heink	88401	Paderewski	88460	Caruso
88284	Homer	88343	Schumann-	88402	Paderewski	88461	Chaliapin
88285	Homer		Heink	88403	Caruso	88462	Chaliapin
88286	Homer	88344	Eames	88404	Hempel	88463	Hempel
88287	Farrar	88345	Caruso	88405	Farrar	88464	Amato
88288	Homer	88346	Caruso	88406	Farrar	88465	Caruso
88289	Farrar	88347	Caruso	88407	Homer	88466	Ruffo
88290	Scotti	88348	Caruso	88408	Paderewski	88467	Destinn
88291	Tetrazzini	88349	Tetrazzini	88409	Farrar	88468	Destinn
88292	Tetrazzini	88350	Battistini	88410	Hempel	88469	Destinn
88293	Tetrazzini	88351	Battistini	88411	Butt	88470	Hempel
88294	Tetrazzini	88352	Battistini	88412	Farrar	88471	Hempel
88295	Tetrazzini	88353	Battistini	88413	Farrar	88472	Caruso
88296	Tetrazzini	88354	Battistini	88414	Homer	88473	Amato
88297	Tetrazzini	88355	Caruso	88415	Butt	88474	Amato
88298	Tetrazzini	88356	Farrar	88416	Schumann-	88475	Bori
88299	Tetrazzini	88357	Paderewski		Heink	88476	Hempel
88300	Tetrazzini	88358	Gluck	88417	Schumann-	88477	Melba
88301	Tetrazzini	88359	Farrar		Heink	88478	Destinn
88302	Tetrazzini	88360	Matzenauer	88418	Gluck	88479	McCormack
88303	Tetrazzini	88361	De Lucia	88419	Gluck	88480	Bori
88304	Tetrazzini	88362	Gadski	88420	Tetrazzini	88481	McCormack
88305	Tetrazzini	88363	Matzenauer	88421	Farrar	88482	McCormack
88306	Tetrazzini	88364	Matzenauer	88422	Farrar	88483	McCormack
88307	Tetrazzini	88365	Matzenauer	88423	Tetrazzini	88484	McCormack
88308	Tetrazzini	88366	Ruffo	88424	Farrar	88485	Melba

No.	Name	No.	Name	No.	Name	No.	Name
88486	Ruffo	88540	Hempel	88590	Gadski	88642	Pareto
88487	Destinn	88541	Hempel	88591	Gadski	88643	Ruffo
88488	Destinn	88542	Gadski	88592	Schumann-Heink	88644	Chaliapin
88489	Amato	88543	Hempel			88645	Chaliapin
88490	Amato	88544	Ruffo	88593	Gluck	88646	Chaliapin
88491	Paderewski	88545	Gadski	88594	Farrar	88647	Bori
88492	Paderewski	88546	Gadski	88595	(unused)	88648	Chaliapin
88493	Caprile	88547	Schumann-Heink	88596	Galli-Curci	88649	Battistini
88494	Paderewski			88597	Alda	88650	Battistini
88495	Gadski	88548	Schumann-Heink	88598	Alda	88651	Battistini
88496	Gadski			88599	Caruso	88652	Battistini
88497	Gadski	88549	Schumann-Heink	88600	Caruso	88653	Battistini
88498	Destinn			88601	Galli-Curci	88654	Battistini
88499	Gadski	88550	Schumann-Heink	88602	De Lucia	88655	Chaliapin
88500	Ancona			88603	De Lucia	88656	Chaliapin
88501	(unused)	88551	Melba	88604	Pareto	88657	Chaliapin
88502	Tetrazzini	88552	Caruso	88605	Pareto	88658	Homer
88503	Tetrazzini	88553	Melba	88606	Pareto	88659	Chaliapin
88504	Tetrazzini	88554	Caruso	88607	Pareto	88660	Ruffo
88505	Tetrazzini	88555	Caruso	88608	Pareto	88661	Chaliapin
88506	Tetrazzini	88556	Caruso	88609	De Tura	88662	Melba
88507	Galvany	88557	Destinn	88610	De Tura	88663	Chaliapin
88508	Tetrazzini	88558	Caruso	88611	De Tura	88664	Hempel
88509	Caprile	88559	Caruso	88612	Caruso	88665	Chaliapin
88510	Destinn	88560	Caruso	88613	Homer	88666	Chaliapin
88511	Farrar	88561	Caruso	88614	Homer	88667	Homer
88512	Farrar	88562	Destinn	88615	Caruso	88668	Ruffo
88513	Farrar	88563	Destinn	88616	Caruso	88669	Chaliapin
88514	Caruso	88564	Gadski	88617	Caruso	88670	Caruso
88515	Gadski	88565	Destinn	88618	Ruffo	88671	Caruso
88516	Caruso	88566	Gadski	88619	Ruffo	88672	Kubelik
88517	Caruso	88567	Hempel	88620	Schumann-Heink	88673	Kubelik
88518	Destinn	88568	Destinn			88674	Kubelik
88519	Destinn	88569	Farrar	88621	Ruffo	88675	Kubelik
88520	Destinn	88570	Calve	88622	Ruffo	88676	Butt
88521	Alda	88571	Gadski	88623	Caruso	88677	Chaliapin
88522	Alda	88572	Calve	88624	Destinn	88678	Chaliapin
88523	Alda	88573	Gluck	88625	Caruso	88679	Chaliapin
88524	Bori	88574	Homer	88626	Ruffo	88680	Chaliapin
88525	Bori	88575	Homer	88627	Homer	88681	Chaliapin
88526	Bori	88576	Gluck	88628	Caruso	88682	Chaliapin
88527	Ruffo	88577	Gluck	88629	Caruso	88683	Chaliapin
88528	Ruffo	88578	Gadski	88630	Pareto	88684	Chaliapin
88529	Destinn	88579	Caruso	88631	Pareto	88685	Chaliapin
88530	Destinn	88580	Caruso	88632	Pareto	88686	Chaliapin
88531	Farrar	88581	Caruso	88633	Bori	88687	Smirnov
88532	Farrar	88582	Caruso	88634	Destinn	88688	Smirnov
88533	Farrar	88583	Gluck	88635	Caruso	88689	Bourchier
88534	Farrar	88584	Homer	88636	Destinn	88690	Lloyd
88535	Farrar	88585	Homer	88637	Ruffo	88691	Lloyd
88536	Farrar	88586	Caruso	88638	Caruso	88692	Lloyd
88537	Farrar	88587	Caruso	88639	Ruffo	88693	Lloyd
88538	Farrar	88588	Hempel	88640	Homer		
88539	Gluck	88589	Caruso	88641	Pareto		

No.	Name	No.	Name	No.	Name	No.	Name
89001	Caruso	89008	Farrar	89015	Farrar	89022	Eames
89002	Sembrich	89009	Abott	89016	Farrar	89023	Eames
89003	Eames	89010	Sembrich	89017	Caruso	89024	Gadski
89004	Eames	89011	Melba	89018	Caruso	89025	Gadski
89005	Eames	89012	Melba	89019	Calve	89026	Farrar
89006	Caruso	89013	Abott	89020	Eames	89027	Farrar
89007	Caruso	89014	Farrar	89021	Eames	89028	Caruso

89029	Caruso	89066	Caruso	89103	McCormack	89140	De Lucia
89030	Caruso	89067	Gadski	89104	McCormack	89141	De Lucia
89031	Caruso	89068	Gadski	89105	McCormack	89142	De Lucia
89032	Caruso	89069	Gadski	89106	McCormack	89143	Domar
89033	Caruso	89070	Gadski	89107	McCormack	89144	De Casas
89034	Caruso	89071	Farrar	89108	Farrar	89145	Galvany
89035	Farrar	89072	Farrar	89109	Farrar	89146	Giorgini
89036	Caruso	89073	Melba	89110	Farrar	89147	De Lucia
89037	Farrar	89074	Melba	89111	Farrar	89148	Paoli
89038	Farrar	89075	Caruso	89112	Farrar	89149	Paoli
89039	Caruso	89076	Caruso	89113	Farrar	89150	Ruszcowska
89040	Farrar	89077	Caruso	89114	Farrar	89151	Ruszcowska
89041	Gadski	89078	Caruso	89115	Farrar	89152	Ruszcowska
89042	Sembrich	89079	Hempel	89116	Destinn	89153	Ruszcowska
89043	Caruso	89080	McCormack	89117	Destinn	89154	Ruszcowska
89044	McCormack	89081	Hempel	89118	Destinn	89155	Ruszcowska
89045	De Lucia	89082	Hempel	89119	Destinn	89156	De Tura
89046	Galvany	89083	Caruso	89120	Paoli	89157	De Tura
89047	Caruso	89084	Caruso	89121	Ruszcowska	89158	Homer
89048	Domar	89085	Caruso	89122	De Casas	89159	Homer
89049	Caruso	89086	Farrar	89123	Battistini	89160	Martinelli
89050	Caruso	89087	Caruso	89124	Gadski	89161	Bori
89051	Caruso	89088	Caruso	89125	Gadski	89162	Bori
89052	Caruso	89089	Caruso	89126	McCormack	89163	Alda
89053	Caruso	89090	Gluck	89127	Bori	89164	Fleta
89054	Caruso	89091	Gluck	89128	Alda	89165	Fleta
89055	Amato	89092	Gluck	89129	Alda	89166	Rachman-
89056	Amato	89093	Gluck	89130	Alda		inoff
89057	Farrar	89094	Gluck	89131	Alda	89167	Rachman-
89058	Ruffo	89095	Gluck	89132	Alda		inoff
89059	Caruso	89096	Gluck	89133	Galli-Curci	89168	Rachman-
89060	Caruso	89097	Gluck	89134	Galli-Curci		inoff
89061	Matzenauer	89098	Gluck	89135	Battistini	89169	Rachman-
89062	Matzenauer	89099	Gluck	89136	Paoli		inoff
89063	Eames	89100	Gluck	89137	Paoli	89170	Rachman-
89064	Caruso	89101	Gluck	89138	Paoli		inoff
89065	Caruso	89102	Gluck	89139	Paoli	89171	Rachman-
							inoff

91000	Calve	91023	De Luc a	91046	Delmas	91068	Renaud
91001	Calve	91024	Kubelik	91047	Affre	91069	Renaud
91002	Calve	91025	Kubelik	91048	Delmas	91070	Renaud
91003	Calve	91026	Renaud	91049	Delmas	91071	Boninsegna
91004	Adams	91027	Renaud	91050	Delmas	91072	Renaud
91005	Adams	91028	Renaud	91051	Note	91073	Paoli
91006	Adams	91029	Garbin	91052	Litvinne	91074	Boninsegna
91007	Caruso	91030	Garbin	91053	Battistini	91075	Bonins. gna
91008	Caruso	91031	De Luca	91054	Battistini	91076	Boninsegna
91009	Caruso	91032	De Luca	91055	Battistini	91077	Boninsegna
91010	Caruso	91033	De Luca	91056	Battistini	91078	Paoli
91011	Caruso	91034	Giraldoni	91057	Battistini	91079	De Lucia
91012	Caruso	91035	Kristmann	91058	Battistini	91080	Paoli
91013	Caruso	91036	Micha iowa	91059	Battistini	91081	Paoli
91014	Caruso	91037	Michailowa	91060	Michailowa	91082	Paoli
91015	Plancon	91038	De Lucia	91061	Michailowa	91083	Destinn
91016	Plancon	91039	Sistine C.	91062	Battistini	91084	Destinn
91017	Plancon	91040	Sistine C.	91063	Michailowa	91085	Gay
91018	Plancon	91041	Sistine C.	91064	Kristmann	91086	Destinn
91019	Scotti	91042	Ackte	91065	Kristmann		
91020	De Lucia	91043	Affre	91066	Renaud	91500	Ruffo
91021	De Lucia	91044	Ackte	91067	Renaud	91501	Ruffo
91022	De Lucia	91045	Note				

92000	Boninsegna	92020	Tetrazzini	92040	Ruffo	92060	Tetrazzini
92001	Boninsegna	92021	Tetrazzini	92041	Ruffo	92061	Tetrazzini
92002	Renaud	92022	Tetrazzini	92042	Ruffo	92062	Van Rooy
92003	Renaud	92023	Battistini	92043	Ruffo	92063	Tetrazzini
92004	Battistini	92024	Batt s ini	92044	Battistini	92064	Ruffo
92005	Battistini	92025	Boninsegna	92045	Battistini	92065	Ruffo
92006	Battistini	92026	Boninsegna	92046	Battistini	92066	Ruffo
92007	Battistini	92027	Boninsegna	92047	(unused)	92067	Tetrazzini
92008	Battistini	92028	De Lucia	92048	Paoli	92068	Tetrazzini
92009	Paoli	92029	De Lucia	92049	Paoli	92069	Tetrazzini
92010	Paoli	92030	Paoli	92050	Paoli	92070	Tetrazzini
92011	Paoli	92031	Boninsegna	92051	Paoli		
92012	Paoli	92032	Paoli	92052	De Lucia		
92013	Paoli	92033	De Lucia	92053	De Lucia	92500	Ruffo
92014	Tetrazzini	92034	Boninsegna	92054	De Lucia	92501	Ruffo
92015	Tetrazzini	92035	Paoli	92055	De Lucia	92502	Ruffo
92016	Tetrazzini	92036	Caruso	92056	De Luc a	92503	Ruffo
92017	Tetrazzini	92037	Ruffo	92057	Destinn	92504	Ruffo
92018	Tetrazzini	92038	Ruffo	92058	Destinn	92505	Ruffo
92019	Tetrazzini	92039	Ruffo	92059	Gay	92506	Ruffo

94001	Melba	95012	Melba	95032	Patti	95206	Caruso
94002	Melba	95013	Melba	95033	Patti	95207	Caruso
94003	Melba	95014	Melba	95034	Patti	95208	Caruso
94004	Melba	95015	Melba	95035	Patti	95209	Caruso
94005	Melba	95016	Melba	95036	Patti	95210	Caruso
94006	Melba	95017	Melba	95037	Patti	95211	Caruso
94007	Melba	95018	Melba	95038	Patti	95212	Caruso
		95019	Melba	95039	Patti	95213	Martinelli
		95020	Melba	95040	Patti	95214	Alda
95001	Tamagno	95021	Melba	95041	Patti		
95002	Tamagno	95022	Melba	95042	Patti	95300	Eames
95003	Tamagno	95023	Melba				
95004	Tamagno	95024	Melba	95100	Caruso	96000	Caruso
95005	Tamagno	95025	Melba			96001	Caruso
95006	Tamagno	95026	Melba	95200	Caruso	96002	Caruso
95007	Tamagno	95027	Melba	95201	Gadski		
95008	Tamagno	95028	Melba	95202	Eames	96200	Caruso
95009	Tamagno	95029	Patti	95203	Caruso	96201	Caruso
95010	Tamagno	95030	Patti	95204	Caruso		
95011	Tamagno	95031	Patti	95205	Caruso		

* *Nos. 94001-7 and 95001-11 are ten-inch; all the others are twelve-inch. Original issues had the following distinctive labels: Victor "Melba" Record (mauve) and Victor "Patti" Record (red) while the Tamagnos each had an individual copy number. Numbers from 95100 on were used for increasingly higher priced concerted pieces.*

INDEX OF OPERAS

The following operas, oratorios and other large vocal works appear in the artists' section without the composer's names which are therefore listed below. The titles are given in the form used in the artists' listings which omit the articles and other words in parentheses. Where the original title differs from the one commonly used, it is included below in brackets.

INSTRUMENTAL INDEX

Music for solo instruments and larger groups will be found in the artists' section under the following names.

A CATALOGUE OF SELECTED DOVER BOOKS
IN ALL FIELDS OF INTEREST

A CATALOGUE OF SELECTED DOVER BOOKS
IN ALL FIELDS OF INTEREST

THE DEVIL'S DICTIONARY, Ambrose Bierce. Barbed, bitter, brilliant witticisms in the form of a dictionary. Best, most ferocious satire America has produced. 145pp. 20487-1 Pa. $1.50

ABSOLUTELY MAD INVENTIONS, A.E. Brown, H.A. Jeffcott. Hilarious, useless, or merely absurd inventions all granted patents by the U.S. Patent Office. Edible tie pin, mechanical hat tipper, etc. 57 illustrations. 125pp. 22596-8 Pa. $1.50

AMERICAN WILD FLOWERS COLORING BOOK, Paul Kennedy. Planned coverage of 48 most important wildflowers, from Rickett's collection; instructive as well as entertaining. Color versions on covers. 48pp. 8¼ x 11. 20095-7 Pa. $1.35

BIRDS OF AMERICA COLORING BOOK, John James Audubon. Rendered for coloring by Paul Kennedy. 46 of Audubon's noted illustrations: red-winged blackbird, cardinal, purple finch, towhee, etc. Original plates reproduced in full color on the covers. 48pp. 8¼ x 11. 23049-X Pa. $1.35

NORTH AMERICAN INDIAN DESIGN COLORING BOOK, Paul Kennedy. The finest examples from Indian masks, beadwork, pottery, etc. — selected and redrawn for coloring (with identifications) by well-known illustrator Paul Kennedy. 48pp. 8¼ x 11. 21125-8 Pa. $1.35

UNIFORMS OF THE AMERICAN REVOLUTION COLORING BOOK, Peter Copeland. 31 lively drawings reproduce whole panorama of military attire; each uniform has complete instructions for accurate coloring. (Not in the Pictorial Archives Series). 64pp. 8¼ x 11. 21850-3 Pa. $1.50

THE WONDERFUL WIZARD OF OZ COLORING BOOK, L. Frank Baum. Color the Yellow Brick Road and much more in 61 drawings adapted from W.W. Denslow's originals, accompanied by abridged version of text. Dorothy, Toto, Oz and the Emerald City. 61 illustrations. 64pp. 8¼ x 11. 20452-9 Pa. $1.50

CUT AND COLOR PAPER MASKS, Michael Grater. Clowns, animals, funny faces . . . simply color them in, cut them out, and put them together, and you have 9 paper masks to play with and enjoy. Complete instructions. Assembled masks shown in full color on the covers. 32pp. 8¼ x 11. 23171-2 Pa. $1.50

STAINED GLASS CHRISTMAS ORNAMENT COLORING BOOK, Carol Belanger Grafton. Brighten your Christmas season with over 100 Christmas ornaments done in a stained glass effect on translucent paper. Color them in and then hang at windows, from lights, anywhere. 32pp. 8¼ x 11. 20707-2 Pa. $1.75

CATALOGUE OF DOVER BOOKS

THE FITZWILLIAM VIRGINAL BOOK, edited by J. Fuller Maitland, W.B. Squire. Famous early 17th century collection of keyboard music, 300 works by Morley, Byrd, Bull, Gibbons, etc. Modern notation. Total of 938pp. 8⅜ x 11.
ECE 21068-5, 21069-3 Pa., Two vol. set $12.00

COMPLETE STRING QUARTETS, Wolfgang A. Mozart. Breitkopf and Härtel edition. All 23 string quartets plus alternate slow movement to K156. Study score. 277pp. 9⅜ x 12¼.
22372-8 Pa. $6.00

COMPLETE SONG CYCLES, Franz Schubert. Complete piano, vocal music of Die Schöne Müllerin, Die Winterreise, Schwanengesang. Also Drinker English singing translations. Breitkopf and Härtel edition. 217pp. 9⅜ x 12¼.
22649-2 Pa. $4.00

THE COMPLETE PRELUDES AND ETUDES FOR PIANOFORTE SOLO, Alexander Scriabin. All the preludes and etudes including many perfectly spun miniatures. Edited by K.N. Igumnov and Y.I. Mil'shteyn. 250pp. 9 x 12.
22919-X Pa. $5.00

TRISTAN UND ISOLDE, Richard Wagner. Full orchestral score with complete instrumentation. Do not confuse with piano reduction. Commentary by Felix Mottl, great Wagnerian conductor and scholar. Study score. 655pp. 8⅛ x 11.
22915-7 Pa. $10.00

FAVORITE SONGS OF THE NINETIES, ed. Robert Fremont. Full reproduction, including covers, of 88 favorites: Ta-Ra-Ra-Boom-De-Aye, The Band Played On, Bird in a Gilded Cage, Under the Bamboo Tree, After the Ball, etc. 401pp. 9 x 12.
EBE 21536-9 Pa. $6.95

SOUSA'S GREAT MARCHES IN PIANO TRANSCRIPTION: ORIGINAL SHEET MUSIC OF 23 WORKS, John Philip Sousa. Selected by Lester S. Levy. Playing edition includes: The Stars and Stripes Forever, The Thunderer, The Gladiator, King Cotton, Washington Post, much more. 24 illustrations. 111pp. 9 x 12.
USO 23132-1 Pa. $3.50

CLASSIC PIANO RAGS, selected with an introduction by Rudi Blesh. Best ragtime music (1897-1922) by Scott Joplin, James Scott, Joseph F. Lamb, Tom Turpin, 9 others. Printed from best original sheet music, plus covers. 364pp. 9 x 12.
EBE 20469-3 Pa. $6.95

ANALYSIS OF CHINESE CHARACTERS, C.D. Wilder, J.H. Ingram. 1000 most important characters analyzed according to primitives, phonetics, historical development. Traditional method offers mnemonic aid to beginner, intermediate student of Chinese, Japanese. 365pp.
23045-7 Pa. $4.00

MODERN CHINESE: A BASIC COURSE, Faculty of Peking University. Self study, classroom course in modern Mandarin. Records contain phonetics, vocabulary, sentences, lessons. 249 page book contains all recorded text, translations, grammar, vocabulary, exercises. Best course on market. 3 12" 33⅓ monaural records, book, album.
98832-5 Set $12.50

CREATIVE LITHOGRAPHY AND HOW TO DO IT, Grant Arnold. Lithography as art form: working directly on stone, transfer of drawings, lithotint, mezzotint, color printing; also metal plates. Detailed, thorough. 27 illustrations. 214pp.
21208-4 Pa. $3.00

DESIGN MOTIFS OF ANCIENT MEXICO, Jorge Enciso. Vigorous, powerful ceramic stamp impressions — Maya, Aztec, Toltec, Olmec. Serpents, gods, priests, dancers, etc. 153pp. 6⅛ x 9¼.
20084-1 Pa. $2.50

AMERICAN INDIAN DESIGN AND DECORATION, Leroy Appleton. Full text, plus more than 700 precise drawings of Inca, Maya, Aztec, Pueblo, Plains, NW Coast basketry, sculpture, painting, pottery, sand paintings, metal, etc. 4 plates in color. 279pp. 8⅜ x 11¼.
22704-9 Pa. $4.50

CHINESE LATTICE DESIGNS, Daniel S. Dye. Incredibly beautiful geometric designs: circles, voluted, simple dissections, etc. Inexhaustible source of ideas, motifs. 1239 illustrations. 469pp. 6⅛ x 9¼.
23096-1 Pa. $5.00

JAPANESE DESIGN MOTIFS, Matsuya Co. Mon, or heraldic designs. Over 4000 typical, beautiful designs: birds, animals, flowers, swords, fans, geometric; all beautifully stylized. 213pp. 11⅜ x 8¼.
22874-6 Pa. $4.95

PERSPECTIVE, Jan Vredeman de Vries. 73 perspective plates from 1604 edition; buildings, townscapes, stairways, fantastic scenes. Remarkable for beauty, surrealistic atmosphere; real eye-catchers. Introduction by Adolf Placzek. 74pp. 11⅜ x 8¼.
20186-4 Pa. $2.75

EARLY AMERICAN DESIGN MOTIFS, Suzanne E. Chapman. 497 motifs, designs, from painting on wood, ceramics, appliqué, glassware, samplers, metal work, etc. Florals, landscapes, birds and animals, geometrics, letters, etc. Inexhaustible. Enlarged edition. 138pp. 8⅜ x 11¼.
22985-8 Pa. $3.50
23084-8 Clothbd. $7.95

VICTORIAN STENCILS FOR DESIGN AND DECORATION, edited by E.V. Gillon, Jr. 113 wonderful ornate Victorian pieces from German sources; florals, geometrics; borders, corner pieces; bird motifs, etc. 64pp. 9⅜ x 12¼.
21995-X Pa. $2.50

ART NOUVEAU: AN ANTHOLOGY OF DESIGN AND ILLUSTRATION FROM THE STUDIO, edited by E.V. Gillon, Jr. Graphic arts: book jackets, posters, engravings, illustrations, decorations; Crane, Beardsley, Bradley and many others. Inexhaustible. 92pp. 8⅛ x 11.
22388-4 Pa. $2.50

ORIGINAL ART DECO DESIGNS, William Rowe. First-rate, highly imaginative modern Art Deco frames, borders, compositions, alphabets, florals, insectals, Wurlitzer-types, etc. Much finest modern Art Deco. 80 plates, 8 in color. 8⅜ x 11¼.
22567-4 Pa. $3.00

HANDBOOK OF DESIGNS AND DEVICES, Clarence P. Hornung. Over 1800 basic geometric designs based on circle, triangle, square, scroll, cross, etc. Largest such collection in existence. 261pp.
20125-2 Pa. $2.50

How to Solve Chess Problems, Kenneth S. Howard. Practical suggestions on problem solving for very beginners. 58 two-move problems, 46 3-movers, 8 4-movers for practice, plus hints. 171pp. 20748-X Pa. $2.00

A Guide to Fairy Chess, Anthony Dickins. 3-D chess, 4-D chess, chess on a cylindrical board, reflecting pieces that bounce off edges, cooperative chess, retrograde chess, maximummers, much more. Most based on work of great Dawson. Full handbook, 100 problems. 66pp. $7^7/8$ x $10^3/4$. 22687-5 Pa. $2.00

Win at Backgammon, Millard Hopper. Best opening moves, running game, blocking game, back game, tables of odds, etc. Hopper makes the game clear enough for anyone to play, and win. 43 diagrams. 111pp. 22894-0 Pa. $1.50

Bidding a Bridge Hand, Terence Reese. Master player "thinks out loud" the binding of 75 hands that defy point count systems. Organized by bidding problem—no-fit situations, overbidding, underbidding, cueing your defense, etc. 254pp. EBE 22830-4 Pa. $2.50

The Precision Bidding System in Bridge, C.C. Wei, edited by Alan Truscott. Inventor of precision bidding presents average hands and hands from actual play, including games from 1969 Bermuda Bowl where system emerged. 114 exercises. 116pp. 21171-1 Pa. $1.75

Learn Magic, Henry Hay. 20 simple, easy-to-follow lessons on magic for the new magician: illusions, card tricks, silks, sleights of hand, coin manipulations, escapes, and more —all with a minimum amount of equipment. Final chapter explains the great stage illusions. 92 illustrations. 285pp. 21238-6 Pa. $2.95

The New Magician's Manual, Walter B. Gibson. Step-by-step instructions and clear illustrations guide the novice in mastering 36 tricks; much equipment supplied on 16 pages of cut-out materials. 36 additional tricks. 64 illustrations. 159pp. $6^5/8$ x 10. 23113-5 Pa. $3.00

Professional Magic for Amateurs, Walter B. Gibson. 50 easy, effective tricks used by professionals —cards, string, tumblers, handkerchiefs, mental magic, etc. 63 illustrations. 223pp. 23012-0 Pa. $2.50

Card Manipulations, Jean Hugard. Very rich collection of manipulations; has taught thousands of fine magicians tricks that are really workable, eye-catching. Easily followed, serious work. Over 200 illustrations. 163pp. 20539-8 Pa. $2.00

Abbott's Encyclopedia of Rope Tricks for Magicians, Stewart James. Complete reference book for amateur and professional magicians containing more than 150 tricks involving knots, penetrations, cut and restored rope, etc. 510 illustrations. Reprint of 3rd edition. 400pp. 23206-9 Pa. $3.50

The Secrets of Houdini, J.C. Cannell. Classic study of Houdini's incredible magic, exposing closely-kept professional secrets and revealing, in general terms, the whole art of stage magic. 67 illustrations. 279pp. 22913-0 Pa. $2.50

THE BEST DR. THORNDYKE DETECTIVE STORIES, R. Austin Freeman. The Case of Oscar Brodski, The Moabite Cipher, and 5 other favorites featuring the great scientific detective, plus his long-believed-lost first adventure — 31 New Inn — reprinted here for the first time. Edited by E.F. Bleiler. USO 20388-3 Pa. $3.00

BEST "THINKING MACHINE" DETECTIVE STORIES, Jacques Futrelle. The Problem of Cell 13 and 11 other stories about Prof. Augustus S.F.X. Van Dusen, including two "lost" stories. First reprinting of several. Edited by E.F. Bleiler. 241pp.
20537-1 Pa. $3.00

UNCLE SILAS, J. Sheridan LeFanu. Victorian Gothic mystery novel, considered by many best of period, even better than Collins or Dickens. Wonderful psychological terror. Introduction by Frederick Shroyer. 436pp. 21715-9 Pa. $4.00

BEST DR. POGGIOLI DETECTIVE STORIES, T.S. Stribling. 15 best stories from EQMM and The Saint offer new adventures in Mexico, Florida, Tennessee hills as Poggioli unravels mysteries and combats Count Jalacki. 217pp. 23227-1 Pa. $3.00

EIGHT DIME NOVELS, selected with an introduction by E.F. Bleiler. Adventures of Old King Brady, Frank James, Nick Carter, Deadwood Dick, Buffalo Bill, The Steam Man, Frank Merriwell, and Horatio Alger — 1877 to 1905. Important, entertaining popular literature in facsimile reprint, with original covers. 190pp. 9 x 12. 22975-0 Pa. $3.50

ALICE'S ADVENTURES UNDER GROUND, Lewis Carroll. Facsimile of ms. Carroll gave Alice Liddell in 1864. Different in many ways from final Alice. Handlettered, illustrated by Carroll. Introduction by Martin Gardner. 128pp. 21482-6 Pa. $1.50

ALICE IN WONDERLAND COLORING BOOK, Lewis Carroll. Pictures by John Tenniel. Large-size versions of the famous illustrations of Alice, Cheshire Cat, Mad Hatter and all the others, waiting for your crayons. Abridged text. 36 illustrations. 64pp. 8¼ x 11. 22853-3 Pa. $1.50

AVENTURES D'ALICE AU PAYS DES MERVEILLES, Lewis Carroll. Bué's translation of "Alice" into French, supervised by Carroll himself. Novel way to learn language. (No English text.) 42 Tenniel illustrations. 196pp. 22836-3 Pa. $2.00

MYTHS AND FOLK TALES OF IRELAND, Jeremiah Curtin. 11 stories that are Irish versions of European fairy tales and 9 stories from the Fenian cycle — 20 tales of legend and magic that comprise an essential work in the history of folklore. 256pp. 22430-9 Pa. $3.00

EAST O' THE SUN AND WEST O' THE MOON, George W. Dasent. Only full edition of favorite, wonderful Norwegian fairytales — Why the Sea is Salt, Boots and the Troll, etc. — with 77 illustrations by Kittelsen & Werenskiöld. 418pp.
22521-6 Pa. $3.50

PERRAULT'S FAIRY TALES, Charles Perrault and Gustave Doré. Original versions of Cinderella, Sleeping Beauty, Little Red Riding Hood, etc. in best translation, with 34 wonderful illustrations by Gustave Doré. 117pp. 8⅛ x 11. 22311-6 Pa. $2.50

MOTHER GOOSE'S MELODIES. Facsimile of fabulously rare Munroe and Francis "copyright 1833" Boston edition. Familiar and unusual rhymes, wonderful old woodcut illustrations. Edited by E.F. Bleiler. 128pp. 4½ x 6⅜. 22577-1 Pa. $1.00

MOTHER GOOSE IN HIEROGLYPHICS. Favorite nursery rhymes presented in rebus form for children. Fascinating 1849 edition reproduced in toto, with key. Introduction by E.F. Bleiler. About 400 woodcuts. 64pp. 6⅞ x 5¼. 20745-5 Pa. $1.00

PETER PIPER'S PRACTICAL PRINCIPLES OF PLAIN & PERFECT PRONUNCIATION. Alliterative jingles and tongue-twisters. Reproduction in full of 1830 first American edition. 25 spirited woodcuts. 32pp. 4½ x 6⅜. 22560-7 Pa. $1.00

MARMADUKE MULTIPLY'S MERRY METHOD OF MAKING MINOR MATHEMATICIANS. Fellow to Peter Piper, it teaches multiplication table by catchy rhymes and woodcuts. 1841 Munroe & Francis edition. Edited by E.F. Bleiler. 103pp. 4⅝ x 6.
22773-1 Pa. $1.25
20171-6 Clothbd. $3.00

THE NIGHT BEFORE CHRISTMAS, Clement Moore. Full text, and woodcuts from original 1848 book. Also critical, historical material. 19 illustrations. 40pp. 4⅝ x 6. 22797-9 Pa. $1.00

THE KING OF THE GOLDEN RIVER, John Ruskin. Victorian children's classic of three brothers, their attempts to reach the Golden River, what becomes of them. Facsimile of original 1889 edition. 22 illustrations. 56pp. 4⅝ x 6⅜.
20066-3 Pa. $1.25

DREAMS OF THE RAREBIT FIEND, Winsor McCay. Pioneer cartoon strip, unexcelled for beauty, imagination, in 60 full sequences. Incredible technical virtuosity, wonderful visual wit. Historical introduction. 62pp. 8⅜ x 11¼. 21347-1 Pa. $2.00

THE KATZENJAMMER KIDS, Rudolf Dirks. In full color, 14 strips from 1906-7; full of imagination, characteristic humor. Classic of great historical importance. Introduction by August Derleth. 32pp. 9¼ x 12¼. 23005-8 Pa. $2.00

LITTLE ORPHAN ANNIE AND LITTLE ORPHAN ANNIE IN COSMIC CITY, Harold Gray. Two great sequences from the early strips: our curly-haired heroine defends the Warbucks' financial empire and, then, takes on meanie Phineas P. Pinchpenny. Leapin' lizards! 178pp. 6⅛ x 8⅜. 23107-0 Pa. $2.00

WHEN A FELLER NEEDS A FRIEND, Clare Briggs. 122 cartoons by one of the greatest newspaper cartoonists of the early 20th century — about growing up, making a living, family life, daily frustrations and occasional triumphs. 121pp. 8½ x 9½.
23148-8 Pa. $2.50

THE BEST OF GLUYAS WILLIAMS. 100 drawings by one of America's finest cartoonists: The Day a Cake of Ivory Soap Sank at Proctor & Gamble's, At the Life Insurance Agents' Banquet, and many other gems from the 20's and 30's. 118pp. 8⅜ x 11¼. 22737-5 Pa. $2.50

CATALOGUE OF DOVER BOOKS

150 MASTERPIECES OF DRAWING, edited by Anthony Toney. 150 plates, early 15th century to end of 18th century; Rembrandt, Michelangelo, Dürer, Fragonard, Watteau, Wouwerman, many others. 150pp. 8⅜ x 11¼. 21032-4 Pa. $3.50

THE GOLDEN AGE OF THE POSTER, Hayward and Blanche Cirker. 70 extraordinary posters in full colors, from Maîtres de l'Affiche, Mucha, Lautrec, Bradley, Cheret, Beardsley, many others. 9⅜ x 12¼. 22753-7 Pa. $4.95
21718-3 Clothbd. $7.95

SIMPLICISSIMUS, selection, translations and text by Stanley Appelbaum. 180 satirical drawings, 16 in full color, from the famous German weekly magazine in the years 1896 to 1926. 24 artists included: Grosz, Kley, Pascin, Kubin, Kollwitz, plus Heine, Thöny, Bruno Paul, others. 172pp. 8½ x 12¼. 23098-8 Pa. $5.00
23099-6 Clothbd. $10.00

THE EARLY WORK OF AUBREY BEARDSLEY, Aubrey Beardsley. 157 plates, 2 in color: Manon Lescaut, Madame Bovary, Morte d'Arthur, Salome, other. Introduction by H. Marillier. 175pp. 8½ x 11. 21816-3 Pa. $3.50

THE LATER WORK OF AUBREY BEARDSLEY, Aubrey Beardsley. Exotic masterpieces of full maturity: Venus and Tannhäuser, Lysistrata, Rape of the Lock, Volpone, Savoy material, etc. 174 plates, 2 in color. 176pp. 8½ x 11. 21817-1 Pa. $3.75

DRAWINGS OF WILLIAM BLAKE, William Blake. 92 plates from Book of Job, Divine Comedy, Paradise Lost, visionary heads, mythological figures, Laocoön, etc. Selection, introduction, commentary by Sir Geoffrey Keynes. 178pp. 8½ x 11. 22303-5 Pa. $3.50

LONDON: A PILGRIMAGE, Gustave Doré, Blanchard Jerrold. Squalor, riches, misery, beauty of mid-Victorian metropolis; 55 wonderful plates, 125 other illustrations, full social, cultural text by Jerrold. 191pp. of text. 8⅛ x 11. 22306-X Pa. $5.00

THE COMPLETE WOODCUTS OF ALBRECHT DÜRER, edited by Dr. W. Kurth. 346 in all: Old Testament, St. Jerome, Passion, Life of Virgin, Apocalypse, many others. Introduction by Campbell Dodgson. 285pp. 8½ x 12¼. 21097-9 Pa. $6.00

THE DISASTERS OF WAR, Francisco Goya. 83 etchings record horrors of Napoleonic wars in Spain and war in general. Reprint of 1st edition, plus 3 additional plates. Introduction by Philip Hofer. 97pp. 9⅜ x 8¼. 21872-4 Pa. $2.50

ENGRAVINGS OF HOGARTH, William Hogarth. 101 of Hogarth's greatest works: Rake's Progress, Harlot's Progress, Illustrations for Hudibras, Midnight Modern Conversation, Before and After, Beer Street and Gin Lane, many more. Full commentary. 256pp. 11 x 14. 22479-1 Pa. $6.00
23023-6 Clothbd. $13.50

PRIMITIVE ART, Franz Boas. Great anthropologist on ceramics, textiles, wood, stone, metal, etc.; patterns, technology, symbols, styles. All areas, but fullest on Northwest Coast Indians. 350 illustrations. 378pp. 20025-6 Pa. $3.50

CATALOGUE OF DOVER BOOKS

MANUAL OF THE TREES OF NORTH AMERICA, Charles S. Sargent. The basic survey of every native tree and tree-like shrub, 717 species in all. Extremely full descriptions, information on habitat, growth, locales, economics, etc. Necessary to every serious tree lover. Over 100 finding keys. 783 illustrations. Total of 986pp.
20277-1, 20278-X Pa., Two vol. set $8.00

BIRDS OF THE NEW YORK AREA, John Bull. Indispensable guide to more than 400 species within a hundred-mile radius of Manhattan. Information on range, status, breeding, migration, distribution trends, etc. Foreword by Roger Tory Peterson. 17 drawings; maps. 540pp.
23222-0 Pa. $6.00

THE SEA-BEACH AT EBB-TIDE, Augusta Foote Arnold. Identify hundreds of marine plants and animals: algae, seaweeds, squids, crabs, corals, etc. Descriptions cover food, life cycle, size, shape, habitat. Over 600 drawings. 490pp.
21949-6 Pa. $4.00

THE MOTH BOOK, William J. Holland. Identify more than 2,000 moths of North America. General information, precise species descriptions. 623 illustrations plus 48 color plates show almost all species, full size. 1968 edition. Still the basic book. Total of 551pp. 6½ x 9¼.
21948-8 Pa. $6.00

AN INTRODUCTION TO THE REPTILES AND AMPHIBIANS OF THE UNITED STATES, Percy A. Morris. All lizards, crocodiles, turtles, snakes, toads, frogs; life history, identification, habits, suitability as pets, etc. Non-technical, but sound and broad. 130 photos. 253pp.
22982-3 Pa. $3.00

OLD NEW YORK IN EARLY PHOTOGRAPHS, edited by Mary Black. Your only chance to see New York City as it was 1853-1906, through 196 wonderful photographs from N.Y. Historical Society. Great Blizzard, Lincoln's funeral procession, great buildings. 228pp. 9 x 12.
22907-6 Pa. $6.00

THE AMERICAN REVOLUTION, A PICTURE SOURCEBOOK, John Grafton. Wonderful Bicentennial picture source, with 411 illustrations (contemporary and 19th century) showing battles, personalities, maps, events, flags, posters, soldier's life, ships, etc. all captioned and explained. A wonderful browsing book, supplement to other historical reading. 160pp. 9 x 12.
23226-3 Pa. $4.00

PERSONAL NARRATIVE OF A PILGRIMAGE TO AL-MADINAH AND MECCAH, Richard Burton. Great travel classic by remarkably colorful personality. Burton, disguised as a Moroccan, visited sacred shrines of Islam, narrowly escaping death. Wonderful observations of Islamic life, customs, personalities. 47 illustrations. Total of 959pp.
21217-3, 21218-1 Pa., Two vol. set $7.00

INCIDENTS OF TRAVEL IN CENTRAL AMERICA, CHIAPAS, AND YUCATAN, John L. Stephens. Almost single-handed discovery of Maya culture; exploration of ruined cities, monuments, temples; customs of Indians. 115 drawings. 892pp.
22404-X, 22405-8 Pa., Two vol. set $8.00

EARLY NEW ENGLAND GRAVESTONE RUBBINGS, Edmund V. Gillon, Jr. 43 photographs, 226 rubbings show heavily symbolic, macabre, sometimes humorous primitive American art. Up to early 19th century. 207pp. 8⅜ x 11¼.
21380-3 Pa. $4.00

L.J.M. DAGUERRE: THE HISTORY OF THE DIORAMA AND THE DAGUERREOTYPE, Helmut and Alison Gernsheim. Definitive account. Early history, life and work of Daguerre; discovery of daguerreotype process; diffusion abroad; other early photography. 124 illustrations. 226pp. 6⅙ x 9¼.
22290-X Pa. $4.00

PHOTOGRAPHY AND THE AMERICAN SCENE, Robert Taft. The basic book on American photography as art, recording form, 1839-1889. Development, influence on society, great photographers, types (portraits, war, frontier, etc.), whatever else needed. Inexhaustible. Illustrated with 322 early photos, daguerreotypes, tintypes, stereo slides, etc. 546pp. 6⅛ x 9¼.
21201-7 Pa. $5.00

PHOTOGRAPHIC SKETCHBOOK OF THE CIVIL WAR, Alexander Gardner. Reproduction of 1866 volume with 100 on-the-field photographs: Manassas, Lincoln on battlefield, slave pens, etc. Introduction by E.F. Bleiler. 224pp. 10¾ x 9.
22731-6 Pa. $4.50

THE MOVIES: A PICTURE QUIZ BOOK, Stanley Appelbaum & Hayward Cirker. Match stars with their movies, name actors and actresses, test your movie skill with 241 stills from 236 great movies, 1902-1959. Indexes of performers and films. 128pp. 8⅜ x 9¼.
20222-4 Pa. $2.50

THE TALKIES, Richard Griffith. Anthology of features, articles from Photoplay, 1928-1940, reproduced complete. Stars, famous movies, technical features, fabulous ads, etc.; Garbo, Chaplin, King Kong, Lubitsch, etc. 4 color plates, scores of illustrations. 327pp. 8⅜ x 11¼.
22762-6 Pa. $5.95

THE MOVIE MUSICAL FROM VITAPHONE TO "42ND STREET," edited by Miles Kreuger. Relive the rise of the movie musical as reported in the pages of Photoplay magazine (1926-1933): every movie review, cast list, ad, and record review; every significant feature article, production still, biography, forecast, and gossip story. Profusely illustrated. 367pp. 8⅜ x 11¼.
23154-2 Pa. $6.95

JOHANN SEBASTIAN BACH, Philipp Spitta. Great classic of biography, musical commentary, with hundreds of pieces analyzed. Also good for Bach's contemporaries. 450 musical examples. Total of 1799pp.
EUK 22278-0, 22279-9 Clothbd., Two vol. set $25.00

BEETHOVEN AND HIS NINE SYMPHONIES, Sir George Grove. Thorough history, analysis, commentary on symphonies and some related pieces. For either beginner or advanced student. 436 musical passages. 407pp.
20334-4 Pa. $4.00

MOZART AND HIS PIANO CONCERTOS, Cuthbert Girdlestone. The only full-length study. Detailed analyses of all 21 concertos, sources; 417 musical examples. 509pp.
21271-8 Pa. $4.50

CATALOGUE OF DOVER BOOKS

HOUDINI ON MAGIC, Harold Houdini. Edited by Walter Gibson, Morris N. Young. How he escaped; exposés of fake spiritualists; instructions for eye-catching tricks; other fascinating material by and about greatest magician. 155 illustrations. 280pp. 20384-0 Pa. $2.50

HANDBOOK OF THE NUTRITIONAL CONTENTS OF FOOD, U.S. Dept. of Agriculture. Largest, most detailed source of food nutrition information ever prepared. Two mammoth tables: one measuring nutrients in 100 grams of edible portion; the other, in edible portion of 1 pound as purchased. Originally titled Composition of Foods. 190pp. 9 x 12. 21342-0 Pa. $4.00

COMPLETE GUIDE TO HOME CANNING, PRESERVING AND FREEZING, U.S. Dept. of Agriculture. Seven basic manuals with full instructions for jams and jellies; pickles and relishes; canning fruits, vegetables, meat; freezing anything. Really good recipes, exact instructions for optimal results. Save a fortune in food. 156 illustrations. 214pp. 6⅛ x 9¼. 22911-4 Pa. $2.50

THE BREAD TRAY, Louis P. De Gouy. Nearly every bread the cook could buy or make: bread sticks of Italy, fruit breads of Greece, glazed rolls of Vienna, everything from corn pone to croissants. Over 500 recipes altogether. including buns, rolls, muffins, scones, and more. 463pp. 23000-7 Pa. $3.50

CREATIVE HAMBURGER COOKERY, Louis P. De Gouy. 182 unusual recipes for casseroles, meat loaves and hamburgers that turn inexpensive ground meat into memorable main dishes: Arizona chili burgers, burger tamale pie, burger stew, burger corn loaf, burger wine loaf, and more. 120pp. 23001-5 Pa. $1.75

LONG ISLAND SEAFOOD COOKBOOK, J. George Frederick and Jean Joyce. Probably the best American seafood cookbook. Hundreds of recipes. 40 gourmet sauces, 123 recipes using oysters alone! All varieties of fish and seafood amply represented. 324pp. 22677-8 Pa. $3.00

THE EPICUREAN: A COMPLETE TREATISE OF ANALYTICAL AND PRACTICAL STUDIES IN THE CULINARY ART, Charles Ranhofer. Great modern classic. 3,500 recipes from master chef of Delmonico's, turn-of-the-century America's best restaurant. Also explained, many techniques known only to professional chefs. 775 illustrations. 1183pp. 6⅝ x 10. 22680-8 Clothbd. $17.50

THE AMERICAN WINE COOK BOOK, Ted Hatch. Over 700 recipes: old favorites livened up with wine plus many more: Czech fish soup, quince soup, sauce Perigueux, shrimp shortcake, filets Stroganoff, cordon bleu goulash, jambonneau, wine fruit cake, more. 314pp. 22796-0 Pa. $2.50

DELICIOUS VEGETARIAN COOKING, Ivan Baker. Close to 500 delicious and varied recipes: soups, main course dishes (pea, bean, lentil, cheese, vegetable, pasta, and egg dishes), savories, stews, whole-wheat breads and cakes, more. 168pp. USO 22834-7 Pa. $1.75

DRIED FLOWERS, Sarah Whitlock and Martha Rankin. Concise, clear, practical guide to dehydration, glycerinizing, pressing plant material, and more. Covers use of silica gel. 12 drawings. Originally titled "New Techniques with Dried Flowers." 32pp. 21802-3 Pa. $1.00

ABC OF POULTRY RAISING, J.H. Florea. Poultry expert, editor tells how to raise chickens on home or small business basis. Breeds, feeding, housing, laying, etc. Very concrete, practical. 50 illustrations. 256pp. 23201-8 Pa. $3.00

HOW INDIANS USE WILD PLANTS FOR FOOD, MEDICINE & CRAFTS, Frances Densmore. Smithsonian, Bureau of American Ethnology report presents wealth of material on nearly 200 plants used by Chippewas of Minnesota and Wisconsin. 33 plates plus 122pp. of text. 6⅛ x 9¼. 23019-8 Pa. $2.50

THE HERBAL OR GENERAL HISTORY OF PLANTS, John Gerard. The 1633 edition revised and enlarged by Thomas Johnson. Containing almost 2850 plant descriptions and 2705 superb illustrations, Gerard's Herbal is a monumental work, the book all modern English herbals are derived from, and the one herbal every serious enthusiast should have in its entirety. Original editions are worth perhaps $750. 1678pp. 8½ x 12¼. 23147-X Clothbd..$50.00

A MODERN HERBAL, Margaret Grieve. Much the fullest, most exact, most useful compilation of herbal material. Gigantic alphabetical encyclopedia, from aconite to zedoary, gives botanical information, medical properties, folklore, economic uses, and much else. Indispensable to serious reader. 161 illustrations. 888pp. 6½ x 9¼. USO 22798-7, 22799-5 Pa., Two vol. set $10.00

HOW TO KNOW THE FERNS, Frances T. Parsons. Delightful classic. Identification, fern lore, for Eastern and Central U.S.A. Has introduced thousands to interesting life form. 99 illustrations. 215pp. 20740-4 Pa. $2.50

THE MUSHROOM HANDBOOK, Louis C.C. Krieger. Still the best popular handbook. Full descriptions of 259 species, extremely thorough text, habitats, luminescence, poisons, folklore, etc. 32 color plates; 126 other illustrations. 560pp. 21861-9 Pa. $4.50

HOW TO KNOW THE WILD FRUITS, Maude G. Peterson. Classic guide covers nearly 200 trees, shrubs, smaller plants of the U.S. arranged by color of fruit and then by family. Full text provides names, descriptions, edibility, uses. 80 illustrations. 400pp. 22943-2 Pa. $3.00

COMMON WEEDS OF THE UNITED STATES, U.S. Department of Agriculture. Covers 220 important weeds with illustration, maps, botanical information, plant lore for each. Over 225 illustrations. 463pp. 6⅛ x 9¼. 20504-5 Pa. $4.50

HOW TO KNOW THE WILD FLOWERS, Mrs. William S. Dana. Still best popular book for East and Central USA. Over 500 plants easily identified, with plant lore; arranged according to color and flowering time. 174 plates. 459pp. 20332-8 Pa. $3.50

CONSTRUCTION OF AMERICAN FURNITURE TREASURES, Lester Margon. 344 detail drawings, complete text on constructing exact reproductions of 38 early American masterpieces: Hepplewhite sideboard, Duncan Phyfe drop-leaf table, mantel clock, gate-leg dining table, Pa. German cupboard, more. 38 plates. 54 photographs. 168pp. 8⅜ x 11¼. 23056-2 Pa. $4.00

JEWELRY MAKING AND DESIGN, Augustus F. Rose, Antonio Cirino. Professional secrets revealed in thorough, practical guide: tools, materials, processes; rings, brooches, chains, cast pieces, enamelling, setting stones, etc. Do not confuse with skimpy introductions: beginner can use, professional can learn from it. Over 200 illustrations. 306pp. 21750-7 Pa. $3.00

METALWORK AND ENAMELLING, Herbert Maryon. Generally coneeded best all-around book. Countless trade secrets: materials, tools, soldering, filigree, setting, inlay, niello, repoussé, casting, polishing, etc. For beginner or expert. Author was foremost British expert. 330 illustrations. 335pp. 22702-2 Pa. $3.50

WEAVING WITH FOOT-POWER LOOMS, Edward F. Worst. Setting up a loom, beginning to weave, constructing equipment, using dyes, more, plus over 285 drafts of traditional patterns including Colonial and Swedish weaves. More than 200 other figures. For beginning and advanced. 275pp. 8¾ x 6⅜. 23064-3 Pa. $4.00

WEAVING A NAVAJO BLANKET, Gladys A. Reichard. Foremost anthropologist studied under Navajo women, reveals every step in process from wool, dyeing, spinning, setting up loom, designing, weaving. Much history, symbolism. With this book you could make one yourself. 97 illustrations. 222pp. 22992-0 Pa. $3.00

NATURAL DYES AND HOME DYEING, Rita J. Adrosko. Use natural ingredients: bark, flowers, leaves, lichens, insects etc. Over 135 specific recipes from historical sources for cotton, wool, other fabrics. Genuine premodern handicrafts. 12 illustrations. 160pp. 22688-3 Pa. $2.00

THE HAND DECORATION OF FABRICS, Francis J. Kafka. Outstanding, profusely illustrated guide to stenciling, batik, block printing, tie dyeing, freehand painting, silk screen printing, and novelty decoration. 356 illustrations. 198pp. 6 x 9.
21401-X Pa. $3.00

THOMAS NAST: CARTOONS AND ILLUSTRATIONS, with text by Thomas Nast St. Hill. Father of American political cartooning. Cartoons that destroyed Tweed Ring; inflation, free love, church and state; original Republican elephant and Democratic donkey; Santa Claus; more. 117 illustrations. 146pp. 9 x 12.
22983-1 Pa. $4.00
23067-8 Clothbd. $8.50

FREDERIC REMINGTON: 173 DRAWINGS AND ILLUSTRATIONS. Most famous of the Western artists, most responsible for our myths about the American West in its untamed days. Complete reprinting of Drawings of Frederic Remington (1897), plus other selections. 4 additional drawings in color on covers. 140pp. 9 x 12.
20714-5 Pa. $3.95

CATALOGUE OF DOVER BOOKS

THE MAGIC MOVING PICTURE BOOK, Bliss, Sands & Co. The pictures in this book move! Volcanoes erupt, a house burns, a serpentine dancer wiggles her way through a number. By using a specially ruled acetate screen provided, you can obtain these and 15 other startling effects. Originally "The Motograph Moving Picture Book." 32pp. 8¼ x 11. 23224-7 Pa. $1.75

STRING FIGURES AND HOW TO MAKE THEM, Caroline F. Jayne. Fullest, clearest instructions on string figures from around world: Eskimo, Navajo, Lapp, Europe, more. Cats cradle, moving spear, lightning, stars. Introduction by A.C. Haddon. 950 illustrations. 407pp. 20152-X Pa. $3.00

PAPER FOLDING FOR BEGINNERS, William D. Murray and Francis J. Rigney. Clearest book on market for making origami sail boats, roosters, frogs that move legs, cups, bonbon boxes. 40 projects. More than 275 illustrations. Photographs. 94pp. 20713-7 Pa. $1.25

INDIAN SIGN LANGUAGE, William Tomkins. Over 525 signs developed by Sioux, Blackfoot, Cheyenne, Arapahoe and other tribes. Written instructions and diagrams: how to make words, construct sentences. Also 290 pictographs of Sioux and Ojibway tribes. 111pp. 6⅛ x 9¼. 22029-X Pa. $1.50

BOOMERANGS: HOW TO MAKE AND THROW THEM, Bernard S. Mason. Easy to make and throw, dozens of designs: cross-stick, pinwheel, boomabird, tumblestick, Australian curved stick boomerang. Complete throwing instructions. All safe. 99pp. 23028-7 Pa. $1.50

25 KITES THAT FLY, Leslie Hunt. Full, easy to follow instructions for kites made from inexpensive materials. Many novelties. Reeling, raising, designing your own. 70 illustrations. 110pp. 22550-X Pa. $1.25

TRICKS AND GAMES ON THE POOL TABLE, Fred Herrmann. 79 tricks and games, some solitaires, some for 2 or more players, some competitive; mystifying shots and throws, unusual carom, tricks involving cork, coins, a hat, more. 77 figures. 95pp. 21814-7 Pa. $1.25

WOODCRAFT AND CAMPING, Bernard S. Mason. How to make a quick emergency shelter, select woods that will burn immediately, make do with limited supplies, etc. Also making many things out of wood, rawhide, bark, at camp. Formerly titled Woodcraft. 295 illustrations. 580pp. 21951-8 Pa. $4.00

AN INTRODUCTION TO CHESS MOVES AND TACTICS SIMPLY EXPLAINED, Leonard Barden. Informal intermediate introduction: reasons for moves, tactics, openings, traps, positional play, endgame. Isolates patterns. 102pp. USO 21210-6 Pa. $1.35

LASKER'S MANUAL OF CHESS, Dr. Emanuel Lasker. Great world champion offers very thorough coverage of all aspects of chess. Combinations, position play, openings, endgame, aesthetics of chess, philosophy of struggle, much more. Filled with analyzed games. 390pp. 20640-8 Pa. $3.50

CATALOGUE OF DOVER BOOKS

INCIDENTS OF TRAVEL IN YUCATAN, John L. Stephens. Classic (1843) exploration of jungles of Yucatan, looking for evidences of Maya civilization. Travel adventures, Mexican and Indian culture, etc. Total of 669pp.
20926-1, 20927-X Pa., Two vol. set $5.50

LIVING MY LIFE, Emma Goldman. Candid, no holds barred account by foremost American anarchist: her own life, anarchist movement, famous contemporaries, ideas and their impact. Struggles and confrontations in America, plus deportation to U.S.S.R. Shocking inside account of persecution of anarchists under Lenin. 13 plates. Total of 944pp.
22543-7, 22544-5 Pa., Two vol. set $9.00

AMERICAN INDIANS, George Catlin. Classic account of life among Plains Indians: ceremonies, hunt, warfare, etc. Dover edition reproduces for first time all original paintings. 312 plates. 572pp. of text. 6 1/8 x 9 1/4.
22118-0, 22119-9 Pa., Two vol. set $8.00
22140-7, 22144-X Clothbd., Two vol. set $16.00

THE INDIANS' BOOK, Natalie Curtis. Lore, music, narratives, drawings by Indians, collected from cultures of U.S.A. 149 songs in full notation. 45 illustrations. 583pp. 6 5/8 x 9 3/8 .
21939-9 Pa. $5.00

INDIAN BLANKETS AND THEIR MAKERS, George Wharton James. History, old style wool blankets, changes brought about by traders, symbolism of design and color, a Navajo weaver at work, outline blanket, Kachina blankets, more. Emphasis on Navajo. 130 illustrations, 32 in color. 230pp. 6 1/8 x 9 1/4.
22996-3 Pa. $5.00
23068-6 Clothbd. $10.00

AN INTRODUCTION TO THE STUDY OF THE MAYA HIEROGLYPHS, Sylvanus Griswold Morley. Classic study by one of the truly great figures in hieroglyph research. Still the best introduction for the student for reading Maya hieroglyphs. New introduction by J. Eric S. Thompson. 117 illustrations. 284pp.
23108-9 Pa. $4.00

THE ANALECTS OF CONFUCIUS, THE GREAT LEARNING, DOCTRINE OF THE MEAN, Confucius. Edited by James Legge. Full Chinese text, standard English translation on same page, Chinese commentators, editor's annotations; dictionary of characters at rear, plus grammatical comment. Finest edition anywhere of one of world's greatest thinkers. 503pp.
22746-4 Pa. $4.50

THE I CHING (THE BOOK OF CHANGES), translated by James Legge. Complete translation of basic text plus appendices by Confucius, and Chinese commentary of most penetrating divination manual ever prepared. Indispensable to study of early Oriental civilizations, to modern inquiring reader. 448pp.
21062-6 Pa. $3.50

THE EGYPTIAN BOOK OF THE DEAD, E.A. Wallis Budge. Complete reproduction of Ani's papyrus, finest ever found. Full hieroglyphic text, interlinear transliteration, word for word translation, smooth translation. Basic work, for Egyptology, for modern study of psychic matters. Total of 533pp. 6 1/2 x 9 1/4.
EBE 21866-X Pa. $4.95

MODERN CHESS STRATEGY, Ludek Pachman. The use of the queen, the active king, exchanges, pawn play, the center, weak squares, etc. Section on rook alone worth price of the book. Stress on the moderns. Often considered the most important book on strategy. 314pp. 20290-9 Pa. $3.00

CHESS STRATEGY, Edward Lasker. One of half-dozen great theoretical works in chess, shows principles of action above and beyond moves. Acclaimed by Capablanca, Keres, etc. 282pp. USO 20528-2 Pa. $2.50

CHESS PRAXIS, THE PRAXIS OF MY SYSTEM, Aron Nimzovich. Founder of hyper-modern chess explains his profound, influential theories that have dominated much of 20th century chess. 109 illustrative games. 369pp. 20296-8 Pa. $3.50

HOW TO PLAY THE CHESS OPENINGS, Eugene Znosko-Borovsky. Clear, profound ex-aminations of just what each opening is intended to do and how opponent can counter. Many sample games, questions and answers. 147pp. 22795-2 Pa. $2.00

THE ART OF CHESS COMBINATION, Eugene Znosko-Borovsky. Modern explanation of principles, varieties, techniques and ideas behind them, illustrated with many examples from great players. 212pp. 20583-5 Pa. $2.00

COMBINATIONS: THE HEART OF CHESS, Irving Chernev. Step-by-step explanation of intricacies of combinative play. 356 combinations by Tarrasch, Botvinnik, Keres, Steinitz, Anderssen, Morphy, Marshall, Capablanca, others, all annotated. 245 pp. 21744-2 Pa. $2.50

HOW TO PLAY CHESS ENDINGS, Eugene Znosko-Borovsky. Thorough instruction manual by fine teacher analyzes each piece individually; many common endgame situations. Examines games by Steinitz, Alekhine, Lasker, others. Emphasis on understanding. 288pp. 21170-3 Pa. $2.75

MORPHY'S GAMES OF CHESS, Philip W. Sergeant. Romantic history, 54 games of greatest player of all time against Anderssen, Bird, Paulsen, Harrwitz; 52 games at odds; 52 blindfold; 100 consultation, informal, other games. Analyses by An-derssen, Steinitz, Morphy himself. 352pp. 20386-7 Pa. $2.75

500 MASTER GAMES OF CHESS, S. Tartakower, J. du Mont. Vast collection of great chess games from 1798-1938, with much material nowhere else readily available. Fully annotated, arranged by opening for easier study. 665pp. 23208-5 Pa. $6.00

THE SOVIET SCHOOL OF CHESS, Alexander Kotov and M. Yudovich. Authoritative work on modern Russian chess. History, conceptual background. 128 fully anno-tated games (most unavailable elsewhere) by Botvinnik, Keres, Smyslov, Tal, Petrosian, Spassky, more. 390pp. 20026-4 Pa. $3.95

WONDERS AND CURIOSITIES OF CHESS, Irving Chernev. A lifetime's accumulation of such wonders and curiosities as the longest won game, shortest game, chess problem with mate in 1220 moves, and much more unusual material —356 items in all, over 160 complete games. 146 diagrams. 203pp. 23007-4 Pa. $3.50

AUSTRIAN COOKING AND BAKING, Gretel Beer. Authentic thick soups, wiener schnitzel, veal goulash, more, plus dumplings, puff pastries, nut cakes, sacher tortes, other great Austrian desserts. 224pp. USO 23220-4 Pa. $2.50

CHEESES OF THE WORLD, U.S.D.A. Dictionary of cheeses containing descriptions of over 400 varieties of cheese from common Cheddar to exotic Surati. Up to two pages are given to important cheeses like Camembert, Cottage, Edam, etc. 151pp. 22831-2 Pa. $1.50

TRITTON'S GUIDE TO BETTER WINE AND BEER MAKING FOR BEGINNERS, S.M. Tritton. All you need to know to make family-sized quantities of over 100 types of grape, fruit, herb, vegetable wines; plus beers, mead, cider, more. 11 illustrations. 157pp. USO 22528-3 Pa. $2.00

DECORATIVE LABELS FOR HOME CANNING, PRESERVING, AND OTHER HOUSEHOLD AND GIFT USES, Theodore Menten. 128 gummed, perforated labels, beautifully printed in 2 colors. 12 versions in traditional, Art Nouveau, Art Deco styles. Adhere to metal, glass, wood, most plastics. 24pp. 8¼ x 11. 23219-0 Pa. $2.00

FIVE ACRES AND INDEPENDENCE, Maurice G. Kains. Great back-to-the-land classic explains basics of self-sufficient farming: economics, plants, crops, animals, orchards, soils, land selection, host of other necessary things. Do not confuse with skimpy faddist literature; Kains was one of America's greatest agriculturalists. 95 illustrations. 397pp. 20974-1 Pa. $2.95

GROWING VEGETABLES IN THE HOME GARDEN, U.S. Dept. of Agriculture. Basic information on site, soil conditions, selection of vegetables, planting, cultivation, gathering. Up-to-date, concise, authoritative. Covers 60 vegetables. 30 illustrations. 123pp. 23167-4 Pa. $1.35

FRUITS FOR THE HOME GARDEN, Dr. U.P. Hedrick. A chapter covering each type of garden fruit, advice on plant care, soils, grafting, pruning, sprays, transplanting, and much more! Very full. 53 illustrations. 175pp. 22944-0 Pa. $2.50

GARDENING ON SANDY SOIL IN NORTH TEMPERATE AREAS, Christine Kelway. Is your soil too light, too sandy? Improve your soil, select plants that survive under such conditions. Both vegetables and flowers. 42 photos. 148pp. USO 23199-2 Pa. $2.50

THE FRAGRANT GARDEN: A BOOK ABOUT SWEET SCENTED FLOWERS AND LEAVES, Louise Beebe Wilder. Fullest, best book on growing plants for their fragrances. Descriptions of hundreds of plants, both well-known and overlooked. 407pp. 23071-6 Pa. $3.50

EASY GARDENING WITH DROUGHT-RESISTANT PLANTS, Arno and Irene Nehrling. Authoritative guide to gardening with plants that require a minimum of water: seashore, desert, and rock gardens; house plants; annuals and perennials; much more. 190 illustrations. 320pp. 23230-1 Pa. $3.50

EGYPTIAN MAGIC, E.A. Wallis Budge. Foremost Egyptologist, curator at British Museum, on charms, curses, amulets, doll magic, transformations, control of demons, deific appearances, feats of great magicians. Many texts cited. 19 illustrations. 234pp. USO 22681-6 Pa. $2.50

THE LEYDEN PAPYRUS: AN EGYPTIAN MAGICAL BOOK, edited by F. Ll. Griffith, Herbert Thompson. Egyptian sorcerer's manual contains scores of spells: sex magic of various sorts, occult information, evoking visions, removing evil magic, etc. Transliteration faces translation. 207pp. 22994-7 Pa. $2.50

THE MALLEUS MALEFICARUM OF KRAMER AND SPRENGER, translated, edited by Montague Summers. Full text of most important witchhunter's "Bible," used by both Catholics and Protestants. Theory of witches, manifestations, remedies, etc. Indispensable to serious student. 278pp. 6⅝ x 10. USO 22802-9 Pa. $3.95

LOST CONTINENTS, L. Sprague de Camp. Great science-fiction author, finest, fullest study: Atlantis, Lemuria, Mu, Hyperborea, etc. Lost Tribes, Irish in pre-Columbian America, root races; in history, literature, art, occultism. Necessary to everyone concerned with theme. 17 illustrations. 348pp. 22668-9 Pa. $3.50

THE COMPLETE BOOKS OF CHARLES FORT, Charles Fort. Book of the Damned, Lo!, Wild Talents, New Lands. Greatest compilation of data: celestial appearances, flying saucers, falls of frogs, strange disappearances, inexplicable data not recognized by science. Inexhaustible, painstakingly documented. Do not confuse with modern charlatanry. Introduction by Damon Knight. Total of 1126pp. 23094-5 Clothbd. $15.00

FADS AND FALLACIES IN THE NAME OF SCIENCE, Martin Gardner. Fair, witty appraisal of cranks and quacks of science: Atlantis, Lemuria, flat earth, Velikovsky, orgone energy, Bridey Murphy, medical fads, etc. 373pp. 20394-8 Pa. $3.00

HOAXES, Curtis D. MacDougall. Unbelievably rich account of great hoaxes: Locke's moon hoax, Shakespearean forgeries, Loch Ness monster, Disumbrationist school of art, dozens more; also psychology of hoaxing. 54 illustrations. 338pp. 20465-0 Pa. $3.50

THE GENTLE ART OF MAKING ENEMIES, James A.M. Whistler. Greatest wit of his day deflates Wilde, Ruskin, Swinburne; strikes back at inane critics, exhibitions. Highly readable classic of impressionist revolution by great painter. Introduction by Alfred Werner. 334pp. 21875-9 Pa. $4.00

THE BOOK OF TEA, Kakuzo Okakura. Minor classic of the Orient: entertaining, charming explanation, interpretation of traditional Japanese culture in terms of tea ceremony. Edited by E.F. Bleiler. Total of 94pp. 20070-1 Pa. $1.25